After The Gold Rush

After the Gold Rush

John Stuart Clark

Five Leaves Publications

www.fiveleaves.co.uk

After the Gold Rush
John Stuart Clark

Published in 2004
by Five Leaves Publications,
PO Box 81, Nottingham NG5 4ER
www.fiveleaves.co.uk, info@fiveleaves.co.uk
Available in the USA via AK Press

ISBN: 0 907123 40 6

Articles based on sections of *After the Gold Rush* have
previously appeared in *Cycle, Cycling Plus, London
Cyclist, Bicycle Business, VeloVision, Rough Stuff
Journal, Adventure Cyclist* (USA) and
Cartoon News (USA).

Five Leaves Publications gratefully acknowledges
financial support from Arts Council England

Typeset by 4 Sheets Design & Print Ltd.,
Printed in Great Britain

Contents

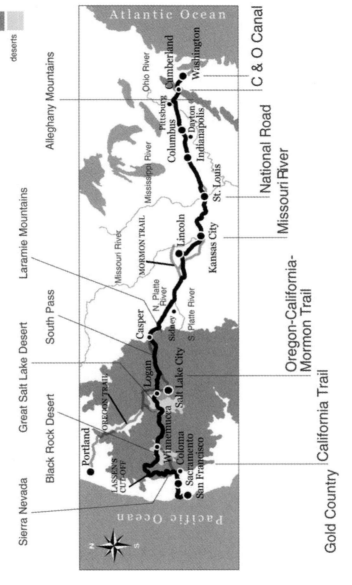

Foreword

I have a tatty box file labelled 'Ride Ideas' where I stash clippings, holiday reviews, tourist leaflets, scribblings — anything which strikes my fancy and has potential for a voyage of discovery, long or short. Four years before I set out to cross America I tucked away a paragraph snipped from a colour supplement which mentioned that the 150th anniversary of the 1848 Californian Gold Rush was approaching. A year later I attached an article about the Mormon exodus to Zion, later to become Salt Lake City. Within six months the paragraph had become a wedge of clips and staples binding newspaper cuttings, notes and downloads from the internet. As the investigation gathered pace, leaflets and maps started arriving from America and the wedge relocated into its own wallet, then to a folder and finally into two drawers of a filing cabinet and a sizable portion of shelf space.

I always wanted to explore America but for nearly half a century resolutely resisted crossing the Atlantic, even for a cheap holiday. Everything I knew about the country told me it had an extraordinary landscape and every American I had ever met struck me as warm, generous and decidedly strange. I was a huge fan of Westerns, musicals and the blues, but was outraged by almost everything Washington inflicted on the world in the name of freedom. The United States increasingly struck me as the most foreign of foreign lands, our shared language only making it the more incomprehensible.

One thing I knew for certain — it would not suffice to drift around that vast country simply sampling things which roused my curiosity. I needed a focus, a project, and preferably one which enabled me to meet the Americans on their own terms. The end of the American Century seemed a fitting time for an expedition into the interior of the sole surviving superpower in the world, but where to go and what to do?

My fascination with the Wild West found me rooting out reproductions of early maps, building a picture of how the European invasion spread across the continent. As I dug deeper into the stories behind these historic movements, I came across trails like Braddock's Road or Sublette's Cut-off, named after people who forged new, possibly better routes across uncharted lands. A picture began to emerge of the pathfinders, pilgrims and migrants who struck out across the New World, and of the society which surfed in on their wake.

While Britain was extolling the wonders of Europe's cutting-edge technology at the Great Exhibition, hundreds of thousands of Europeans were an ocean away, trudging through the wilderness in search of a promised land. Some of these immigrants were fleeing religious intolerance, famine or conflict — issues which occupied me in my day job as a political cartoonist. The majority were simply economic refugees, searching for improved opportunities. The most fascinating group, however, were the hundreds of thousands who crossed the continent with no intention of staying where they arrived any longer than was absolutely necessary. Their reason for walking anything up to 3,000 miles across some of the most inhospitable terrain on earth was simply to strike it rich. Their dream was to arrive, bend down and scoop up a nugget of gold which would set them up for life. If that wasn't the ultimate expression of the American Dream, at that time I didn't know what was. It seemed to me nobody was more obsessed with easy money and the power it bestows than Uncle Sam.

Aware of the limitations of the research material available to me in the UK, I went back to the old charts and mapped a provisional line which would take a gold seeker across the middle of the United States, from sea to sierra. I allowed myself £1,800 for a four month adventure — a derisory amount in consumer heaven, but equivalent to what some of the gold seekers could afford. I would cover the distance on a nineteenth century vehicle I knew Americans had long since dismissed as inappropriate, outmoded and strictly for kids — a vehicle which contributed more than any other to their humiliation in Vietnam. I would travel on a bicycle, with one wheel in the past and one in the present.

What the future held in store when I took off from London that July was more than my family and I bargained for. An excursion projected to take four months came to be spread over two years — six if you add the time spent in researching, planning and dealing with the fallout on my return. The actual ride took me across searing deserts and the poorest of America's inner cities, through dramatic storms and winds which drove me insane. Along the way I met billionaires and gangsters, oilmen and hoboes, cowboys and, of course, gold prospectors. I travelled at a time when the worst tornado on record struck the mid-West, the worst school massacre shook the nation, and the worst case of a president caught with his flies open was slobbered over. And I journeyed amongst a people openly critical of their country and, in most cases, thoroughly welcoming, arriving home a year before 9-11 exposed America's vulnerability and radically changed the mood of the nation.

The terrorist attack on the Twin Towers also radically altered the attitude of some British publishers, who suddenly became very wary of handling anything vaguely

3

critical of America. This book isn't particularly, but not one of the six publishers who expressed enthusiasm for the project before I departed held true to their desire to have first refusal. None would even read it, and my agent only found one which went so far as producing a supportive reader's report. At a time when the best selling book in the country was Michael Moore's polemic ripping into the country's 'Stupid White Men', this unique record of retracing one of the most formative folk movements in the history of the United States was stonewalled.

If that isn't enough, my journey was also through a family tragedy which shook the foundations of my relationship with my wife and took us three years of heartache to get through. In following a historic trail undertaken overwhelmingly by men, I was forced to take a long hard look at my role as husband, companion and father. If I had known what I was getting into when I began making travel plans, I would have stuck at the drawing board.

And so I extend my heartfelt thanks to all the Americans who took me in, fed and sheltered me along the trail, to the Borcherts, Fells, and Cohens, who understood the mess I was in, and especially to the Grodecki family, who opened their arms to a total stranger and came to my rescue. At the UK end, Fi and Karen were stalwarts for my wife and myself, and my parents went the extra mile or several hundred. To all the magazine editors who have published extracts masquerading as articles, my thanks for confirming this is a story worth telling, and to Ross Bradshaw of Five Leaves, a high five for venturing where the big boys feared to tread.

After the Gold Rush is for my wife, Sandy, who gave me undying support in exchange for buckets of grief, but it is dedicated to her mum. We miss you, Pauline.

Chapter I
Washington D.C.

"You can't get out of here you know."

The voice was deep, dark and authorative. I looked up from tying my shoes to see a gargantuan customs official waddling towards the men's room.

"The only way out is by bus," he called back, already fumbling at his flies, "but you'll have to box your bicycle before they'll take it."

Between checking visas, this same official had spent three quarters of an hour watching me unbox my bicycle, rebuild it, load up the pannier bags, dispense with the box, disappear into the men's room and emerge dressed as Lycraman. Only then did he decided to tell me the good news. There were only two ways out of Washington Dulles Airport, by air or by freeway, "and bikes ain't allowed on the freeway." There was no rail terminal or service road, no footpath or track. I was trapped.

In the terminal car park, I shared my problem and a lighter with an elderly African-American couple recently arrived from Los Angeles and craving nicotine. They were dressed formally, DJ and gown.

"You could put you bicycle in the trunk," the woman offered, "and we could run you to the end of the freeway, couldn't we, honey?"

5

By the size of the limo which arrived, they could have put the bike in the boot with me sat on the saddle. Where I had just flown in from, black folks were lucky if they could hail down a cab.

"Hey, man," the dinner jacket replied to the surprise on my face, "this is America!"

"Really? Just the airport, or is there more?"

It wasn't a good start for somebody aspiring to ride 3,000 miles across the North American continent.

One hundred and fifty years after the *St. Louis Republican* carried the first report east of the Rockies that gold had been discovered in California, I touched down in the U.S. of A. In a week's time, if I could break free of the airport, I would begin my journey shadowing the route of the 1849 Gold Rush from Washington D.C. to Sacramento. In a country forged on the back of westward bound wagon trains and lone saddle tramps, I planned to retrace one of the most extraordinary migrations of them all, and was damned if I would be propelled into the capital at a speed greater than that of a galloping horse. I had every intention of beginning my journey the way I meant to continue.

I rode off to the start of Interstate 267. As I approached, the superintendent of toll booths stepped forward with an arm raised.

"Before you say anything," I said, "I've talked to a couple of cops. They said I could to take the freeway."

It was the truth, but the super' eyed me with suspicion. "Okay, you can ride as far as that," he said, pointing to a slip road up to a fly-over five hundred yards down the interstate which the police had already warned me fed back into a different section of the airport. I cycled up the slip road and down the other side, back onto the interstate.

My journey into the capital was a baptism by fire. Between dodging flayed tyres, broken bottles and shattered windscreens, I rode the interstate hugging the gutter of the emergency lane for dear life. How I escaped being sucked into the slipstream of convoys of trucks defies physics, and my memory of free-ranging across eight lanes of rush hour traffic to reach a far embankment and a county road remains locked in a post-traumatic amnesia. Monitoring my progress through traffic cameras, I imagined the Highway Patrol were doubled up with paroxysms of mirth.

Four hours later, with darkness drawing in fast, I arrived at the south bank of the Potomac River shaken but unscathed, wondering if it was such a good idea to undertake this journey by bicycle. In theory, pedal power would enable me to cross the first half of America at approximately the same speed as a Forty-Niner travelling on horseback. In practice, it appeared parts of the country were now only accessible to drivers. I had a nasty feeling I was set to become a familiar source of light entertainment on CCTV.

Across the Potomac, Georgetown was jumping, the sidewalks bustling with night shoppers and boisterous parties hunting a restaurant which wasn't heaving. The road was an assault course of chatty kerb-crawlers, sloppy parking and meandering pedestrians, but the streets became calmer the further east I rode. The closer I got to the city centre, the quieter Washington became. By Thomas Circle, a handful of blocks from the seat of government, the imperial capital of the most powerful country in the history of the world fell silent. As if downtown had been zapped by a neutron bomb, nothing stirred. Except that the stillness was now contained within acres of office blocks and mausoleums, Washington was as lifeless as it was a century and a half ago.

Though already the administrative centre of the United States, the capital wasn't much more than a rat infested sewer in the middle of the nineteenth century. Burgeoning cities like New York and Philadelphia might have been obvious choices for the headquarters of the new republic, but politics demanded a custom-built capital, then struggling to rise out of the marshes at the fork of the Potomac and Anacostia Rivers. Labelled the 'City of Magnificent Distances' by Charles Dickens, who visited in 1842, it was

7

a wide open street plan — full of promise but short on buildings. What people called blocks were squares of wasteland waiting to be blocked in. Streets started nowhere, ended nowhere and were unpaved. Washington was nearly sixty years old, but Pierre L'Enfant's great master plan for a showcase capital was painfully slow in revealing itself.

Public buildings appeared to be plonked as far from the public as possible. If there was any reason why two departments need have a close relationship, it was also good reason to site them at opposite ends of the city. A clerk with a memo to deliver had to walk through fields and climb fences, hold his nose crossing congealed sewage and claw his way through the ankle deep mud of the ploughed street on which the next administration block was located.

Along the way, he might have passed his boarding house, where the clerk shared a room with six and a bed with one other, invariably a stranger. It was probably in a row of three-storey Georgian terraces which also contained homes, workshops, stores and maybe a hotel. The block was one of a number of isolated hamlets struggling to weld together to form the residential and commercial districts of the aspiring capital. For eight dollars a week, the young clerk was fed and roomed. According to Dickens, dinners were an all-in wrestling match and floors were splattered with bile spreading out like yellow lava from festering spittoons. Reading his *American Notes*, you get the impression Washington was awash with phlegm.

The Hostel International on 11th Street had a lot in common with a nineteenth century boarding house. Meal times in the self-catering kitchen were pandemonium. If the floor wasn't slippery with phlegm, it certainly squelched with grease. Residents were wedged in ten to a room, cooking, eating and sleeping on top of each other. Aside from the continual tide of overnight guests, there were interns, students, contract workers and drifters shacked up for the season at a residential discount. The place stank of sweat but I couldn't have wished for a more appropriate base camp from which to launch my expedition into the heart of America.

Most of my week in the capital was spent locked in the vaults, making full use of the vast resources held by the Library of Congress, the National Archive and the Smithsonian Museums. Despite numerous raids on university libraries in Britain, there were gaps the size of the Grand Canyon in my knowledge of the Gold Rush, and as diligently as I tried to fill them, it seemed Americans were filling the gaps in their knowledge of the Old Country. In the Local History and Genealogy Reading Room, fellow researchers were buried under piles of bound editions which appeared to contain nothing more than lists. On the walls, the only pictures were clan and tartan maps of Scotland and a reproduction chart of nineteenth century Ireland.

The frumpy woman sat opposite assured me the British were wrong to believe the Americans were obsessed with researching their family trees. "I only come here two weeks in a year. I stay with my sister in Georgetown but I'm not on vacation. I spend vacations visiting the places my relatives came from in Scotland and Poland."

I was to meet scores of her countrymen and women eager to chronicle their European genealogy for me. Most were either direct descendants of Mark Twain, the King of Sweden or had just stepped off the *Mayflower*. And she was the first of many who were amazed that anybody from "Ingerland" could get sufficiently fired up about American history to undertake the sort of odyssey I was about to launch into.

"I guess the Gold Rush might be kinda interesting," she said, tapping her pencil, "but why would you wanna pedal all the way to Sacramento? We got planes."

In the mid-nineteenth century the city's broadsheet was *The Washington Intelligencer*. While bars, boarding houses and markets would have been rife with rumour in the fall of 1848, it was to this august publication that the

9

chattering classes turned for authentication. Early reports from the Far West were more Chinese whisper than observed reportage. They were reports of reports from newspapers closer to the source. Editorial comment doubted California was the El Dorado described, and suggested the size of the strike had been greatly exaggerated to entice Easterners to rush into the newly acquired territory. It was, after all, a little too good to be believed. Nine days after gold was unearthed, California was ceded to the United States by the treaty ending a two year war with Mexico. In seven decades of Spanish and Mexican control, not a glimmer of yellow had been seen. America gets hold of the territory and suddenly the Far West is a blaze with gold. It was just too close to the American Dream come true.

Ten months after the find, President James Polk was sufficiently convinced by the evidence to go public. On December 5th, he stood up in Congress and stated, "The accounts of the abundance of gold in that territory are of such extraordinary character as would scarcely command belief were they not corroborated by authentic reports of officers in the public service." Despite this endorsement from the top, it wasn't until residents started to read firsthand accounts of what was going down half a world away that gold fever really took a hold of the city.

The first time the Washington public got to study an accredited report direct from California was a three column letter from the Quartermaster General of the Army in San Francisco entitled 'Further from the Gold Region'. Like a Christmas present, it appeared on December 25th.

'In the latter part of February 1848, a mechanic named Jas. W. Marshall was employed in building a saw-mill for John A. Sutter, Esq. on the south branch of a river known in California as the American Fork... While employed in cutting a mill race or canal for its improvement, Mr. Marshall discovered the pieces of gold as they glistened in the sunlight at the bottom of the sluice.

Pieces of considerable size were taken from the water, and in a few days gold of the amount of $150 were removed in this manner. Examinations were prosecuted at other points along the stream, and almost everywhere with success.'

Quartermaster Folsom saw 'no prospect of exhausting the mines', and stated that 'From all that I can learn as to similar deposits of gold elsewhere, I believe these to be the richest placer mines in the world'. He went into great detail about the finds, citing examples of clerics and military men, 'New Mexicans', Californians and prospectors from the Sandwich Islands who had decamped from the sierras with up to $30,000 in gold after just three days panning. He described how coastal towns and villages had been 'almost absolutely deserted' by their male population, how crops were left to rot in the fields, and how 'extended agricultural or mechanical improvements (to California) are at an end for some time'. Of those that remained, Folsom bemoaned the extraordinary wages he needed to pay to keep men working on the repair of a government lighter and the ship *Huntress*. 'The wages of clerks have advanced at least two hundred percent', he reported.

Despite the President's endorsement and what I read in the newspaper, it would have taken more than the lure of gold to induce me to undertake a 3,000 mile hike across the unknown, particularly when the riches at the end of the rainbow were anything but guaranteed. Regardless of the growing fever on the streets, I certainly wouldn't have sold my business, spent my life savings or borrowed heavily off friends and family to pay for the trip, as many of the Forty-Niners did. And yet here I was, about to retrace their epic voyage, knowing much of it would be across vast wildernesses and thoroughly gruelling. Did I have more in common with the argonauts of 150 years ago than I was aware when first inspired to follow their wheel ruts?

11

Contrary to impressions gleaned from authors like Mark Twain and films such as *Ride the High Country*, the early days of the Gold Rush were not peopled by down-at-heel reprobates. Judging from the numerous 'Gold Rush Diaries' I dipped into in the Library of Congress, the majority of those who set out in 1849 were skilled professionals and articulate artisans. They were farmers, lawyers, merchants, bankers, craftsmen and public servants — people not driven by poverty to seek their fortunes. They were men with families, responsibilities and a standing in the community. Largely United States citizens, they were more accurately Euro-Americans — Scottish, French, German, Dutch, Irish and Russian immigrants who had come to North America to build a new life and were now on the trail of the means to greatly improve it. 'Off to Sacramento with my wash bowl on my knee', they thought they would be back home in a year having become unimaginably rich.

But for many it was the pure adventure of the proposed expedition which grabbed their imagination more than the gold at the end of the trail. A number of diarists thrilled at the prospect of new vistas, exciting challenges, unforeseen dangers, encounters with strange people and months on the hoof sleeping under canvas. As one wrote, 'Never having been far from home, the thought of an adventure of such magnitude... possessed my mind more forcibly than any expectation of getting rich from gold digging.' '(I want) to see something of Indian life,' another records, 'and indulge in hunting on the plains, and all that sort of thing.' A big country was waiting out there and they wanted to taste it. I too would have probably scrimped and saved and gone along for the ride. I had already crossed the Atlantic, as hundreds of thousands were to do when news of the strike spread abroad.

American ship owners were quick to advertise passages to California round Cape Horn or via the Isthmus of Panama in the capital's broadsheet. For those with memories of a dreadful trip across the Atlantic, the overland trail undoubtably looked a calmer option. My proposed route across the continent was historically authentic though not necessarily the one every gold seeker from Washington took. From the capital, I intended to follow the Chesapeake and Ohio Canal into the Appalachian Mountains. At Cumberland, Maryland, I would pick up the National Road and follow it all the way to the Mississippi River. From St Louis, I hoped to bum a lift on a river boat up the Mississippi and Missouri Rivers to Independence, the leaping off point for the Oregon, California and Santa Fe Trails. I planned to follow the gold seekers as closely as legally possible, allowing for a few serendipitous detours. Unfortunately, the modern American road maps spread around me in the cartographic department of the Library of Congress left a lot to be desired. There was no way of telling how feasible my line would be, particularly on a bicycle.

My walk to the libraries each morning took me past the Court House on Pennsylvania Avenue. Opposite the entrance a thick crop of mike stands sprouted from a temporary platform a pavement away from an arc of outside broadcast vans. In the shade of the trees, packs of yawning journalists waited for the latest twist in the Monica Lewinsky scandal. The whole world was watching as 'Zippergate' piled humiliation on the President of the United States but, back at the hostel, it was all rather a bore.

"You've got to be living with your head in the sand not to know Clinton's got the loosest damn grip on his libido," a Smithsonian intern told me.

"Hey, it goes with the territory," a medical student from California said with cynical resignation. "Okay, Clinton's told a porky, but that's what politicians do. He ain't the first president to screw around in the White House. What about George Washington?"

Among the residents who congregated outside the hostel for an after dinner natter, the general consensus was that, peccadilloes aside, Clinton was doing a damn good job.

Economic growth in the U.S. was spectacular, inflation was negligible and unemployment at its lowest in thirty years. As a consequence, crime figures had plummeted and social peace was the order of the day. Only one voice in the hostel was consistently and vehemently critical of the President. It belonged to a tight skinned man in his fifties with electrocuted hair and a General Custèr beard. He dressed like a vagabond, spent his time hovering in dark corners avoiding conversations and, unfortunately, slept in the bunk above me. When I finally got Mike Smith to talk, it turned out he was a lobbyist for Made in America, a Stateside version of the Buy British movement.

"I dress like this to deflect attention," he confided. I couldn't work out if he was top of the CIA's Most Wanted list or simply an attention seeker.

Mike spent much of the week trying to encourage me to ditch my plans in favour of picking up a pen to draw cartoons for "the cause." Exactly which cause and for what purpose remained a mystery, but barely a night went by without him leaning over his bunk and hissing, "Are you in or out?"

The day before I was due to leave he whispered that he had the okay from "some important people" for me to attend a meeting the next morning at which I would "get the full picture." I postponed my departure and joined him at the Economic Policy Institute (EPI) on L Street, an imposing suit of offices where you had to crab walk to avoid the power shoulders. Mike was still in disguise but had run his fingers through his hair in deference to the twenty besuited men and women from different monitoring groups, trade unions and think tanks who had come together in an oak-panelled boardroom for an update of the nation's trade figures, released that morning.

In the month that the Russian economy had been declared a dead duck, there was deep concern about the U.S. pumping money into propping up the faltering Far Eastern economies, the World Bank and the debt crisis in Latin American. In all three zones — Russia, South

America and the Far East — the United States was the largest host country for direct investments, totalling more than $117 billion. The country was surfing an unprecedented wave of prosperity, but it skimmed on desperately dodgy investments and was importing more of every major commodity than it was exporting (bar plastics and paper).

"This staggering shortfall in the balance of trade signals real trouble ahead for the U.S. economy," Thea Lee from the *Trade Deficit Monitor* declared. "Clinton's building a humdinger of a headache for whoever follows him into the White House, and Joe America thinks he's never had it so good."

"Until his job gets pulled from under him and relocated to Mexico," Bill Klinefelter from the United Steel Workers of America added.

The Achilles Heel of America's Nineties boom was the North American Free Trade Agreement (NAFTA), which Clinton had signed up for in 1994 despite virulent opposition from his own party. A sort of North American European Union, NAFTA was a god-send for American multinationals. Relocating production south of the border, they reaped an instant windfall from savings on their wage bill. Rather than provide the thousands of new manufacturing jobs Clinton promised it would, 200,000 jobs had been lost to Mexico since joining NAFTA.

At the end of the meeting, I followed Bill Klinefelter out onto L Street. On the sidewalk, the headlines on all the newspaper vending machines were making a meal of Lewinsky's dress arriving at FBI headquarters for analysis of the alleged stain. The union man scanned the displays and shrugged his shoulders in disbelief. Not one of the papers that day contained a word about the disasterous trade figures. In *The Washington Post*, Herblock's cartoon summed up the media's prevailing obsession. It depicted a little man clutching a paper labelled 'Latest on Lewinsky, Starr, Clinton' while his other hand extended to halt a massive revolving planet. The caption read, 'Hold everything!'

All was not well in the Land of the Free. Currently filled by a huff and puff scandal, it seemed a big black hole was opening up at the heart of the sole surviving superpower. The United States I was heading across presented a far more complex picture than Clinton's high rolling boom had Americans believing, and I was curious to see if signs of the rot setting in presented themselves. It was an opportune moment to explore a country generally accepted as the wealthiest and most powerful in the history of the planet.

On Sunday afternoon, I took a final stroll along the Mall in the shade of the avenue of elms and tried to focus on the journey ahead. At the time the gold seekers began assembling their kit, the north side of the Mall was a canal — the Washington Canal — a marginally more disgusting cesspit than the rest of the flat wasteland which was then a putrid marshalling yard and is now a splendid promenade.

When I reached Constitution Gardens, 750 cyclists pedalled over the small mound footing the Washington Monument to complete the final furlong of the Big Bike Ride Across America, the longest charity ride the world had ever seen. They were greeted by a PA system of Woodstock proportions blasting out 'America the Beautiful' and a thousand cheering supporters wearing T-shirts proclaiming 'I'm proud of you Harvey' and 'Great butt No. 436'. Parked up the length of the Mall was the convoy of rental trucks, coaches, 'Hummers' and articulated rigs which carried the 110 members of the support crew, the canvas town, medical tent, personal effects, portaloos, washing machines, kitchen and, of course, the media centre where riders could email home and download the day's digital snaps. From the podium, a grateful representative for the American Lung Association eulogised the cyclists' achievement, equating their 3,454 mile odyssey to those undertaken by Lewis and Clark, the pioneers of the Oregon Trail, and Neil Armstrong landing on the moon.

I stretched out on the grass, relieving the knots of anticipation and worry which precede every epic voyage. As the final stragglers on the charity ride effortlessly cruised in and punched the air, I wondered if I would feel half as elated at the end of my solo, unsupported transnavigating.

Chapter 2

Chesapeake & Ohio Canal

Though thousands took off across America unaccompanied in the spring of 1849, many more Forty-Niners formed themselves into joint-stock companies or partnerships before joining the Gold Rush. Knowing nothing about organising expeditions themselves, they employed guides with outback experience who had an eye for purchasing the best equipment, animals and supplies. For anything up to $700, they bought into the company, had a joint share in its assets and paid for their passage to the Far West. Each had a Board of Directors, a Treasurer and a Secretary, and articles of association or company constitutions set down legally binding rules and codes of conduct for along the trail. Right from the start, the Gold Rush was a business venture. The companies provided security, companionship and a sense of commitment to a journey into the unknown which wouldn't actually begin until four months down the line, when they arrived at the Missouri and the start of the California Trail. For friends and family left behind, they provided a reassuring moral framework which would protect their loved ones as they ventured beyond the bounds of civilisation.

Many companies pulled out amidst great public celebrations and proudly marched up Pennsylvania Avenue to the accompaniment of brass bands. Several set out in full military regalia, wearing uniforms which identified their chain of command. Some got to shake the hand of President Polk, who told the gold seekers that the hearts and minds of America went with them. It was as if the men were marching off to war, the destiny of the United States striding into the unknown beside them. Across the country, in cities, towns and villages, similar rituals took place between spring and early summer for at least the next ten years, but the frenzy which engulfed the nation in that first year of the Gold Rush was never more exuberant and jingoistic.

Whether they travelled alone or in a convoy of ox-drawn wagons, the Forty-Niners left in dribs and drabs, the flow increasing as spring matured. Many set off for George Town (as it then was) and the start of the Chesapeake and Ohio Canal (C & OC). Some would follow its towpath, as I planned to. Others would hustle a ride on a barge returning empty into the mountains. If a channel groper wasn't the fastest vehicle for somebody in a rush to reach California, in the month of April, it made good sense. In the mid nineteenth century, roads out of Washington did not run straight up the Potomac Valley, but travelled north to Baltimore then west to pick up the main thoroughfare through to Cumberland in the Alleghenies, where the canal terminated. At that time of year, overland routes were heavy going, even on horse back. In the quagmire of unpaved roads churned up by an appalling winter, every step was going to be a struggle through cloying mud.

With just a grunt from Mike Smith, I set off for Georgetown along the north avenue of the Mall, riding on gravel above the old Washington Canal. It was early but the promenade already jittered with power walkers and joggers. Independence and Constitution Avenues were steadily filling up with sports utility vehicles (SUVs) and yawning suits scurrying towards a day shuffling papers on the Hill. Where the Washington Canal once joined the Potomac River at Tiber Creek sat Abraham Lincoln, doe eyes staring down his nose at the Capitol and another Washington farce. I wondered if Abe knew that the guide books now promoted a 'Scandals Stroll' which could wear out a pair of Timberlands.

Aiming for Rock Creek, the first inlet above the Tidal Basin, I presumed it would be obvious when I arrived at the stream. Behind the Georgetown Sailing Club, a nasty little concrete bridge carried me over stagnant water which nobody would have reason to give a second glance. Once the busy link between the C & OC and tidal waters, Rock Creek was pinned by overhanging trees and choked by a carpet of pond weed.

As the fledgling capital slowly emerged from the mosquito infested marshes, the need for a dependable passage to sources of food and building materials became ever more urgent. Before the War of 1812, work started on a national road linking the Ohio and Potomac Rivers — the line I planned to follow at the end of the canal. After the war, the idea of building a navigable canal from the Appalachians down to D.C., independent of the river and financed by the federal government, gathered support. Nobody believed hacking a trough through the mountains was going to be easy, but the rewards were never in doubt. America was a country heavily depended on 'wet roads' or rivers to transport freight and, further north, the Erie Canal from Buffalo to the Hudson River had proved a major fillip for New York city. It had paid for itself in under a decade.

In 1849, the C & OC was still a year from its official opening, but virtually all of it had been cut and flooded and barges were already providing a steady turnover at the George Town terminus. When the argonauts set out for the interior, the basin was log-jammed with boats all the way to the Alexandria Aqueduct (now the Francis Scott Key Bridge). On the busy towpath, boatmen and stevedores dodged mules, fishwives, and derricks unloading timber. Factories that walled in the water for eight blocks were animated, rattling with knitting machines and spitting steam from dyeing vats.

By comparison, the terminus I rode into was a haven of quietude dappled by leafy shadows and framed by the soft lines of a shambles of original clapboard houses. The Victorian factories had turned their faces to the bisecting streets and become fancy sea food restaurants or craft shops. Moored in the canal, a reproduction packet boat waited to mule-drag customers through the first lock and back, but it was too early for tourists. A couple of homeless people warming their stiff bones stretched out on benches next to the bronze bust of Court Justice William Douglas. The judge led the campaign in the 1950s to save the disused canal from becoming a highway. Thanks to his efforts to preserve the green corridor as a nature reserve and National Historical Park, I wasn't fighting four lanes of traffic to get out of Washington.

Within an hour of leaving the hostel I was the other side of Georgetown, rolling beside still waters. Except for a row of Canada geese curled up like coits, I had the towpath to myself. On the north bank, above a ragged cliff, a concrete wall muffled the rumble of the Clara Barton Parkway running parallel with the waterway. It was the last lump of concrete I saw for ten miles. Long graceful curves winding through dense sycamores carried me blind past the suburban sprawl of Senate Heights, Foxhall and Palisades. To my left, a wooded bank slipped down to a cycle path, then another wooded bank and the Potomac River, relaxed in its maturity. To my right, the canal was broad and clear but for an occasional log colonised by basking turtles. By the first feeder lock at Little Falls, five miles from the terminus, the crisp edge of the waterway had blurred under thicket, the waters had become a swamp, and I was travelling down a corridor of vaulted forest which ran virtually unbroken for the next 180 miles.

Approaching Great Falls, I was suddenly released from its grip and found myself riding a high causeway, cool waters shimmering either side of me. The towpath was all that separated the C & OC from the Potomac. A dry sun began roasting my covered shoulders. Hot rock on the far bank of the canal sucked floods of sweat out of me. After a mile, the river swung wide for the Mather Gorge, the big attraction at Great Falls and the only attraction along the canal's length to merit a hotel.

Although still in the piedmont of the Potomac Valley, the pillared rocks through which the Potomac has carved a gorge is the most formidable barrier along the river's entire course. Conservation work prevented me clambering along the Billy Goat Trail down to the chasm but, from the towpath, I could see a frightening array of the sort of navigational hazards eighteenth century helmsmen faced before the canal was cut. Calf deep rapids, dives over fault lines, fomenting rushes between grizzly outcrops — while a responsive riverboat might have made it, these were not the waters to coax a channel groper down.

Mostly taking advantage of the cool, I mooched around the Visitor Center, once the old Crommelin Hotel. In its hey-day, the well-heeled from the city took weekend breaks up here to admire the falls, sometimes with their own wives, but it was a slow day for Park Ranger Rod Sauter. Delighted with the nature of my quest, he told me the Forty-Niners could have saved themselves a journey and a half if they hadn't been in such a hurry.

"Thirteen years later a Union soldier with the 71st Pennsylvania discovered gold right here," he said, wagging his finger above his head. "After the Civil War, a bunch of them bought the land and began a mining operation that remained in business, off and on, until 1940. It was never wildly lucrative, but they did pretty good."

It was my mother-in-law's birthday. Pauline was sixty-nine and I had every intention of giving her a ring at home, in the English market town of Louth. She wasn't well. Six weeks before my departure, she turned bright yellow, we thought with jaundice. Admitted to the Lincolnshire County Hospital for tests, she was diagnosed with cancer of the bile duct and given between six months and six years to live. After a minor operation to enable her to eat properly, she was discharged. The plan was to build up her strength in preparation for a major operation. Meantime, my mother-in-law had returned home to be nursed by Sandy, my wife.

I left for the States with Pauline's blessing. Though booked to travel with me for the first month of my journey, Sandy had decided she wasn't leaving home until her mum was well on the road to recovery. Reluctantly she agreed I should continue with the American trip and be back in time to make Pauline's Christmas (possibly her last) unforgettable. But I should have phoned to wish my mother-in-law Happy Birthday while I was still in the city. The maps didn't prepare me for what lay ahead. The last place I was going to find a payphone was beside the Chesapeake and Ohio Canal.

The towpath plunged back into the forest and the trail inland became deserted again. For hours I ploughed down the tunnel before meeting another human being — another ranger. It was a short but intriguing exchange. Appearing out of nowhere to help me lift my bike up a temporary flight of steps on a detour round flood damage, the burley official recoiled at the weight and asked, "Got enough food to last the length of the canal?"

A moment of uncertainty skated across my forehead. Either this guy ate like a paper shredder or he knew something I didn't about the availability of provisions along the trail. I was riding through Maryland, for heaven's sake, a state not renowned for food shortages.

When it was in operation, there were over thirty places where the Forty-Niners could pick up provisions beside the canal. Bargees bought most of their supplies from lock keepers who supplemented their wages with the sale of vegetables from smallholdings adjacent to their homes. The majority of lock keepers' houses were now boarded up, maintained in mothballs and smartly decorated in a coat of whitewash, but there were still facilities beside the towpath. The first was a snacks cabin sixteen miles from

Georgetown at Swains Lock. Originally the lock was operated by a Swain, and the family still ran the cubicle and canoe hire.

Fifteen miles on, the verdant tunnel was ruptured again, and a grocery and bait store appeared beside Whites Ferry. Things were looking good on the supplies front, and I would have filled my panniers. Instead I was wrong footed by an old lag who held forth eight centimetres from my face with an agitated monologue. I couldn't decipher a word but frankly he terrified me. I pedalled away with more spit on my glasses than food in my bags. It was the last canal side store for 150 miles.

A couple of miles from Point of Rocks, an ominous drone crept up behind me. For hours, the massed choir of crickets had backed what few songs ran through my head, familiarity reducing their racket to a *sotto voce* accompaniment. Since the only mechanical sounds which managed to pierce the leafy canopy were generated by aircraft, I presumed a Jumbo was struggling to gain height from Dulles Airport. The drone became a rumble and got louder. A rattle was added, then a clatter with a discernible beat underpinning a cacophony of grating metal and clanging couplings.

I hadn't noticed the rail embankment creep up on the canal's festering carcass, and was taken aback when the freighter drew alongside. By the time I reach the road to the village, the two engines had slowed to a crawl and the noise diminished to a ponderous clickety-clack. I grew old waiting at the level crossing for the train to pass. It was pushed by as many locomotives as pulled the mile long vertebrae of coal wagons.

Even as President John Quincy Adams and invited cronies were celebrating the ground-breaking ceremony of the C & OC, the canal company were locked in a race with an arch rival that was to try and trip them every inch of the way to Cumberland. On the same day, July 4th, 1828, Charles Carroll of Carollton, the sole surviving signatory of the Declaration of Independence, was performing a similar initiation ceremony fifty miles north on behalf of the Baltimore and Ohio Railroad (B & OR).

The railroad was conceived as a response to Baltimore's anger that Washington's vision of a waterway didn't extend to including Maryland's premier city. The canal was projected to terminate at the capital which, unlike Baltimore, was neither a major sea port nor a commercial centre, let alone a centre of population. Until the canal was proposed, everything bound for the capital travelled via Baltimore and the port retained the bulk of western trade — a commercial advantage Baltimore wasn't prepared to give up without a fight.

Injunctions started flying weeks before either company moved the first shovelful of earth. The dispute was about rights of passage through Point of Rocks, a narrow section of the Potomac Valley which happened to be part of Charles Carroll's extensive Maryland estate. Legal wrangling held up the canal for four years. By the time Carroll's attorneys finally ran out of writs, the railroad was leaps ahead in the race to Cumberland. The B & OR crossed the finishing line eight years before the C & OC and commercially outstripped it for the remainder of its active life.

A mile beyond Point of Rocks I shared a campsite with a backpacker who was taking the opportunity to educate her two cousins in the delights of nature. The Bald Eagle Island site was one of thirty-six free pitches spaced less than six miles apart along the length of the canal. Little more than a patch of muddy ground cleared of undergrowth, each was equipped with a water handpump, a chemical loo, a table or two and a steel barbecue. Inaccessible to motorists and tailored for hiker-bikers, we would have been sleeping on the towpath without them.

Preparations for the evening's campfire began early and we didn't have to walk far to collect dead timber. Either side of the clearing, debris brought down by the Potomac was piled high around stout trunks which had held fast against the spring floods. Cracked and twisted amongst the severed branches were building parts. There were window frames, door jambs, broken chairs, shingles and lengths of splintered shuttering. On Bald Eagle Island itself, the clapboard wall of a summer house lay limp as wet cardboard with its balcony still attached. I was to cross aqueducts bridging tributaries of the Potomac where wide parapets of Seneca Red Stone had been ripped away by the ferocious waters, exposing the canal trough and the ballast within uprights. When it had a mind to be, the Potomac could be one mean river.

Between where Wills Creek and North Branch merge into something substantial enough to carry cargo from Cumberland, the Potomac River drops some 600 feet in about 200 miles to the Georgetown wharfs. While the ridges of the great divide are ranked north-east to south-west, the river runs north-west to south-east draining 10,000 square miles of the Appalachian Mountains and eastern piedmont. Much of its course is over rapids and shallows, and it is a rare spring when the thaw doesn't invade the banks and a rare decade when persistent rains don't at some point overwhelm the canal and drown the flood plain. Laid on embankments inland from the canal, the Baltimore and Ohio Railroad remained relatively unscathed by the highest of floods. The canal, however, was regularly overwhelmed and, ultimately, vanquished by a horrendous washout in 1889.

I paddled into the cool of the Potomac for an evening dip. A powerful current raised white horses upstream of my ankles as I hobbled across the shallows. Any second I expected to step off the pebble bar and sink into deep and dangerous waters. In midstream, with the water barely over my knees, I sat down, rolled over and stretched out with hands anchored to rocks to let the bubbling river wash over me. My first day on the trail had been a strange one. It had been a relief to be shot of the clamour of the big city, to meander along a peaceful line carving through temperate jungle, but it was disconcerting to be crossing the most densely populated portion of America and not see more than a handful of Americans.

At Dam Four, eighty-five miles from Georgetown, the C & OC made use of the Potomac. Barges slipped out of the canal and into the river made deeper by the weir, then round an impassable rock headland and back into the canal three miles upstream.

Four cyclists heading east were cooling off beside the water, moaning about the arduous detour they had been encouraged to take by a ranger up at Opequon Junction. The road had swung inland to climb serial hills for five miles which felt like ten. They couldn't recommend it any more than the official could recommend taking the path beside the river. He told them it was difficult even for walkers. Suspecting this had more to do with a non-cyclist grossly underestimating the capability of experienced riders to steer the thinnest of lines, I set off on the riverside route.

Until the guard lock at Big Slackwater where barges used to feed into the river, it was plain sailing and very entertaining, mostly for the devilment of chasing groundhogs from the towpath. As the track became a thin trail then an overgrown path, I sensed Mother Nature had something wicked up her sleeve. The path shrank further, the trees peeled away and I wobbled out onto a narrow ledge ambushed with hawthorns. Sandwiched between sheer rock on one side and a short drop into the river on the other, I dismounted, leant the bike against the cliff face and slid it along at an angle, pushing from behind. I tied a stick to the handlebars to assist steering and thought I was being very clever. Then the whole caboodle disappeared with a splash.

It took me half a day to cover the next couple of miles. In places there was something one might generously call a path, but more often I was scrambling over boulders dislodged from the bank or up to my thighs stumbling through the river. I removed the panniers, carried them forwards ten metres, returned for the bike then repeated the performance. Tidal waves of sweat blurred my glasses, lubricating their persistent slide down my nose. A bush hooked and flicked them to a landing spot which took me quarter of an hour to uncover by methodically uprooting and inspecting at nose length every shrub in the vicinity. Shins and elbows were torn and bloody. Clothes were saturated and filthy. It was more adventure than I needed this early in the trek.

As evening approached I reached a pontoon at the bottom of a grass track disappearing up through a break in the cliffs. A quarter of a mile round the river's bend, I could see the next leg of the canal. I walked ahead to check if the path improved, returned disappointed, strode onto the pontoon, took off my specs, and threw myself fully clothed into the Potomac. It was sublime. The dying sun had left a sliver of evening warmth glowing at the foot of the pontoon and I wallowed in its small mercy.

I should have unfurled my sleeping bag and given up on the day, but I wanted to see the back of this bad mistake. At right angles to the river, a grass track twisted through the rocks, across a field and into the garden of a large bungalow where, for some reason, a Vietnamese woman was watering her concrete driveway. I asked for directions and she called her husband. A Schwarzenegger of a man with crew-cut and flack jacket stepped out of the house. I was about to learn that the average American is useless at giving directions to anybody other than a motorist.

"First left, second left, follow it round to the left, then take the second left after the mill and follow the road down to Opequon Junction," I repeated Schwarzenegger's instructions. "Got it. Thanks."

Had I hell.

Between every left I should have taken were a whole load I shouldn't have. An hour later, with darkness closing ever deeper, I was still taking lefts and ending up in spacious cul-de-sacs where vast lawns radiated out to encompass dimly lit mansions. I hadn't a clue where I was but round here you needed a compass to find your mailbox. Then a motorist failed to notice me pottering along in the dark, swerved at the last moment, shot across the road into a field, scythed a row of corn, lurched back onto the tarmac and accelerated away as if completing a standard overtaking manoeuvre. I figured it was time to call it a day and rode up the first floodlit driveway.

A young lad opened the door onto a beautiful log cabin the size of a warehouse. The settee wrapped round the widescreen TV could have sat an American football team and yet, despite its intimidating open plan, the place felt cosy. Everything that wasn't furniture was log or stone.

"Pa" came downstairs with his stomach hanging over his shorts and tossed me a beer. Three cans later, he got dressed in his flip-flops, hustled Junior into the pick-up and led me to a short-cut that I hadn't got "a Christmas turkey's chance of finding." The turnings were all to the right this time.

That night I slept at the Opequon Junction hiker-biker site and dreamt I was eating groundhog like you do melon. It had taken me nine hours to cover six miles.

At the Georgetown Visitor Center back in D.C., I had inquired about interviewing a park official regarding the canal, and was directed to Debbie Ayres, the Chief Interpreter. Told she was based at the Williamsport Visitor Center, I had made arrangements by phone to see. Striding into Cushwa's warehouse, now housing the Williamsport centre, I explained to the old salt behind the desk that I had a flexi-time appointment with Debbie. "Is she in?"

"Possibly, but she's at Park Headquarters, Shepherds-town," he said, opening a collapsible Zimmer frame and gingerly rising to his feet.

Shepherdstown was thirty miles back the way I had come. The ranger dialled Debbie's office for me and handed me the phone. I explained the confusion to her secretary, apologising for my reluctance to pedal all the way back for a chat. "Is she heading this way at all?" I asked.

"Dunno."

"I see."

The phone went dead. I handed it back and thanked the ranger for his assistance. "That's a-okay," he said, "We're here to help."

I was beginning to get the feeling that the park authorities were less then conscientious in their attitude to the public. Harpers Ferry, their biggest attraction, was made inaccessible to me by a bridge across the river which was off limits to cyclists, even if I had the strength to lug my rig up the huge flight of steps. And it would have been nice to see an occasional information board identifying the different flora and fauna along the self-proclaimed nature trail, not to mention the odd finger post pointing to the nearest store or diner where hiker-bikers on a two hundred mile trek could get something more substantial than the dehydrated cack of their survival food. But, as Bill Schoenadel, owner of the Orleans Grocery, Little Orleans, explained, directing walkers and cyclist towards the nearest source of nutrition conflicted with the non-commercial ethos held dear by the National Historical Park Service and their masters, the U.S. Department of the Interior. "A sign post might suggest the federal authorities were endorsing us," Bill said, disclaiming all responsibility for the graffiti under the railway bridge which led me to him.

Bill's store-cum-diner was a living museum which had featured in National Geographic's *Vanishing America*. It was the sort of place the National Historical Park should have been keen to promote. Originally the offices of a timber yard supplying the canal, it was now crammed from ceiling to floor with all kinds of memorabilia. There were rusty flintlocks, fading photos of fishermen and hunters, old railway signs, stuffed animals, ancient fishing rods, enamelled adverts, printers' forms, team pennants, broken paddles, and everywhere clumsy witticisms like, 'If you don't want to smoke you can go outside and not do it'. The ceiling was covered in historic dollar bills signed by the likes of Fingers Magee, Cold Feet JJ and The Big Bird, and the furniture looked like the work of the Shakers.

A fisherman came in for bait and asked, "How're they running?" Bill waffled. The phone rang. Bill agreed to hire out a couple of kayaks, drive them up to Town Creek and run the customers back to their car when they floated into Little Orleans a couple of days later. Three women camping beside the river came in for sodas and he entertained them with a paper tearing trick. Bill and his wife Ethel had a nice little earner in the Orleans Grocery. They had been there since Bill's early retirement from the printing trade and, although most of their business was at weekends, they were happy to be out of the rat race and "doin' alrighty." I told him that, in the UK, a facility like the canal would be heavily promoted and busy right through summer, if not the year.

"That's the National Park Service for you," he nodded his head. "Don't know what they've got hold of."

Bill directed me up aways to St. Patrick's Church and a graveyard where men lay buried beneath headstones which gave their name and date of birth but no further details. It seems an enterprising monumental mason travelled the canal during its construction, carving and selling to workers who figured a headstone with half an inscription was better than none. "But you won't find anything about that in no Park's literature," Bill spat.

Twenty-five miles from the end of the canal, the Green Ridge Mountains shaped the Potomac into a series of tortuous twists and turns around Paw Paw Bends. Up until Sorrel Ridge, the canal rarely ran further than a few hundred meters from the river's northern bank. The torrent fed it, the valley shepherded it, and dry river beds made construction easier for it. Where the two entered the Green Ridge range, surveyors decided to take the canal off on an independent course. The result was a 3,000 foot tunnel rather than a six mile meander which would have carried the canal no further westwards than a mile. The short cut took ten years longer to build than estimated, came in 300% over budget, and cost many an Irish and German navvie his life.

Completed the year before the Forty-Niners passed through, the Paw Paw Tunnel is rated as the most remarkable feat of engineering along the canal's length. By European standards it is underwhelming, though it did give me palpitations half way along when, walking in total darkness, the hand rail suddenly disappeared. But for me the most remarkable feature of the old C & OC remained how far I had come to see so little of Maryland, never mind her people. It wasn't until ten miles from Cumberland that the sycamore shutters slid back to reveal a broad flood plain surrounded by truncated whalebacks held at bay by wild swings of the river. At the junction of Wills Creek and North Branch, wheat fields and stud stables gave way to estates or 'sub-divisions' of ticky-tacky bungalows. Up an embankment and going my way, a freight train was decelerating into town. I raced it down the track and round a corner where the skyline of Cumberland suddenly rose up before me. About the size of an English market town, its blanched civic buildings stood proud against the browns and greens of interlocking Allegheny ridges. At first glance, it looked like a thriving little community.

The end of the Chesapeake and Ohio trail led to the old Western Maryland Railroad station. At the platform, a locomotive stood sentry, just to remind me who won the race to Cumberland. The building was now home to the tourist office and the last and first National Park Visitor Center. Beneath an ugly concrete flyover, a shabby picnic park was invaded by thirty Boy Scouts from 965 Webster Maryland pack. They were about to spend a week cycling down the C & OC to Georgetown. Judging by the quantity of spring rolls, burgers and soda-pops they were shovelling down, they had insider information on the canal's acute shortage of catering facilities.

Chapter 3
Braddock's Road

When the American revolutionaries booted out the British and finally celebrated their independence, the United States was a divided nation, split in two by the dense forests and disjointed backbones of the Allegheny, Appalachian and Blue Ridge Mountains. Tracks and trails meandered through the hardwoods for foot and hoof, but bulk trade between west and east had to travel a tortuous route down the country's great riverways. For example, to get from Pittsburgh to Philadelphia, two cities in the same state, cargoes were floated down the Ohio River into the Mississippi and then south. At New Orleans, loads were transferred from flatboats to keel boats, which sailed into the Gulf of Mexico, round the Florida Straits and back up the Atlantic coast. An overland journey of some 300 miles became a 4,000 mile odyssey. The emergent nation desperately needed a passage to what was then the West or the Old West. It needed it for trade, immigration and political bonding.

The man who best understood this was a young surveyor employed by the Ohio Company called George Washington. On company business, Washington had travelled extensively around the Old West and knew how frustrated farmers were with the limitations of the 'wet roads'. He had also had a bad time fighting the French in the mountains and realised the strategic importance of uniting the country. In his cabin, still standing across the river from the Cumberland tourist information centre, he began devising alternative routes for what would become the National Road of America. After years of argy-bargy by self-interested parties in Congress, a line from Cumberland to the Ohio River was finally selected for the country's first federally financed highway.

The woman with the expensive dental work in the tourist office explained that Cumberland's good fortune lay in its position at the foot of the two strongest outflows east of the Allegheny Mountains — Wills Creek and the North Branch of the Potomac. The Ohio Company's fortified trading post became a key junction for road and river traffic and, when black gold was discovered in the surrounding mountains, the settlement blossomed into a major industrial centre on the back of the railway and canal. What most distinguished Cumberland from hives of industry like Baltimore, however, was the size of its itinerant population. Strolling through downtown in search of the stagecoach offices, Forty-Niners bumped into a world of nations in transit from the eastern seaboard. The kaleidoscope of cosmopolitan apparels and tongues on the streets encouraged one diarist en route to California to observe that he had arrived at a 'the crossroads of the world'.

By the end of the twentieth century, the coal was about as played out as the demand for fossil fuel, the canal terminus had been replaced by a vast freight yard for the successor to the B & OR, and the pedestrianised streets of downtown were empty. Businesses were in the final days of closing down sales and vacant premises were plastered with 'To Let' signs. Once Maryland's second largest and most prosperous city, Cumberland had been relegated to the National Register of Historic Places. Outside of the architecture, there was little to delay me from venturing onto my first stretch of American blacktop since the Ride from Hell from Dulles Airport.

The traffic on the National Road, otherwise known as Route 40, was light but constant, and getting out of Cumberland was unexpectedly easy. As the town receded, the road swung right to pair up with the contra-flow of Wills Creek and started to climb. Tarmac and spewing river breathed in as they squeezed between two mighty headlands which reared up like sperm whales breaking through the swell of the flood plain. Either side of me, Haystack and Wills Mountains were freeze-framed, poised at the apex of their leap, ready to come crashing down as soon as I was through. Once the Gateway to the West when the West was still in the east, the Cumberland Narrows were like the nozzle of a funnel, accelerating everything that flowed through, including my legs.

Beyond the chicane, the valley opened out to allow a sibling of suburbia to spread its wings. Unkempt yards surrounding shabby homes became progressively more groomed as I climbed towards La Vale. An extraordinary number of families were holding porch, yard or garage sales, possibly pending the sale of the rest of the house, and it was election time. Small polythene banners promoting candidates were planted in verges and the fixed grin of James 'Jim' Stakem started to bug me as his road-side plaques repeatedly stared me down like targets on a firing range. The incline was long and steady, igniting twisted knots in my quads which burned hotter the higher the road ascended.

Whether the Forty-Niners travelled by stagecoach, mule or Shanks's pony, the road they took across the Appalachians was the best maintained and best serviced turnpike in the country. It was the mail road to the Old West and the highway that opened up the mountain wilderness to settlers. Although half a century away from being paved, stage lines boasted they could cover 100 miles a day on the crushed stone, even over the highest cols. As frequently as every mile, the roadside was punctuated by inns, taverns and drover stations. Anybody who could cook could hang out a shingle and make money out of travellers in a hurry to eat and move on. If anything delayed progress down the pike it was the drovers herding pigs, sheep, cows and geese to market. A decade before the Gold Rush, the flow of livestock was somewhat reduced by the introduction of road tolls, but drovers quickly forged 'shunpikes' which looped round the hexagonal toll booths, designed to provide a clear view of the turnpike but not the back of the building. The La Vale Toll Gate House had been carefully restored in a brash coat of white with black highlights, but the little museum inside was closed when I arrived.

According to the map, the road I climbed was U.S. Route 40. At Clarysville I stood before a blue and white shield confirming that. Another sign on the same post indicated I was on the National Road. A third, pointing to a side road off to my left, said I was at the junction with the Old National Pike. In Cumberland, the woman in the tourist information centre had called it Braddock's Road, but said it should rightly be called Washington's Road. Confused? I thought I was on the Cumberland Road. That's what the Forty-Niners called it in their diaries. I sat myself down beneath the signs, pulled out notes made in Washington and tried to unravel the highway's genealogy.

Wills Creek had cut an obvious line for an Amerindian mountain trail leading from the Shawnee camp that later became Cumberland. When the Ohio Company set up shop, the trail became known as Nemacolin's Path, after the Delaware Chief hired by the company to recce a westward passage up the valley for prospective settlers. As the French moved in on their turf, the company sent the inexperienced George Washington to warn them off. Little more than a squiggle of squelched leaves and snapped branches, Nemacolin's Path was inadequate for the passage of a large platoon. Washington and his men had to cleave a way through the tangled mountain chaos — a delay which proved disastrous when they encountered the French.

When Washington's expedition failed, the British sent in the big guns under General Braddock. Setting out with nearly two thousand troops, Braddock similarly found Washington's Road too narrow. He likewise lost time hacking back the forest and had to lay a corduroy road of felled tree trunks for his heavy wagons. The route Washington recommended and Congress later approved for a national road followed pretty much the same line as Braddock's Road, and there were cast iron plaques beside the highway that were not going to let me forget it. The Old National Pike was the new name for the old National Road after it was handed over to the states it passed through and became a toll road. Its route was the sole line through the mountains until Maryland became over-run with automobiles in the 1920s and began building by-passes of numbered roads.

I continued my flog up the National Road, Route 40, climbing through the drab linear developments of La Vale, Eckhart, then Frostburg — small towns with a big litter problem. A large rock scarred with an engraving slipped into view. It was one of a spaced row of boulders marking the boundary of a small colonial house which sat like a painted island in a painted sea of perfectly manicured lawn. Nearby were the metal uprights of the old turnpike barrier. The rough engraving said, 'J.B.H. March 20 1871 G Z I'. My spirits lifted. I had seen the La Vale tollhouse and old cast iron mile posts beside the highway, but this was the first indication that I journeyed where real flesh and blood pilgrims had gone before.

As the waning sun cast long shadows across the road like palm leaves before my donkey, I achieved the summit of Big Savage Mountain. To my chagrin, it was barely a thousand metres up, but I was whacked, and slumped beneath a solitary rowan to stuff fuel into empty legs. For the first time since leaving Washington, I had reached a vantage point. Unfurled before me was a panoramic view of the panhandle of Maryland. It reminded me a lot of Bavaria. Rolling hills the height of Britain's tallest mountains were crested with dense forests which flowed like green mud slides into the valleys below. Etched in deep shadow, the contoured harvest rings of yellowing corn fields nudged into the green goo dominating the landscape. Here and there the sun picked out whitewashed farmsteads and Dutch barns planted in the corn.

The National Road swooped off the watershed and wandered forth like a lackadaisical eel exploring the seabed with no mind for the line of least resistance. Beside its thin grey trail, a fault line as straight and cruel as a Samurai's slash split the panorama between north and south. An even newer new National Road had appeared on the scene, thankfully sucking the traffic away from my route. Big Savage Mountain had been tamed and wrent in two by Interstate 68, the latest update on U.S. Route 40, which the interstate was also called. To add further confusion, my road now became Alt. 40.

The tank hadn't been filled. Three cheese triangles and a bottle of Gatorade weren't going to get me far over the hurdles Alt. 40 had in store. Half an hour later, with a pit in my stomach the size of Hades, I caught a glimpse of a Miller Lite neon flickering in the window of a long sullen shed which was more of a deserted workshop than an inviting roadhouse. It didn't look promising but the neon sign cast zany reflections on a row of dusty pick-ups parked against the boardwalk.

Round an L-shaped bar, men were absorbed in a raucous conversation with women who gave as good as they got about a barn dance which had degenerated into a fist fight the night before. The men were of the denim dungarees and check shirt variety, with sleeves rolled up exposing the grubby long arms of a once white grand-dad undershirt. The women were of the tight jeans, tight top, big bones, deep cleavage type. They had 'don't-fuck-with-me' writ large across their foreheads. Pausing long enough to satisfy myself they weren't going to eat me alive, I pulled up a stool next to the only geezer who wasn't wearing a baseball hat and ordered a beer.

The chatter rounded on Joanne, a dead ringer for Susan Sarandon sitting between a couple of square jawed bookends who would have crushed her if they leant inwards. Everybody seemed to have a take on her sex life. Her guy was a heel (general laughter) and had left the roadhouse the previous Wednesday with another woman ("What's new?" "Shelley ain't no woman!"), never to be seen again ("I give it a week." "Nar. He'll be in tomorrow. Sunday. Shelley's Lutheran."). Joanne said she was definitely going to move on this time, and a couple of the boys offered up their beds. Each got a clip round the ear. It was Happy Hour and then some, and the rumbustious bar-flies included me in their banter in the same way that the father rapers in *Alice's Restaurant* included Arlo Guthrie when he sat in the prison reception. I might have been wearing lycra, but we all reeked of sweat and were caked in grime.

Jack (the guy without the baseball hat) had just finished a day down at Meyersdale laying a cyclepath. He worked for a local contractor, but the project was for the Rails-to-Trails Conservancy. Similar to Sustrans in the UK, "R2T" (as Jack called them) had converted over 10,000 miles of abandoned railroads into recreational corridors and traffic-free cycle routes in the last decade. The old Meyersdale station was going to be renovated and transformed into a café, maybe with dormitory accommodation. Jack hoped the route would attract tourism into an area wounded by the demise of the coal and farming industries. Like the rest of the lads round the bar, Jack used to be a farm worker. "Only Big John is now. His Pa owns a place over towards Accident."

Pushing aside the bookends, Joanne slid round the bar and gently interrogated me. Clapping her hand on my thigh, she informed me I "sure got the legs" for crossing America.

"I can't ride a bicycle myself," she said, "Impossible. The only time I tried riding a bike I rode into a cow."

"I don't suppose that happened in Accident?" I asked. The alcohol was kicking in fast.

"Nar, Ohio." The dime dropped. "Oh, I get it. No... you know why they called it Accident?" I couldn't wait and cracked another can.

Sometime during the Civil War, two engineers from the opposing camps were lined up, facing each other, in two locomotives. They were on the same single stretch of the B & OR track running through Garrett County, and each wanted to proceed. Neither was prepared to back up to a passing point, so each stoked up the fires, built up a head of steam, and let the locos rip. If we are to believe Joanne, where they met was where Accident was born, on the back of an enterprising farmer's wife who set up a lemonade stall to cater for the folks that poured in to survey the devastation.

The state I was in by the time I staggered out of the roadhouse, I would have believed Bill Clinton had he stood before me claiming to be an avowed monogamist. I had trouble steering a straight line and threw my sleeping bag down on the first bit of sheltered ground to present itself. This turned out to be an island of land between where the Old National Pike prescribed a sharp left-hand bend and the younger National Road, Alt. 40, smoothed it out on Negro Mountain, known as Nigger Mountain during the Gold Rush. Close by, several Forty-Niners from the coastal plain stayed at a 'stand' or hostel run by William Sheets. Short of sleeping by the side of the road, stands were the simplest, cheapest, most unsavoury accommodation available along the National Road. Catering for drovers and teamsters, they provided pens out back for their herds, while inside the two-story cabin, road weary men flopped down for a night on the floor of the bar, feet pointing towards the fire. With five cans of Bud and a double portion of Joanne's spicy wings inside me, I was toasty enough beneath the stars.

If not as long and grinding as the haul up Big Savage Mountain, the hills on Alt. 40 kept coming like storm waves rolling towards a beach the following day. The blacktop cleared a path through tangled sycamores in their bottoms and Sitka spruces on the tops. At the end of long driveways to hidden farmsteads, election flags promoting Chester H. Sines for sheriff and Russel T. Sines for commissioner suggested the family was something of a Family in local politics.

Five miles before I reached Keyser Ridge, a McDonald's sign protruded high above the canopy of Savage River State Forest like a cocktail stick thrust in green froth. When I reached the crossroads, a dozen cars were parked beneath the 90 metre pole and the plastic diner was packed. Across the intersection, next to the Highway Department's yard, Little Sandy's Truck Stop looked a more tempting choice, recommended by a parking lot stuffed with 18-wheelers. I placed my order and took delivery of a small chicken salad which could have fed an African nation.

I hadn't anticipated having problems finding good food in America, but was discovering that fresh fruit and vegetables were a rarity in town stores. Eating out, your options were severely limited if you discounted fast food. Little Sandy's was the first café I had passed since leaving Washington whose menu wasn't restricted to the frier and microwave. At Keyser Ridge, I set myself the challenge of crossing the country without anything so naff as a McDonald's, Wendy's or Burger King passing my lips. Little did I realise what a tough task I was setting myself.

Mealtimes might have been an unholy scrum, but the food the Forty-Niners fought over in the taverns and roadhouses would have stretched Dean & DeLuca. One diarist catalogued the fare on offer at the Neil House, a hostelry further down the National Road. Starting with oyster soup, diners were invited to choose from nineteen entrees, six different pickles, sixteen savoury pastries, thirteen creams and jellies, six confectioneries or fresh fruits, and eight preserved fruits. On top of that came the main course of Indian corn and venison stew or cock-a-leekie, swilled down with applejack or a quart of good metheglin. It is difficult to understand how burgers became the American staple.

The Old National Pike slipped away from Alt. 40 and I followed it on a meander into the historic logging town of Addison. 'Village' would have been a more accurate description for this delightful backwater, but it was not a word I had heard a lot of, and 'hamlet' didn't seem to exist in the American lexicon. Few of the communities I rode through lived up to the title of a town. Somewhere along the line, the European hierarchy of terms for settlements had been dropped, perhaps in the hope that calling a hamlet a town or even a city would will it into being. Addison hadn't expanded much since the Forty-Niners traipsed through. A peaceful couple of rows of clinker built houses were wrapped like a girdle round a pregnant Allegheny mound before tying back onto the main road. Midway round its girth, another tollhouse was preserved but again its museum was closed.

Since the episode at Williamsport where I missed linking up with the Chief Interpreter of the C & OC National Park, I had not had a lot of luck with heritage sites and interpretive centres. All the National Road toll-houses I called at on different days of the week were closed. In Jocky Hollow, I arrived at the National Road Visitor Center on the dot of 11.30am and discovered that, despite a large notice stating it opened on Sundays from 10.00am until 5.00pm, it was also locked and barred.

Most of these small tourist sites rely on volunteer staff from organisations like the Daughters of the American Revolution, a kind of Women's Institute with attitude. Established over a century ago, the Daughters are a non-profit making, non-political, voluntary service group dedicated to the memory and spirit of American Independence. Or, as the Pennsylvania chapter put it when I phoned them to enquire about the tollhouses, "We believe in honouring the flag of the United States of America, in the education of children and adults, in preserving history for future generations, in a strong military, in perpetuating the memory of men and women who achieved American Independence, and in God, Home and Country."

The lilting voice on the end of the phone had to be reading a script, but it was pretty hard to square the beliefs she listed with the Daughters' incorporation as a non-political organisation. Their "categories of common service" included committees for Historic Preservation, Patriotic Education and Genealogy. Lonely hours in a damp old tollhouse waiting for the American public to show any kind of interest in their only National Road must have seemed a fairly low priority by comparison.

Chapter 4

Six miles north of the old federal road lay the little Pennsylvanian holiday village of Ohiopyle, hidden in a cleft in the Alleghenies. It was not a stop on any argonaut's itinerary but I had been on the road for a week and took the detour for a bath, a washing machine and recuperation. Four streets of seasonal lodgings and cute wooden homes were serviced by a church, fire station, post office and the Falls Market grocery store. At the bottom of the hill where the village perched, the thoroughfare was bordered on one side by a crush of outdoor leisure stores side-lining in bicycle hire and whitewater rafting. On the other side, beyond a park, a bend in the Youghiogheny River growled. The hills surrounding the community were a State Park laced with forest paths and mountain bike tracks. For the less physical, there was a cycle trail along the old Western Maryland Railroad line which pottered west to Connellsville or east to Confluence and beyond, where Jack from the roadhouse was working on its extension.

The warden of the Ohiopyle hostel was just minding the store while the official warden took a few days off. With a hang-dog expression, Don Stone apologised, but the place was fully booked for a troop of twenty-five Girl Scouts. He was expected to give up his own bed for the party and would be sleeping on the couch. Not relishing a hostel monopolised by women, he invited me to pitch my tent in the grounds, "but beware of the poison ivy. Pennsylvania's infested with the damn stuff. Darn weed can get you even when it's been dead five years. I knew a guy once..." Thinking about my nights sleeping rough beside the turnpike, my skin began to itch.

It bucketed down the following morning. Undaunted by sheet lightening and a heavy sky poised to flatten the mountains, the Girl Guides bundled into microbuses and

46

set off for an outdoor centre somewhere to the south. They left the hostel spotless. With nothing to do, Don dragged me into his beat-up dormobile and took us on a tour of the countryside. The condition of the van was a symptom of the condition of the highland tracks he confidently batted down. He knew the area well, he said, but at every undistinguished intersection Don paused long enough for me to doubt he had any idea where we were. If there was a phone line looping down the side of one of the tracks, he invariably turned right and followed it.

The lines led to isolated trailer homes set back in dark clearings hacked out of the forest. Some were 'double wides', or two trailers joined along the length like Siamese twins. Many were surrounded by a chaos of wrecked motors, partly dismantled tractors and rotting school buses now serving as chicken roosts. A few showed pride in outward appearances and had made a stab at nurturing a garden. Since nothing but rhododendrons and ground elder thrived in the gloom, plastic flowers and artificial lawns were the solution, generally guarded by gnomes, Bambis and Barbie Dolls.

During the course of a day rattling across the high country, we hit tarmac a couple of times and cruised through 'frontier towns' which weren't on either of our maps. Amounting to no more than a handful of houses, it was difficult to work out if these places were growing up or dying on their feet. They had the appearance of being temporary. Families lived in glueboard shells which, by the height of the rising damp, had been waiting for some time to be clad in sheets of plastic clapboard. With a sneer, Don explained the insanity of this modern method of construction. Apparently he used to be an architect, before his wife of twenty-three years ran off with his best friend.

"In the East, the earliest American homes were made of wood. Not only were they quick and easy to put up, but the wood was there for the taking. Also — something most people don't appreciate — those houses were never meant to last. People were still moving west. They were temporary shelters for people feeling their way into a new continent, built to last a generation or less. Variations on the early clapboard or board-and-batten style of building have trickled down the ages. Ironically, they've ended up in a computerised vacuum former in a push-button factory churning out non-biodegradable repros of the frontier days of impermanence. The original houses were organic. If properly maintained, they would settle and survive for centuries. As you can see, plastic sheeting doesn't live. As the glueboard settles, the outer shell simply cracks. So the house built to last less than a generation lasts for generations, and the one built to last generations lasts less than a decade. Crazy, yeh?"

One frontier town which was an established settlement — unrecognised by Rand McNally but on everybody's shopping map — was Pechin. Named after a family which had done well out of selling supplies to the surrounding settlers, Pechin's hot spot was a large sloping car park surrounded on three sides by a shanty town of seedy breeze block sheds housing a grocery, bakery, hardware store, delicatessen, clothes shop and 'sports emporium'. We were there to stock up the hostel's larder. As I walked bent double along the dark fusty aisles of the grocery shed, dodging the warped ceiling boards and the water dripping from damp patches onto sacks of flour, I made a mental note not to eat with Don that night.

How Pechin's stores passed the environmental health inspectors surely didn't bear investigation. The tarred floor was slippery with mould, the fridges were rusty inside and out, the place reeked, and saturated palettes sagged under the weight of caterers' packs of goods you had to wipe the condensation off to discover what they contained. The fire exits were blocked by more piles of caterers' packs, but the grotto was shoulder to shoulder with eager shoppers filling multiple trolleys with enough food to fill the back of a pick-up. Pechin's was cheap but certainly not cheerful.

"You think this is bad," Don said, picking up on my expression of disgust, "wait 'til we go to the restaurant."

That night I had trouble with my bowels. I finally dragged my sleeping bag into the hostel and slept on the toilet.

Steam rose from the valley floor as from a Turkish bath. Above a couple of hundred feet, the mountains faded into an olive haze, merging into a pale yellow wash where the sun struggled to burn through the dense mist. Nothing stirred in Ohiopyle save for a couple of chipmunks having a tug-of-war over the remains of a sandwich which hadn't made it into the litter bin. It was 5.30am on a schleppy morning and I was stood in the gloom outside the Falls Market store, waiting for the payphone to ring, poised to do a live interview with BBC Radio Nottingham for their mid-morning show.

The interview went well and I was animated, flapping my hand up and down, pacing around the sound booth at the full extension of the telephone cord. When it was over, I carefully worked my way through the dialling marathon for Nottingham, England. If everything was going to plan with her mum, we had agreed Sandy would be working at home to receive a regular Tuesday call. The morning sun was winning its battle, and I could now make out the railroad through the billowing steam still rising from the Youghiogheny. It was going to be a fabulous day.

Sandy's voice came over the line as clearly as if she was on the next block. She sounded low, forcing herself to be chirpy about hearing me on the radio. My excitement at being alive and well and in Ohiopyle for the start of another chapter of the Forty-Niner's story evidently wasn't infectious. Her voice was wobbly. She was struggling to surf on any part of my wave of vivacity. I stopped gushing and asked, "How's your mum?"

A terrible sigh blasted through the ear piece.

"They took another blood test." Her voice was breaking up. "She's had to go back into hospital. I've just heard. She's really poorly, John."

A chasm opened up and Ohiopyle fell in. While I tumbled through desperate thoughts, Sandy explained how her mum had picked up after returning home, allowing Sandy to get back to work in Nottingham. The phone call from the hospital came three days later, just as she was beginning to feel more positive about her mum's prospects. The news had gutted her. I clung to the phone, hugging Sandy tight. "It's not fair. It's just not fucking fair."

It was all we could think to say to each other. Without knowing exactly what had set Pauline back, we thought the worst but couldn't speak it. Sandy had to get to the hospital immediately. I promised to call again in a couple of days when she had more details, blew a kiss, put the phone down and slumped against the back of the bench.

I needed caffeine and shuffled into the store by the side entrance. It had yet to open but, under a couple of naked light bulbs, five men in denim overalls were forking up hash browns and knocking back black coffee. I didn't feel sociable and declined the invitation to join them. It wasn't simply that I was upset about Pauline and feeling useless for Sandy. I sensed the prospects for my adventure were at best tentative, at worst terminal, and I wasn't even a quarter the way across America. I became maudlin, and left before finishing my drink.

I sloped back to the hostel lost in confused thoughts. The valley was bathed in rays of gold but a small black cloud sloped along above me, raining down stair rods of anguish. The day-sack which never left me began to slip off my right shoulder and I gave a mighty shrug to flip it back into place. A sharp pain stabbed my lower abdomen and I buckled. A second stab and I was on my knees, arms outstretched like a sprinter in the blocks, holding my breath until the pain subsided. I rose gingerly, brushed off the gravel embedded in my palms and knees, and discovered a slight bulge had appeared below my appendix. Shuffling along like I was scanning the pavement for butt-ends, I returned to the hostel and slid into my tent. I felt miserable. On top of everything, I had torn a muscle, so I thought.

Before I flew out, Sandy and myself half-heartedly discussed the possibility of my having to abort on account of her mum's health. My mother-in-law's fight against cancer had now accelerated into what sounded like a losing battle. My soul mate was running about like a blue arsed fly, desperate for support from hubby. Hubby was on the other side of the Atlantic locked into something totally selfish and inconsequential. Neither women wanted to be the cause of my jacking in the American odyssey. I didn't want to drop everything and jet home to discover there had been another reversal and Pauline was back on her feet. I was at a loss to know what to do.

I spent the day at the picnic table in the grounds of the hostel trying to be productive. I worked my way through back issues of *The Milepost*, the National Road heritage paper, but little sank in. I brought my notes up to date, but had problems recalling recent events. I tried to do some maintenance on the bike, but found nothing amiss.

Some of the new intake of hostel guests stopped by my table to chat. They helped take my mind off things. Pete and Mami Marshall were newly married and probably hadn't let go of each other since the priest said, "You may kiss the bride." Pete was a crooner for a swing revival orchestra doing big things in Pittsburgh. Mami was a landscape architect and the serious one. She navigated our conversation round to talking about race, "probably the most compelling social issue in modern day America."

She was Japanese-American and Pete was "Scotch-American, descended from Jocks who were planted in Ireland then emigrated as Scotch-Irish," he explained. "Yeh, I know. It gets complicated." Mami said that her and Pete were already "eighth-breeds."

"When you think of the stigma attached to being a half-breed in the nineteenth century, then realise how few Americans are now ethnically or nationally pure, you realise we are creating a quite extraordinary nation of mixed blood castes. We're a bunch of mutts!"

"Today's Americans just don't look like yesterday's Americans," Pete said. "Speilberg discovered that when he tried casting *Saving Private Ryan*. No John Wayne looka-likes."

With each new generation, Americans were moving further and further from the largely Euro-American roots of the nation, whose prejudices Pete felt still dominated the power elite in the capital. Mami believed there was a ground swell of resentment against paying federal taxes and therefore being seen by the world to subscribe to what Capitol Hill does around the planet in the name of the American people. "Do you realise that, since the Second World War, we've bombed twenty foreign countries?"

"We're kind of a nation of nations," Pete said. "It's almost impossible for the U.S. to stage a war anywhere in the world without upsetting a vociferous minority of our own people."

Two days earlier, somebody had blown up the United States embassies in Kenya and Tanzania killing over two hundred people, twelve of them Americans. The CIA were blaming an Arab terrorist cell led by the little known fundamentalist Osama Bin Laden.

"You wait," Mami said, "We'll do a Libya on some poor Third World country. A load more innocent civilians will die and Arab investors on Wall Street will pull the plugs."

"Hey, what was George Washington if not a terrorist!," Pete exclaimed with arms outstretched, as if hitting the final note of *My Way*.

Of those who joined me to shoot the breeze, only Dan and Harry picked up that all was not well. They were an odd couple who could have been *The Odd Couple* had Harry looked more like Jack Lemmon. Don was the embodiment of Walter Matthau at his most sardonic, and could have done voice-overs for the great ham without anybody being the wiser. They fed and fussed over me, prizing out details of the drama unfolding back in the UK

Both in their seventies, they had been through the trauma of their parents' deaths and were, in the gentlest way possible, preparing their children for their own. Meantime, they were batting around on pushbikes exploring Pennsylvania's Rails-to-Trails.

Harry's advice was to, "Get it done, John, get it done. No point sitting round here stewing, son. Get on that bike and get pedalling."

"You've already given up," Dan cajoled me. "Nobody knows what's happening at home. As long as you sit wallowing in self pity, you're sending out negative vibes that don't need a Boeing 747 to cross the Atlantic."

There were barely four hours of daylight left but I took their advice. Bundling my gear together, I headed off along the Western Union cycle trail following the Youghiogheny downstream. Almost immediately I was clasped in the same embrace of dense forest which had inhibited my appreciation of the Appalachians along the C & OC, but it felt good to be eating up the miles. I stormed down the R2T, eager to get back amongst the diesel fumes and motor rumble of the National Road. The physical activity induced a degree of optimism and a torrent of sweat. When I burst from the trees and swung into Connellsville, I celebrated with a coffee and donut. At the corner of a gas station, on the steps of an old railroad guard's van selling used CDs, I set about planning the next couple of days of my journey. I was reacquainting myself with the argonauts' trip through Pennsylvania when a motorcycle cop roared into the centre of the main crossroads opposite the music shop. Stopping the traffic, he waved through a cavalcade of twenty cars, each with a small flag of a white cross on a blue background flapping from their aerial. Right then, a funeral cortege was the last thing I needed to see.

A day later I returned to the National Road along leafy Appalachian lanes which hammered muscles and carried me to blind heights. Swinging into the heritage site of Fort Necessity, I hoped that a swift injection of American history would help me focus back on the job in hand. I had reached the end of Washington's Road and the site of his desperate encounter with the French.

Dispatched in 1754 by the Ohio Company to stall the advancing French, Washington was invested with the task of establishing a fort at the junction of the Allegheny and Monongahela Rivers, south of the French line of forts at what is now Pittsburgh. Delayed by the constrictions of Nemacolin's Path, he continued to press forward, despite intelligence that the French had already reached the river junction and built their own stronghold. Near Great Meadows, where I now stood, the young surveyor made a series of bad tactical decisions.

He set up camp on land he thought was 'a charming field for an encounter' but was actually a bog. He ambushed a reconnaissance party which included the brother of the commander of the French forces, killing ten and capturing all but the one who scurried back to raise the alarm. Now equally alarmed, Washington set his men to build an impromptu stockade in the marshland, dangerously close to tree cover. When the French eventually arrived and surrounded Fort Necessity, the heavens opened flooding the meadow. Outnumbered four to one and after a day of terrible casualties, Washington finally surrendered. He was imprisoned, ridiculed and forced to sign a confession stating that he had assassinated the commander's brother. Only then were he and his men allowed to return to Virginia.

The tape-slide show in the Visitor Center glossed over Washington's humiliation and somehow presented him as a conquering hero. Down the hill from the centre stood a small log cabin surrounded by a circle of upright logs, seven foot tall, pointed and shaved flat on the outside. It was the most recent in a series of reproductions of Washington's hastily erected stockade which began in 1932 with the archaeologists getting it wrong. Based on their reading of ground impressions, they originally erected a diamond shaped fort. Then somebody thought to check eye-witness accounts and discovered the structure was a 'Small Stocado Fort made in a Circular Fform (*sic*) round a Small House that stood in the Middle'. Further digging revealed the charred stumps of the original uprights and an accurate reproduction was finally put in place.

Addressing the problem of wood rot and the need to rebuild the stockade every ten years, the National Park Service had now found a way to erect "an authentic historic fort that will be cost effective to maintain," the ranger assured me. "The next Fort Necessity will be wood above ground level and non-biodegradable plastic beneath. In Europe I guess you wouldn't waste your time on such a project. Over here, this is an ancient site, as meaningful to us as Stonehenge is to you guys. In America, three hundred years takes us back to our prehistory."

A mile up Alt. 40, on the opposite side to the stockade, lay Braddock's Grave, possibly the last resting place of the man the British sent in to rectify Washington's bungled attempt to halt the French. Forty three years in the regiment previously commanded by his Major General father of the same name, General Edward Braddock was an old style Coldstream Guard, clueless about forest fighting and guerrilla tactics, and a staunch member of the British aristocracy. He loathed Americans and had no time for the tactical recommendations of their Amerindian scouts.

Despite superior forces, Braddock was outflanked, defeated, and mortally wounded by the French not far from where they captured Washington. He died during a frantic retreat and his last words are said to have been, "We shall better know how to deal with them another time." Whether he was referring to the French, the Americans or the natives we will never know. He was originally buried in the path of the road his troops helped to improve. There the general turned in his grave for over fifty years before workmen dug up what were thought to be his bones.

I walked down the short, evocative length of Braddock's Road where the general had been hurriedly interned. For less than a hundred yards, it arched gently into a scrubby little valley, stopping before a creek and a mesh of tangled forest. It was barely the width of an artillery wagon and wheel ruts were etched in the roadbed. On a small knoll between the track and the modern National Road stood a twelve foot monument to Braddock. Looking like a plinth awaiting a statue, it was erected by the Coldstream Guards in 1913 on the site of their commander's second grave.

I couldn't resist the hope that the arrogant old duffer was still rotting somewhere down in the damp valley and that an American irregular from Maryland was the unknown soldier receiving all the honours.

Chapter 5
National Road

Another interminable ascent carried me to a continuation of Chestnut Ridge, the densely forested spine I had explored with warden Don Stone. Rattling around in his dormobile, I had seen little of Pennsylvania beyond a whole lot of maples, but here, at Laurel Hill, the western aspect afforded a breathtaking view. If I couldn't see California, whatever was glistening on the distant horizon had to be the Mississippi. Ahead of me, America appeared flat as a pancake, though of course it wasn't. Chestnut Ridge was simply the last pinnacle over 2,000 feet for the next 2,000 miles. At the foot of the ridge, Uniontown, the first proper town since Cumberland, carved out a space in the forest. Relieved to be out of the mountains, I sped down the edge, shooting past traffic held back by 15 mph speed limits.

Jammed between prefabricated blocks housing Expert Tyre, Super America and the Columbia Energy Group, I stumbled on Uniontown's Old West Schoolhouse, a log cabin erected in 1810. Currently owned by the National Road Heritage Park, the schoolhouse contained a two room information centre which was actually open. Inside I found Rachel Vaughn sat at a blank computer, engrossed in a John Grisham novel with the soundtrack from *Titanic* buzzing through her headphones. Rachel was nineteen, bright, helpful, and delighted to have somebody to talk to. Her summer job was proving stunningly dull, with considerably fewer visitors than her employers had led her to expect. She ran through the origins of the federal road for me, outlined the battle in Congress over funding, and explained how senators whose constituents lived a thousand miles from the proposed thoroughfare were reluctant to stump up for something they would see no direct benefit from. "It was kind of like asking Hungary to put in for a freeway from Cork to Dublin funded by the E.C.," she observed.

Not only did Rachel know her history, she had a grasp on things European I had previously not encountered in America. She was good and knew it, and had no intention of making a career out of working for the Heritage Park.

"I'm tired of living round here," she told me. "It gets worse every year. I'm getting out. I'm at Jackson School — sort of half way between here and Brownsville — training to become an elementary teacher for the hearing and sight impaired. There's no demand for it round here. I'm hoping to move to Philadelphia. My boyfriend's there. This place is terminal."

A promotional paper for Uniontown made great play of Beesontown — its original name — being born on the same day the nation was founded. When the National Road came through, Henry Beeson's hamlet of rural cottages was transformed into a ferment of industry, with stagecoach factories, blacksmiths, stables, leather workers, and all the ancillary services needed to tend travellers, animals and vehicles which had survived or were about to take on the rigours of crossing the Appalachians.

It wasn't a big place but, since the 1950s, Uniontown had been on the skids. I didn't have to walk far to see disheartening signs of boarded up buildings, flattened blocks and structural decay defacing the impressive facades of once illustrious department stores. The town's motto, 'Uniting tradition with innovation', was only in evidence around the imposing stone courthouse. Built in the 1890s and resembling a stern English public school, the court was the focus of all legal activities appertaining to Fayette County. Either side of the building, along Alt. 40, a swarm of law firms were getting fat on the pollen of county crimes and misdemeanours. According to Rachel, attorneys were about the only people keeping Uniontown alive.

It was a familiar story of community meltdown after the implosion of the coal and steel industries, and the narrative dragged on through the remaining urban areas of Pennsylvania and the short ride across the panhandle of West Virginia. The bleakest town was Brownsville, eleven miles down the road and perched on a steep eastern bluff carved out by a broad bend in the Monongahela River. Picture a ski jump 300 feet wide flanked by flat faced, characterless shops and bars, and you've pretty well got Brownsville, at least where the National Road lunges over the river. The swoop was a funnel for a chilly wind which prowled menacingly through the town. Behind the top of the jump, peeking above a sycamore canopy, the bluff still supported the surfeit of ecumenical architecture which once blessed the town with the grand title of 'The City of Spires'. Glittering they were not.

Cranking through the foothills of the Appalachians might have taken me to lower heights, but now the climbs came with disheartening regularity. After Beallesville, I gained the spine of Twelve Mile Ridge and was relieved the highway clung to the backbone all the way to Washington, PA, the third town on my route thus far to be named after Georgie-boy. Either side, the wooded slopes of Pennsylvania slipped down to lush valley bottoms jewelled with sparkling corn hoppers. The road became scarred with thin lines of tar sealing a shattering of cracks. Its scabby trail flowed from one side of the ridge to the other, through small communities like Scenery Hill which had found new life in old jugs. Antique shops abounded among the white wooden houses, each a chaos of farm tools, furniture and knick-knacks which barely looked second hand.

The character of the road was changing. It was now almost continuously marshalled by spick and span bungalows and small brick houses sitting pretty in acres of lawn. As I rode west, the tinny clatter of mowers cumulated to the pitch of feedback and the air was heavy with exhaust. Everywhere I looked people were sat on or striding behind grass cutters. Every last square centimetre of anything which could vaguely be called grass was diligently weeded and lovingly trimmed until a green fit for Tiger Woods was sculpted. It wasn't difficult to see how America consumed more petrol in a year of mowing lawns than the UK did in a year of motoring.

The bleakest stretch of country was the short leg through West Virginia following the Ohio Creek down to Wheeling. A long gradual descent between high wooded cliffs ricocheted the road from one side of Valley Gorge to the other. In the space between rebounds, manky trailer homes had been levered nose-to-tail onto the verge. In the two metre strip between trailer and road, power and telephone poles were planted at drunken angles. From gaps beneath the trailers, children's trundle toys overflowed onto the congealed oil and mud of the strip. The valley reminded me of one I had ridden down in Slovakia, except there the poverty was clean and house-proud.

Arriving in Wheeling should have been cause for celebration. Located beside the slothful Ohio, it was the river crossing surveyors on the first section of the National Road set their theodolite sights on. Built concurrently in short sections, the length from Cumberland to Wheeling was completed in 1811, seven years after the ground-breaking ceremony. By then, lobbying was well advanced for Congress to shell out for the second phase, across the forested undulations of Ohio, Indiana and Illinois to the banks of the Mississippi.

Unlike the Chesapeake and Ohio Canal, the federal highway was an immediate and outstanding success. After riding its length in 1816, Uriah Brown summed up what most farmers, civic leaders, entrepreneurs and members of the travelling public undoubtedly felt. 'The goodness of God must have been in Congress unknowns to them; when they fell about to and Erected a Lane for the Making of this great Turnpike road which is the Salvation of those Mountains or Western Countrys and more benefit to the human family than Congress have any knowledge.'

And I would have celebrated reaching Wheeling, had it shown me one iota of welcome, but the town was as hostile to modern cyclists as it was to eighteenth century whites. Legend had it that 'Wheeling' was Delaware Indian for 'Place of the Skull', supposedly named after the indigenous people decapitated the first settlers and stuck their heads on poles.

Initially the ride into town wasn't too harrowing. Where the Madonna of the Trail stood on an eight foot plinth in a lay-by beside the municipal golf course, the road was lined by walled gardens and large redbrick houses held high by mock doric columns. Possibly they were occupied by lecturers employed at the Jesuit University down the road. One conscientious academic with flowing grey locks, a crumpled white suit and deep Alabama drawl made it his business to give me a roadside tutorial on the sculpture. It was the second Madonna I had come across, an exact duplicate of one at Beallesville located opposite another golf club. Ten foot tall and cast in algonite stone, the statue depicted a pioneer woman nursing a baby while her young son clutched at her skirt. According to my professor, the statue was erected by the Daughters of the American Revolution in the late 1920s.

"A decade earlier," he said, "the Daughters had set up a National Old Trails Committee in order to waymark some of the nation's historically famous land routes. A metal plaque was initially proposed but it was thought this heroic sculpture by August Leimbach would stand out more."

61

It certainly did. Missouri granite mixed in the algonite coloured the Madonna shocking pink.

Since departing Washington, PA, the line of the National Road had been shadowed by Interstate 70. An eight lane girdle strapped round the midriff of America, I-70 crosses nine states, falling two short of a coast-to-coast thoroughfare. Laid in the Fifties and Sixties, it by-passes all of the villages, most of the towns and some of the cities on Route 40, summarily retiring settlements which once fed off the National Road. They have become sleeper communities, their reveries disturbed twenty-four seven by the incessant whine of rubber emanating from the interstate a quarter of a mile to the north.

On the edge of Wheeling's town centre, the interstate smothered the old highway. Off to the right, a more recent Route 40 took me round the back of the metropolis, through a cacophony orchestrated by panel beaters, exhaust fitters and tyre retreaders. The highway climbed a cliff face builders of the National Road would never have attempted to a vantage point on Mount Wood overlooking the whole grotty city. Wheeling was a steel town, home to an outpost of the Pittsburgh Steel Corporation, but it was the rusting hulk of an abandoned mill which dominated the skyline. It hung in the balance how long rolled steel would continue to flow from Wheeling's remaining foundries. Half of Pittsburgh Steel was owned by Don Yang Tinplate Ltd and Nittetsu Shoja, names which suggest the collapse of the Tiger economies could have more than a passing concern for workers in West Virginia. Outside Big Boy Restaurant & Market, a hand-written sign read, 'Support the Soup Kitchen of Greater Wheeling by Buying a Tomato for a Dollar'.

Wheeling gave me my first taste of having to fight for space on the American blacktop. By the time I reached the river, I was a hardened campaigner, deaf to abuse and skilled at dodging drivers trying to carve me up. I thought I was surviving well, making sustained if dangerous progress, until I reached the river crossing. At Wheeling I discovered cyclists are prohibited from entering America west of the Ohio.

There were two bridges thundering across the river, both exclusively for interstate traffic. Somewhere in Wheeling there had be a way for cyclists to cross to the west bank, and there was, according to those I asked, if I was prepared to ride five miles south to a toll bridge out of town or a further twelve miles to the bridge at Moundsville. I manhandled my bike over the concrete barrier onto I-70 and ignored the blaring of car horns.

On the far side, beyond Wheeling Island, I caught my breath on a bench trying to sell me 'Happy Hubcaps' to cheer up your auto, and soaked up the atmosphere. I had reached the historic artery which once kept the heart of America pumping. Down the 'wet road' flowed trade with the north and south. Across it, ferries hauled creaking Conestoga wagons full of whiskey, corn and timber to the start of the new trans-Appalachian highway. Thirty years later, the Forty-Niners crossed the other way over the first suspension bridge, completed that year. Travelling in coaches and wagons, on horseback and foot, they crossed the Ohio River and entered the Old West. The frontier was ever on the move, heading for the Pacific, and Wheeling was the second Gateway to the West I passed through.

I gave those thoughts about five minutes. Any longer and the atmosphere I was soaking up would have asphyxiated me. The bench was on a lonely island of concrete prowled either side and overhead by a continuous stream of articulated rigs belching clouds of black smoke. Wheezing from an overdose of exhaust, I left Wheeling feeling depressed and angry. It wasn't just that the town was utterly awful or that its drivers had been unbelievably intolerant. Nor was it that my injured abdomen was beginning to make itself felt. Since Ohiopyle, my mother-in-law had never been far from my thoughts. The uncertainty of her condition made it impossible to focus on what I was supposed to be doing in the States, let alone enjoy it.

My increasing negativity was further fuelled by the problem of finding suitable places to kip. The National Road was studded with hotels, motels and B & Bs, many of them contemporary to the time of the Forty-Niners but, like them, I was travelling on a shoestring. Between impenetrable forests, insurgent lawns and fields deep in corn, there wasn't a lot of spare land for wild camping, and doors I knocked at mostly weren't answered. If they were, the occupant wasn't going to entertain a Brit sticking four pegs into their sea of lovingly rolled green. This was made abundantly clear in East Richmond when the door of a log bungalow swung open to reveal a middle-aged woman striking a pose straight out of a John Ford Western. She was holding a pump-action shotgun angled to blast my knees away. Her response to my entreaty was repeated flicks of the shotgun and something akin to, "Getaway with you over the hill." She didn't see me for dust.

Twenty-five miles into Ohio, the National Road was again gobbled up by Interstate 70, forcing me onto a loop of country roads which swung south past Senecaville Lake. The map indicated it was a State Park with official campsites. After three nights of sleeping in ditches, I rode like a man possessed towards a steaming hot shower.

Speeding down the tight hills clasping the reservoir, I swept into the first site and stopped just beyond the doorway to the reception booth. As I dismounted, a security guard lunged out of the cubicle, hand on revolver butt, and charged towards me. I swung round to see who he was chasing, but it was me. "Resort Grounds is a private site," the sexagenarian panted, his hand on my shoulder more leaning than grabbing. He said he would have "plugged" me had I set a foot inside the compound.

The second ground — a State Park site — was busy with weekend campers, but the warden had no space for a single person tent. Had I arrived with a fifty foot RV, a speed boat, a couple of tents for the kids, a barbecue with table, chairs, strings of outdoor lighting, fold-out patio and a selection of illuminated garden ornaments, like any normal camper, she had a couple of plots vacant at an overnight price equivalent to two nights in a hotel.

The third and last site was also run by the State Park and did cater for hiker/bikers. Unfortunately a tornado had swept through the valley the week before and swamped the mini plots. Though dry, the rangers were reluctant to allow me to pitch on the hard mud. It took four of them to come to this decision, a conference involving myself and the warden sandwiched between two squad cars summoned by her shortwave radio. Exhausted, mad and oozing sweat from every orifice, I rode away cursing, determined to crawl into bed that night smelling sweet and awake someplace where I could chill for a couple of days.

Even the Forty-Niners, hell bent on reaching the gold fields, took one day in seven out. For those in a joint stock company, it was written into their constitution that Sunday was a day of rest when the men would repair and maintain, and observe the Sabbath. Until things began to fall apart in the wilderness west of Kansas, they staged interdenominational services, often joined by independent travellers who likewise took the Sunday off, if only because teamsters and stagecoach companies shut up shop on the seventh day.

As the dull chill of a whimpering evening triggered a longing to be home and curled up with Sandy, I returned to a National Road released from the suffocation of I-70. Two and a half hours later, I staggered into Spring Valley Campground, south of Cambridge. I was met by a broad smile and a warm bowl of butterscotch popcorn, freshly exploded in a sliced off oil barrel slung over a roaring wood fire. Happy campers stuffing their faces welcomed me out of the dark like a prodigal son. On a day when I felt thoroughly harassed and unwanted, it was nice to know not everybody in the East was a miserable bastard.

Spring Valley had been chewed up by the same tornado which wiped out the backpacker plots at the Senecaville campsite. Sat under the awning of a recreation vehicle which hadn't driven anywhere in five years, a retired couple told me about popping down from their home in Wheeling to clean up the mess.

"We found our picnic furniture wedged up there in the woods," the old boy said, jerking a thumb at the canopy of beeches behind the site. "The neighbour's RV lay on its side with our washing pole through its windshield and a load of torn branches over it."

Saplings had been ripped up, van roofs prized open and the ground swam in water sucked up by the twister at Senecaville Lake and spun out at Spring Valley. Signs of the destruction remained in the shredded canopies, snapped lattice fences and trees stripped of leaves a season before autumn.

Although favouring a belt from Texas to Nebraska known as Tornado Alley, twisters are not uncommon in states located between the Appalachians and Mississippi River. The previous year was not only the hottest on record by a length, it was also the worst for tornadoes. Ohio had been hit by sixteen. On a sliding scale of one to five, the twister that swung through Spring Valley was a baby, barely reaching F2 on the Fujita scale, but it had taken a life. It was one of maybe a thousand unremarkable tornadoes which would swirl across the States that year. If unremarkable in their intensity, they were remarkable in their number. Climate change had triggered an increase in local activity in recent years, particularly between April and July, and everybody I spoke to at Spring Valley agreed the weather was turning vicious.

As I was to discover the further west I travelled, the weather in this country is the one force people cannot ignore. While the media indulged anybody who could string together an argument purporting to prove there was no link between exhaust emissions, global warming and climate change, those I met at Spring Valley were not convinced. But as a woman who sagged in all the wrong places said to me at the poolside, "Hell, we're just as worried by climate change as you guys but, hey, we're resigned to it."

While basting his skin in Aftersun Lotion which sizzled on contact, her husband added, "Issues like global warming have become big yawns in this country. To do anything about them requires sacrifices Americans and the multinationals are simply not prepared to make. Sacrifice is for losers and every American wants to be a winner, regardless that ultimately all of us lose. It's all very petty-minded."

I left Spring Valley a new man, smelling more human than primate and feeling more optimistic about my journey. On a day when temperatures were nudging into the forties and you could spit-roast a groundhog without a flame, I rode fully clothed, every inch of me covered or shaded. On the radio, a public service announcement by the Environment Protection Agency worked hard to encourage the nation to save energy by turning off the TV when not watching it and turning off lights when leaving a room. Their *coup de grâce*, however, was clearly designed to make a major dent in America's generous contribution to global warming. "And, folks," the voice said, "decide what you want out of the fridge before opening the door and being indecisive."

If it seems a strange thing to clip onto a handlebar, I rarely make a long journey without my FM radio. Aside from the news and weather forecast, a little on-bike entertainment goes a long way when the road ahead has nothing to offer but a whole lot of tarmac. In foreign countries, it is also invaluable for getting a handle on the lingo. I could now say, "Hey!" as fluently as any American, but today I was in the mood for a sing-a-long. The landscape had changed again. Pedalling was no longer hard work. Gone were the suffocating rows of bungalows, the short crippling hills and dark forests. I rode across gentle undulations, rolling between bean fields and leatherwood copses. For the first time, the vast expanse of the deep blue sky impressed itself upon me.

Chapter 6

I had now completed a third of the 600 miles of the National Road, undoubtably the longest, thinnest national heritage site in the United States. It had a governing body, Friends who support it, and an annual festival in May which included covered wagons travelling down it. In co-operation with Americorps, efforts were being made to improve the National Heritage Park in the hope of attracting more tourists. Eye-sores were being beautified and dilapidated houses were being renovated but, despite all I read in *The Milepost*, it was difficult to believe anybody gave a hoot about the old turnpike. Aside from an occasional stone bridge and the tollhouses, I saw little that indicated I was journeying down the country's most prestigious land route.

America was dragged westwards along this highway. The ideas and traditions hauled in on the back of it shaped the future mind set of the nation. You could trace styles of architecture down it, how they matured and mutated, and follow lines of migration specific to certain nationalities or even regions within the homeland. In 1849, it was the artery prospective gold diggers travelled north or south to join, before turning left or right to swell the stream of migrants heading west. The National Road carried the American Dream to the rising sun. It was the original Main Street, USA, and the expanding American empire's Appian Way, but only the regular mile markers pressed home that I was riding a historic line, and they had become sporadic since entering Ohio.

The National Road Museum outside Norwich, however, was an oasis of enlightenment I hadn't expected. I was shown round by volunteer Dick Baltzly, a retired school master from Zanesville whose grandfather-in-law had the dubious distinction of being the first motorist to be killed overshooting an S-bridge. Shaped in a double curve and built during the 1820s, only a handful remained beside Route 40, though I doubt the motoring public paid them much heed. I thought their unusual design was to control runaway horses.

"It used to be said they were crooked bridges to carry crooked politicians to Washington," Dick explained, "but the kinks simply straightened out the road. When you're cutting stone, it's easier to bridge a river at right angles. But with the advent of automobiles and speeds of fifteen miles an hour, they became death traps."

Dick delighted in bringing the story of the National Road to life, and our tour of the museum kept me enthralled for four hours. Impressed that I was pedalling the length of the old highway, or those sections not under interstates, Dick told me how indebted the motoring public should feel towards cyclists and the League of American Wheelmen.

"If it wasn't for you guys, the road would probably still be a dirt road. In the way these things happen in this country, people had abandoned the National Road by the 1860s and taken to the new railroads. The road fell into terrible disrepair."

He showed me a faded photo of a length through Scenery Hill, then called Hillsboro. The mud was knee deep. Four men were trying to lift a buggy out of the mire while a fifth pulled at the horse.

"For a short time we got the cycling bug and ran 'century races' (100 miles) up and down the road. When the League of American Wheelmen got going, a major plank of their advocacy was for the improvement of the National Road. Ten years later the authorities laid the first length of concrete, just the other side of Zanesville."

When the twenty-five miles laid to Hebron was completed in 1916, it became the first road in the world gridlocked by motor cars. Of a Sunday, almost all of Muskingum County's 1,557 car owners were out there battling for the space to enjoy the smoothest ride in the land.

Interstates and Wheeling aside, pedalling through America had so far been pleasurable. Unlike the British, drivers were generally courteous, relaxed and gave me a wide berth, possibly because cyclists were less in evidence than Amish horse and carriages. Except for those on the Big Bike Ride, I had yet to see one, but I was about to cross my first major city since leaving Washington. I wasn't thrilled by the knowledge that the National Road had an eighty-three year old tradition of tailbacks.

When President Thomas Jefferson finally gave the nod for construction of a national road, he signed a document which stipulated the highway would run through the capitals of all the states it traversed. At the beginning of the nineteenth century, the only state capital along its route worthy of the title was Columbus, Ohio, some twenty miles west of Hebron. Today the streets are littered with monuments to Christopher Columbus and a replica of the *Santa Maria* is moored downtown on the Scioto River, but the city has never managed to attract visitors in the way Cleveland or Cincinnati have. In 1992, the civic elders attempted to put this to rights by capitalising on the quincentennial of its namesake. Unfortunately, the celebrations back-fired when Native Americans pointed out that Columbus was not somebody any right-minded American should wish to eulogise.

If the great explorer's reputation is somewhat tarnished by his record as a genocidal maniac and bulk exporter of slaves, he was also the man who instigated the world's first gold rush. What Columbus 'found' in Haiti set France, Britain, Portugal, Holland and Spain pitching against each other in a race to rob the Americas — plundering which totally changed the course of world history. Almost overnight, gold and silver replaced land and property as the basis for European wealth. A 400% increase in inflation utterly undermined the continent's economic *status quo*, giving rise to a powerful new merchant class. Their merchantile system of trading around the Atlantic rim laid the basis for what was to become global capitalism.

But these heady leaps across 300 years failed to register with the ranks of gold seekers hauling through Columbus in 1849. None were the slightest bit interested in how the find in California would impact on anybody but themselves, and they were eager to keep moving. On a day when all I set myself was to cross Columbus on the main thoroughfare, I was solely concerned with reaching the far side in one piece.

The lead-in started at Reynoldsburg, a dozen miles from the city centre. It was a suburb of sharply defined lawns and well maintained bungalows, many occupied by professionals operating from home. There were doctor and peredontic practices, monumental masons and insurance agents, beauticians and dieticians, and legions of chiropractors. You could find a cure for every American ill beside the National Road. Two miles on, the road became pregnant, spasmed across the ring road or beltway of I-270, and gave birth to another raft of lanes. Suddenly I was no longer pottering down a quiet highway. In front was a bus whose air conditioning unit blew sickly hot air straight into my face. Behind was a queue of roasting motorists disappearing back into a shimmering heat haze heavy with pollution. To my left I was boxed by lane after lane of flustered drivers. Nobody could overtake between traffic lights which appeared as regularly as the joins in a railway track, and nobody could overtake me because I was cycling at their speed. To use the lingo, they were 'pissed'.

We entered the chaos of the plastic shanty town euphemistically called an 'out-of-town development'. To my right, the perspective was crammed with vinyl throw-ups, each fast food outlet formed in a corporate mould which uniquely identified them from their nearest competitor next door. To call them buildings besmirches the word. Throw-ups better describes their construction (and what their culinary chemistry can do to a stomach).

71

Each housed a corporate interior selling corporate junk which corporate marketing men had duped Americans into calling food. There were hundreds of them, each with their own driveway and excessive expanse of parking. There wasn't a player missing.

Having ridden along a mile of single acre lots containing one run of junk food joints, the pack was reshuffled and a second deal of the same throw-ups appeared in a different order for a second mile. Then a third, and so it went on. I ground my way down five miles of sprawling plastic before I reached anything approximating a brick building. There was no hard shoulder and the verge was a long thin pin cushion of neon signs and utility poles strung with a chaos of wires like spaghetti trees. A small civic road sign travelled past my shoulder — 'Keep Franklin Beautiful'. I rode on, half expecting a follow up to say, 'Too Late'.

My eyes were stinging, my cheeks streamed with tears, and I wheezed like a climber with altitude sickness. The air was foul, laced with exhaust and rancid fat from kitchen extractors. Nobody who smelt the stomach churning odour would ever eat at these places, but everybody except muggins was sealed in a tin can, breathing air conditioned sweetness.

The road ducked under a railroad bridge and emerged at Whitehall, once a white middle-class suburb of outstanding town houses, now a black ghetto of multiple occupancies going to rot. On a third floor balcony, a family were having lunch beneath the ribs of a roof covered with black polythene holed as a vagabond's vest. Porches were crudely shorn up with six-by-fours. Windows were glazed with flattened cardboard boxes. On the sidewalks (the first I had seen since the previous town of Wagram), loiterers gossiped amongst festering piles of garbage. A florid mural depicting black heroes had 'LIFE SUCKS' sprayed across one corner.

Around Capital University there was a respite and the traffic slackened off. Thrusting above the crumbling brickwork of old Columbus, the great white hopes of new

Columbus reached for the stars and caught the sun. But the first all-American skyscrapers I had seen remained at a distance and dazzled. Route 40 hung a right away from the old federal pike while I continued straight on, the wrong way up a one-way street. Swinging onto the sidewalk, I collapsed on a patch of grass opposite Uncle Sam's Pawn Shop, strategically located next door to the Central Benefits office. It took two litres of water and a thorough face wash in a municipal fountain before I felt capable of continuing.

Crossing the river and leaving the towering infernals behind, I started the ride out of the city. Somehow I had by-passed the heart of Columbus and seen nothing of the 'broad boulevards and green spaces' described in the guide book, to say nothing of Christopher Columbus. The traffic swelled and congealed with commuters heading home.

Initially I thought I had been spared the horror of riding through another plastic shanty town. Then the road became smooth as glass and the progression of fast food outlets began its wretched repeats. This time each outlet had a filtration lane, encouraging the impatient to speed past me then violently swing right. With a raucous blast of its air horn, an eighteen-wheeler forced me off the road. I shot across the verge, through a scrubby patch of bushes, jumped a couple of kerbs and came to rest on the forecourt of a gas station.

Propped panting on my handlebars, I watched a woman fill her car and squeeze back behind the wheel. Her girth made the obese look lithe. Having driven the twenty metres from pump to kiosk, she and her two fat children painfully extracted themselves and took four steps to the raised platform the kiosk was set upon. After a couple of failed attempts to mount the foot high kerb head on, they turned sideways, lifted one leg outwards, made contact with the platform and were hauled up by their elephantine mother. As I edged back towards the highway, they emerged from the kiosk clutching handfuls of styrofoam containers. Their determination to join the 280,000

Americans who die prematurely each year from excess body weight was admirable.

Nobody was going to let me back into the stream of traffic. I rattled along a stone grip exposed between the tarmac and dying grass verge. Like an ellipsis squashed to a full stop, the end of the urban sprawl was marked by a three car pile up which missed me by five seconds. It was sixteen miles between the eastern arc of the beltway at Franklin and the western arc at Lincoln Village. Housing a population of 633,000, Columbus has about the same population as my home town of Nottingham. From the furthest limits of its urban sprawl, Greater Nottingham is roughly seven miles across. I could only presume the 'broad boulevards and green spaces' in Columbus were mighty broad and spacious.

That evening, camped in a field sandwiched between I-70 and Route 40, I tuned in to hear the 42nd President of the United States admit to the American people that he had been economical with the truth about his relationship with "that woman," Monica Lewinsky. I tuned in to WRUTS Radio, a Christian channel which warmed its audience for Clinton's address by inviting callers to contribute to a studio discussion. Interspersed with musical interludes from the Haven Quartet, the panel of four emphasised what the Bible had to say about admitting our sins before God. "If he's lied, he should come clean," was one contributor's unfortunate choice of words.

To my surprise, the first hour of reactions phoned through to WRUTS were rather tepid, despite efforts by the studio team to raise the temperature. Christian America was forgiving and ready to accept Clinton's admission. They knew which side their bread was buttered on, and drew a clear distinction between Clinton the President and Clinton the family man. "As a Christian, the man needs to re-examine his faith, rebuild his relationship with his family, and prey for forgiveness," Ralph Richards, Senior Pastor of the Calvary Memorial Church, intoned. "As a president, he need's to get the devil back to work."

I crawled out of the tent at daybreak feeling as jaded as America hoped Bill Clinton was feeling. As I stretched the old limbs, a large bulge beneath my appendix popped out to say good morning. I tried pushing it back in, but the mutant appendage picked up in Ohiopyle was adamant it wanted to take the morning air.

My physical condition mirrored my mental condition. Although it had its moments, my adventure was turning into a grind. Mindful of events unfolding back in the UK, I was travelling through a tunnel of anxieties and viewed America behind a plexiglass of grey emotions. I wasn't enamoured with I was seeing. Unable to shake the panic, I wasn't pausing to talk to people. I hadn't phoned home in a week, ignoring the hundreds of payphones I must have passed since leaving the mountains. There was no denying it, I didn't want to hear the news. I sensed it wasn't good.

But today was a Tuesday and, at Harmony, I swung into a gas station to dial up Nottingham. I was nervous and feeling guilty, praying that the name of the sleepy little village would prove a good omen. The phone rang and rang.

Nine miles later, on the far side of Springfield, I stopped to dial the UK once again and discovered I had left my purse at the payphone in Harmony. It contained only a $30 running kitty, but my negligence was disarming. On the road, vigilance of the little things keeps the larger thing together. Losing the damn purse took on a significance greater than its worth. My journey was falling apart as rapidly as my innards were falling out. I was phoning the wrong town. Something had happened. Sandy wasn't in Nottingham.

Sixteen miles on, I pulled into a drive-thru at Brandt and made contact with Louth. My mother-in-law was fading fast and the family was gathering. I was going home. Seventeen hours later and twenty-two days after I first landed there, I called Sandy from Washington Dulles Airport with the news that I would be landing at Heathrow, London, around tea time. My gear was stashed, and I had been fed, comforted and enjoyed a night between sheets, thanks totally to the open-hearted hospitality of Paul and Debbie Grodecki.

I had camped next to Paul, Debbie and their three children the previous weekend at Spring Valley. It was the Grodecki's annual get-together, when the family met up with brothers Bill and Ed and their respective partners midway between where each couple lived. In the course of a weekend spent kidding around, pitching ball and ribbing each other like they were still on their parent's back yard in North Ridgeville, Ohio, the brothers had pulled me into their circle. When they decamped, middle brother Paul thrust his business card into my hand saying, "If you are ever in the vicinity of Dayton..." Brandt is less than a dozen miles due north of Dayton. With nowhere else to turn, I threw myself on his charity.

By the time I reached the plush offices of the development company where Paul practiced property law, his travel secretary had produced a list of forthcoming flights out of Dayton International. Paul couldn't do enough for me that evening and handled me with all the care and concern one might a lost little boy. But when we finally reached the family home south of the city, I sensed his wife was less than ecstatic about my dumping on them in such a dramatic fashion. Debbie's response to my profuse apologies said it all however. "If I was in Sandy's position, I know I would want my husband at my side, whatever it took."

A week after I returned home, Sandy's mother died. It was agonising, but I couldn't immediately visit Pauline. Like the Angel of Death, my appearance at her bedside would have confirmed she had lost the battle. I finally got to see her when she was drifting on morphine and on the run in to the tunnel. I was shocked and deeply upset. Sunk low in her emaciated face, Pauline's eyes were the clearest expression of raw terror I had ever seen. She wasn't ready to die.

"Oh, you've come back," she said weakly.

The following day Pauline passed away.

Chapter 7

For seven months, Paul and Debbie Grodecki stored my bicycle and kit in the cellar of their executive home on a new sub-division called Brookside, just outside Springboro, Ohio. During that time Sandy and myself tried to heal ourselves. She was weighed down with grief and dragged deeper by the gradual emergence of some shocking family skeletons. I was informed my torn muscle was actually a hernia and that it would cost more than I budgeted for four months in American to have it stuffed back in. By the new year I was fit again and Sandy was over the worst, or so I thought. She tried hard to talk me out of returning to the gold trail, but I couldn't make sense of her arguments or maybe didn't want to. Such was my obsession, it never crossed my mind that she simply wasn't ready to be left on her own again.

I flew back to Dayton on the 19th of April. After a night catching up with the Grodecki's, I hit the road in a hire car heading east to Cumberland and the start of the National Road. To get back in the swing of things, I intended retracing my tracks, returning to spend a relaxed weekend in Springboro before climbing back on the saddle to continue where I left off at Brandt. Turning round at the terminus of the C&OC, I picked up Route 40 again heading west. I stopped at Little Sandy's truck stop on Keyser Ridge again and took a stool at the counter next to a trucker venting his spleen about America committing troops to peace keeping in Yugoslavia.

"What the hell we doin' in Kosovo?" he asked. "Why does this fuckin' government think we gotta police the world? We got reservists on standby ready to fly out to Yugoslavia. Did y'know that? I mean like, who the hell's protectin' *us*?"

His concern about national security was shared by two other drivers at the counter, one of whom recently received a call from his son in an engineering corps of the U.S. Army. The accumulation of supplies, tents and plant suggested they were gearing up to deposit a large military base somewhere in the trouble zone.

"We're gonna have more troops in the Middle East than in this country," the father said. "Anybody can just walk into America and take us!"

It wasn't the last time I heard somebody express the fear that Clinton was laying the country wide open to invasion by becoming involved in Europe's problem. Nor was it the last time an American relocated Yugoslavia. Before my journey was through, the country had been sited in Egypt, Turkey, Russia and "somewhere near Thailand."

I left the cafe, climbed into the Mazda and switched on the radio. As I cruised through the mountains of Pennsylvania, a terrifying story unfolded over the sound waves. A high school in Littleton, Colorado, was under siege from an army of police. Somewhere inside, two, possibly three teenagers were shooting the place up and hurling bombs. The explosions were audible and accompanied by screams. The death toll was being estimated at twenty-five.

The live broadcast slowly pieced together what was happening from interviews with frantic parents, harassed cops and distraught students who had escaped the carnage. When the noise of gunfire and explosions finally ceased, the culprits were revealed to be two members of a bunch of youths known as the Trench Coat Mafia. Distinguished by their Gothic clothing, the two had been systematically bullied by the 'jocks' (the sports stars of the school) and had chosen Hitler's birthday on which to wreak revenge. Armed with an Uzi, a shotgun, various handguns and home-made bombs, Eric Harris and Dylan Klembold strode into Columbine High School, killed twelve, then shot themselves dead.

The America I drove through over the next few days was in shock. Wherever I stopped, Columbine monopolised the conversation. While the deaths were appalling, people were stunned more by the backgrounds of the two assailants. These maniacs were not white trash, Yardies or Hispanic drug dealers. Harris and Klembold came from secure, respectable, white middle American homes. They were loved, spoilt and their parents were long term opponents of firearms.

In a café in Concord, waitress Trish shared the problems she was having with her five year old daughter. "I can't get her to go to school. She's terrified. I took her in today and she said, 'Please don't leave me here, mummy'. I've left her with my mother, but there's no telling when I'll be able to get her back into that place. These kids, you know, they have fire drills and tornado drills. Now they're having what the school calls 'emergency drills', in case a gunman attacks."

The odds were quite good that some fruitcake would assault her daughter's school. One in ten educational establishments in America reported serious crimes, often violent crimes, in the previous year. Large schools were now equipped with surveillance cameras, metal detectors and employed a police presence, sometimes during lessons. As a Sheriff at a gas station in Old Washington, Ohio, told me, "We got us a deadly problem that defies logic or solution. In the last two years, we've had fifteen kids shot dead by other kids, and that's just in schools. Our society's built on bullets," he said, before quickly reassuring me that, of course, both gun and bullet were "inanimate objects."

Talk shows on the car radio rammed home this message again and again, feeding America the old line that it wasn't the gun that killed, but the shootist with his finger on the trigger. On WFRB Radio, Rush Limbaugh ridiculed the inevitable calls for stricter gun controls.

"That isn't going to do nothing!" the living legend growled into the microphone, "These kids — no, they weren't kids — these monsters would have got hold of guns regardless. What does Clinton know? He's never been in the military — probably never held a gun. He's had people protecting him all his life. What's his solution, huh? More conflict resolution programmes? What, y'mean like we've got lined up for Slobo? Ha!"

Pronounced 'Slow-bow', Rush was referring to Slobodan Milosevic and NATO's bombing campaign of Kosovo. In the course of an hour long monologue he ripped into Clinton, the United Nations, Slobo, and the Trench Coat Mafia. He argued a case for disengagement in Yugoslavia on the basis that "the invasion force" set a bad example, "undoubtedly influencing the monsters of Columbine. What are we doing in Far East Europe if we can't protect our own at home?"

Back in Springboro for the weekend, I walked into the Grodecki household to find Paul and his two daughters, Melanie and Alicia, up to their elbows in pots of paint and bits of wood scattered across the dining room table. They were putting the finishing touches to two elaborately decorated little boats made of blockwood. On Sunday, the Miawashi Indian Princesses were meeting up to judge the best dressed galleon and race them down a local creek. Joe, the boy in the family, used to join in the activity but now, at the grand old age of twelve, he had no time for "kids stuff."

After a week sleeping in the car, I was grateful to Joe for giving up his bed. Heavily into 'collectables', his room was an exciting splash of brash football posters, baseball memorabilia and unopened packets of Cheerios. These had attained the status of collectables by virtue of the sports stars featured on the packaging. I surveyed his immaculate room with a critical eye, picturing it as the healthy tip I hoped it was when a guest wasn't staying. Materially, Joe had everything a kid of his age needed and a good deal of what they crave to make growing up fun. He wasn't spoilt, but he wanted for nothing.

What I could glean from the media suggested Klebold and Harris were equally well provided for at Joe's age. In the intervening years, they had become big fans of demon metal music, gory movies and Doom video games, much like millions of other teenagers. Predictably, commenta-

81

tors wagged arthritic fingers at the bad influence of shock lyrics and violent images, citing how his skill with a computer joy stick turned Harris into a marksman. Their arguments were as fatuous as suggesting that Joe's walls ought to be stripped of sports icons for fear he would grow up to become a jock, a bully or worse — the President of the United States. Something far more complex was at work in the minds of the Columbine killers — something which was suppressed with medication and anger management counselling until April 20th. Why didn't they just target the jocks? How could they produce home-made bombs in the cellar without their parents knowing? Where did they get their firepower from? America was reeling with questions.

After church on Sunday, the Grodecki family, accompanied by grandparents and foreign guest, joined the Miawashi Indian Princesses for the annual boat race in Springboro. Established back in the Twenties as a way for fathers to bond with their daughters, the Princesses normally met in smaller 'tribes', but today was the big jamboree to which all were invited. Over a hundred people had turned out.

At the back of the local school a brook had been cleared for a short, swift course. Proud grandparents lined the banks and nattered. Sizzling barbies, bowls of salad and lashings of relish fed milling parents and ravenous kids. On a couple of picnic tables, the fanciful creations of young imaginations and hours of labour were laid out for judging prior to entering the heats. Throughout the afternoon, exaggerated whoops and "Go-gettem"s rang round the creek as the good-humoured racing unfolded. By the end of the day, enough classifications and tribes received a Miawashi Indian rosette or feathers for all to feel they had been in with a chance. There were no tears or tantrums, and I didn't see a single parent lose their rag with an obnoxious brat. It had been a great family occasion. On the day that 100,000 people gathered in the suburbs of Denver to remember the Littleton dead, it was also immensely reassuring.

My first day back on the bike was bright and warm, but spring was struggling to break through. Blossoming redbuds gave warning that the new season was in the air, their exuberant purple splash making the rest of nature look drab. The gently undulating, unerring straight of the National Road forged through sweet hamlets ignored by the map and fields of maize stubble ignored by the plough. Grey rows of dry stalks stretched to the horizon like vanquished troops returning from battle. Five miles before the Indiana state line, Interstate 70 returned to haunt Route 40, sidling up with a roar after dipping south to service Dayton. Except for pottering tractors, my road was empty. It was a day for the rhythm of the crank and the purr of the chain.

Remembering my difficulties when last on the road, I began my search for somewhere to lay my head early. On the far side of Centreville, I pulled up outside a shabby wooden farmhouse, knocked on the side door and rattled through the patter I had scripted back in the UK, devised to solicit the sympathy vote. This time out I was determined to stay with the locals. Nine times out of ten it was to prove a winner.

"Good evening, sir/mam. My name's John and I'm from England. I'm cycling across America following the route of the Forty-Niners to the Californian Gold Rush. Have you a spare corner of land where I could throw up a tent for the night? I'd be ever so grateful and I'll be gone by the morning. All I ask is water."

My first success was a stocky man in overalls who looked like he had just finished eighteen hours on a Detroit production line. His name was Jessie Collins and his ancestors were English, he immediately informed me.

"It ain't my farm, but the owner won't mind," Jessie said, "She ain't never here. We got a pavilion up on the hill. Jump in. I'll run you up there."

83

Sliding through waterlogged fields along a pitted track, Jessie drove his pick-up quarter of a mile to the top of a knoll overlooking a small lake. On the crest were a few dodgy picnic tables, the shelter and the remains of a bonfire. In the lake, two men were fishing from a row boat. Jessie waved and hollered something indecipherable. They waved back and hollered something equally indecipherable. "The guy's a total nutcase," Jessie said, "but I've got your dinner sorted."

Back at the farmhouse to meet the family and appear impressed at their family tree, there was a knock at the side door. Jessie answered it to the accompaniment of a lot of indecipherable hollering. The door closed, things went quiet and Jessie returned to the sitting room with a bucket.

"There y'go. Dinner," he said, setting it down beside me.

In the bucket were three carp and a catfish barely covered by water.

"What am I supposed to do with that?" I asked, knowing the answer.

His wife and two teenage daughters chuckled and yawned as Jessie prattled on about gutting and boning and starting an open fire.

"I thought you were following the Forty-Niners?," he said. "So act like a Forty-Niner!"

I was back on track.

Chapter 8

My journey needed to be completed in the anniversary year of the first mass migration from the East, but why I returned in April rather than July, the month I left off, eludes me. The immediate goal of the Forty-Niners was to reach the frontier town of Independence, Missouri, by mid-summer at the latest, allowing time to cross the prairies and mountains before winter set in. I was less than a month's ride from what was then the western border of the United States and could have given Sandy and myself more time together. The moment I crossed into Indiana it seemed the weather was going to make me pay for my monomania. It lashed it down, bitter and cold, and there was no cover.

In the small towns and villages I was able to nip between junk shops and antique stores, some the size of flea markets. The National Road was now the 'Antiques Roadshow' and the sale of Americana appeared to be the only trade plied beside Route 40. But unlike the other states I had passed through, Indiana was making a valiant effort to preserve some of its more humble historic buildings associated with the heritage of the road, such as banks and saddleries, and the two storey Houston Brick House at the corner of the main crossroads in Lewisville. As another thunderstorm unleashed its retribution, I was shown round the building site by Sue Saunders, President of the Lewisville Town Board.

"We saved the property from becoming a parking lot," Sue explained, walking me through rooms in various stages of restoration. The attention to detail had necessitated scouring the country for craftsmen. "The morticians next door wanted to buy it and tear it down, but the Houston House has a special meaning for the town. Houston used to be a tanner in Uniontown, Pennsylvania. He married Fanny, set off down the National Road to find somewhere to live and became a successful merchant here. He was a generous philanthropist, particularly towards the children. Lewisville owes him a great debt. This is kind of a way of repaying him. It'll become our Community Center."

In a makeshift office shrouded in dust sheets hung an impressive portrait of William Houston. Willy was a stern man, with a clean shaven upper lip and a long square beard hiding his neck. He and Fanny were good examples of how America spread west along the federal highway. The year the road was completed, 200,000 immigrants travelled towards the Mississippi along the pike. Indiana and Ohio received 90,000 settlers a year for a decade after it was laid, most of whom journeyed down the National Road before peeling off north or south to build new lives.

The rain had let up and Lewisville glistened in a pool of steaming sunlight. Except for the one hole, the sky was black and bubbling like boiling tar. Enormous thunderheads reared up like horses of the Apocalypse teetering on their hind legs. I leapt onto my bike and pumped the pedals. A hundred metres down the blacktop, a sudden rush of wind pushed me onto the sidewalk and another deluge hammered down. Next stop, Susie's Antique Café, empty except for the proprietor and her friend, Valerie. There wasn't an antique in view. Susie adopted the name because the building used to be the Wildley Hotel, the village's one prestigious night stop in the days of the Model Ts.

I spent a couple of hours with the women, drawing their caricatures, devouring chicken and fries, waiting for the weather to let up. As closing time approached, Valerie peered out at the monsoon and asked, "Are you really going to cycle off in this? You know there's a tornado warning out?"

I didn't.

"Look, we've a trailer round the back. Why don't you put up in there for the night?"

It was a nice offer, if I hadn't known that the majority of Americans killed by twisters were caught in trailer homes. I quizzed the women about last minute warning signs and what to do when it arrives.

"The sky turns green, the birds stop singing and the cows shit themselves," Susie sniggered.

"Yeh, and what you do is find the nearest storm drain, crawl into it and kiss your bicycle goodbye," Valerie added. "Whatever you do, don't make a run for a grain silo. I rode out a twister in one once. The noise was terrifying. I was deaf for three days."

That evening I cadged a floor beside a John Deere harvester in a galvanised barn barely six miles down the road. It was as far as I got between downpours. During the night, the tornado blew over a mile to the north but the racket of the wind, rain and debris crashing against the corrugated steel had the mice and myself hugging each other in fear of the barn taking off. According to the farmer, the year was shaping up to be the worst he had ever know for tornados, and the season had yet to begin.

My challenge for the new day was to cross Indianapolis, a city Paul Grodecki rated as "kind of okay." Since it was not much more than a village before the advent of the motor car, there was nothing I had reason to stop for. Its nickname of 'Naptown' suggested the metropolis would be a lot easier to fight my way through than Columbus, but it still took me the best part of the day to reach the far side. Getting lost before I was even close to the near side didn't speed my passage. An hour after discovering I was 'turned about' (as the wagon masters put it), I was still baffling over my ability to lose my way on a line which ran straight as an arrow for over 600 miles.

I was at a gas station in Gem, fourteen miles from the big city, placing a call through to Sandy. At the same time, I was fielding questions from a bunch of cops poking round my rig. When I finished on the phone, I gave them a tour of the state-of-the-art features on my expeditionary bicycle, and they gave me a tour of the high-velocity hardware in their squad cars. When we parted, I paid more attention to looking cool from behind than looking where I was going.

After ten miles the highway began twisting and turning through marsh land — bends not in keeping with the National Road west of the Ohio River. I hadn't seen a Route 40 shield for some time and the wind no longer pushed me from behind. Then a railroad crossed my path. I couldn't believe any north-south line would by-pass a city the size of Indianapolis. I strode into a caboose converted into a barber's shop and learned I was in McCordsville, north-east of Naptown. According to my map, there was no umbilical linking McCordsville to Gem. It dawned on me that the payphones at Gem were set to one side of the gas station, on the corner of the non-existent crossroads. I had set off north believing I was still riding west, pushing off from the side rather than the front of the pumps.

So I took a left and rode down Route 36, cycling south-west along the Pendleton Pike. I followed the railroad all the way into Indianapolis, through the obligatory black neighbourhood and fast-food shacks, over the beltway and onto a single lane highway where the cycling almost became enjoyable. I turned a corner and the sky shut down. Traffic coalesced and suits suddenly thronged the sidewalk, pouring in and out of posh lobbies like flood water. The steel and glass Goliaths of the city's towering skyscrapers made me feel like an ant at David's feet. They mocked me and herded me along with sly shuffles. I had no doubt they meant to squash me.

Already thoroughly intimidated by the burly metropolis, I punctured outside the Indiana World War Memorial — a monument the size of an office block in the heart of downtown. What morsel remained of my self-esteem fizzled away. Surrounded by the clamour of power dressers, power architecture and power advertising, me and my humble puncture repair outfit felt totally emasculated. I stripped the wheel and suddenly found myself being interviewed by a cub reporter on her way back from lunch. She whipped out her mobile. Minutes later I was being snapped through numerous view-finders by a photographer with hyperactive sweat glands. All I could think about was repairing the hole and fleeing Indianapolis.

The National Road kinked left beyond the city centre and realigned itself on a south-westerly course. Caught in the rush hour, I battled for space, rattling through the outskirts over fractured tarmac. This side of Indianapolis held a candle to the days when it was a great motor city, second only to Detroit as a manufacturing centre. Workshops and garages abounded, each forecourt featuring a souped-up banger plastered with product endorsements and Speedway stickers. Between them, run-down motels from the heyday of motor tourism sported zany neon signs and extraordinary fins projecting from their flat roofs — precursors of the shark fins which were to grace Chryslers and De Sotoes a decade later. In the gathering gloom, it seemed I was riding through a *film noir* set.

Drawing away from Indianapolis, I rode through mile upon mile of rotting maize fields and realised I had seen nothing but fields of corn, soya and sunflowers since entering crop country. Few houses had vegetable plots and such things as allotments and small-holdings didn't appear to exist. Round here, they grew nothing edible which didn't first have to be processed.

Every four to eight miles, I rode through a 'pike town' like Lewisville. Even at a cyclist's pace, the journey had a rhythm set by the distance between service stops for the stage lines. Villages had grown out of taverns franchised to cater for passengers and provide a change of horses. Artisans set up beside the inn to supply tack, black-smithing and animal feed, and by the time the Gold Rush began, each wayside pit stop had grown into a sizeable community. By the time it petered out, the horseless carriage had made regular engine changes unnecessary. Speeds increased, distances shrank, and suppliers to the redundant technologies of horse and carriage, ox and cart, withered away. The only commercial undertaking which had bent with the winds of change and survived was the village store. It had down-sized, diversified and ticked over, sometimes moving premises into the grain merchant's, the tackler's or, in the case of the Stilesville store, the farmers' bank.

Bill von Axelson wore a striped apron like some men wear a Marines' uniform. He was sat at a roll top desk doing the accounts when I walked in. Grey and balding, he wore silver arm bands and just needed the eye shade to complete the effect. When he stood up, he stood tall and erect and looked me straight in the eye.

Bill's store reflected his military bearing. Around three walls, lines of cans, boxes and packets stood shoulder to shoulder without a label looking anywhere but to the front. Along the fourth wall, spit and polished counters, coolers and glass displays were ranked, each a self-contained detachment — the deli, the pizza parlour, the café, the hot dog stand. Closest to the door was command HQ — the roll top desk and ornately embossed cash register. Arranged in the centre of the room, tables and chairs were camouflaged in gingham with condiments grouped in a central fall-back position. The General Store and Soda Fountain, Stilesville, Indiana, looked ready for a photo shoot for *Picture Post*. There were even a couple of crinklies hunched over a table arguing in heated whispers.

"I used to live in Bridgeport, just over the state line," Bill told me. "Used to drive this way quite regular going up to visit our son. My wife noticed they were renovating the old Roberts Bank. Over the period of a year or so, we watched them doing it up. We thought it was a good site for a store. It's a wonderful building — real character. A couple of years ago we bought this and the place next door. Once we're on a sound footing, we're aiming to expand into there. Roberts' old vault is still there. I use it for a meat store."

Bill was the first of several owners I met who had recently taken on village stores to side-step the rat race.

While he showed me the vault tagged 'E.R. Roberts Bank — 1886', I asked how business was shaping up.

"Pretty damn good. There's a restaurant over the road, but the guy don't care if the sun don't rise in the morning. We get all the local trade, and since we've had the pizza franchise, we got people driving thirty miles to get themselves a Noble Roman's Pizza."

The population of Stilesville currently stood at 183 but, in the years of toing and froing, Bill and his wife had noticed the exponential growth of new sub-divisions in the area. On all sides, Indianapolis was expanding into the farmlands, particularly along Route 40. Exclusive estates of 'ranch style housing' were springing up around artificial lakes stocked with carp. Set in beautifully tended acres, they appeared with the regularity of staves on the sheet music of the National Road.

"Last year was the worst for the farmers. There are fields round here haven't been reseeded in four years. Can't sell their corn so don't bother growing it. If a developer should offer to buy some of their land to build a sub-division — sure they're going to sell. Of course the downturn hits the town, but with all these inter-urban commuters moving in…"

Bill ran a slick ship which would appeal to a commuter population who liked a touch of nostalgia with their Noble Roman's Pizza. While he took in deliveries from a soda truck, the arguing pensioners rounded on me. Apparently the day marked the climax of a series of 'copycat' incidents trying to find fame on the back of the Columbine shootings. "It's just kids, I tell you, whadda y'think?" the one with the thick white moustache asked me.

On Tuesday a nineteen year old strode through Northview High shouting that there was a bomb on the third floor of the school. He was arrested and charged with making a false report. There is no third floor to Northview High. On Wednesday, two elementary kids were arrested in a Montezuma school. One was arrested for threatening to surf the web for instruction on how to build a bomb.

91

The other had his collar felt for threatening to shoot a fellow student, though he owned no gun. Today, a thousand pupils from South Vermilion High had been evacuated by a bomb hoax. Predictably the police and fire service had made a meal of it, and the assembled kids had congradulated them with mock applause.

"'Just kids', you say? Aagh! Monsters they are, not kids... monsters," the crinkly with the bifocals growled.

Rush Limbaugh's talk show had at least found a sympathetic ear in Stilesville.

After three days of almost constant rain the sky cleared, the sun shone bright and Indiana became a sauna. I warmed my bones on the grass verge of a gas station at the intersection with the main north-south drag between Lafayette and Bloomington. Longitudinally the world was in a hurry. The highway heaved with a steady stream of tractors and trailers and mothers ferrying kids away from the school on the opposite corner. Along the National Road, drivers were more relaxed, the left arm hung out of the window getting a tan. Those turning off Route 231 noticeably eased back on the accelerator to continue their journey east or west.

A scrawny, frizzle haired woman in her late thirties approached me, shuffling across the forecourt from the gas pumps. She clutched a roll of tape and a hand-written poster for a rummage sale at the local Peace Lutheran Church, probably intending to stick it on the signals control box at the junction. Stopping at a safe distance, she inquired about my bike trip.

"Aw, my husband and myself are majorly into backpacking and mountain walking."

She spoke like the commentator of a horse race, building up speed as the full stop approached. Her sweatshirt depicted snow capped mountains — 'Wilderness Country'.

"And you do that round here?" I asked, looking around at a landscape which had drawn closer contours, but not that close.

"Nar. We used to live in California."

"Really, so why did you move?"

While the race was under starter's orders, I noticed her ears were a pin cushion of holes. It wasn't long ago she extracted a small jewellery store from them. Then she was off, pacing herself for the first few laps. As the tempo of her monologue picked up, she edged closer, sat down on the grass and pulled her feet beneath skinny thighs. On the final furlong, words galloped out quicker than her lips could form them.

Her father abused her. Her mother was an alcoholic. In her youth, she ran with the space cadets, moving between communes, sleeping around. She had tried every drug going on the West Coast.

"Man, I was in orbit, but when I came down — my life was spiralling into deep shit. I was turning into my parents. Hell, I just wanted a normal life, y'know. Whatever normal is. I wanted kids and a home."

She went to see the priest at her aunt's Lutheran Church and pleaded for help. She got the calling, became a church stalwart and met her future husband at bible reading classes. He was in the latter stages of rehab after a methamphetamine habit. They married, had three children and decided to move to Indiana before their protégés reached gun toting age.

"The schools in California — man, they're boot camps for gangsters. Our youngest knew how to hot-wire before he could spell Porsche."

Fifteen minutes later, while the lapsed junkie was galloping through a damnation of all things Californian, an elderly woman came across the forecourt looking concerned.

"Excuse me, young lady," she said. "Are those your children in that van? I think you need to attend to them. They're running around naked."

The mother had walked away from her wagon leaving the pump pouring petrol into the tank. The pipe wriggled and spasmed as her naked brats leapt about inside the van like hyperactive kangaroos in a bouncy castle. Splayed on the forecourt was a litter of children's clothing.

"Gotta go," the woman said. "Been nice talkin' to you."

She walked back to her van, scooped up the clothes, replaced the nozzle and drove away. At the exit onto 231 the vehicle jerked to a halt, the door flew open and the woman ran back to the kiosk, presumably to pay. She finally pulled away without replacing her petrol cap or sticking up the rummage sale poster.

It had been depressing listening to the grounded space cadet, but refugees from California who felt compelled to regale me with tales of terror in the Golden State were to become familiar figures. None were quite so wired, though all appeared to be damaged in some way or other. The closer I rode to the 'Wilderness Country' of the Gold Rush, the more intrigued I became about why California was such a popular place to flee from.

Between the end of Indiana and the beginning of Illinois lay a belt of chaos which would trigger earthquakes in Japan if a butterfly tried crossing it. I remember pulling away from the town of Terra Haute and wondering why local traffic had evaporated, but the hows and wherefores of suddenly finding myself in the thick of Interstate 70 were immediately smacked out of mind by a convoy of pantechnicans bulleting by.

Air horns blared and slipstream shockwaves blasted me into the verge. In a moment of panic, I leant into the salvos and attempted to outrun the traffic, sprinting towards a heart attack. There was no going back. At least going forwards I benefited from the sling-shot effect of being sucked in and blown out. Grit pinged off my glasses and stung bare skin. The noise was painful. I turned my shoulder to the maelstrom and pedalled cowering, frantically searching for an escape. Beyond the embankment ran an empty country road. Between me and it stood a four metre fence stranded in flood water twenty metres wide. Two awful miles later, a slip road took me and my palpitating heart back to the National Road. I figured I had earned a quiet night.

Less than a mile from the interstate, I turned off Route 40 up a snaking driveway to the first house in Illinois. The small ranch was set in rambling grounds and surrounded on three sides by sycamores. Warped wooden sheds and buckled wire pens were dotted around the back, and a child's tricycle lay on its side near the garage. Two yappy dogs bounded out of nowhere and criss-crossed in front of me as I approached the front door. Feeling lucky, I rapped a confident rhythm. After a few moments, a toddler with a mess of blond hair appeared from around the back.

"Hello. Is your daddy in?"

"My daddy's dead," the boy said without a moment's hesitation.

A man in his thirties appeared and gently took hold of the youngster.

"What can I do you for?"

I went through my patter.

"Aw, y' hit a real bad time, man." His expression was pained.

A young girl, maybe ten years old, and a man with a thick black moustache appeared. He was slightly older than the first bloke but there was clearly a family resemblance.

"What he want?" the newcomer asked.

The first explained my request to the second, who immediately turned away and raised his arms. "Heck, I can't be doin' with that," he said, disappearing back into the house.

While the first man repeated that this wasn't a good time, the young girl wrapped one arm round his legs and the other round the little boy's neck. "Hello," she said slowly, as if asking a question. I smiled and acknowledged her, then said to the man, "No problem. I'll just keep rolling."

As I reached the road, I heard somebody hollering. They were beckoning me back.

95

"I'm real sorry, man," the man said, "Didn't mean to be unsociable an' all. Sydnee here'd really like you to stay." He placed a hand on the girl's shoulder.

"Are you sure?" There was something in the air which said I really ought to try somewhere else.

"Ain't Christian to turn away a traveller, even when times are bad. It's my little brother, Josh's dad." He took the hand of the boy. "He's done himself in."

"Oh, my God. When?"

"This morning. Me an' my bro' just got back couple o' hours ago. Didn't hear nothing 'til then."

I should have moved on, but Sydnee already had my hand and was leading me across the grounds to the side of the ranch. Little Josh pushed the back of my bike and giggled.

On the evening of the day their kid brother ended it all, Mark and Doug extended hospitality to a total stranger. It was an extraordinary and potentially disastrous situation but, without thinking, I slipped into the support role I found myself in with Sandy's family in the immediate aftermath of my mother-in-law's death. This time it involved baby-sitting responsibilities, and was made easy by the children's enthusiasm for something exciting to do at the end of their miserable day. I let them erect the tent, helping Josh push in the pegs, holding the loops for Sydnee to feed the pole through. While I passed gear over for Josh to stow away, Sydnee sat on the grass playing with my radio and told me about her uncle's death.

"He put a gun to his head and blew himself away."

I hoped it was a line she had overheard.

Beyond the words, "My daddy's dead," Josh hadn't a clue what was going on and Sydnee was doing her level best to keep it that way. With Josh and the dogs running along beside us, she took me on a whistle stop tour of the spread. She introduced me to Wilbur, her pot-bellied pig, showed me her "team room" in one of the barns, and dragged me round a ramshackle workshop where the brothers renovated old ranges, grandfather clocks and

96

period furniture. Done with the outbuildings, she raced Josh and myself round her bike track, weaving through the woods at the back of the house. Emerging on the far side, Sydnee was off and running, charging across a field of corn stumps. Lifting Josh onto my shoulders, I followed her back across the state line and half way round Indiana. The grand tour completed, we returned to the house to find Mark and Doug looking anxious and angry.

"Didn't y'hear me hollerin'?" the younger brother chastised Sydnee. "We been callin' ya. What have I always told ya about goin' off with strangers?"

"No offence, mister," Doug said, "but we don't know you from shit. You could be cool, but we don't know that."

They were right. I had thought to mind the children so the lads were free to field phone calls, talk to their folks and agonise, but it would have been a good idea to make public my intentions. I told Sydnee we were both guilty and apologised all round.

"Enough said. I got the steaks sizzling away... so let's go eat!"

Mark playfully chased the kids into the house, immediately dispelling the heavy atmosphere.

"You too, John," Doug said.

I was never more reluctant to accept an invitation, but it made sense in the circumstances. Try as they might, Mark and Doug were never going to rise to the level of jollity Sydnee had manufactured for her little cousin.

The house was not what I expected of a couple of welders. Orderly, comfortable and furnished with taste, it actually belong to their parents. This was their retirement home, but the boys lived in while the folks made up their minds when to call it a day. No mention was ever made of the children's mothers. The boys were self-contained. With a helping hand from their twin sisters, Jane and Joan, Mark and Doug worked their shifts so they could share in household chores and the responsibility of Sydnee's up-bringing. "Ain't sure who'll take on little Joshie," Mark whispered as he served up dinner. I got the feeling something tragic had also happened to Josh's mum.

For an hour after dinner, I entertained the children in the den down in the cellar. Upstairs the brothers talked, paced and made phone calls. Now and then, there was a yelp or curse, mostly from Doug, who was evidently finding the death more difficult to get to grips with. Perhaps for distraction, he came downstairs to show me some photographs of California taken by his parents on a recently holiday. Amongst photos of the folks in front of their hotel, in front of a baseball stadium and so forth, a picture of his youngest brother appeared. Elbows on the table, Doug peered at it for a brittle moment before leaping up saying, "Dunno what that's doin' there. That's my kid brother." Ripping up the pack of photos with venom, he charged back upstairs screaming, "Gotta trash em!"

A lie-in would have been most welcomed the following morning. I was thoroughly drained but, well before the morning sun cleared the horizon, the kids were tugging at the zip of my tent. They snuggled up on my sleeping bag while I came to, then helped me strike camp.

"We're gonna garden today, ain't we, Joshie?" Mark said, throwing open the back door as the kids wheeled my bike to the driveway. Doug emerged looking like a zombie. Neither brother had got much sleep and scarlet eye sockets indicated they had spent a deal of the night crying.

"We're gonna plant radishes," Sydnee elaborated. "I wish you could stay longer, Mr. John."

I saw Doug tighten up and immediately made a big play of departing. After lots of hugs for the kids, I rode down to the tarmac and turned left onto Route 40. The family stood at the bottom of the low rise and waved while the dogs bounded around barking. I was relieved to be back on the road but felt confident the boys would make the day swing for Josh and Sydnee, and benefit from the effort.

Chapter 9

Challenging leaps and bounds carried me up to the Illinois plateau across which Route 40 would complete its journey through the Old West. The ground was sodden and fields were swamped with pools of stagnant water. Lawn dogs attacking a grass bank rode mowers with chains on their rear tyres. On top of the bank a track appeared, running parallel to the road. Sometimes it was just a couple of wheel ruts, more often short lengths of brick road flocked with weeds. Where Route 40 took embankments over valley and creek, the track dipped in and out of the contours. Stone bridges which once spanned the streams had disappeared, probably reappearing later as stone houses.

I swung across the blacktop, jumped the kerb and rattled across a lumpy verge to take the red brick road. A quarter of a mile on, it arched steeply down and came to an abrupt halt at a swollen creek. I rode back and into a driveway to ask about the track.

"It's the Cumberland Road," a man on a lawn mower told me.

"The Cumberland Road?" There was that name again.

"Yeh, the old National Pike."

Apparently in Cumberland County the National Road was still known by the name used by the gold seekers of '49.

With the thrill of an archaeologist discovering a length of Roman paving, I rode west along Route 40 watching lengths of the original turnpike come and go. Some farmed either side of it and used the line as an access road. Others had ploughed it in, though a long shallow depression in the bean tops indicated the pike wasn't going to be obliterated that easily. Illinois was now flat as rolled metal, intensively cultivated and a checker board of ruler straight roads running towards the four points of the compass.

Going my way, the life lines of different epochs of transportation ran parallel. To my left was the original National Road, *circa* 1820. Beyond that was the railroad which superseded it, *circa* 1860. I cycled on the upgrade of the old pike, U.S. 40, which attracted people off the trains and into cars, *circa* 1930. And on my right, a little way off, I could see trucks bowling down I-70, the upgrade on the upgrade which put the 'inter' into 'state highways', *circa* 1960. The four lines were less than a couple of miles apart and aiming dead west. On principle, I took the original brick line wherever possible.

Beyond Greenup, principles got me into problems when a sign at a road block informed me the bridge across the Embarras River was under repair. Nine times out of ten, this means you can walk or cycle across the building site, but not drive. Five miles further down the old pike, not even a rope was strung across the writhing flood. I heaved the bike down to the river bank and set off across country to intercept Route 40. There was no path or trail, and it struck me as odd that a river on the outskirts of a town didn't have a footpath running beside it. I was to see remarkably few paths beside rivers and creeks. The absence of human beings walking in town or country was perhaps the most unsettling feature of cycling through America. In the 250 miles since leaving Dayton, I doubt I had seen a dozen people on the sidewalks of the forty-six small towns and villages I passed through and I still hadn't encountered a single cyclist. Aside from a regular turn on the lawn mower, it seemed the gaps between home and car, car and supermarket, office or fast food joint were the closest most Americans got to taking the air.

But east of Effingham I was picked up by a grey haired pedal-pusher riding a recumbent, a bicycle you sit in rather than on. We crossed paths, stopped and talked men's talk — gears and tubing. He offered to show me to the local camp ground, then changed his mind and invited me back to his place.

John Fearday was a second-hand car dealer, mostly of sports utility vehicles. He told me this was the first year that sales of SUVs had outstripped that of ordinary cars. After the oil crisis had frightened Americans into scaling down the family saloon, the motoring public was now getting back into gas guzzlers in a big way. He took me to see K & F Cars, his lot on the south side of town, then east on 40 to his home, a large modern bungalow at the entrance to a cul-de-sac of cloned modern bungalows. His wife was circling a tree on a mower. It was that time of day.

Betty Fearday took husband John to one side in their car port and whispered. She wasn't happy about the filthy looking stray John had brought home. I dug out my passport. Betty looked it over.

"Well, if it's alright with John, I guess..." Peeling off her gardening gloves, she held open the front door. "You'll find the bathroom down the corridor on the left."

Betty's fears were dispelled after I gently bounced on the spare bed and professed undying appreciation of their home comforts. She quickly opened up.

"We've been riding recumbents for about four years now," she told me. "After two balloon heart operations, John's doctor recommended he take up gentle exercise. He prescribed cycling. John now rides about a hundred miles a week for his health, but he also takes a load of pills. Rat poison and stuff."

She held up a plastic dispenser the size of a slide box sectioned off into days of the week. Each section was the size of a matchbox and packed with medication.

"Beyond minor fibrillations, John hasn't had any more heart problems, but we've become health freaks. I admit I'm now obsessive about what we eat."

We were joined by their daughter-in-law and grandson for dinner, which involved jumping in the ubiquitous black SUV and driving three cloned bungalows down the road to the restaurant. Health kick or not, it was obviously a house too far to walk.

"The fish is good here, but I'll have mine without the batter," Betty said.

She interrogated the waitress about the ingredients and cooking of each dish the five of us selected, but had no problems with the quantities. I was stuffed after the entrees, a shallow segmented bowl the diameter of a satellite dish holding corn, broccoli, spaghetti, bean and cabbage salads. Then came the real salad course, with enough lettuce to feed the rabbit population of Norfolk. By the time the rockfish in American batter and French fries arrived, I was eating for the next week.

On a mobile, John placed a call through to Jeff, one of their sons and husband of the daughter-in-law. He was pulling out of Columbus, Ohio, driving a transporter full of cars destined for somewhere west of Effingham on I-70. His family wouldn't see him that night. After dropping off wherever, he was then heading north to pick up another delivery for somewhere in the south-east.

"We're delivering wholesale," John explained. "It's just another arm of the business."

Between John, Betty and Jeff, they ran the car lot, a car rental business, the car wholesale and delivery business, and held the agency for CellularOne mobile phones. They were busy people, but had just been through a poor year, largely a knock-on from the disastrous year for farmers.

"You got to work all hours in this country to get ahead," Betty said. "We went round to a young couple's place the other evening for dinner. I couldn't believe it. 'Where did we go wrong?' I thought. They had all the latest kitchen equipment. The house was like a show home, wasn't it, dear? We do all this work. Heck, we're fifty-seven years old and look at us."

I couldn't see anywhere John and Betty Fearday had gone wrong. Their house was pleasant, comfortable and wanted for nothing which plugged or plumbed in. Photographs on the sideboard showed they had a beautiful family of four grown-up children, all but Jeff in universities up north. But whatever inadequacies Betty and John worried about had evidently taken their toll on a couple who looked twenty years older than their age. Bodily, they were in good shape, but lines of anxiety on fresh faces had not been smoothed away by their recent regime of healthy eating and exercise.

Back at the house, John put on an apron and sat in front of the television cracking nuts. He placed a high sided metal tray on his lap, with two extended sides of perspex to catch flying shells and a corner cup holding dental tools. It had been made for him by his father. While we talked, John extracted hickory nuts — apparently a difficult task which made buying them expensive. He collected the walnut-like seeds on his bike rides, took them to the car lot to crack in a vice, then brought them home to remove the kernels. The dinning room table was covered with Tupperware containers full with hickories.

"It's stress management therapy," he conceded. "If I get wound up at work, I go crack a few nuts. When I'm home, I watch documentaries and pick them out. It keeps me sat down away from the paper work."

John had worked himself into the ground. He had twice paid the price for striving too hard to earn the mighty dollar but, "Thank the Lord, I've been given a third chance. It could have been worse, I guess. I used to be a farmer."

John's story wasn't unusual. Compared to the British, it seemed to me the Americans worked their socks off, more often than not to the detriment of family life. I had yet to meet a family who weren't thoroughly giving and caring of each other, but apparently that wasn't the norm.

"Look at the parents of those kids at Columbine," Betty said. "It isn't hard to understand how they hadn't the slightest idea what their kids were doing down in the cellar. They were making bombs, for pity's sake. How do you hide a bomb making factory in your parents' house? They were hard working, absentee parents is all."

The massacre had made Americans take stock of the time they spent with their children. In the newspapers, a string of ludicrous polls revealed the average father spent less time with his kids than with his boat, at the golf club or watching ball games. Betty said the women on the close were beginning to worry about how well they really knew their children. What did their latch-key kids get up to before they arrived home, and what exactly were they doing during the hours they disappeared into their bedrooms after dinner? It had been revealed the Columbine killers ran a white supremacist web site. Half the school and the Sheriff's Department appeared to know, but not their parents.

Betty's rolling conversation about food continued at the breakfast table. It was hard to see where the tower of pancakes fitted into her scheme of healthy eating, but I wasn't complaining. She said it was difficult to find the ingredients for what Europeans would consider a wholesome diet. Grains, pulses and wholefoods in general were in short supply, and some vegetables and fruits the British take for granted were unheard of. She had never seen a cauliflower and never heard of watercress or aubergines.

"If nothing else," she sighed, "I guess we've always got hickory nuts."

Main Street, USA, was fast running out on me, but the end of the National Road was not where Capitol Hill intended it to be. The highway was projected to run clear across the Old West to St. Louis on the Mississippi River but, when work was completed in the 1850s, it fell short by over sixty miles. A mess of squabbles related to funding, alignment and the highway's brief caused the great federal project to fizzle out at Vandalia, two-thirds the way across Illinois. By then, railroads were in the ascendant and few brownie points were to be gained by state representatives supporting the old modes of transportation. On a day when I was looking for any excuse not to be riding the line, the political intrigue surrounding the shortfall would have made fascinating reading. Unfortunately it was a Saturday, and the town library and most everywhere else in Vandalia was closed. Touring empty streets I could find no plaque, statue or memorial celebrating the beginning and end of the historic highway. Opposite another Madonna of the Trail, there was just the Trail's End Saloon. I strode in to hold my own celebration and caught a Jack Daniels slid down the bar to me.

Ignoring the months spent back in the UK, it had taken me twice as long to travel the length of the National Road as it would have taken a Forty-Niner with the price of a stage coach ticket. Since few independent travellers squandered their money on such luxuries along a road which was well travelled and easy to bum a lift on, I figured my timing was about right. Today was May 1st. The keenest of the argonaut companies were now setting off from the trail head at Independence. I expected to be crossing the Kansas River in a couple of weeks, well within the time frame for a safe crossing of the Wild West.

From the end of the National Road, St. Louis was a little over fifty miles as the crow flies south-west and easily attainable in a day. Unfortunately, forty of them were exclusively on I-70 and inaccessible to me. The meandering detour added at least another twenty miles to the journey, presuming I could ride straight across the Mississippi from East to west St. Louis. The map indicated seven bridges crossed the lazy river. Three were for interstates and three for ordinary highways only accessible from interstates. That left just one, the McKinley Toll Bridge, which appeared to be open to bicycle traffic.

Between the end of Route 40 and the Gateway City, quiet country roads led me through lush rolling farmland. Apple groves were new features on the landscape and the winter wheat was calf high, looking the better for a couple of days of sunshine after a week of downpours. Fields of red clover and soya beans were thickening up, but there were still acres of sodden ground lying fallow. Pedalling along beside his spluttering Farmall, a leather-skinned farmer told me that a northerly wind blowing up the Mississippi valley was beginning to dry out the soil. "In a week we should be able to seed a second crop of soya and set about planting the milo. It's been a real wet spring, but hopefully the weather's on the turn."

The route I devised to feed me into St. Louis was a flanking movement which snuck up on the city through a series of sleeper towns and suburbs. As I spun through Troy and Glen Carbon, traffic began to accumulate. The boys were returning home after a weekend with their toys. Pick-ups and RVs towed speed boats, ATVs and gliders. Small packs of motor bikers cruised the blacktop, ankles on foot rests, molls on pillion. I stopped a cyclist in U.S. Postal Service lycra riding several thousand dollars worth of Greg Lemond dream machine and asked about getting into St. Louis.

"I don't think you can from this side," he said. "I've never tried it, but I'm pretty certain they won't let you across the toll bridge. You gotta swing up to Alton and come in on 67."

Alton was north of where the Missouri joined the Mississippi, and a good thirty mile detour I couldn't afford. I had to get into the city before the working week began and the streets became manic with business traffic. If the worst came to the worst, I would do as I did in Wheeling — hoist my bicycle onto an interstate and pedal like the clappers.

The road through the outskirts of East St. Louis wound through chintzy sub-divisions and short bursts of pasture, but at Granite City things turned ugly. For over a mile, I rode beside the grim blast furnaces of Stein Steel, their fearful black structures held upright by a tangle of pipes and girders caked in black gunge. It looked like the factory had recently relocated from Hades or somewhere in Romania. Ghastly black cooling towers belched out grey steam and splattered me with sooty droplets. Everything in the vicinity was black and the definition of the kerb was lost under a solidified layer of coal dust.

I emerged from a cloud of steam spitting something phosphorous and found myself in a vast marshalling yard. Mountains of coal reared up on my left, dwarfing earth movers and tipper trucks the height of a house. Beyond the black tracks, a row of miserable stores appeared. If their windows weren't grilled, they were boarded up and plastered with ripped posters for blues gigs and dance parties.

I asked a lad the way to Venice, where the toll bridge took off, and followed his pointers up a fly-over across another expanse of woven railway lines. Hanging a right, I was suddenly very alone, cycling across derelict land. Large rectangles of shattered concrete indicated the area was once an industrial estate, now overrun by knee-high weeds and burnt out cars. In the middle of the wasteland stood a tin shack. Pacing outside, a black woman bursting out of a crimson top and cling-film skirt was squabbling down a mobile phone, doing the business.

At an ungated level crossing, St. Louis' Gateway Arch emerged above the forest of weeds, framed by the two Xs of the warning signs. Surrounding the giant hoop and almost as tall were the slender columns of downtown skyscrapers. It worried me that I was so close to the heart of the city yet so far from anything resembling civilisation. Surrounded by undergrowth and trees, I might have been a Forty-Niner arriving on the east bank looking across to the wharfs of the old city.

I had no problem picturing store keeper Bill von Axelson, architect Don Stone, school master Dick Baltzly and others like them milling around the banks of the Mississippi 150 years ago, waiting to ferry across. There would have been hundreds of them bottle-necked at the gateway to the most westerly city in the old United States. On 'wet roads' they had come from the Great Lakes and Deep South. Overland they had travelled from points east, funnelling into the National Road. The overwhelming majority were men, but there would have been a Betty Fearday and Debbie Grodecki, heading further north with their husbands and children to settle the virgin pastures of Oregon. Argonauts and pioneers mixed with merchants, missionaries, carpet baggers and opportunists, swanning between encampments where fiddles played, men gambled, dinner was served and the weary simply stared into the fire, thinking of home.

Don Stone had told me that the reason Americans are so easy to get to know (superficially at least) resides in their history as travellers. Certainly it was expedient to be friendly and polite along the trail. You never knew who you might bump into, able to give you a leg-up. But most of the people congregated on the east bank of the Mississippi in the spring of 1849 were more than travellers. They were taking a step into the unknown, caught up in a heroic movement and aware that they were writing the history of America. Full of enthusiasm and hope, I think they genuinely cared about each other, at least until going their separate ways the following morning. Certainly that was the sense I got from the Americans who had sheltered me, but such concern and charity was a far cry from what I rode into beyond the wasteland.

The tarmac took a couple of bends and brought me into a run-down area of shabby condominiums and dilapidated tenements. I felt a thousand eyes exploring me, as if swimming through frog's spawn. Kids throwing a football stopped running and stared while the ball was in flight. In a crescent of grotty condos, everybody on the street froze and turned to marvel at me. To a person, they were black, which usually wouldn't have bothered me, except this was America and I had read *Bonfire of the Vanities*. I could have been snapped in two by the tension in the air.

Aiming for the meanest, most muscle-bound beefcake on the block, I dropped the bike on the sidewalk next to where he was doing callisthenics and fished out a bag of John Fearday's hickories. Nobody on the crescent moved. A woman washing a car unwittingly let her hose wander onto a laundry basket of clean clothes. I offered the hulk a nut and explained I was lost.

"Gee, hickories!" he said, holding out a plate of a hand.

The tension evaporated. Quickly surrounded by a circle of young bloods, I surrendered the bag and did my level best to field a bombardment of questions. On learning how far I had ridden, a gangly youth wearing a Bob Marley T-shirt hissed, "Hey! Respect, man," and the circle fell to murmurs while the big man gave me directions.

Apparently I was in Brooklyn, East St. Louis, and there was only one place more deprived in America — Venice, next stop down the line before the bridge. Two months later, the President visited the neighbourhood on a nation-wide tour of the country's most severely depressed areas. Targeting the worst Indian reservation, the worst area of rural poverty and so forth, East St. Louis was selected as the worst inner city ghetto.

I turned to pick up my bike and found it in the hands a couple of homeboys giving it the once over, trying to work out what and where everything was.

"Y'lucky y'ain't got 'ubcaps, man," the big fella said with a beam.

The commercial district of America's worst inner city ghetto looked like a Middle East ceasefire had just been declared. Beside a rubble strewn blacktop, a series of low sheds housing dive bars and porn cinemas had survived. Roxy's was 'Only a Kiss Away' from ecstasy for some suit from the city and Leonardo Bo Peep's guaranteed to satisfy his black meat fantasies. Beyond the seedy blow-ups outside the Platinum Club, the Antioch Baptist Club and Lincoln High School were pontoons of morality sinking in a sea of decadence. Vacant looking black men shuffled down the street, stoned or pissed or vanquished. Caucasian drivers steered their way round craters in the road with windows glued up and eye's firmly fixed to the front.

Taking a left onto Broadway, I pedalled up to the toll booths for the McKinley Bridge and tendered my 50 cents through a hole in a booth held together with gaffa tape and hastily nailed sheeting.

"Where ch'you fink you're goin', man?" the gargantuan sister in the cubicle asked. "Man, ch'you can't go across there. What ch'you finkin' 'bout?"

A ripple of chuckles came from two other elephantine women lolling over the crash barriers. I tried reasoning.

"What ch'you gotta do is haul your bi-cycle onto a pick-up an' cross in a veh-icle, man."

"Right, like anybody driving through Venice is going to stop," I said.

I applied pressure, threatening to cycle across regardless, knowing none of the women had it in them to give chase. The sister finally took my cash and told me to "ride like th'Devil."

The bridge was a rusting girder construction carrying a lane either side and two within the curved superstructure. It looked like it should have been condemned twenty years ago. The roadbed was concrete and crumbling, laid on a mesh of metal stresses. In places, there was no road and I clattered across the mesh with a clear view of the Mississippi swirling beneath me. Expansion joints were like tectonic plates with a sharp six inch lip I had to lift my bike over. Shards of brown glass littered the outside of the lane and the northerly sweeping up the valley pushed me into their path. I heard crunching but the explosion never came.

On the west bank I pulled into a gas station to get a bearing on South 12th Street, where the Hostel International was located. The guide book said it was 'on the edge of a dodgy area', and where I was fitted the bill. The cashier in the gas station was surrounded by more bars than a Brinks-Mat vault. She directed me back onto Broadway and told me I was on the wrong side of the city.

But for a squad car, Broadway was empty as the warehouses which lined it. These weren't any old warehouses however. Maybe it was the evening sun hitting them full frontal or the wind's quiet winnowing of the street litter, but the moment I turned into the street I felt in the presence of something once great. They were just brick blocks, some six stories tall, flat faced with zig-zag fire escapes, but there were touches of splendour in the details. Swirls and flourishes on the blocking course at the top of the buildings, geometric brick reliefs along the walls, and mock Grecian reliefs worn like epaulets at the upper corners told of an era when St. Louis was a flourishing trade centre. Now almost the whole ten blocks were disused.

The cop waited for me to draw along side, leaned across the passenger's seat and asked where I was aiming for. She followed me to the next intersection then swung left. For the remaining blocks of the warehouse district, she tracked me on a parallel road. I saw her pause at each intersection. The officer was keeping an eye out for my safety, bless her, but I didn't feel in the least bit perturbed by the stillness of the deserted streets. If anything, I would have liked to explore deeper, but no doubt she knew something I didn't.

I rode into downtown, past swanky hotels and the Old Court House, between steel edifices and austere state buildings. The traffic on sidewalks and tarmac was light, though a couple of Yellow Cabs had still managed to collide. Beyond the Busch Stadium, a span carrying I-64 over the city and another carrying Broadway over a marshalling yard separated the prestigious from the poor as surely as a Berlin Wall. I continued into an area of distressed condos and dejected semis, passed Hope IV and the ten acre site of a gutted housing project built to 'Prepare for Tomorrow', according to the buckled sign. It seemed 'Building a Community of Opportunity' had proved a hollow clarion call, as with Hopes I through to III presumably. Finally I found South 12th Street and realised I had just ridden through the 'dodgy area' mentioned in the guide book. By comparison with Venice, it was posh.

Chapter 10
St. Louis

There were more residents than itinerants staying at the Huckleberry Finn Hostel, St. Louis. When I signed in, I signed on for a guest appearance in a soap opera featuring the comic turns of a colony of Bohemians. Set in adjacent houses and a large back yard, the principle characters of the hostel show fell into two groups.

There were those who were sufferable in small doses and appeared to be unemployed, namely Rudi, a wizened Costa Rican who never stopped trying to please, and a lad from Chicago for whom everything was "awesome" or "way cool," nicknamed The Dude. Rudi said he knew everybody it was important to know, but barely took a step outside of the place and spent much of his time prattling on the phone. The Dude was down here on some business to do with entertaining children. He claimed he was a professional clown but fancied himself as De Niro in *Taxi Driver*. Both were lonely souls who generously cooked for everybody when they cooked for themselves. For travellers stopping off over night, they were the perfect hosts. For anybody staying longer, they rapidly became irritating.

The second group of players were a fast talking, wise-cracking threesome pivoted around a systems analyser for Anheuser-Busch, brewers of Budweiser. René was in her late twenties, wore her hair like a geisha and had a chin which could punch holes in hardboard. Recently relocated to St. Louis, she was working to amass the collateral to buy her own pad. On one seat of the seesaw was Jim, a card carrying cynic and ex-UPI journalist whose halcyon years were spent in Vietnam covering the war. Disenchanted with the media, he now spent his days exercising race horses for a millionaire friend from his college years. On the other seat, Terry was a wheeler-dealer; stocky, tough, with a wayward left eye. He made his crust from recycling wood ripped out of condemned buildings. Both men had been divorced several times and clucked around René like competing stepfathers.

My week away from the trail began calmly enough with a lie-in. I brought my diary up to date, did the laundry, slobbed out and worked my way through a water melon. Between long breaks at the yard table helping me demolish the melon, Rudi worked at lowering his rent by slapping a coat of paint on every splint of woodwork in the place. Meanwhile Terry was stripping out a second floor dormitory, hurling the debris out of the window in volleys aimed at flattening The Dude.

Around mid-day, I started to catch news flashes on Rudi's radio and switched on the TV in the kitchen. By mid afternoon, sensational images of twisters were beaming in live from storm chasers in the mid-West. A complex of tornadoes was ripping through Oklahoma. An unprecedented three touchdowns were cutting a trail of destruction a mile wide and thirty-eight miles long through the heart of Oklahoma City. It had never been known before, but one touchdown was to last for four hours. It barely travelled, ripping into the earth like a buckled power drill. The force of the twister was rated at a rare F5 on the Fujita scale. This was later upgraded to F6 or 'inconceivable'. No tornado had ever surpassed F5.

The news appeared to be water off a duck's back to Rudi, Terry and The Dude. When he got back from work, Jim was full of his day swanning with the rich and cut short my attempt to initiate a conversation about twisters. Tom, the warden, expressed a little more interest, mainly because he had heard on the news that the system were heading for St. Louis. That evening, he made a thorough inspection of the hostel's storm cellar.

We only saw René briefly that night, and I didn't discover until the following evening that she was a native of Oklahoma City. René didn't learn about the disaster until she arrived at work on Tuesday morning to find a string of messages on her ansaphone. Her parents lived in Bethany, a suburb of Oklahoma City, trapped between the paths of the most powerful and a lesser tornado. With the lines down, René had an anxious morning trying to get through to the authorities. Finally she received a call from her Aunt Jessie who lived in Tuttle, south-west of the city and dangerously close to the line of most destruction.

"Everybody's fine," René later told us with tangible relief. "Their houses are a mess and they're badly shook up, but they're okay."

She looked pretty shook up herself, but managed a smile.

"My aunt's family had kind of a lucky escape. The twister took them by surprise. They sheltered in the bathroom — in the shower. It took two hours to pass and when they opened the bathroom door, the house was in chaos. Amazingly the walls and ceiling were still standing. When they opened the front door, they discovered the whole building had been picked up and moved two blocks."

In the wake of Oklahoma, four dozen minor tornadoes swarmed across a broad front which pushed through three states during the next twenty-four hours. Over St. Louis, the sky took a day to mutate from bright and breezy to threatening and evil. By mid afternoon Tuesday, churning black clouds were thundering across the heavens bringing daylight to an early close. Frantic to break loose, the tangles of telephone lines and power cables strung across the yard began whipping violently like screeching oscillator waves. The atmosphere was oppressive and everything on the street lighter than a full dustbin became airborne.

It was Cinco de Mayo, Mexican Independence Day, and that evening Terry, Jim, René and myself dined out. Having seen the celebratory road accident Rudi and The Dude were cooking up in the kitchen, we fled to a little Mexican place opposite Lafayette Park. During dinner the storm gathered pace. When we emerged, we stepped onto a sidewalk flayed by a tempest. In the park, trees and shrubs were being ripped to shreds by hurricane winds which splattered us against the restaurant wall. Broken branches bounced like tumbleweed down Park Avenue, splashing along the washed out street, ploughing into parked cars. In the space of the dozen difficult steps between the exit and our vehicle we were soaked to the skin.

"Are you ready for this, John?" René shouted, turning her palms to the weather. "It just keep getting better the further west you go!"

The new morning was glorious, without a whisper of wind in the air. The city smelt fresh and clean, as if driven through a car wash. It was a good day to play the tourist and ride up the huge parabola known as the Gateway Arch. St. Louis was the third American town or city I had ridden into laying claim to the title 'Gateway to the West' but, by 1849, Missouri was already incorporated into the United States. The boundary of the Old West was several hundred miles further on, where the Missouri and Kansas Rivers merged. However St.Louis was the last big metropolis the Forty-Niners would see before clapping eyes on San Francisco. For those from the backwoods, it was their first experience of a big city but, as one gold seeker observed, downtown wasn't the most beautiful of places. 'The business part of the city is dirty, with black, narrow streets filled with carts drawn by mules. It is a bare heap of stone and brick, covered with coal smoke, with which the air of the city is black all the time'. It sounded like Granite City today.

By the middle of the nineteenth century, St. Louis was already a powerhouse of industry and commerce, well in advance of most other cities west of the Appalachians. It had a head start, so to speak. The trading post Pierre Laclède established beside the Mississippi in the 1760s was built on the European demand for fashionable beaver skin hats. Once a year at a handful of 'rendezvous' in the Green River valley, Wyoming (then part of French Louisiana), trapper and fur trader haggled over how many pelts for how much whiskey, cloth and supplies. Wagon loads of skins were hauled out of the mountains and across the prairies to be sorted, cured and tanned in St. Louis before shipment downstream and out through New Orleans. Decades later, the scars those wagon wheels left on the wilderness steered the great migrations westwards. Following the California Trail, I would cross the Green River in about a month's time, and my excitement for the journey ahead took a bound on my way to the arch. Opposite the Old Courthouse, I found myself outside the International Fur Exchange. While prowling gaggles of day-trippers snapped each other in front of the clone of Capitol Hill, I stood in awe of an unremarkable redbrick high rise block on the opposite corner of Market and N 4th. Now redundant, the Fur Exchange was undergoing a well deserved face lift. Behind the scaffolding and fluttering splash sheets, I was sure I caught a glimpse of the Rockies beckoning.

I was on a high, which the view from the top of the 192 metre croquet hoop of the Gateway Arch made spectacular. Looking east through binoculars, I tried to make sense of the terrain I had covered since leaving Vandalia. Immediately beneath me, in the deep brown flow of the mighty Mississippi, a reproduction paddle steamer the size of a jelly bean was drawing along side another converted into a McDonalds. Turning to the opposite porthole, I peered across the crosshatch of the city to where I was heading. It looked like I could be spending the coming month just trying to clear the metropolis.

A hundred and fifty years ago, the vantage point would have afforded a bird's-eye view of one of America's busiest crossways. From the east, a stream of pioneers, pilgrims and argonauts crossed the Mississippi, swelling the city for as long as it took them to find passage on a steamer bound for Independence. Up and down and across stream, the river was frantic with flatboats, keelboats, rafts and steamers. In came molasses, sugar, coffee and dry goods. Out went flour, salt, bricks and furs. What the line of migrants brought to the city was cholera and hell raising. The year the Forty-Niners arrived, the resident population of St. Louis was decimated by the one and a third of the city went up in smoke, possibly a result of the other.

Symbolically if not geographically I had reached the halfway point of my trek. Although not the trailhead for the way out West, the Gateway City was where the Forty-Niners first appreciated the size of this folk movement they were a part of. A city of 65,000 people was suddenly swelled by as many as 15,000 itinerants a day, and everywhere they walked, the gold seekers were bombarded with placards and hustlers trying to sell them something 'indispensable' for the journey ahead. Their excitement is tangible in their diaries. Despite the threat of cholera, many confessed they had never been happier, "free from care, enjoying good health, mind contented, enjoying... a mild spring climate," as one from New York state wrote. Whether by 'wet road' or overland, their travels thus far had been entertaining and made easy by the support of settlers and communities along the way. To a large extent the Old West was tamed, but beyond St. Louis there was only a vast emptiness supporting nothing but herds of buffalo and tribes of hostiles, or so they were led to believe. The great American adventure properly began on the banks of the Mississippi, and it was here that most of the Gold Rush diarists began their entries.

So it was with heightened anticipation that I entered the Jefferson National Museum of Westward Expansion, bunkered in the base of the Gateway Arch. At the centre of the museum was a striking bronze of the president who bought Louisiana off the French for a song in 1803, thus linking the Old West with the Far West to create a national territory from 'sea to shining sea'. Radiating out from Jefferson was an area the size of a football pitch where a series of semi-circular time zones chronicled this most extraordinary period of American history. But I might have been reading a telephone directory for all the exhibition moved me. Elevating turgid to an art form, walls of endless text successfully hammered dead the very spirit of adventure the museum was supposed to be celebrating. Few artefacts were authentic, the stuffed animals needed a good dusting and the only sparks of life in the place were four talking automatons which sounded drunk.

For four days I walked the streets of the city and the corridors of its mausoleums trying to paint a picture of what St. Louis was like in 1849. In the American Frontier room of the Museum of Art I finally found one. *View of St. Louis — 1846* was about as compelling as its title, but Henry Lewis had produced a workmanlike record of the skyline the Forty-Niners would have seen from their camp on the opposite side of the Mississippi three years later. The city looked like an *arrondissement* of nineteenth century Paris. In the foreground, a family of migrants were settling down for a night on the east bank before catching the ferry across. On their wagon was daubed the words, 'Overland to Oregon'. The river was busy and forty paddle steamers were moored five deep against the wharfs. Framed by the leaves of cottonwoods, certain buildings on the west bank stood head and shoulders above the roof tops of the commercial waterfront. I asked an attendant if she recognised any.

"Now that's an interesting question," she said, peering at the picture. "Y'know, I've never really looked at it properly. Why don't you try the Resource Department. They're sure to have a list of the buildings."

I left her puzzling over the cityscape and went to talk to the Resource Department. The receptionist had a leaflet about Henry Lewis but said, "Y'know, that's an interesting question. You ought to go talk to the Registrar's Department, upstairs."

The registrar also thought I had an interesting question, but could offer no answers. It seemed nobody had ever raised the question of whether any of the buildings featured in Henry's 1846 painting remained standing after the Great Fire of '49, let alone until today. Were the citizens of St. Louis really that disinterested in their heritage or was I turning into an irrepressible anorak? Probably the latter. It transpired that Henry Lewis was a bit of a discovery.

Henry was an English cabinetmaker who found success as a landscape painter, mostly pedestrian renditions of the unopened country. In 1848, inspired by a local newspaper editor, he embarked on a 'Great National Work'. He kitted out a boat as a studio and set off down the Mississippi to paint one huge continuous panorama of its shoreline. Completed the year the Forty-Niners passed through, the work was exhibited in St. Louis before touring around the country and, from 1851, overseas. To display it Henry gave a performance, reciting a narrative while winding the canvas between two upright rollers. During those first exciting years of the California Gold Rush it seems Henry's travelogue was doing the rounds of American and European cities, whipping up recruits for the great westward trek like a forerunner of the TV travel show.

After each frustrating day of foraging, I returned to the hostel to find a debate in progress. By evening, the yard table had been transformed into a Montmartré café where the Bohemians discussed whatever was brought to the round by the trickle of overnight guests from Japan, Germany and Holland. Like casualties to E.R., the constant drip of itinerants kept the hostel show bubbling.

Wednesday evening was unusual in that the guest was an American. Scott had flown in from Boston to visit a Max Beckmann exhibition at the Museum of Art. He was a struggling artist whose work was concerned with what he called "the American condition," the topic under discussion when I pulled up a chair.

"Let's face it," Scott said, "Americans are like a spoilt teenager. As fast as he unwraps one new toy, he's looking around for the next. We consume like breathing depends on it. We're immature, barely out of shorts compared to a civilisation the age of Europe's. The punk rejected his parents (you guys, the British) when he was in diapers and now he's strutting around attention seeking — looking for somebody to show him what to do and where to go next. He's badly in need of a role model, but there ain't nobody. Except for wanting more, the kid's aimless. That's kind of dangerous when you're a super power."

"Explains why he's been trashing hotel rooms from Saigon to Managua," Terry chuckled.

Though barely a thousand miles into the country, I had to admit the United States didn't look much like a superpower. If the Manhattan skyline was the image America liked to project of its status in the world, the fabric of the nation I had ridden through was overwhelmingly low rise, tacky and looked recently assembled from a flat-pack. Entire towns were held upright by strings of utility cables any mature nation would have buried. Pockets of deprivation were more squalid than anything I had seen in the old Eastern Bloc, and Bombay's lingering smog was a coastal breeze by comparison to the air quality in most towns and cities. Had I dropped into America blindfolded, I would have guessed I was travelling through an underdeveloped country, not the world's richest.

The relentless pursuit of the new had certainly had a less than beneficial impact on the historic highway I travelled, but there was evidence Americans were becoming disenchanted with what passed for progress. Nobody I talked to thought the fast food joints were in the fine tradition of the taverns and inns which once lined the National Road. Many were appalled by the plague of franchise shanty towns squeezing the commercial life out of town centres. Maybe the economic boom was providing a breathing space, but people seemed to be taking stock of their quality of life in America. Many had regaled me with severe misgivings about the ubiquitous motor culture, the rush to tear down anything erected pre 1950, and the environmental impact of the country's voracious consumption of energy. I was surprised how vocal people were about all the things the British take a poke at Americans about, including their lousy diet. What best illustrated Scott's point, however, was the epidemic of concern about the 'Columbine syndrome', where parents found it easier to furnish their kids with the latest technology and send them packing, rather than sit down and engage with them.

"For all its failings, you've got to remember our democracy is an ongoing experiment," Scott continued. "We might be one of the youngest countries in the world, but we're one of the oldest democracies."

"Hey, we wrote the manual on democracy," Jim cut in, "which mostly means wishing the federal government would take a hike and leave the states to go their own way. Fifty percent of Americans are registered to vote but only fifty percent of the fifty percent get out and do it." He reckoned Capitol Hill was generally regarded as an irrelevance, except when it came to dealing with the rest of the world. "Then we expect Captain America to fly in, grab whatever we need and get the hell out fast. It's the mentality of your Gold Rush guys, John, except now we go plunder some other poor bastard's country."

"The Founding Fathers didn't like what they saw going down in Europe," Scott jumped back in, trying to maintain a thread which was shaping up to be a protracted history lesson, "so they came over here and had a go at something different — something they thought was better."

"Provided you're white," Rudi hissed, flicking open a can of worms guaranteed to poison polite conversation.

For a moment, things became sticky. Jim donned his 'weary journalist' hat and Rudi became the consummate victim, wilfully misinterpreting everything the old cynic said about the white man's conquest of North America.

When Rudi postured for a fight, Terry mutated into Don King, I rattled through the Queensbury rules, and The Dude pissed everybody off by incinerating our corn cobs on the barbie. As Scott retreated defeated to his bed, René assumed the role of peacemaker, cooling things down with a gag she said summed up the redneck perspective on race, certainly in her home corner of the Bible Belt.

"The President of Mexico, Jesse Jackson and a Texan are each granted one wish by a genie. The Mexican President says, 'I want to bring my people home and make them rich'. Jesse Jackson says, 'I want to lead my people back to Africa and make them rich'. The Texan listens to this, thinks and says, 'Shoot! I'll just go for a Bud!'"

I was going to miss the hostel show, and on my last night cooked them a traditional English roast. I was leaving early. After four days in the Gateway City I had spent more money than in four weeks riding through the American mid-west. Like many of the westward bound who stopped off in the nineteenth century, I simply couldn't afford to stay a day longer, no matter how much I needed to recharge the batteries. As one of the Forty-Niners wrote, 'Many a green'un who has started for the gold mines has been relieved of his tin by the time he has been in St. Louis three days, and has had to forgo his golden dreams and return to the old diggings.'

Chapter 11
Missouri River

Most of the Forty-Niners completed their journey to the western fringes of the United States by paddle steamer, heading north up the Mississippi River then west along the Missouri for three hundred miles to the frontier town of Independence. I planned to follow their route, hitching a ride on a river barge returning upstream, but a couple of phone calls during my time in St. Louis confirmed what I feared when I first saw the Mississippi through the mesh of the MacKinley Bridge. This spring was as wet as the spring of 1849 was dry. The rivers were running dangerously high and fast. Nothing was moving up the Big Muddy and the one barge I saw struggling up the Mississippi I overtook while strolling along the quayside.

The opportunity to begin my Wild West adventure with a lot of lounging around on deck wasn't going to happen, but the warden of the Huckleberry Finn Hostel had drawn my attention to the Katy Trail, a Rails-to-Trails cycle path which began at St. Charles and hugged the north bank of the Missouri for 150 miles to Boonville. Where it swung south back across the Big Muddy, I would have to find my own way west to Independence along whichever country roads and tracks ran closest to the bend in the river defining Saline County. According to my map, the only road cut the curve like an arrow through an apple.

Sad about leaving the cast and feeling uncomfortably alone, I rode away from the hostel show on a line through the Gateway City I hoped would be hassle free. Despite assurances from Tourist Information, The Dude was so convinced I was riding into a repeat of my frustrations at trying to cross the Ohio and Mississippi rivers, he offered to truck me across the Missouri. We wouldn't have got far. Dropping off the bluff supporting St. Louis, I swept into the flood plain to be confronted with my first challenge in the wild and woolly West. The plain was a washout. For a handful of miles, I chanced I knew the course of the road and cycled through flood waters up to my axles. Mid-way, I passed a driver sat on the roof of a drowned pick-up who had chanced the same thing and slipped into a ditch.

From the Mississippi westwards, I could expect to chew up roughly four times the daily mileage the overlanders were to achieve in the coming months. While I would be continuing alone, solo travellers on the trail of gold were now in the company of hundreds of fellow argonauts, on a boat whose deck was jammed to the railings with wagons and carts, mules and oxen, supplies and mining equipment. Every table, chair and inch of floor space was occupied by a man who talked about nothing but the sudden and immense fortune he was going to find, and who dreamed of spending it anyway but wisely. Whatever the differences in their background or nationality, all silently shared deep concerns about entering the uncharted lands of the American West. Their diaries reveal they had little doubt that the boat trip was carrying them from the rule of law to the law of the jungle.

I crossed the Missouri River and found the Katy Trail with few problems beyond wet feet, but the converted railbed of the old Missouri-Kansas-Texas (MKT) Railroad was a different ball game to the line beside the C & OC. It was a hiker-biker trail and a State Park, but there were no free camp sites and any hope of pitching wild were hampered by flooding on my left and a steep wooded bluff beyond a ditch immediately to my right. By the time I reached Greens Bottom, six miles west of St. Charles, evening was drawing in early under a slurry of thick clouds. Between the bluffs and the Missouri half a mile away, the land had opened out to contain a minor road to Jefferson City, a wheat field polka dotted with flood water and a dozen mysterious tumuli which could have been Native American or Top Secret. Thrusting into the field was a gravel car park and a chemical toilet block servicing the Katy Trail, with enough dry space to place a small tent but no cover to hide it. I pulled over, noted the 'No Camping' sign and fed myself, waiting for darkness to fall before pitching.

Around eleven o'clock, my deep slumbers were rudely interrupted by car tyres spinning through gravel, headlights panning across the flysheet, and the sort of whoops and hollers which precede grievous deeds in redneck movies. Nervously, I dressed and peered out. The car park was ablaze with the headlights of pick-ups, jeeps, compacts and coupés. Silhouettes were jostling between the beams, huddling in clinches, leaping on bonnets. People were shouting and passing bottles between hands. It was a rave or maybe a prelude to some ad hoc drag racing, but nobody appeared to have noticed the tent yet. It was inconceivable these rebel rousers would turn up the chance for a bit of fun with an illegal camper. I decided to approach them before they approached me, and introduced myself to a body leaning into a chrome enhanced 4X4 parked at the edge of the melée.

"Oh, yeh, yer from Ingerland, huh?" Unbent, the body barely reached up to my chest and was more boy than man. "We've just graduated. We're having a party. You're cool."

Relieved that I was cool, I joined a small circle of youths clutching bottles in paper bags and soggy spliffs. We were just getting to know each other when a couple of them exclaimed "Oh, shit!", dropped the booze and bolted.

Suddenly everybody was leaping about, bottles and butt-ends were flying, car doors were slamming and engines revving.

Down the driveway to the car park a police car eased forward — no siren, but with lights flashing. It pulled up half way. From the car park an orderly queue of headlights lined up and began filtering out right, heading back to St. Charles in convoy. There were forty-three vehicles, most of them probably owned by a parent, all occupied by teenagers. When it had emptied, the cop moved onto the car park, flipped the trunk open, climbed out with a flashlight and began picking up bottles. I slipped back into the tent, hoping he wouldn't spot me.

A good ten minutes later, I heard the car door slam and tyres crunch across gravel. Then the crunching stopped, there was a pause and I was spot lit.

"How y'doing?"

"Better if you hadn't stopped," I muttered, before shouting, "Okay, thanks."

"Stand away from the tent, please sir."

The interrogation was conducted with the utmost politeness, but with the flashlight never leaving my eyes. The cop was just a dark shape that wasn't buying my excuse about arriving at night and seeing no signs. He needed to check an ID and searched my tent while I searched pannier bags for my passport.

"English, huh?"

"Close enough." The torch was back on my eyes. He needed to see an ID with a social security number on it.

"Er... we tend not to use them. Haven't a clue what mine is."

"Can't run you through the computer without a social security number, sir."

"Even if I had it, I'm from the UK remember."

"Date of birth?"

"Three, ten, forty-nine."

"Born in March?"

"Sorry. I forgot you guys write it arse-about-face. Born October."

That was uncool. The cop stepped back and politely ordered me to walk to the front of the police car, tracking me from a safe distance, never dropping the torch beam.

"Stand in the headlights, sir, and drop the bum bag. It's making me jumpy."

"The only thing in it that shoots is a camera," I said, beginning to get annoyed. I had strapped on the camera bag to facilitate easy removal of my press card.

"Maybe, maybe not. Place your hands on the hood, sir, and spread your legs please."

He took the press card, garbled into the radio, then walked back into the headlights. It was my first proper view of my inquisitor. He was a kid, not much older than the youths who had just graduated. He too had just graduated, having learnt the book from cover to cover on how to be a pig. From a utility belt bristling with armaments, cuffs and radios hung an immaculately pressed green uniform, black stripes down the side of each leg and embroidered badges puckering the new top. His crew cut was so sharp it was a weapon.

The computer had turned up nothing on me.

"So what y' gonna do. Y'can't stay here and the nearest hotel's in Dutzow, twenty miles away. Got lights?"

I shook my head.

"You mean you gotten all that gear but no lights?"

"Why would I want to ride through America in the dark? You don't see anything."

"Well y'can't stay here."

The conversation went round in circles until I suggested loading my bike and kit into the patrol car for him to run me up to Dutzow. Finally he caved in.

"Well, I've told you to move on. It's your responsibility. It's not my fault if those kids come back."

"They won't come back."

"Oh, they'll be back with their beer and drugs. They're out to party." Then he turned the screw. "Don't blame me if they shoot you."

Brilliant! With Columbine still headline news, it was exactly what I didn't need to hear. It never entered my mind that I was rubbing shoulders with graduate assassins, but the cop had planted a seed in a brain which was tired, anxious and angry. I was guaranteed an appalling night's sleep, awaking at every bark of a dog and growl of an engine, dreaming of bloodbaths and body bags. The kids never reappeared.

On the dot of 7.00am, I was joined for breakfast in the car park by three lassies preparing to pedal the twenty-six miles to Defiance and back before heading off to work. I expressed surprise at their dedication to cycling, and mentioned how few pedal-pushers I had encountered on my trip.

"Aw, but the Katy Trail's great," one of them said. "Y'won't catch me cycling on the highway but, man, I love this trail. You'll see lots of bikers between here and... where y'going? You're kidding, right?"

I did see an exceptional number of cyclists that day, largely because the American Diabetes Association were running a Bike-A-Thon. At times I was engulfed by so many dawdlers I switched from the trail to the highway running beside it. I was learning that this was the way Americans cycled — in a pack, on a cycle trail, or to fetch their mail from the end of the drive. Participants I spoke to thought I was clinically insane to ride on the road without the security of 1,000 other charity cyclists, but they assured me they had been in training for the event and rode it every year. Today they would tuck all of forty miles under their belts.

They were probably wise to attempt no further. While occasional avenues of trees shaded the trail from a sizzling sun, the prevailing wind was a westerly. It blew straight down the track, cranking up the temperature, lifting hot dust into eyes, nose and throat. Michael Bauermeister told me he had ridden across America several times, but hadn't once enjoyed cycling from east to west.

"Damn wind. I rode a recumbent each time. Better streamlining, but a pin ain't streamlined enough for the winds y'get out west. And the damn dogs, man. Got bitten by one crossing Kansas. Y'know, low down in a recumbent, y'kind of a tasty meal on a plate. I was in hospital three days being jacked full of anti rabies vaccine."

Michael was a sculptor who worked out of a small wooden farmhouse unusually located on the south side of the Katy Trail. In the window of Noama Woodworks he displayed large wooden vases the shape of a trumpeter's mute and the size of a trumpeter. Walking me round a workshop stuffed with ancient lathes and wood working tools, Michael told me about the flood of 1993, when the Missouri burst its banks and turned the north of the state into a fast flowing reservoir.

"The flooding drowned the ground floor of the house and barn. It was kind of freaky to walk downstairs and find the river lapping half way up 'em. It did less damage to us than to other folks. When the water subsided, most of my tools were still around, but I had to strip down the lathes and spent weeks trying to get rid of the sand. Didn't take too long to clean up the workshop, but it's bare wood walls and floors. The flood kinda gave 'em a good sanding and cleaned 'em up."

The Missouri was one river I was not going to take a dip in. In places a mile wide, it seethed with more undercurrents than the House of Representatives. Dense as pea soup and fast as a boy racer, it carried a flotilla of wood down stream. I watched thick tree trunks career down the river, stop dead, up-end and slip into the depths like the Titanic, never to be seen again. Michael told me about a light aircraft piloted by a flying student with an instructor which ditched in the river a year ago. According to those who witnessed the accident, it was a perfect crash landing on water but, before the pair could jump clear and be rescued, the Cesna was sucked under. Nothing was ever found of aircraft or occupants.

The Missouri is the longest river in the United States. It flows out of Montana and drains over 500,000 square miles of the north-west, east of the continental divide. North of 40° latitude, it absorbs all the main flows eastward bound from the Rockies, including the Platte and Kansas Rivers. For over fifty years, environmental agencies have been attempting to tame the Big Muddy, but the enormous quantity of silt it spirits away continues to frustrate the country's efforts to channel it into a fixed course. When the Missouri has a mind to rebel it does so with moral abandon. In the summer of 1993, the floods killed over fifty people and devastated more than twenty million acres in the Missouri and Mississippi valleys.

"Around here," Michael said, "the flood mark is twenty-five foot. That August, the river reached forty foot."

The following day, a Sunday, I came across bulldozers busy shovelling earth up a stout levee which curved in towards the trail on the western edge of Montgomery County. At a soda stall opposite, I was informed that the levee was the first bend in the Missouri after the junction with the Osage River. While the woman struggled to get the coffee machine working, she explained how the "Great Flood" caused a "real bad feeling" between those living on the banks of the Big Muddy and those in the Ozarks, a hundred miles south-west of us.

"The Osage is dammed, okay? Hydroelectric power. The turbines don't provide much electricity these days, but it switches in when St. Louis goes crazy with the air conditioning. Anyway, '93 was a real wet summer after a dreadful spring, and the people in the Ozarks were getting concerned about the lakes overflowing. Without any warning, they open the sluice gates. 'Course a tidal wave comes racing down the Osage, enters the Missouri, hits the first bend and blasts away the levee."

"They called it the 500 Flood," her husband butted in, pouring me home-made lemonade in lieu of coffee. "Rain like that's only supposed to happen once every 500 years. Two years later, we had another big rush flatten the levee. Thought it was set to happen again last Friday, but we were lucky."

A short distance from Portland, between the outflow of the Osage and the vulnerable first bend, the trail was still flooded from the deluge which thundered in after the Oklahoma twisters. South of the old rail embankment, roads and fields were obliterated, forcing local farmers to use the Katy Trail for access. Tractors had chewed up the surface and I had to wade through a current up to my knees. For three tense miles, I nervously scanned the waters for the tell-tale wake of predatory 'snappers' (turtles) homing in on my ankles. Somewhere in the back of my skull, double basses started in on the theme from *Jaws*.

It was May 9th or 'Mommy's Day', as the cards insisted on calling it. Nobody was cycling or hiking down the Katy Trail that morning, but I certainly didn't have the grit line to myself. First a green and black diamond-back snake crossed my path, followed by a tortoise and a muskrat with something slithery dangling from its jaws. A racoon darted out from the bracken, stopped to stare at me like a confused highwayman, then bounded off down the trail. In the swamps, large snappers plopped into the stagnant waters as I rode by, cracking open the mat of pond weed. Smaller box turtles basked on rotting logs with their backs to the sun, undisturbed by loose formations of indigo buntings and martins dive-bombing them. Higher on the wing, turkey vultures criss-crossed on the thermals, cranes casually flapped through the deep blue and a couple of silhouetted eagles spiralled closer to the sun.

After the previous day's throng of Bike-a-Thoners, it was a relief to have elbow space, but Mommy's Day, celebrated two months later than in the UK, turned out to be a depressing day. Except for the couple at the farm yard soda stall, I didn't see a soul and imagined Missourians were otherwise occupied making their mum's dinner. I couldn't shake the memory of Sandy's miserable first Mothering Sunday without Pauline, and imagined my own mother was probably worrying herself stupid about the pair of us. Discovering the café in Hartsburg was closed and with no inclination whatsoever to cook, I resolved to get well and truly drunk.

The Hitching Post was the first Western-style saloon I had entered. A long walnut bar stretched the length of the room. Behind it were ceiling high mirrors. The floor was bare boards and the lights were mock kerosene lamps. Occupying most of the room, a mess of round tables and chairs with curved backs looked like 'The Duke' might have recently dealt a hand at them. The place just needed a 'Joanna', but the Hitching Post played loud honking rock music instead.

Eyeing the anarchic crew holding up the far end of the bar with misgivings, I kept to myself at the opposite end and knocked back a couple of beers. I was served by different people. Since the gang readily alternated between both sides of the bar, helping themselves to drinks, it was hard to know which of the five men and two woman actually worked there. The guys looked mean and wore everything which identified them as whatever the American equivalent of sheep shaggers might be. The women looked like they had stepped out of *Beavis and Butthead*.

The ice was broken by Chris, an ex-Marine with the handshake of a boa constrictor. Then Dayla slid along the bar and wrapped herself round my neck, slowly followed by Sean, who fell over a couple of tables en route. In transmitting the news that I was from England and a cartoonist, Chris ensured the remainder of the crew gathered round in a crush. Three bottles of Sierra Nevada suddenly appeared on the bar in front of me.

"Geddim some paper, man," a hulk called Brandon said, "anna pen. Hey, draw d'bitch, man. Make d'tits like humungus." He tickled Dayla, who spilt her drink and writhed around the bar giggling.

I drew Dayla as I saw her, like something out of *Beavis and Butthead*. The sketch went down a storm, and then there were four bottles racked up in front of me. Next up, I had to draw Sean, otherwise known as Twinkie. Twinkie could have crushed me with his little finger.

"Draw him with his twinkie sticking out," Dayla demanded.

I obliged. More guffaws and screams, and then there were five bottles.

If it was possible, Brandon's bulk was even more gross and threatening than Twinkie's. I could have painted the Last Supper on his bicep and still had space for the frame. He had a Devil's mask tattooed on his forearm, but Brandon (aka the Big Bitch Banger) was a softy and a pin head, which is how I depicted him. The place erupted.

I looked at the bar and saw ten bottles. There were then two bars. Somebody thrust twenty bucks in front of my eyes and they became forty.

"Will you draw a portrait of my daughter, John? I'll pay you."

If I wasn't already out of it, I was teetering in the doorway.

"I'm sorry. I can't do it any more. I've got to eat," I said to the time dissolve wavering before my eyes. "And somebody give me some water!"

"You want food?" Chris asked. "Get the man a pizza. Now. Go!"

Time passed, maybe with Dayla soothing my brow. Talking Heads asked what a psycho killer was, Hendrix fed back through the crossroads, and the boys were on the bar, dancing like tarts. An elderly gent walked in, looked aghast and walked right back out again. My pizza arrived, swiftly followed by my first 'shotgun'.

"Okay," Twinkie barked, stabbing a hole in the base of a can of Bud, "what y'do is hold the can upside down over your mouth, release the ring-pull, and swallow like a whale."

Three shotguns later, I passed out.

Considering the amount of alcohol which gushed down my gullet that night, I was bright as a button when I opened my eyes the next morning, if a little surprised to find myself half naked and in my tent. When I tried crawling out and standing up, however, I discovered the bones had been removed from my limbs. Wobbling round the tent like David Byrne in his rubber suit, it slowly registered that I was pitched in the middle of Hartsburg's baseball diamond. Chris stopped off on his way to mow his dad's lawn. He hadn't a clue how I came to be where I was or who had put me to bed. He had passed out shortly after I had.

Unlike my ride up the Missouri valley, the Forty-Niners' voyage up the Missouri River was written off as 'monotonous'. Though the scenery was observed to be 'finer' than that of the Mississippi valley, there was little to occupy the men trapped on board except poker, talk and the 'trashy, obscene' literature available at the purser's office. The gaming tables were never empty, twenty-four hours a day, and many an argonaut lost everything to the card sharks before they had set foot on the California Trail. The trip was laboured and took far longer than the captains estimated, partly due to powerful spring currents and partly because the over-loaded steamers regularly ran aground on submerged sand bars.

If anything livened up the journey and gave the gold seekers a taste of what was to come, it was rampaging cholera. There were examples of shipfuls of men being struck down, of boats being abandoned and left moored on the shore. On a crowded dirty steamer where the water supply and food came from uncertain sources, passengers were immensely vulnerable, if not to cholera then to the panic which followed a diagnosis. Some passengers recorded how the bodies were wrapped in blankets and lined up on deck until sufficient had accumulated to moor against one of the river islands and dig a mass shallow grave. But the sick and dying were well attended. An extraordinary number of doctors and ministers had been smitten with gold fever and joined the exodus to California.

Either a full body transplant or the last rites would have been most welcomed the way I was feeling, sat on the Hartsburg pitcher's mound. The prospect of packing up and moving out filled me with rigor mortis

Chapter 12

In a thousand miles, I had seen nothing outside of museums and advertisements which indicated America had ever been inhabited by anybody other than immigrants. There had been a few names of rivers and a couple of brief encounters with folk claiming to have traces of aborigine blood, but I had to wait until I was west of the Mississippi before meeting my first Native American. A big man with short grey hair, sleepy eyes and a paunch, he was sat in front of signs for fishing bait and fresh donuts on the porch of the Easley store, rocking gently on the back legs of a plastic chair.

David Geurts was a full-blooded Oneida Indian, married to an Anglo-American for twenty-five years, with three children, all doing well at college. He was one of only 1,500 pure Oneida's left, but the tribe and his brothers and sisters shunned him.

"They think I've sold out. They think any Indian who isn't drunk and lying around the reservation is an Uncle Tom."

David had only recently taken over the tenancy of the store and was still straightening it out. The place had stood empty since the 1995 flood, and he had been shovelling out loam and washing down surfaces off and on for eighteen months. Although he spent most of his time there, he also ran a successful flooring business which had him fielding phone calls from his manager while we talked. David was a grafter but it had been a struggle. When he first left the reservation to become a building labourer, he was fluent in Iroquois, the Oneida's tongue, but his English was limited. Fellow workers labelled him a liar because his lips never touched when he spoke, as they wouldn't when speaking Iroquois. Having mastered the language, however, the racism didn't let up, so he changed his name and took himself back to the reservation to get a higher education. At the Indian college, he learned the "White Eye's ways of doing business." His plans for the store included bike hire and camping, each successful diversification increasing the hostility he would receive from the tribe he was keen to remain a part of. Next month he was off to Wisconsin for the Oneiga's annual pow-wow and was curious to see what kind of reception he would walk into.

But the KATY Trail meant more than an opportunity to diversify for David Geurts, inveterate survivor. Despite the fact that the old railroad bridges carrying the Katy Trail across creeks were too narrow to drive a Hummer through, David had it on unassailable authority that the cycle path doubled as a military artery.

"As soon as the lights go out, you're gonna see the army streaming down that trail. Convoys of 'em. You heard of the FEMA plan?"

The Federal Emergency Management Agency plan was apparently something dreamed up during Richard Nixon's tenure to subvert the democratic process. In essence, it laid the ground for a military take-over of the United States led by the Commander-in-Chief, the President. Financed by the Rothschilds, Rockerfellers and Kennedys, sixty-five internment camps capable of holding 60,000 people had been built somewhere in the wilds of the deserts to incarcerate counter insurgents. According to David, the plan was so hush-hush that, when a newspaper got hold of the story, the FBI stormed in, smashed up the presses and bulldozed the office to the ground.

(FEMA was actually established in 1979 as a rapid response force for coping with federal natural disasters like the Great Flood, and has nothing to do with internal security conspiracies. During the '93 flood it set up vast trailer parks known as 'FEMAvilles' to house those who lost their homes.)

"Have you heard Mr. C. on the radio?" I asked, fanning the flames.

"Good man. Does good work consciousness raising."

Mr. C. is a basket case who regularly insinuates his way onto right-wing talk shows to rant about the New World Order and their conspiracies. My favourite was the one about the impending conquest of the United States. As more and more U.S. troops were flown out to Kosovo, so more and more Russian troops were amassing on the Mexican and Canadian borders. With orders to attack Uncle Sam while his back's turned, the Ruskies planned to link up with the Peace Troops, a foreign military force who were already active in the country covertly preparing the ground for invasion. But come FEMA or Peace Troops, David Geurts was ready for anything.

"I've been stock-piling food, sleeping bags, arms, survival gear, and we've just finished my dune buggy. We've got over 200 built so far. They're hidden in different places along the Missouri. That was my job — the logistics of stockpiling and mapping."

David belonged to a group of local survivalists who weren't going to take a White House coup lying down. They communicated with other groups through the internet, where there were over fifty survivalist web sites. In one day, the FBI closed down twenty-five sites but David assure me new ones were continually appearing, particularly from churches like the Southern Baptists whose Armageddon scenario neatly dove-tailed into the FEMA scenario.

Or rather, they used to communicate through computers. A nerd in the group recently discovered the hardware doubled as a receiver/transceiver and that Microsoft Excel was a thinly disguised tracking software sponsored by the U.S. government. David told me of his horror when his friend managed to punch up a digitised image of a bird's eye view of his home (where the computer was based), his yard, even his dog running around the yard. David said Bill Gates was the Devil incarnate. It was the first thing he had said since we began talking about the KATY Trail which I had no dispute with.

Shortly after New Franklin, the Katy Trail arced south and crossed the river to Boonville. My route continued on the north bank, into the headwind and along a dirt road at the foot of the bluffs. I was aiming to bridge the Missouri at Glasgow. The road from there to Independence was the closest I could get to tracking the river. Within eight miles of New Franklin I was grinding my way up a cut through the cliffs, climbing into a Missouri landscape which had me gasping for breath.

After the gentle swell of Illinois, I presumed Missouri would be much the same. It wasn't. As I reached the summit, a roller coaster complex of pastoral wolds stretched before me like a stormy sea. Big dippers slid steeply down to valley bottoms where new leaf copses queued up for a ride. It could have been the Scottish Borders, except the farms sprinkled across the upland were clapboard and white, and the trees were broadleaf. The cattle, however, were Angus.

With black clouds galloping up on my heels, I turned into the first farm and rode up a driveway where a school bus was parked up for the night. Ally Boggs, aged ten and killing time before tea, leapt off the swing and dashed inside to fetch her mum. I went through my begging routine. Ally's mum scrutinised me. "Two days ago we had a murder in town, y'know."

On Saturday night, somebody had walked into the home of a Boonesboro couple, shot the husband dead and "raped the wife every which way," she said. "But, you're okay by me if you're okay by my husband. Melvin's up in the far field, mowing hay. Can you cycle on tracks? Do you mind taking Ally with you? She doesn't often get to cycle up the track."

I was in.

The Boggs family farmed 250 acres of rolling upland. They grazed twenty-five head of beef and a dozen young calves which Melvin called "my babies." Thanks to the European embargo against the import of hormone treated beef, the bottom had dropped out of the market, costing

American cattlemen $500 million in lost revenue. Although Melvin didn't treat his herd, he did think it was a lot of fuss about nothing. He wasn't over concerned, though. He had retired, and the farm was just something to keep him ticking over, supplementing his pension. He thought about moving into cereal crops but, with soya and corn mountains growing, the picture wasn't any rosier on the arable side of the fence.

Melvin Boggs was a lot older than his wife, and I would have confused Ally for his grand-daughter. Considering he was supposed to be taking it easy, the Boggs family annually nurtured five acres of tobacco, planted out from a seedbed about the size of a kitchen garden. For Howard County, this represented a sizeable stake in a crop which is labour intensive and very fickle. At different times in the cycle, Mr. and Mrs. Boggs and their two daughters were bent in the back-breaking work of planting out, harvesting, hanging and stripping tobacco, all by hand. Only the drying period provided respite and a little recuperation before the stripping that Ally so loathed. For a month after the sacks had gone to the agent, she found herself hacking up tobacco dust. For that, I had never felt more guilty about being a smoker.

Ally quizzed me about England, Robin Hood and my two dogs with seven legs, well past her bedtime. In front of us, dominating the driveway, the big yellow school bus caught the last rays and bounced them down to the lawn where we sat. It looked magnificent, every inch the star of the blacktop and symbol of all that is safe, secure and routine in American family life. Every adult has memories of riding the school bus and tales of woe or happiness to tell. Twice a day, it was a halfway house between the suffocation of home and the discipline of school, full of friends and enemies, intrigues and japes. The school run was the last time most Americans regularly travelled in a community of passengers, and they remember it fondly.

Though it put her in the unenviable position of having to be a goody two shoes, Ally was proud that her mum drove the school bus. Each new school day began with Mrs. Boggs sat at the steering wheel testing the whistles and bells.

"After a tragic accident," her mum explained, switching the lights on and off, "we now have an arm that swings out from the bumper so children crossing in front of the bus are always visible to the driver."

She pressed a button and the arm swung out. She pressed another and a Stop sign flicked out. In a design barely altered since the Reo Safety bus of the 1930s, there was nothing digital on Mrs. Boggs' bus.

Everything double checked, Ally and her sister jumped aboard with their school bags, ready to start the morning run. Through the window, Ally pleaded for me to stay a second night, but I was anxious to keep moving. The Boggs' came from a dynasty of small farmers whose roots were buried deep in Howard County. Their story might have filled some of the huge omissions in the Jefferson National Museum of Westward Expansion, but it was the stories of sculptor Michael Bauermeister which had been gnawing at me. What was up ahead that transformed his rides to the Pacific into such an ordeal? Surely not a couple of snarling dogs and a spot of wind? And if it was so terrible, why repeat the performance? While the going was good, I felt I needed to put miles behind me, to buy time for whatever was up ahead preparing to pounce.

There were steel fabricators and agricultural suppliers on the outskirts of Glasgow, USA, but the town itself was easily missed. The main road took a left at a high railroad embankment and crossed the river adjacent to the girder rail bridge. The two features were as a castle wall hiding the high street, but a narrow arch provided a discreet access I initially didn't see. Beyond the portal, I found myself on a quay side among huge silos, grain elevators and warehouses. A little further on, the high street was lined with stores sporting several strings to their bow, like a laundromat doubling as an insurance agents.

I stopped off at Charlie's Quik Chek to pick up supplies. Behind the deli counter, Charlie kept flicking his eyes up at the Scottish flag emblazoned on my baseball cap.

"Say, ain't the original Glasgow in Scotland?" he asked. Shouting down the aisle to attract the attention of a customer, he hollered, "Hey, Sam, you wanna interview this guy. He's from Scotland. Y'know, Glasgow, in Scotland."

With his wife Barbara, Sam Audsley was the publisher and editor of *The Glasgow Missourian*. He was also the photographer, proof reader, advertising manager and star reporter, plus the manager of the custom printers which pushed out wedding invites and business cards. The headline news for the week was the resumption of grain barges leaving Glasgow.

Sam interviewed me down at The Outlook — a picnic area overlooking the river jammed between a row of workshops. I asked about the grain barges, explaining my disappointment at not being able to catch a boat upstream from St. Louis.

"The last fourteen days of April were the wettest on record. The river rose five feet above the high water mark for spring. We can't get the barges in when it's that high, but things are starting to settle down. A couple set off down stream last week carrying a million bushels, but nothing's coming up. Mind you, the farmers can't get into the fields, so what the hell. Until the river drops, the surface water behind the levees won't subside. We've already passed the optimum date for planting out corn and we're getting mighty close to the final date for soy beans. If the current weather persists, we're are going to have another disastrous year."

According to his own *Missourian*, farmers in the state had planted the lowest acreage of winter wheat since the 1970s. Last year's harvest fetched the same prices as twenty-two years ago, but the soya and corn crop had flourished. Unfortunately that meant a glut and a buyer's market, with huge surpluses enabling the big food processors to push down prices. A few farms had gone to the wall, Sam said, but the main victims were those companies supplying agricultural equipment, seed and fertilisers. The town had lost several businesses over the last twelve months.

Sam blamed interstates for distorting the public's view of the countryside. In batting between cities on smooth blacktops which iron out contours, modern day motorists had lost the interaction they once had with the landscape and the small farming communities the old highways linked. With no communication between town and country dwellers beyond what they glean about each other from the media, the problems and frustrations of farmers were increasingly seen as the whinging of the well heeled.

"Most Americans don't equate food with farming," Sam said, "but then most of what they eat is so heavily processed you need five years at Yale to make sense of the ingredients label. The public just see farmers as people with a lot of land. They must be wealthy. The reality is patently otherwise. You say you stayed with the Boggs'. In this corner of Missouri the majority are like them, small farmers living hand to mouth."

I crossed the river and climbed back into the hills riding through large areas of farm land either under water or dense with spring weeds. And I did ride through the fields — on farm tracks. I was determined to stay close to the river but between the bridge at Glasgow and the hamlet of Malta Bend, forty or so miles away, the Big Muddy squiggled in a twitchy arc to the north while the tarmac dipped to the south. The gap between road and river was a blank on my map and too big to venture into blind. I found my way through thanks a large-scale plan of the area nailed to the office wall of the Missouri Farmers Association depot outside Gilliam. It was a good move — the chart revealed I was entering 300 square miles of a maze as regimented and baffling as Hampton Court's.

For several hours, I struggled through water-logged tracks and ankle deep mud across a bleak landscape of fallow fields. As darkness closed in, thunder rumbled along the Missouri valley and stars in the sky were extinguished. Through a thinning of woods to the north, the horizon suddenly pulsated with bright flashes which animated the trees into dancing shadow puppets. Like a night attack at the Somme, thunder and lightning reached a fever pitch. For nearly two hours, I huddled in my hastily erected tent and monitored the storm.

With an almighty crack, the ground jolted and the heavens opened. A second shaft of lightning struck the earth and shook it, lighting up the tent for a split second in which I saw my glasses case leap in the air like a genetically modified jumping bean. A third bolt grounded and the case leapt a little lower. I peeked through the fly sheet to check the heavy drumming was still the monsoon and not hail. Back in Indiana I had learned that hail was invariably an overture to a tornado.

The hail stones held off, but the deluge didn't let up until early afternoon the next day. I lay in bed rereading Sam Audsley's grim predictions about what would happen to the local economy if the weather didn't rapidly take a turn for the better. When I finally decamped, I rode into a ferocious westerly heavy with freezing droplets which stung me like swarming bees. For twenty miserable miles there was no protection or shelter and my wheels were picking up mud like a rolling snowball collects snow.

At Malta Bend, the tarmac swung back up to shadow the Missouri. I left the mud behind but the wind blew stronger, unobstructed as it careered down the broad valley. I spent the afternoon fighting it and a telephone company. In an effort to call home, I tried the payphones in every village along Route 65, but couldn't make sense of the recorded message which cut in as I dialled. At a couple of stops, a local popped up to see if I had got through. Expressions full of hope changed to resignation. It seemed Saline and Lafayette Counties were incommunicado.

I rode into the small town of Lexington and continued my efforts to contact Nottingham. Having again failed, I stopped a couple of blue rinse babes and inquired if there was a payphone in town which wasn't owned by the Sprint telephone company. The women, both in their seventies and wearing figure hugging denims, explained that Sprint had the monopoly and I would probably have to cycle into Independence, thirty miles away, to find another supplier.

"We do have a lot of trouble with them," the deary who looked like Nancy Reagan said, "but you could try the Chamber of Commerce. They might let you use their fax machine."

It was important I made contact with Sandy. Since my return, something disturbing had haunted our weekly conversations — something she wasn't telling me. Thanks to Sprint, I had missed our regular link-up by a couple of days and knew she would now be as worried about me as I was about whatever was going down with her. While waiting for the commerce office to finish with the one phone in town which didn't connect to a pre-recorded message, I wrote my fax, concerned there would be no reply.

"I could let you talk to your wife," the woman on reception said, "but if word got out they'd be queuing back down to Malta Bend."

Not knowing what joyous little ghetto I might have to pedal through, I wanted to reach the Independence-Kansas City conurbation with daylight to spare, and was disappointed that I couldn't give Lexington the time it deserved. It was a curiously impressive backwater of historic buildings and historic people, mostly well preserved. At some point it must have been an important town, but I couldn't figure out why. Set high on a bluff overlooking the Missouri River, it certainly wasn't a bridging point in the old days. Along the cliff edge, however, the beautifully restored antebellum mansions on Highland Avenue suggested somebody had made a lot of money here in the early 1800s. At the top of Jack's Ferry Road leading up from the river's edge stood another

Madonna of the Trail. Lexington was once an important staging post on some historic highway, but which?

It was inevitable that, in researching such a convoluted journey, I would miss something significant. Five miles out of town, a modest historical marker beside a lay-by put paid to the mystery. I was now following nothing less than the Santa Fe Trail. If the swollen Missouri had cheated me out of sailing up to Independence, this simple plaque was ample compensation.

Along with the Oregon and California Trails, the Santa Fe Trail shared Independence, Missouri, as its starting point. One branch of the pioneer and argonaut trails adopted the line of the Santa Fe Trail into what became Topeka before peeling off north-west to snake through the midriff of America. The Santa Fe Trail meanwhile angled south-west to present day New Mexico. What I hadn't appreciated was that the trade route south originally started in Franklin, near Boonville. Shortly after it was established in 1821, however, the Missouri section was washed away by the river and the jumping off point was shifted west to Independence.

Sooner than I was ready for it, the old Santa Fe Trail fed me into the outskirts of the Kansas City conurbation, past the gauntlet of throw-ups and into the tatty outer limits of Independence. The word on everybody's shop front was 'Thrift'. There was a Thriftway, Thrift Autos, Thrift Clothing and the Kingdom Come Mission Thrift Center. Second to 'Thrift' was 'Pawn'. Avenue Pawn, Value Pawn, and plain Pawn were loosely interspersed with a rich selection of restaurants representative of the faces I saw cruising the sidewalks. Chinese, Mexican, Tex-Mex and Vietnamese outlets overwhelmed the burger bars, and it said something about the constituents of the borough that the Viet Tien Video store was doing a brisk business though it was only mid afternoon.

I should have stopped and walked around Independence, but knew nothing significant remained of its formative days as an assembly point for the start of the three great trails. In 1849, the present town of 120,000 souls was a village of a little over a thousand. Known as an 'outfitting town', the place was totally geared to the needs of the overlanders. If you required twenty wagons for your journey, they could be ordered at a price from Chicago. For a radius of a dozen miles around the village, over 10,000 people were camped up, preparing their kit and caboodle for the long haul through the American wilderness. More arrived by the day, mostly up the Missouri River, an eleven day journey (depending on how many sandbars they ran aground on). It had taken me six.

If not already convened in a joint-stock company, new arrivals scouted around for one to join. A sizable American city was camped in the grasslands, a conglomeration of neighbourhoods with names like the Boston and Newton Joint Stock Company, the Washington City Company, the Spartan Band and the Helltown Greasers. Having bought their way into a company of anything up to three hundred men, the argonauts spent the first couple of weeks on the trail going nowhere. They accumulated supplies (500 pounds of food per person), strengthened the simple farm wagons deemed most appropriate for the rough trail, sought advice on whether to use mules or oxen, and practised driving their 'covered wagons'. They made tents, filled cartridges, salted beef, and learnt how to cook and play faro. When they were finally ready to leave, traditionally from Independence Square, many found themselves delayed by the cholera which rampaged through scores of camps. Their sick finally dead and buried, they pulled out crying, "Ho for California!" That spring, more than 35,000 apprentice prospectors set off from the banks of the Missouri to seek their fortune in the Sierra Nevadas.

My attempt to strike out from Independence was blocked by Route 24 feeding into another blessed interstate. Snared in the middle of a cloverleaf of motorways, I stopped a Mexican burdened down with shopping and asked him how to get to Kansas City.

"You sure you wanna go there?" he asked, "They just had a quake. Only a 2.8, but it's left an eight foot deep crack in the hospital car park."

Once again I was riding into a metropolis severed by a large river, this time the Kansas. Once again the map wasn't showing me a bridge I could legally take to cross it. What was a little earthquake to add to my troubles?

Vaguely aware that downtown Kansas City had recently been revitalised but baffled why anybody would want to write a song about the place, I improvised my way down to the river's edge. A cabby directed me to stick on 12th Street until it hit Route 169, my escape across the Kansas. From wherever I had arrived, I could see the bridge flying high, but no way to it. I cycled up and down the east bank, feeling my way through a ramshackle area of light industry and redundant meat packing plants. Finally I noticed a two storey box girder bridge carrying one of four interstates across the divide. The lower level was a disused road linking with nothing but a grass verge and concrete barriers. I pushed through the blockade and gingerly tested the roadbed. From over my head the reverberations of the interstate shuddered through the structure. Compared to the McKinley Toll Bridge, this flyer was solid as the Rockies.

Kansas City, Missouri, was the fourth and last Gateway to the West I passed through. For the Forty-Niners, it was the undisputed end of the United States and beginning of the wasteland. As one voyager wrote, 'Here all the rules of the game changed, where a culture accustomed to travelling on a network of rivers adapted to an ocean of prairie'. Having crossed the great divide on my own private span, the rules of the game only altered because I immediately became lost. I pedalled up 3rd Street into a sprawl of shabby bungalows and littered sidewalks where groups of hooded youths eyed me with menace. On a street corner, a Sixties stereotype of a pimp openly handed over little packets to a nervous twitcher who was already well out of it.

Thinking the road out west lay due north, I rode deeper into the ghetto, past a barricaded Baptist Chapel and the church bus, parked in wasteland within a high security corral of chain link and razor wire. Finally I arrived at a leafy dead end where I received a friendly warning from a couple playing with their baby outside the last bungalow. Apparently the road west lay due south. "Ch'ou better ride, man," the woman said, looking at her husband's watch, "Ch'ou don't wanna be round here whenna sun goes down."

The Kansas River was the last major flow I would have to cross in an urban setting before reaching the Sacramento River in California. It was the last impediment I envisaged to my progress across America, but K.C. had one final trick up its sleeve. With a sense of relief, I returned to Route 24 and pulled away from the city, trapped in a flow of rush hour traffic black in skin and exhaust colour. Passing under the beltway of I-435, the road fell ominously silent. A quarter of a mile from the interstate, the tarmac came to an abrupt halt. A detour sign instructed me to backtrack onto I-435. Not just the road had been ripped up. For as far as I could see through binoculars, the landscape had been shaved by a fleet of earth movers parked the other side of the 'KEEP OUT' signs. I had no option but to hit the low gears and strike out due west, following caterpillar tracks between high banks of mud. Somewhere in front of the setting sun, I presumed the continuation of R-24 lay in wait.

A short distance into the crossing, a pick-up appeared from behind an escarpment and pulled up beside me. A thick set man who looked like an office worker leant out of the cab and gruffly informed me I was on private property. I told him I was going west and he told me to take the detour, so I told him I wasn't allowed on the interstate and he told me that was my problem. I suggested that, since everybody had stopped work for the day and gone home, it was surely perfectly safe crossing the site. He suggested that was "totally fucking irrelevant. This here's private property," he repeated. "I can't let you through. You've been told."

He backed up and disappeared, leaving me weighing up no options what-so-ever. Then a maintenance wagon appeared from behind a different escarpment, this time containing a site worker wearing flick-up sun glasses. We went through the same arguments. He assured me there was a detour I could take, albeit slightly longer, and I assured him that I could be across this lot in quarter of an hour. "I'm running out of daylight," I pleaded.

Finally he relented, warning me to keep a look out for earth movers putting in overtime.

"Thanks," I said. "This country just isn't geared for cyclists."

"Yeh. Well, we growed up."

Two thirds of the way across the site, with the continuation of the highway now in sight, I noticed a police car pull up in front of the far barriers. A copper climbed out and raised his binoculars. Jobsworth Number One had called in the law. While I resigned myself to spending the night in the cop shop, an earth mover slowly scraped a path in front of me. By the time it had passed, the police had disappeared.

Chapter 13
Oregon Trail

When the Forty-Niners pulled out of Independence, they first travelled south-west following the heavily rutted Santa Fe Trail. Three days later they turned right, crossed the Kansas River at present day Topeka, then headed north-west to meet up with a second branch travelling due west from Fort Leavenworth, further north round the Missouri bend. The two tributaries of the Oregon-California Trail merged on the banks of the Big Blue River, just north of its junction with the Little Blue, the river which would steer them to the Platte Valley and thence into the mountains. Whichever route they took, argonaut and pioneer found themselves in a queue of wagons strung out across the grassland all the way to the horizon. Nose to tail traffic was a feature of American travel long before the National Road was paved.

Covered in lush grass and colourful carpets of spring blooms, the wilderness they entered was rich in feed and water and seemingly boundless, with precious little disturbing the smooth curves of the horizon. Only the valley bottoms were delineated with thin lines of cotton-woods and elm. The oceanic swell of the prairie and the open expanse of deep blue sky filled the travellers with optimism. They talked of returning to farm this beautiful country as if their riches were already in the bank.

Although rain regularly transformed the trail into a muddy path, the going was relatively easy for wagons heavily laden with supplies and equipment. The only adversity was cholera, and the idea that the pestilence could be out-run quickly took a hold. If a wagon broke an axle or became stuck, those behind would race to overtake and jump ahead. So the narrow trail across the Great American Desert was widened until, in some places, the Oregon-California Trail was anything up to fifteen wagons wide.

Until they became strung out beyond the prairies, the wagon trains didn't really need maps, though accurate charts of the route across the great emptiness were readily available. Back in the Library of Congress I had been privileged to handle the maps of Captain John C. Frémont, the foremost explorer of the uncharted lands between the Missouri River and California. Known as 'The Pathfinder', Frémont had covered more miles than any contemporary explorer and the maps he produced with the German cartographer Charles Preuss were to inspire thousands to follow his paths. 10,000 copies of Preuss' topographical charts were published in the early 1840s and, in accuracy and execution, they were works of art. Preuss employed modern mapmaking techniques to plot peaks and troughs using clusters of fine lines radiating from the edge of escarpments. At a glance, it was easy to get a picture of the lie of the land. Further information was provided by a table of 'Meteorological Observations', lists of flora and fauna, and a general description of the area focusing on 101 useful things the traveller in these parts needed to know to survive the journey. Finally, dotted at angles around the map, Preuss placed Frémont's dated observations of notable landmarks.

Looking at my thoroughly uninformative road map of the state of Kansas, I imaged the landscape was something like the pancake of Holland. Certainly that was the received information from people I met in Missouri. A few roads bent and curved, but the predominant layout was rectilinear. Running rigidly north to south or east to west, the grid gave the impression there is nothing out there, not even contours, to get in the way of laying arrows of tarmac. With no line presenting itself as an organic shadow along the river banks, I decided to approximate the northerly trail and dog-leg my way north-west up to Marysville, the nearest town to the junction with the branch from the Santa Fe Trail.

On the way into McLouth, I was hailed from the side of the road.

"'You riding to California?"

"I am indeed."

"Following the route of the Forty-Niners?"

"How did you know that?"

"Whoa, hot dog!" The woman turned on her heel towards three friends and clicked her fingers. "I told yoos!"

One woman clapped her hands together and held them in prayer. Two others beamed with congratulations. They were stood outside a dilapidated wooden house of Toy Town proportions, on a front garden which was a roadside verge more than a lawn. Over the grass, a couple of plastic awnings sheltered a row of small tables forming one long banqueting table seated with a hotchpotch of chairs. Around the corner, on a short dirt driveway, a giant of a man in muddy dungarees was prodding charcoal in the bottom half of a hinged oil drum. They were having a barbie. 'They' included two more women, a man, and a girl with learning difficulties who came running from the house when the woman whooped. Over the next couple of minutes others emerged to form a semi-circle round me. It didn't seem possible so many could squeeze into such a diminutive building, but more were to appear.

"Could you eat a burger?" one of the women asked me. "Sling y'bicycle and pull up a chair."

I had gatecrashed a graduation party thrown by the Nowak family for kith and kin. Beyond a porch stuffed with logs, tools and work boots, teenagers Jessica Nowak and Katie Crawford were hemmed in the kitchen by giggling girlfriends. While the tables were laid I was invited to "rest up" next to an old lady in her nineties whose face was an artist's dream of creases, wrinkles and veins. She was the matriarch of the clan and had adopted the pose.

"We heard about you on the radio," she whispered. "Left St. Louis about a week ago, yeh?"

"I did, but I didn't talk to any radio station."

"Yeh, we know all about you," she winked.

While I tried to get to the bottom of both the media mystery and the confusion of who was related to whom, even more people appeared from the house of mirth carrying large tureens of salad, bowls of relish and gherkins, and copious bags of buns. Two lavishly decorated, calorie concentrated but no doubt absolutely delicious graduation cakes were placed at the head of the serving table. The jolly giant (who I think was Jessica's dad) deposited the first plate of sizzling burgers and covered them in foil. By then I had learned enough to know I hadn't a hope of remembering any of what the old girl was explaining. Jessica's family ran to twenty people, several of whom had just driven up, but that didn't include the matriach's great-great-grandchildren. The youngest child at the party was four generations on from the oldest adult.

We adjourned to the tables, where I was placed between a middle-aged couple who lived on the north side of Kansas City, Kansas. I told them about getting lost somewhere around 3rd Street. The man whistled through his teeth and chuckled.

"And you got away? Man, you're blessed. There was a shooting there two nights ago."

He knew the ghetto well. He was the odd job man for an unique housing project where residents bought shares in the property when they moved in, then sold them on at the market price when they moved out. As owners of a slice, they had a vested interest in maintaining the place, keeping the peace, fostering a community and — most important of all — talking to each other. His job had more to do with brokering race relations than fixing the guttering but, after careers in the army and as a trucker, he relished the work.

"Nice people," he said with a smile, "but at sundown I leave and go home."

Amongst the new arrivals was David Showalter, pastor of the McLouth Church of the Nazarene — the family's church. He had been in the parish barely three years, having accepted the position over the more tempting offer of a tough district in Los Angeles. David had ministered in China, Romania, Albania and throughout Europe. Los Angeles was a great challenge for him, but his family came first. They were tired of his challenges and his wife refused to move into "another war zone," albeit one in America.

Pastor Showalter was keen to talk and he took me to one side. As our conversation progressed, it became clear he was the genuine article. Although barely in his forties, he practised that old time religion where the social welfare of his parishioners came before their spiritual welfare, much to the annoyance of those who didn't need social support. McLouth was overwhelmingly a poor community of dirt farmers, few of whom owned the land they farmed. In his travels, David had seen enough deprivation and suffering to know any hope provided by the church was meaningless until tangible humanitarian aid was first put in place. People at the party mentioned he was a nuts-and-bolts, sleeves-rolled-up sort of pastor, but I didn't expect such pragmatism.

"It's the old story. The quickest way to a man's heart is through his belly, and the heart is the resting place of the soul."

David relished his time abroad. In visiting so many different countries, he felt he had learned a lot about America.

"Americans really should travel. We are such an arrogant nation. There is something totally humbling about visiting countries where people have taught themselves two or more languages by simply coming across a book. They read everything they can get their hands on. They're hungry to learn, and so resourceful. We don't want to know nothing. If the air conditioning breaks down, it's the end of civilisation."

I asked him if he thought American civilisation was coming to an end.

"Come, John, you've cycled through East St. Louis. You tell me."

He thought it was great that, in Europe, you could ride the equivalent distance from K.C. to Chicago and travel through four countries.

"It's kinda people sized, with such a great variety of cultures so close together. Oh, and I love your mass transit systems. Whenever I travel beyond America, I get a sense of community we just don't have in this country outside of rare family gatherings like this. We're a nation that lives life in little boxes, except when we go to the mall, where we lose ourselves in a big box full of little boxes."

David said he felt honoured to be invited into the Nowak family circle. It was the first of several calls he was expected to make that day on the graduating sons and daughters of his parishioners, but this was the party he most looked forward to.

"These are real good people, poor as church mice you guys would say, but with hearts full of riches and a sense of family the middle classes have lost."

I told him that most of the people I stayed with along the road were church goers and asked him how a country weighed down with so much religion could shape up to be so irreligious.

"Well, John," his volume dropped, "I honestly believe the United States is the most godless country on the planet. Why, I've been to pagan countries that have more spirituality, more humanity, more human bonding than America will ever have. But you've gotta understand that the church was the first building the settlers put up. It was the glue which held together the embryonic community — the foundation on which a new society was built. These days, particularly for those on a higher income, the church is just another network to tap into. It's a social club, like the golf club or the Elks. It's another means to an end, and the end is the American Dream, and don't ask me what that is." He gave a deep sigh. "Do I sound cynical?"

Long after David had left to visit members of his flock he sounded cynical about, I gathered up my camera belt, took a few snaps and did the round, expressing heart-felt thanks. I had been at Jessica and Katie's party for nearly five hours. During that time something like thirty members of the Nowak dynasty had passed through.

Beyond McLouth, the long flat straights promised by the Kansas map weren't happening. The roads were long and straight alright, but the landscape was corrugated, each crest a little bit higher than the last, each trough a little further above sea level than the previous valley bottom. It was hard, frustrating cycling. No matter how fast I zoomed into the hollow, I could never quite muster the speed to climb out without having to change gear. I calculated that in three days of cycling my longest respite between changing gears was about four and a half minutes.

For oxen, wagons and people on foot the terrain had rapidly become exhausting and, if not potentially lethal, certainly damaging. What few trees inhabited the draws were gradually being felled to repair rolling stock splintered as overloaded wagons strained through muddy bottoms. To reduce weight, anything the wagon masters considered unnecessary for the journey was dumped overboard. Local store keepers, many of them Native

Americans, were delighted. They restocked their shelves with regular sorties to scavenge along the trail.

The character of the landscape if not the contours I bounded through had changed significantly in 150 years. Aside from the whole state being hacked up into squares and farmed, the wilderness was now bushy with immature varieties of broadleaf. In the Thirties, what was known as the Great American Desert came very close to becoming a real desert. Poor farming practices and a series of droughts reduced the land to a dust bowl which encompassed 150,000 square miles of Kansas, Colorado, New Mexico, Oklahoma and Texas. On exposed reaches, the wind lifted more than ten centimetres of top soil into the atmosphere, sometimes obliterating the midday sun. To prevent such erosion ever happening again, President Roosevelt introduced a program of tree planting in the prairies known as the Shelterbelt Project. The leafy avenues I was riding along were the sixty year old legacy of that hectic period of setting windbreaks.

It is sometimes easy to forget how young the face of America really is. The idea that the prairies were an open wasteland worthless for agriculture was originally suggested by the diary of Vásquez de Coronado. Two hundred years before the Gold Rush, the Spaniard entered the interior of North America in search of gold and became very lost in a wilderness bereft of landmarks. The notion of a wasteland was later reinforced by the American explorer, Zebulon M. Pike, who reported, 'These vast plains of the western hemisphere may become in time as celebrated as the sandy deserts of Africa.' Pike considered the grasslands were a good buffer between the Americans in the east and Spanish in the west, and would peg back Americans, 'so prone to rambling', to the borders of the Missouri and Mississippi. On nineteenth century maps, the Great Plains west of Independence were therefore labelled the Great American Desert. It was only after the Civil War that settlers began to realise the prairie's potential as the bread basket of the United States.

Despite its reputation as a wheat state, Kansas generates three times more income from its cattle farming. I was deep in beef rearing country, but rode across an oscillating prairie of predominantly empty pasture. The few herds of Herefords, Simmentals and Longhorns I saw looked lost and a little nervous, perhaps aware that the end of the beef season was fast approaching and their time was running out. For many spreads the game was already over. Empty farm buildings strained to hold it together against the tug of creepers. Fields which hadn't been grazed in years ran wild. But I also saw vegetable gardens and farmhouses with flower beds, and hoped I was moving into a region where village stores stocked nutritious local produce. When I interrupted a Saturday siesta to ask a farmer for water, however, I noticed lunch had been a take-away. I looked on the map. The nearest town likely to have a fast food outlet was forty miles away.

I rolled through Winchester and Boyle, cross-hatched dirt road settlements of peeling wooden bungalows and service garages, but no grocery stores. A few lawn dogs were hard at it and Winchester's church was being white-washed by a man on a ladder who kept peering skywards. Overhead, the mantle had turned black as the Devil's robe and a wet wind began streaming in from the south-west. I leaned into it, straining towards a dull glow on the western horizon which seeped from a tear in the black hood. Thunder rumbled across a worried prairie and the humidity was dense. Turning south at Valley Falls to cross the Delaware River, I was instantly soaked by a waterlogged broadside borne on the wind. I rode into town, out of the gale, and took an instant shine to the place.

Doing the rounds along Broadway, the sharply decked but grossly over-weight local plod told me Valley Falls was definitely on its last legs. Twenty years ago an evening round checking the lock-ups used to take a full hour. Tonight he would be back in the police station by the quarter after. "Businesses come and businesses go," he said, "but the wrong ones come and the wrong ones go."

161

Broadway was definitely broad — about the width of a dual carriageway — but the shopping centre only amounted to three depleted blocks containing such inappropriate outlets as an office suppliers, Coleman's Jewellery and the Glacial Hills Gallery. Like a row of rotting teeth, each block had a gaping hole and premises in need of filling. What buildings remained were beautiful two storey structures from the 1880s sporting delicate patterns along the pediment and little pelmet-like touches around the windows. Watched by an elderly woman and her two grown-up children, all wearing horn-rimmed glasses, I sketched the elaborate finials capping the Historical Society's gable end.

"The empty lot behind you used to be the hotel," the mother told me, "'cept it burnt down fifteen years ago. Everybody came out to watch it burn. It was the last time I seen the street full."

Broadway was still surfaced in brick, the preferred hardtop for the National Road. The old bird claimed she could remember the dirt road being upgraded.

"It were done by a negro with no legs working from a trolley," she said, pronouncing the n-word "nehgra." But she had to tell me she was "no racist. Heck, I moved around. I seen things. I were born in Muscotah, came to Valley Falls with ma folks, then to Holton where I worked, then Mayetta, then back to Valley Falls. You could say I been around a lot."

She had indeed. The towns she listed were within a radius of eighteen miles of each other.

The tedium of the hills didn't let up the further I travelled north-west. They were racked up before me like cue balls arranged for a trick shot. At odd times and for no particular reason, the linear tarmac turned a sharp left-right-right-left and continued in a line directly opposite where it had thrown a wobbler. A dirt track invariably closed off the fourth side of the square. I began to ignore the detours and kept straight ahead. Then I ignored the tarmac and its direction altogether. I set off across country, navigating from town to town using a compass. If there were more than two sets of tyre tracks running down it, I took the gamble that each unplotted dirt road linked with another farm or county road leading roughly in my direction.

Of the communities I rode through, only one was bigger than a hamlet. Horton was a big city by comparison to its satellite towns, with a population of nearly 2,000. Throw-ups were starting to appear along Route 75 clustered around a Wal-Mart but, half a mile down a tree lined avenue to the east, Horton's town centre retained much of its original charm. Whereas every other Kansas town I entered had grown up along a thoroughfare or at an inter-section, Horton's centre was a delightful rectangle of late nineteenth century store fronts facing onto a ghastly neoclassical town hall. Before a committee of notables decided they couldn't function without this stone eye-sore and its fall-out shelter, the town square was presumably a civic park. Somewhere there would have been a store selling locally grown produce, but what did for a grocery store these days was the Casey's gas station.

I bought the healthiest food I could find there, and sat outside chomping a 'chicken salad on wheat bread, net weight 5.0 oz' according to the label on the front. On the back, a second label listed the ingredients as:

Chicken salad (cooked light and dark chicken meat, water, salt), chicken flavor (salt, wheat starch, carrageenan, modified food starch, sodium phosphate), celery dressing (soy bean oil, water, egg yolk, vinegar, sugar, salt, spice, potassium sorbate and sodium benzoate), cream cheese (cultures, salt, carob bean cum, honey, water), bread-crumbs (bleached wheat flower, yeast, sugar, salt), non-dairy creamer (partially hydroginated vegetable oil (coconut and soybean oil), corn syrup solids, potassium casienate, sucrose, dipotassium phosphate, mono-diglyc-erides, sodium stearoyl lactylate, carrageenan, artificial flavour, turmeric extract (color, yellow #6), vinegar, sugar, salt, glucono-delta-lactone, whole milk, natural chicken flavour (maltodextrin, salt, corn oil, beef extract, thiamin

*and flavouring), spices, modified food starch, hydrolyzed
vegetable protein, tomato paste, guar gum, xanthan gum,
onion powder, garlic chives, garlic powder), wheat bread
(enriched wheat flour (wheat flour, malted barley flour,
niacin, reduced iron, thiamine mononitrate (vitamin B1),
riboflavin (vitamin B2), water, crushed wheat, high fruc-
tose corn syrup, stone ground wholewheat flower...*

...followed by another list of nineteen ingredients present
in quantities of less than 2%. At only $2.59, I certainly got
a lot for my money.

It was a Sunday and at the toll of 12.00 o'clock St.
Dominic's turned out. Suddenly the gas station was busy
servicing the congregation of automobiles which queued
round from the church car park like communicants lining
up for bread and wine. Men in their Sunday best man-
made fibres were grabbing newspapers, wiping
windscreens, valeting upholstery, kicking tyres, and
topping up sugar and gas levels. Nobody turned their
engines off and smokers ignored the warning signs, but
then this was men's work. The women stayed put, fanned
by air conditioning, chomping candy, flicking through the
funny pages. The hoagies were separated from the townies
by a white band across the top of their bronzed foreheads
where the baseball cap had been pulled down while at
work. Their trucks and cars were distinguished by a
Sunday shine ruined by splatters of red mud fanned up the
doors. Farm workers were in the minority. For most of St.
Dominic's flock, Horton was a dormy town for jobs in the
city.

As I left the square, the Trinity Lutheran Church
emptied, followed by the First Methodists. I had a feeling
some Committee of Interdenominational Churchgoers co-
ordinated the conclusion of services so the town wasn't
instantly grid-locked and Casey's swamped. One of the
multitude who thronged the sidewalks making for their
cars shared the joy she felt at spending time with her
saviour.

164

"You have a lovely cycle ride today, y' hear," she shouted.

I assured her I'd try to, but it was going to be difficult. By mid-afternoon the wind was whipping up a storm and I found myself pushing hard to ride down hill, never mind up. There were no storm clouds in the sky, no billowing grey matter or solid cap. It was clear as a bell, the temperature was withering and sand by the side of the road was dry enough to be scooped up and thrown at me. I turned north and spent the rest of the day riding at an acute angle, leaning into the wind.

Chapter 14

Long before the Forty-Niners set out for the sierras, there was a slow but fairly dependable mail service between Mexican Alta California and the United States. *Gringos* who had emigrated from the States were in regular communication, encouraging friends and family to join them in the land of perpetual sunshine. Their letters were carried by ship via Panama, and generally took about thirty days to filter through the U.S. postal system. With the sudden influx of prospectors in 1848 and the frenzied growth of business, there was a pressing need for something quicker. California joined the Union the year after the Forty-Niners invaded and a decade before anywhere else west of the Missouri. It was crucial that the state felt closer to the federal capitol than the 3,000 miles between them suggested.

In 1858, the Butterfield & Fargo Stage Company won the overland mail contract and significantly reduced delivery times, but what the government had in mind was something more akin to the speed of the telegraph which terminated at St. Joseph, Missouri. Two years later, the haulage company of Russell, Majors and Waddell came up with the idea of a relay of horse riders galloping non-stop across the wilderness, carrying the mail in a specially designed saddle cover. Each courier would ride seventy-five miles, changing horses every ten to fifteen miles at one of 190 way stations established between St. Joseph and Sacramento. The first outing of the Central Overland California and Pike's Peak Express (aka the Pony Express) was on April 3rd, 1860, and the first home station, where riders changed over, was Fort Markley. More of a trading post than a stockade, Fort Markley used to be a couple of miles west of the small farming community of Seneca. The town has since expanded but Fort Markley is still there... of a sorts.

Though it was early evening when I arrived, it could have been midnight. The fort was a jumble of black shapes, but it seemed whoever ran the trading post now offered camping. On the gate was one of those 'Pitch and we'll catch you in the morning' notices. A seedy block labelled 'Cowboys' and 'Cowgirls', and a row of eleven unoccupied hook-ups indicated I was in the right place, but nothing stirred except a nosy possum. I erected the tent next to a lean-to sheltering a tractor, and settled back in its seat for the evening's aerial display.

The firmament was a mat of grey clouds layered in quarrelsome bands. To the south-west, a broad column of cumulonimbus seethed, its innards churning like a full stomach, its capital supporting an alien skyscape which looked like the underside of a weld of melted ping-pong balls. In front of me, a shelterbed of birch trees was taking a drubbing from a furious wind and behind me the road was a blur of drivers rushing home to secure garden furniture. Out of the gloom, three people ran into the lean-to carrying the camping sign. One of them said, "See you in the morning. Good luck," and was gone.

A black aura encircled me and the birds fell silent. Sheet lightening started strobing in the west and thunder rode across the prairie. With the crack of a deity's whip, the heavens rained down water bombs for ten minutes then stopped abruptly. Enormous swirling thunderheads slid lazily towards the north-east, occasionally throwing out bolts of electricity to prod the front runner along. Again rain fell as from an upturned water butt, followed by a gale which stapled the hoop of my tent to the ground. Then the fireworks started in.

In an impressive show of nature's whizz-bangs, lightening forked down with such rapidity the landscape appeared to pulsate between a negative and positive. Some were crazy inverted Ys and some were shattered single shafts. Many grounded, held fast and shuddered with psychotic convulsions. For an hour they licked down like exposed nerves flicking out from the heaven's cranium.

There was no thunder, just explosions and the lingering smell of burning.

In the quiet light of morning the fort was revealed to be a bit of a joke, albeit one which somebody had put a lot of effort into. The historic Pony Express home station was now a ramshackle collection of sheds with signs locating the 'Jail', 'Stables', 'General Store' and so forth in that dreadful Playbill font which has become irretrievably associated with all things Western. It could have been the set for a B-Western but, inside each building, genuine articles provided a feast for woodworms. In the stables stood an immaculate example of a Conestoga wagon, complete with hoops and a new canvas, but it was draped with mouldy yolks and an accumulation of junk which should have been binned decades ago. Beside a humorously inauthentic gallows stood a rusty metal cage labelled the '1st Jail in Bern, Kansas', a companion piece to the 'Oldest Cowboy Jail Door'. No less contrived than Washington's Fort Necessity beside the National Road, Fort Markley was a lot more fun.

Behind the flat fronted facade of the 'Saloon' was a real breakfast bar and Mary Jane Markley, the widow of Jim Markley who built the sorry little theme park. Jim was a direct descendent of the Markley who established the original trading post, but somewhere in his blood line there was Kiawa Indian. He had been given the name White Eagle by his relative Red Eagle, and must have been something of a big chief in Seneca once upon a time. On the walls of the café were photos and press clippings of Jim locked in a pow-wow with Ronald Reagan, with Gerald Ford and with other white hairs who looked like VIPs.

Mary Jane was from Spanish stock, from before independence and the birth of Mexico. Prior to marrying Jim she taught school, but now ran the fort and did some sort of community work in the afternoons. Short and compact with a frizz of shiny black hair, she was a single-minded cookie, currently locking horns with town planners who wanted to absorb her humble spread within the urban

168

limits. But Mary Jane kept a horse, which wasn't allowed in town, and she wanted to keep the spirit of the rural outpost alive.

"Heck, five years ago we had thirty to forty head of buffalo roaming out there," she told me.

The town golf course was directly opposite her now and, on the fort's side of the road, Seneca ended a hundred yards away. It wouldn't be long before the site of the home station was gobbled up by a shanty town.

Anxious to hang onto her one paying guest as long as possible, Mary Jane provided me with a list of sights I really couldn't leave Seneca without seeing. I took a day out of the saddle to absorb it all, and spent a full hour walking down Main ticking off the ploughing mural in the post office, the 1922 Stutz engine at the fire house, the Pony Express memorial plaque, and the Preservation Society's window display. Mary Jane was a founding member of the Pony Express Preservation Society, but the museum wasn't due to open until Memorial Day, in twelve days time. Through the window I saw my first *mochilla*, the over-saddle with four locked pouches which held the letters. Like small bicycle panniers joined by a throw of leather, the *mochilla* was designed for easy removal so the dismounting rider could hook their arm under, whip it off, run to the next horse, and flip it back on while in the process of mounting. I always wondered how they did that.

I took a break at Hard's Drug Store and Soda Fountain and stepped into an Edward Hopper painting. At the back, sat round a chromed bar, the lunch crew were sipping floats and discussing the weather. One of the women couldn't wait for the vagaries of spring to settle down.

"Get that wind dryin' out them fields after all this rain so the boys can get out in 'em. They're driving me plum crazy, all their moanin' an' all."

She was a thick-set woman in her forties, who was probably a local beauty before frequent visits to the soda fountain built up copious chins. The headline in the *Seneca Courier-Tribune* published the day before the

169

storm read, 'Farmers Hope Rain Goes Away'. Barely twenty per cent of Nemaha County's corn crop had been planted to date, when usually sixty percent was in the ground. The soya bean planted out amounted to no more than five per cent and nobody had begun to think about sticking in their sorghum.

"It's the darn soil we got round here," said a wildly bearded man with fingers thick as carrots. "Too much darn clay in it. Don't drain so darn good."

"If'n we do get a run of hot weather," the fountain maid added, "it'll blight the darn wheat, is what."

Everybody had a opinion about how the darn weather affected the darn farmers, presumably because they had plenty of experience of how both affected the darn fortunes of Seneca.

At the bottom of Mary Jane's list was a church — St. Mary's of St. Benedict — four miles from town at the end of a solitary ribbon of tarmac. I saw the steeple long before the valley where it was rooted. By comparison with everything ecumenical I had seen in the countryside, St. Mary's was a cathedral. Surrounding it was a junior school, rectory, graveyard and an L-shape of eight bungalows which comprised the community of St. Benedict, originally called Wild Cat.

Inside the limestone shell, the church was an outstanding celebration of religious art and decoration. Despite six transept windows rich in ochre, amber and crimson, the nave was uncharacteristically light and uplifting for a Catholic church. Every architectural feature which could be delineated, floriated and illuminated was, and every arch of the vaulted ceiling incorporated a delicately painted Christian symbol. I'm not keen on religious art, but St. Mary's was exceptional. What I didn't understand was how a community of less than a hundred people could afford such a magnificent palace of worship.

While she supervised a playground noisy with hyperactive children, the local school marm explained that the real community were the farming families in the outlying district. She had taught in American cities and in Germany, when her husband was overseas with the Forces. They had settled in Nemaha County because it was "quiet and stable, and there's a lot of caring." There were no divorcees amongst the parents of the kids at St. Benedict's, and none of the problems the majority of American schools were grappling with after Columbine. Most families could trace their ancestors back to the first settlement of the county, and many still lived on the ancestral farm. Almost everybody was German-American and devoutly Roman Catholic.

I zig-zagged my way from the little cathedral on the prairie trying to figure a way to ride west without riding into the westerly wind. While I was talking to the teacher it had picked up apace, diffusing the landscape behind a veil of sand. I rode fully clothed with a bandana tied over my nose and worried that this was the bad news Michael Bauermeister had alluded to back in Missouri.

At the Easley store, survivalist David Geurts had warned me about the Spirit of the Wind or Ga-oh, as it was called in Iroquois. Of the three upper powers (which included the Spirits of Thunder and Echo), Ga-oh was the meanest. When he was created, the Spirit of Good was so concerned Ga-oh would tear the heavens to shreds he confined him to the northern sky, where he now lives with his 'watchers', the four winds of the planet, tethered to his hands. The winds are embodied in animals — the Bear is the north wind, the Moose is the east and the Fawn, the south. It was my luck that the west wind was that most ferocious of animals, the Panther, Da-jo-ji.

According to the *North American Indian Reader*, when Ga-oh summoned Da-jo-ji,

'...all the sky seemed threatening; an ugly darkness crept into the clouds that sent them whirling in circles of confusion; a quarrelsome, shrieking voice snarled through the air, and with a sound of claws tearing the heavens into rifts, Da-jo-ji, the Panther, sprang to the gate.

Said Ga-oh, "You are ugly and fierce, and can fight the strong storms; you can climb the high mountains and tear down the forests; you can carry the whirlwind on your strong back, and toss the great sea waves high in the air, and snarl at the tempests if they stray from my gate. You shall be the West Wind."'

I had seen storm clouds which whirled in circles of confusion, but the Panther I faced had yet to start tearing down forests. It had taken its toll on my left knee though. Only once in the ten days that Ga-oh had been bugging me did a Moose wind propel me from behind, and something under my knee cap was wearing thin. An unfair share of cycling accidents had left my knees vulnerable and the Panther was gnawing away at the weakest. A dull throb pulsated ominously in the region of the patella and sharp pains started shooting up my thigh. With two thousand miles to go and the worst of the terrain lying in wait, this was not what I needed.

But the wind wasn't exactly whipping up a fury. It was just there, leaning against me, making life difficult on a blisteringly sunny day when I should have been skipping through Kansas singing, "We're off to see the Wizard..." According to the weather report, it was gusting at 18 mph — barely Force 5 on the Beaufort Scale. Though the Panther stalks silently and the wind has no sound, the noise was deafening. It is only when something gets in the way — something like the fleshy bits around your ears — that the whining, moaning, and shrieking of the Panther is heard.

The line I now followed linked the three stages the Pony Express rode between Seneca and the crossing of the Big Blue River. The landscape had softened and become more like the prairie I envisaged from reading the Gold Rush diaries. The lows were broad and shallow, and any tree cover was reduced to small spinneys or scraggy lines shadowing creeks. The boldest uprights in a flowing grassland were the isolated billboards erected by the good Christians of Nemaha and Marshall Counties — 'Every one who believes in abortion has already been born', 'Life/Abortion.

Choose Life', and the one with the weird kid who looks destined to become a paedophile, 'Abortion Takes My Life'.

I swept into the flood plain of the Big Blue and on to the crossing at Marysville, a town whose main claim to fame is its association with the Pony Express, memorialised on the west side of town. Surrounded by a circle of tarmac and flanked by the Stars and Stripes, the larger than life sculpture of a rider in full flight had become the icon gracing every leaflet, plaque and tourist trinket relating to the Pony Express. It took 125 years before Kansas thought to commemorate the heroes of the old mail run, but Richard Bergen's bronze captured the thunder and fury of men who relied on speed alone to ride clear of 'dem pesky Injuns'.

Pony Express employees rode armed with a Bible not a gun. For emergencies, they carried flour, corn-meal and bacon, and a medical kit of turpentine, borax and cream of tartar. With luck on their side, the 2,000 mile mail run took ten days to delivery but many didn't make it. In a dusty display case at the Pony Express Barn-Museum on Elm Street, a fading photocopy of a contemporary advert in a San Francisco newspaper couldn't have been more honest about the vicissitudes of the job.

WANTED

Young, skinny, wiry fellows not over eighteen. Must be expert riders willing to risk death daily. Orphans preferred.

On a mezzanine running round two sides of the converted home station half a dozen room settings claimed to show the sort of quarters where the riders ate, slept and received their orders. It was difficult to believe the company provided such luxurious accommodation for a bunch of mavericks who were dispensable.

West of Marysville, beyond Bergen's statue, Route 36 bridged the Big Blue River. Where the wagons once crossed, a deep cut sliced through the east bank down to what one diarist described as a 'big blue river, twenty

173

yards across and four feet deep, rushing over a stony bottom'. Fording today he would have called it the Little Muddy. While companies waited their turn at the ford, the men did their laundry and aired items against cholera contamination. They fed well and joined together for an evening of banjo driven song. At sunrise they herded their cattle through the river and set course for the Little Blue, which would feed the Oregon-California Trail and the Pony Express north-west into present day Nebraska. I turned right onto Route 77 and tracked the Big Blue up to Wymore riding at 30° from the perpendicular.

Cycling into a headwind is easy by comparison with the annoying fluctuations inherent in a broadside. As long as the wind was striking me somewhere in an arc from my left round to my right temple, the force appeared to be constant. Sideways on I presented a bigger target, and the Panther made intermittent rushes which threatened to topple me if I over-compensated when it suddenly backed off. Any traffic coming between the predator and myself introduced confusing eddies, backdrafts and slipstreams which had me continually shifting body position to keep the bike on the straight and narrow. The effort of concentration was exhausting and further frustrated by the change in road surface the moment I crossed the state line. Midway between 'Leaving Kansas Come Again' and 'Nebraska The Good Life' the smooth tarmac abruptly became concrete slabs joined in a seal of bitch which reverberated up my spine each time I bumped over the weld. For the next 500 miles I was to judder across Nebraska going Ba-Dum Ba-Dum every four to seven metres.

On only my second detour from the road to gold, I was rolling north to Lincoln, the state capital of Nebraska, to call in on Paul and Arlene Fell. Paul was a fellow cartoonist, but it was Arlene I was most excited about meeting. Correspondence before I left Britain suggested Arlene's family history might help me get a handle on how 'The Indian Territory' of open prairie was transformed into a checkerboard of white farmsteads. Since so much of

174

this journey was proving to be a narrative about rural America, it was a long diversion I was happy to make. Following the same dirt track logic which saw me through Kansas, I crossed the Big Blue and set the compass for Adams, dog-legging north-by-north-east to swing into Lincoln from the east.

Once again the landscape changed and with it agriculture turned from pastoral to arable. Except for half-hearted efforts at an occasional shelterbed round a cowering farmstead, I rode a high wold stripped of tree cover (if ever there was any) and dangerously exposed to the Panther. Out here, the black cat had jabbed a paw and left plankwood barns reeling at an angle to the east, racked up across the landscape like frozen falling dominoes. The stubbled fields were still saturated, and large ponds had formed at the bottom of drainage channels cut up hill, across furrows ploughed into a spiral of contours.

At the two-bit town of Filley, the woman behind the counter of the café explained why one side of the short street was boring new blockhouses while the other was traditional Western linked by a boardwalk.

"We had a tornado come through two years ago. Ripped along that side of the street and stopped half way through smashing up our barn."

The barn looked like a behemoth had stamped on one end of it without even shaking the other.

In the slightly larger community of Adams, the railroad sidings and enormous grain elevator explained how the village merited a bank of city proportions, resplendent with doric columns. From a series of loud speakers dangling off lamp posts and electricity poles, country music accompanied me down the street. I was reminded of villages in East Germany I had ridden through before the end of the Cold War, where tannoys blasted out propaganda. I asked a contractor mowing a corner store's lawn if the Adams system was similarly used for public announcements.

"No need. In a place like this, if you drive into a ditch out of town, word gets back before you do."

Since Illinois, I had been collecting witticisms about small town America. There was the storekeeper in Weaver, Illinois, who said, "Round here, you miss a Sunday at church and folks send you a get well card." The owner of the café in Boonesbro, Missouri, thought the best indicator of the size of a place was the state of the baseball diamond. "If they're playing on dirt, you're in a small town." In Seneca, Mary Jane Markley had said, "If you managed to cycle further than 3rd Street without reappearing in farmland, you're in a major city."

The vast majority of these rural communities were established at the end of the nineteenth century by whichever family in the area had the most land and could afford to give over eighty odd acres for the creation of a Main Street or Broadway. Frequently they named the town after themselves, like Steinauer (pronounced "Steener"), a village twenty miles north-east of Wymore and the ancestral home of Arlene Fell, a Steinauer (pronounced "Steiner") through her mother's side of the family.

Once upon a time, Steinauer was big enough to support a newspaper (*The Steinauer Star*), a bank and an opera house where Saturday night was polka night. At different times in its development, the Pony Express and the railroad ran through, and Czech entrepreneurs swelled the population to an all time high of 350 souls. If that sounds small, it has to be remembered that the residents of Steinauer were totally outnumbered at weekends when the outlying farms came in to buy supplies, exchange gossip, worship and party. At the end of the twentieth century, the population was struggling to hold at ninety, and most of those were either commuters or working land no longer theirs. At weekends people now leave Steinauer to purchase supplies.

Chapter 15

Paul and Arlene Fell lived in a new 'open house' duplex (semi-detached) off Old Cheney Road to the south of Lincoln. They remembered Old Cheney when it was a dirt road ten years ago and everything south of it was squares of agriculture. What I rode down that afternoon was a four, sometimes six lane highway serving as an inner beltway. Hanging off it was now a vast complex of new sub-divisions sprinkled with malls, plazas, gas stations and low rise office blocks. The new development alone was larger than any town I had passed through since leaving Kansas City.

Ranked across the hills were homes clustered by styles which ran the gamut from modest to The Ridge, a pretentious enclave where orthodontists, doctors and bank managers lived in ugly architect designed properties costing anything up to four million dollars. The whole area was landscaped with attractive parks and ponds, and was expanding south at a rate of knots. From Old Cheney, the southern panorama was solid with roof tops. Beyond it, sidewalks, lighting and a sprinkler system were already in place beside strips of lonely tarmac which charged off across a countryside braced for further invasion. In the last fifteen years, Lincoln's population had nearly doubled. Unless they were mopped up by the insurance corporations which had recently relocated to the city, the question was, where did all these people work? According to Paul Fell, there had been no commensurate growth in any other sector of Lincoln's blue-collar employment base.

Paul and Arlene were the first couple I stayed with who hadn't spawned children, and their attitude to work was a million miles from that of recumbent fanatics, John and Betty Fearday of Effingham, Illinois. Arlene was frantically trying to do as little work as possible. Having been the Alterations Manager at a prestigious department store in town, she now ran her own business from a premises in the historic quarter of Lincoln. Turning away tailoring and dress-making commissions, she preferred the flexibility inherent in the quick turnover of alterations and repairs. I think she secretly wanted more time to shop. Paul meanwhile was as neurotic as most cartoonists are about their work — wishing to slack off but convinced everything would dry up if he did. Until 1992, he was the staff cartoonist on the *Lincoln Journal*, the city's biggest paper. After eight years service and with no warning, he felt the cold steel of the axe which had lopped off so many editorial cartoonists in Europe and America of late.

"Newspapers aren't run by newspaper men any more," Paul observed with an anger I shared. "They're run by bean counters who haven't a fucking clue what the function of an editorial cartoon is."

Now back with the *Lincoln Journal Star*, his old newspaper renamed after a take-over in 1995, Paul had survived the lean times by freelancing, lecturing at the university and, most imaginatively, by airing his cartoons on a radio show. *Fax Fix* on Radio KFOR Lincoln provided listeners with a number they could dial for a free fax of a weekly editorial cartoon Paul later discussed on a phone-in programme. It was an innovative idea destined to go national until another bean counter moved in on KFOR.

Breakfast at a cartoonist's table is typified by hunting for the peanut butter under a truck load of newspapers and hurling abuse at the radio or TV news. On the first morning of my stay, the headline story came from Conyers, Georgia, where a teenager had walked into Heritage High School with two guns and fired discriminately below the waist. He shot six youths, none fatally, and as the heavy brigade arrived, he dropped to his knees, stuck the barrel of a .22 in his mouth, and didn't pull the trigger. Apparently his girlfriend had jilted him.

It was exactly a month since Eric Harris and Dylan Klebold became infamous. Regardless of what was happening with the American economy, Columbine was still the most discussed story on the street, receiving commensurate column inches and regular revisits from the cartoonists. While producing his fair share, most of Paul's work was concerned with events in Nebraska more than with national and world news. With the State Legislature just down the road, he was ideally placed to receive the nod on how senators were manoeuvring around particular issues. The couple took me for a look round the State Capitol building. From the snatches of conversations he had with a few of the staff, it was clear Paul was a recognised face and his cartoons impacted on those who walked the corridors of power. I was given the grand tour, which mostly consisted of checking out the iridescent murals of Nebraska's history and the busts of famous notables, work which was of the highest order.

Considering the state was the butt of so many urban American jokes, Nebraska was a backwater of outstanding talent and innovative ideas. The very building we were in was mold-breaking. It was not a poor copy of the federal Capitol building in Washington, like so many other state capitols and town halls. Instead of the obligatory golden dome, a 122 metre tower topped with a little crown and a six metre statue of a sower lunged out of the ground rectangle of the main block. It deserved its honorary as 'the penis of the prairies'. From a hole in the helmet I looked west towards California hoping to see a ripple of the Rockies on the horizon. The line between heaven and earth couldn't have been smoother if Jesus the Carpenter had planed it himself. At the foot of the big dick sat the unique single chamber where state senators did the business, as against the two house system of senators and representatives which operates in every other state. Walking the main corridor, inspecting the photographs of senators through recent ages, just one black face appeared again and again, getting older by the administration. This, I was told, was the legendary Ernie Chamber, who probably knew more about the workings of Nebraska politics than any other public servant.

Before leaving the building, we called in at the office of Senator Vrtiska, Arlene's cousin, whose politics she was less than enamoured with. Vrtiska was a short, ruddy man with a demeanour that oozed power. He was the owner of a large ranch somewhere in Nebraska which featured in an aerial photograph prominently displayed over his desk. It was the last-but-one day of business before the summer recess and Vrtiska had just come from the chamber having voted in favour of a two year moratorium on the death penalty. Senator Vrtiska voted against his usual party line.

"You know where I stand on the death penalty, Paul." He was a law and order merchant. "But Kermit put up such a darn convincing argument. Okay, so I don't agree with Ernie, but I think Kermit has something worth exploring."

Nebraska was the first state to have second thoughts about legalised murder since 1973, when the U.S. government reinstated it as a state option. Ernie Chamber, the living legend, had always been opposed to the death penalty on the grounds it inevitably disposed of a disproportionate number of African-Americans because they were poor, vulnerable to involvement in crime, and couldn't afford a smart defence team. At the other end of the political spectrum, white conservative Kermit Bashear argued that the death sentence was being applied 'unjustly', citing examples where expensive briefs had helped guilty whites side-step their just deserves (according to the yardstick set by sentences handed down to poorer sections of the community). While their arguments might have been subtly different, for once right and left were united in calling for a suspension of executions while a study of all homicides and capital sentences since 1973 was conducted. The day's vote fell in favour of the moratorium, 27-21.

"This means it'll go to the governor for his vote," Vrtiska explained. "If he vetoes it, it'll come back to the chamber and Kermit will have to find three more supporters. And Johanns probably will veto it, eh, Paul?"

Governor Johanns was a conservative, new to the office and (according to Paul) proving to be even more of a plonker than his political track record suggested. Over the weekend he threw the moratorium back to the chamber. With just one more day of legislative business before the summer recess on Monday evening, the moratorium was going down to the wire, and Paul was in the thick of it. It was a joy to witness him pumping Vrtiska and taking the piss out of the senator's knee-jerk liberalism.

I was also having problems with a jerking knee and had started to limp. On an unaccompanied visit to the University of Nebraska State Museum it suddenly collapsed and sent me crashing into a display case, but I tried to disguise my infirmity in front of Paul and Arlene. I didn't want to become any more of a burden than I already was. The Fells were spending money on me like it was ink and, by day two, I was becoming embarrassed by the number of times we ate out. Paul dismissed my concern, maintaining that, "We don't normally do this. It's kind of a nice break for us, not cooking. If you feel so bad about it, you can pay for the Runzas when we're next in town."

"You simply can't leave Lincoln without tasting a Runza," Arlene added, vamping it up.

"Most Americans eat out most of the time," Paul went on. "We all have hi-tech kitchens with the latest gizmos and watch TV cookery shows until they come out of our ears. But there isn't the time in most people's lives to cook, even if they knew how, or at least that's what they believe. Nobody bottles or bakes any more. Look in anybody's fridge and all you'll find is beer, soda pop and doggy bags from the meal they ate out the night before. The kitchen is as modern and over-equipped as it is purely for it's realty value."

In the *Lincoln Journal Star* that morning, U.S. Agricultural Secretary Dan Glickman was bemoaning

181

America's lack of support for their farmers. 'For every dollar spent on comestibles,' Dan maintained 'only 8¢ is spent on purchasing food for home consumption'. 92¢ went on eating out and the preferred breakfast, lunch and dinner was taken at one of the big throw-ups, which did its grocery shopping overseas.

The opportunity to sample a Runza, Nebraska's native fast food, came on the day when Arlene would reveal all about her roots. After trucking round the Museum of Nebraska History listening to her repeat, "Oh, I remember those," as if half the exhibits were Steinauer heirlooms, we tumbled into the Runza Rock 'n' Roll Café. If the restaurant didn't exactly rock, the waitress at least rolled to our table on skates. Considering the chain had been operating since 1949, they were seriously under-achieving in their pretensions to becoming another Wendys or Taco Bell. Everything about the packaging of Runzas suggested they weren't quite cutting it, but the food was excellent. Modelled on a German-Russian recipe brought over by the Everett family when they emigrated to Lincoln, the Runza was a meat or vegetarian concoction, heavily laced with sauerkraut and wrapped in something like unleavened bread. It looked like a jumbo spring roll before frying, but was substantial and didn't taste of MSG. I was further impressed that the current owner of the Nebraska chain and a man of millions, Donald R. Everett, was the guy wiping tables across the aisle from us.

Somebody amongst the Steinauers had done a heap of research. On our return to the house, a loose leaf folder containing 500 pages of family history, genealogies, obituaries, photos and memories of the old country landed on the table like a stamp hammer. The story it revealed was not very different from that of hundreds of thousands of other European families who settled west of the Missouri in the middle of the nineteenth century.

"The Steinauers were economic refugees," Arlene explained, "funded by the Swiss government to relocate across the Atlantic. In 1856, Antony, Nicholas and Joseph Steinauer paid a dollar twenty-five an acre for 480 acres of land where Turkey Creek runs through. At the end of a journey halfway round the globe, they found nothing but wind and grass and spent the first year living in a cave dug into the mud banks of the creek."

The Steinauer brothers were amongst the first wave of sod busters who struggled to create a home and livelihood in the Great American Desert. They broke land to grow corn, potatoes and wheat, and later raised cattle, pigs and oxen. Their first buildings were log cabins and sod houses — amazing organic constructions made from slabs of turf, sometimes as many as four storeys high, with shingle or sod roofs on which the grass continued to grew. They survived droughts, washouts, bitter cold, torrid heat, sandstorms, blizzards, fires and plagues of grasshoppers. Hailstorms frequently decimated their crops and their finances fluctuated from neck deep in debt to barely floating.

As the existence of Steinauer town suggests, the brothers worked hard and came good. They married girls from back home and the family tree blossomed. More land was incorporated in 1904 when the Kincaid Act permitted farms to expand to 640 acres — the one square mile that the prairies are still divided into by the dirt roads I travelled. The Great War brought prosperity but during the Great Depression of the 1930s chronic droughts brought on the dust storms. For the first time and after a number of violent demonstrations, farmers received government subsidies to stave off mortgage foreclosures.

"At the turn of the (twentieth) century, thirty-eight per cent of Americans were farmers," Paul said. "Today it is less than two per cent and the Agricultural Department expects 40,000 farms a year will disappear for the foreseeable future, mostly absorbed into big corporate operations."

Since the Forties, one innovation after another has seen farm acreage increase as the number of farmers decreased, "but there is still a Steinauer working land around Steinauer," Arlene proclaimed.

I saw him in a documentary about the family recently made for European TV, a copy of which Arlene and every other American Steinauer had on video. Those interviewed spoke in a mishmash of American, English and High German, even the youngest generation, much like the Asians I live amongst in Nottingham speak Urdu, Gujerati or Punjabi with a streak of English woven through. Although Arlene was only distantly related to the three brothers, I couldn't help noticing her facial characteristics were pure Steinauer.

"Yeh, she's got the big nose and sticking out chin," Paul said, milliseconds before a flying cushion attacked him.

I rode away from Paul and Arlene's wishing I didn't have to, fearing I was headed wide-eyed and limping into some kind of a mauling. If the Panther was going to run wild anywhere it would be across the prairies, but concern for my mental and physical well-being didn't top my list of worries. In a link up at the Fell's place, Sandy had told me she was faxing through a letter which tried to express all the things she was having trouble saying over the phone. The fax never appeared, I presumed because she had second thoughts. It would have only taken a phone call to check but, I didn't want to make it. I had become too wrapped up in my Boy's Own adventure, and would pay the price.

Ten miles south of Lincoln, I hung a right and set course for the town of Hastings, a hundred straight miles due west on Route 6. Beyond it I would cross the diagonal of the Oregon Trail, pause to say, "Hi! Remember me?" then work my way south-west on another diversion to the Pioneer Village at Minden. I had no idea why I was going there, except people at Jessica Nowak's graduation bash said it would be a mistake not to call in if I was interested in pioneer history. My eventual goal was Fort Kearny, an important staging post for the overlanders on the banks of the River Platte, a dozen miles north of Minden.

West of Crete on Route 6, the undulating terrain of eastern Nebraska softened into a ripple which lapped so gently it is understandable that drivers consider the state to be flat. I was also gently but consistently climbing. At a rate of two to three metres a mile, I was ascending the foothills of the Rockies, hidden beyond the flat horizon over 700 miles away. According to the map, the average height of the eastern plains was around 700 metres above sea level while, in the west, they reached 1,500 metres. More accurately, I was creeping up a ramp of debris — a vast alluvial fan of sand and gravel washed away from the Western Cordillera over the millennia, spreading out across the whole mid-west of America. Remarkably, the bedrock deep beneath my wheels sloped in the opposite direction, from east to west.

Yellow irises nodded in a wind heavily laced with the stench of cattle pens and mulched sorghum. In fields which appeared to know no bounds, small herds of Simmentals counted their lucky stars they weren't packed in corrals with the hundreds waiting to take the final truck ride. To my right, the sky was so deep and blue I wanted to jump in and swim around. Far off to the south, white puffs suggested surf breaking over a coral reef. Between the two, on a line running straight down the highway, an isthmus of clouds tapered down to sand dunes on a beach which looked distinctly like a storm front. It was going to be a short day.

Since leaving Indiana, everybody who talked about the weather confirmed this was the worst spring they could remember. The blame was squarely laid on the shoulders of Il Ninã but I was assured things would change for the better by next weekend, the Memorial Day holiday weekend, marking the start of summer in the minds of Americans if not that of the seasons. Since Missouri, the weather had fallen into a pattern of days which started with blue skies, high cirrus clouds and tolerable humidity. Day two started dull and became dark as night. Churning grey clouds, dense humidity and an atmosphere I had to machete my way through set the scene for the morning. Around mid afternoon, the plot was thickened by a crescendo of rolling thunder, sheet lightning, fork lightning, then a short sharp monsoon. The dramatics were followed by a day of clear skies, searing heat, lethal sun and low humidity. Everybody rushed into the fields that day, mending and tinkering, if not actually ploughing. Then, like somebody cleaning off a brush of white emulsion on blue canvas, tell-tale cirrus wisps reappeared, and the cycle began over.

As I pedalled into Friend, an old boy on a tricycle swung out from the main drag, rode like the clappers down the wrong side of the street and shouted, "Better put up for the night, son. It's a-coming." Judging from the main street set at right angles to Route 6, Friend was going to be a cool place to knock off early. On both sides of the broadway, buildings had recently received a lick of paint, but what the local art teacher and his team had done amounted to more than a little redecorating. The fine detail of every decorative pediment and window head was picked out in brilliant white with highlights of mushroom grey. The frontage of each bar, store and office had a separate colour scheme, co-ordinated to complement the colours either side. Signboards were smartly and simply lettered in classic serif faces. On side walls reaching above younger buildings in the block, small murals remembered past glories such as pony trotting at the Friend Races of 1911. Tubs of variegated blooms mellowed the harsh line between office and sidewalk and, every thirty paces, new olde worlde lamp standards added a finishing touch of class. There wasn't a blemish of litter anywhere.

I downed a couple of Busch Lites in the Broken Spoke Saloon, and chatted to three bikers on their way to a Harley Davison gathering in Hastings. One had once shipped his machine to Europe to cruise the continent. He'd been away for ten days and figured he'd seen it all.

"Didn't like Europe," he told me with a grimace. "Too old."

At the back of the bar in the car park, an obscure Country & Western radio station was setting up a live transmission for a hootenanny that evening. Nobody was too concerned about the impending downpour and the joint was a-rocking. It seemed the whole town had knocked off early.

Five blocks south of the bar, the town park had a swimming pool, baseball diamond, swings, pavilion and the Friend Community Center. Under the trees outside the centre, a young man was grilling burgers and wieners on a park barbie surrounded by a gaggle of kids. We exchanged greetings. I told him I was camping overnight and he said, "You betcha. C'mon over for a burger when y'ready." The only other people around were an elderly couple sweeping the grass with metal detectors. They were out for the summer in their RV, metal detecting their way towards Colorado. I asked if they had found much.

"Oh, nickels an' dime stuff. Hair clips, brooches, sometimes an arrow head, Roman coins. Once I found me a watch..."

"Hang about," I interrupted. "You've found Roman coins?"

"Yar."

"In Nebraska?"

"Nar. Oklahoma."

In the community centre, eight adults and ten kids ranging from toddlers to eight year olds were celebrating the first birthday of Jessie Stutzman. Jessie hadn't a clue what was going on, but there were lots of plastic cups to throw around and the wrapping from his presents tasted scrumptious. While he gurgled cheerfully in his dad's arms, we all played musical chairs to Bruce Springsteen. In the middle of the first manic round, lightning flashed, thunder crashed, windows rattled and the kids screamed louder as the speed of the chase accelerated. Within minutes of the monsoon falling, a boy came charging into the centre shouting, "Ma! Ma! The pool's overflowing! We're gonna be flooded." The chances of the centre being overwhelmed were slim, but the prospects for my sorry little tent didn't look good. Floodwater from the swimming pool was pushing towards it in a series of mini tidal bores.

A police car cut a wake along the perimeter road, slowing to a crawl to rise over a traffic calmer. I dashed out, splashed across the lake that used to be a lawn, and stopped him. The window rolled down on an unshaven dude in a Levi jacket, checked shirt and hair which hadn't seen a comb in a month.

"Sure y'all can camp here, but I ain't no real po-lice off'cer. He's away on vacation. I'm just a-fillin' in, but I'll be sure 'n' let him know when he gets back," the guy said, being helpful. "When y'leavin'? There's a party on in town t'night, but y'should be okay out here."

The park was bordered by three tarmac roads. The two along its length changed to grit as they stretched away from the village into the back of beyond. The one close to my tent linked the two others and was rippled with traffic calmers. As the shindig at the Broken Spoke wound down, revellers drove home. Dozing in my tent, I could hear that the road in front of me was the main drag out of town. Some vehicles turned left along the link road running by my head, then right onto the grit before fading into the distance.

Around midnight, a different pattern emerged, with occasional vehicles driving up the road behind me, turning right past my head, clunking over the calmers, then back into town in front of me. People were still cruising as I drifted into sleep. An hour later I was sharply awakened by two objects hitting the side of the tent and a vehicle roaring away past my head. A couple of minutes passed before a third missile landed, a vehicle revved, tyres plopped, and a voice shouted, "Go home!" Then a third vehicle and a fourth projectile. I was under attack.

Since the incident at Greens Bottom, Missouri, and the graduation kids partying in the car park, I had learned to accept that the growl of a souped-up engine was not synonymous with prowling rednecks whacked out on moonshine and armed with sawn-offs looking to exact evil against some 'nehgra' — or a Scotsman if an African-American wasn't to hand. At Friend, however, the old Hollywood stereotype came rushing back to mind. I lay rigid in the tent, acutely aware that two layers of ripstop nylon offered no kind of protection.

During a lull, I slipped out of the tent and crouched in the doorway of the toilet block, maintaining a watch over the roads. Two more vehicles crawled round the three sides of the park. Then a pick-up slipped onto the link road, bridged a traffic calmer and paused. Somebody stepped out, hurled something at my tent and jumped back into the cab. With a blood curdling screech and in a cloud of burning rubber, rear wheels spun and the chassis bucked before the driver slipped the clutch and shot away. A fourth vehicle followed the same routine and roared off drowning calls for me to leave town *pronto*.

The streets fell silent and, after a judicious pause, I crept back to bed. Splayed around the tent were quarter full bottles of soda. My assailants were chicken-shit teenagers! Checking they didn't contain urine, I sat in the tent and chain smoked, sipping Coke, 7-Up, Mountain Dew and Kool Aid. It was ironic that I had cycled safely through two of America's worst ghettos only to be attacked by pop bottles in a country village called Friend.

Chapter 16

Despite the fearsome brazier raging in a petrol blue sky, there were indications that the new dawn heralded problems which had nothing to do with grilled flesh. A row of emperor butterflies were lined along the edge of the tarmac with their wings parked up like F-14 Tomcats packed on the deck of an aircraft carrier. Above a church, the Stars and Stripes flew without flapping, like a steel plate, and empty cattle trucks batting down the highway leaned at a southerly tilt. The Panther was charging in from the north-west and everything indicated I was in for a day of hard graft.

Settling into the grim task of carving through the air stream, I slid up and down the wave band, searching for something on the radio to occupy my mind. Between ranting fundamentalists, bigoted talk shows, music from the sixties and everything escaping from Nashville, American radio can induce a coma, but Nebraska Public Service Broadcasting was airing a talk about Crazy Horse, Chief of the Lacota, the nomads contained in this part of Nebraska when it was the Indian Territories. The Lacota were one of the tribes which made mincemeat of General George Custer and the Seventh Cavalry at the Little Bighorn, but their initial position on the great white migration was to help it along, steering the pioneers right when they got lost, providing food when they ran low. For Crazy Horse, the Oregon-California Trail was a Holy Road. It was forbidden to attack it or hinder the travellers in any way which might cause the U.S. Army to rain down upon the tribe.

As with most of the indigenous and relocated tribes the wagon trains encountered, the Lacota were no threat. It was only later that the natives became incensed about the white man stealing their crops, scaring off the buffalo, spreading cholera and destroying the woods which provided summer shade. When settlers began nicking their lands, Crazy Horse and his people joined Red Cloud's Oglalas in raids on American civilians but, during the transition from migration to colonisation, what most disturbed the natives were the 'singing wires' — the telegraph lines being strung across their homelands to replace the Pony Express. The Lacota used to try out-racing the Morse code, galloping like fury to overtake the songs travelling down the line. In my case, I was having trouble overtaking the telegraph poles, and was now struggling between towns at barely six miles an hour.

Since Crete, Route 6 had been tracked by the Burlington Northern Santa Fe (BNSF) Railroad line. With the stone embankment running less than a hundred feet from the edge of the road, I soon discovered that the enormous length and slow progress of an American freight train made for a marvellous wind break. On a few occasions, I even managed sufficient speed to keep pace and enjoyed anything up to fifteen minutes unimpeded pedalling. It was a busy line, and every driver hung on his horn and waved encouragement. For the first time since my knee had been playing up, I enjoyed my cycling.

The railroads played a decisive role in the conquest of the West, and historical markers had started to appear beside the road where the Iron Horse had been attacked by natives. The strip of land on which the Burlington Northern was built was originally provided by the federal government. Land either side of the track was sold on to incomers from the east and, every ten or so miles, a town was mapped out, the distance between settlements governed by the miles a horse drawn wagon could travel on a day return. Burlington Northern demanded the towns be named in alphabetical order. Thus the places I ticked off included Crete, Dorchester, Exeter, Fairmont, Grafton and... Sutton. Did the town stick their heels in and say to the railroad, "Don't be so daft!"?

Beyond Crete, fields became noticeably larger, sometimes as big as four miles squared, and the terrain ironed

191

out a little flatter. Clumps of fir trees, lines of telegraph poles, irrigation systems and a rare farm house were the only items sticking above the ruled line between heaven and earth. As I pedalled out of one town I could see straight down the road to the next. Above its tight cluster of trees and roofs, the water tower and grain silo stood like white plant markers in a tray of seedlings. Only once were the miles of emptiness disrupted when a row of billboards suddenly appeared informing me I was ninety miles from Howard Warp's Pioneer Village at Minden. Each billboard featured something different I should get excited about — fire wagons, kitchens, agricultural equipment, numismatics. What the hell was this place I couldn't afford to miss?

After Sutton came an unusually long gap of twenty-eight miles before we got back on the alphabetic track with Hastings. The town itself was an uneasy combination of red brick college community on the inside and agricultural service industries on the out. Turning my nose up at the official KOA camp site on the edge of town, I went in search of the Adams County Fairgrounds, hoping there would be space to slip a tent between the caravans of travelling entertainers.

The fairground was a jigger car park lousy with weeds and oily puddles behind the stands of a modest county showground. In the ground, circus people were grazing Shetland ponies and elephants, and practising juggling. The tigers' cage and their living wagons were parked within a circle of carnival trailers forming a separate encampment away from those who permanently inhabited the car park. I joined the permanent residents and was told I could pitch anywhere amongst the battered caravans dotted around the gravel. The guy who gave me the okay reeked of bourbon and fell out of his van when he answered my knock. Every beat up trailer was surrounded by a small scrap yard and paired with an beat up banger. There was nothing on the car park younger than thirty years old. Most of the humans were the worse for drink and looked twice that age. I was down amongst the Hastings down and outs, the cream of Nebraska's trailer trash.

As I unpacked, Leroy and Neal wove across the car park from their respective hovels, homing in on me like confused Cruise missiles. They plonked themselves on the ground beside my bike and started rabbiting, passing a Coke bottle between each other. Offered a swig, I first established the contents were one part Kool Aid to three parts vodka, receiving the added information that the invention of Kool Aid was Hastings' great claim to fame. It tasted good. I had a few more swigs and we became bosom buddies.

Neal was bearded, well built, mean looking and wore a tatty quilted combat jacket, despite sweltering heat. He was thirty-six years old, going on 106, and filthy.

"He never fucking washes, dirty bastard," Leroy said to his face.

Leroy chain smoked. Everything he said was punctuated by nasal snorts and hefty gobs of nicotine tainted phlegm.

"Oh, is there a bathroom?" I inquired.

"Showers, man, but don't use the toilet with the fucked cistern. It's fucked," Leroy explained. "They're over there, behind the cattle pens."

I pictured wash facilities splattered with faeces and swimming in urine, but they were sparkling.

Neal lived in the smallest caravan on the planet.

"Yep, just enough room for a bed and my TV. Wanna see?"

I gracefully declined.

"Last night, the wind pushed his van sixty fucking yards across the car park," Leroy said, "So we've chained it to a fucking pylon."

Neal arrived in Hastings a year and a half ago, nobody knew where from. He pitched a tent on the car park and survived winter to winter under canvas. At the beginning of spring, his tent was shredded by a storm and he took to sleeping in the toilet block. Then Leroy found him the matchbox he currently occupied. He received social security for a "mental problem," which he and Leroy immediately pissed against a wall.

"Hey, we're drunks, man, but we ain't fucking moochers."

I think this meant they weren't beggars or scroungers. Neal certainly was a grafter. While we were talking, his boss drove up in a pick-up laden with lawn mowers.

"His name's Elton Hughes," Leroy told me between coughing fits, "Like Howard fucking Hughes's cousin, yeh? Never saw any of the money. The guy's a city farmer. Lays sod."

Boom-Boom came running up to Leroy and clung to his jeans. Otherwise known as Alan, Boom-Boom was Leroy's one year old and a remarkably advanced child to say that his father was an alcoholic and his mother, Judy, was illiterate. Judy was in her thirties, had a chubby face and a drinker's nose though she never touched the stuff. She was badly disabled from birth and didn't stray far from their caravan, but Leroy loved her, he said, and brought her talking books from the free library to educate her. It was Judy's welfare cheque that supported the family.

"Hell, I can get me seventy-five bucks an hour when I work," Leroy said, competing with the $25 Neal earned for a full day's toil. "It's getting the fucking work is the problem."

Leroy was a qualified refrigerator mechanic trained in the penitentiary, or what he called the "grey bar hotel," who could also turn his hand to washing machines and spin driers. He kept his tools in the boot of a 1956 Plymouth which listed at an acute angle under the weight. Having spent eleven of his forty-eight years inside, he was probably an expert at his trade and totally trustworthy. Except for scamming petrol from almost every gas station in Hastings, he had turned away from thieving now that Boom-Boom was on the scene. "Okay, so I drink, but I don't need no trouble with the law." I still couldn't see the college fraternity of Hastings falling over themselves to ask Leroy to mend their whiteware.

The family lived in a thirty year old caravan which was larger than Neal's but tiny by American standards. They filched electricity through a cable jerry-rigged to the lights above the cattle pens and were terribly house proud. Accepting Leroy's invitation to join them for evening popcorn, I had to take my shoes off in the doorway before padding into a fluffy love nest where everything which had a place was trimmed in pink, including the toaster. We drank unadulterated Kool Aid and the smell of booze was noticeable by its absence.

Married for sixteen years, Judy and Leroy had spent the last two living on the showground car park. They previously rented a house in Colorado, but set off one day to visit Judy's dad in Minnesota. On the way home, the car broke down east of Hastings and the police impounded the vehicle. Because they had no money, they were dumped in separate crisis centres. Leroy felt grossly insulted. Two days later he had fixed the car and they set off to continue the drive home to Colorado. Four miles west of Hastings, they broke down again.

"I kinda figured that if God had meant us to leave this place, we'd be long gone. Two breakdowns, either side of town — man, you gotta reason God wants you to stay."

They celebrated settling into a new town by having Boom-Boom despite the Medicare doctor advising them against parenting.

Route 6 had a bend in it twenty miles west of Hastings. Nebraska is not a place where the joy of travelling includes the thrill of seeing what's round the next corner. It wasn't even a proper corner — more a lazy curve gently realigning the highway to the south-west. Before it, the BNSF railroad switched to the left hand side of the road, stealing away my windbreak. I quickly gave up on the exposed tarmac and slipped across a level crossing to pick up the grit service road running the other side of the tracks. At Hastings, the single track had expanded to four and barely five minutes elapsed between one or more freighters rumbling by. Between windbreaks, I rode huddled over the handlebars beneath the height of the rail embankment, revelling in the thought that the Panther couldn't see me.

I rode into Minden anticipating great things and was immediately greeted by a huge white arrow supporting a Model T Ford twenty feet above the ground. In the back seat of the car sat a plaster cast grandma losing her rag with her middle-aged son, who was crouched before the radiator ready to give the hand crank a whirl. A second enormous arrow labelled 'Entrance' pointed to a long, low, brick and glass building in the vane of car showrooms of the Fifties. On the roof stood a Conestoga wagon. At around eleven in the morning I stepped into Harold Warp's Pioneer Village and didn't leave until thrown out at sundown.

Harold Warp made his millions out of glazing and was the president of Flexo-Glass, Chicago. His dad, John Nelson Warp, settled near Minden in the 'south-west quarter of section 10, township 5, range 14' purchased off the Chicago, Burlington & Quincy Railroad Company. At some point, young Harold started to collect bits and bobs which the farming family were throwing away. His hobby grew into an obsession with amassing anything telling 'The Story of America and How It Grew'. Harold collected everything from thimbles to churches and blades of grass to a Pony Express relay station. To contain his trinkets, he bought twenty acres of Minden and expanded to include a functioning motel, camp ground and restaurant. On the edge of town, he also owned an airstrip, from where courtesy cars delivered visitors down to his Village.

Harold's was a magnificent obsession, now spread around attractive grounds where even the trees were exhibits and labelled. Splayed around a circular green, transplanted buildings hid a row of two-storey hangers packed to the rafters with clobber. There was no way anybody could appreciate a fraction of what the site held unless booked into the motel for a week. The main building alone contained over 10,000 items, and each hanger was so tightly packed you couldn't get near half the exhibits. I followed a family around the Homes and Shops Building, eavesdropping in on their memories of this type of kitchen which they had before the kids were born, and that type of bedroom, so like great grandma's. Outside the sod house, I waited while a husband took a snap of his wife standing in the doorway. On her father's farm there were the remains of the two storey sod house her grandparents built. Where the Smithsonian focused on the extraordinary, Harold Warp concentrated on the common and garden. His hoard provided the whole family with a chance to wallow in nostalgia while those too young to know the meaning of the word whizzed round the oldest U.S. steam powered merry-go-round, still only 5¢.

Harold's collection of wagons put the Smithsonian's to shame. It provided me with an opportunity to study the rolling stock which crossed the virgin plains. On the Oregon-California Trail, light farm wagons were preferred over the chunky Conestoga wagons because of their ability to negotiating tight canyons and steep bluffs. Around three metres long and one and a half wide, the bed of the wagon was a simple wooden box protected by a hooped canvas top, capable of carrying around a ton. To improve manoeuvrability, the front wheels were generally smaller than the back, but the rigs had neither a brake nor springs. On steep descents, chains were used to lock the rear wheels and provide a drag.

Of course, all manner of wagons, buggies and two-wheeled *carretas* carried the gold hungry west. In the rush to join the migration, anything which was light, manoeuvrable and load bearing hit the trail, often with dire consequences. I was now nine days out from Independence and the Forty-Niners had been on the go for just under a month. Already the rigours of the prairies were taking their toll on the weaker vehicles and some wrecks had been hacked in two to form a *carreta*. Where most companies left the Missouri with a wagon to every three men, some were now forced to double up, which meant dumping supplies. By the end of the journey, twelve per wagon was not uncommon and most people had crossed the West on foot. Walking was quicker than riding. Though mules were faster than oxen, they weren't as powerful, so which engine you chose to hitch your wagon to depended on your approach to driving the trail. Horses were never used for pulling, though they accompanied some wagon trains in much the same way that today's RV owners tow a car. For reconnaissance, hunting and rounding up stray cattle, the horse was a useful accessory but not essential.

Reeling with an overdose of Americana, I staggered out of Harold's place and headed north to rejoin the westward trails. As the evening sun hovered low over miles of feeder pens and shimmied in the heat rising off thousands of cattle being fattened for slaughter, I swung into the Fort Kearny camp ground. Three college students were lounging around the office shed, all working holiday jobs at the State Recreation Ground. While I checked in and bought papers from the vending machines, they brought me up to date with what was happening in the world. I learned that America was fighting the "commies in the Middle East" (Yugoslavia) and that the city of Lincoln had just agreed to house an intake of Armenians. Public opinion (the lads) was concerned that America was about to be swamped with refugees, "and what do they know about democracy?" Pointing out that the United States was built on refugees, it was explained that that was different. "They brought civilisation to this country."

The camp site was bordered on one side by the Platte, the river which came to mean so much to those undertaking the long haul west. For nearly 500 miles, they and I would track it to the doorstep of the Rockies. As early as 1842, John Frémont recommended the U.S. government establish a fort south of the flow to protect the pioneers. Three years later, Congress approved plans for a chain of military outposts stretching from the Missouri to the

Rockies, but what the army erected at Fort Kearny was more a collection of barracks, warehouses and officers' quarters than a fully fortified stockade. At the historic park next door to the camp ground, stubby markers located the four corners of the original buildings. A sketch drawn by a traveller in 1849 showed just a handful of disparate sod buildings, a few tents and an adobe brick sutler's store. (A sutler is a civilian licenced to sell provisions on an army base.) Twenty years later, another contemporary drawing indicated the outpost had grown into a small brick village.

Bright and early the next morning, I joined a group of second grade school kids and their teachers for the slide presentation in the Visitor Center. The show was introduced by Paul Hendrickson, an elderly volunteer dressed in the Yankee uniform of C Battery Artillery, Fort Kearny. After an over-long history of the fort, the lights went up and Paul introduced somebody sitting at the back of the room as, "A very interesting young man who is from overseas and following the trail of his ancestors." I looked around for the guy Paul was inviting to step up and say a few words. Once again, who I was and what I was doing had somehow travelled before me.

As I made to leave, Eugene ("Call me Gene") Hunt beckoned me back into the Visitor Center. Gene was the Superintendent of Fort Kearny, bespeckled and moustached, and bubbling with enthusiasm for his corner of American history. He was one of those people for whom breathing and full stops get in the way. He brought out maps of the area plotted by Frémont, Lt. Woodbury (the fort's original surveyor), and the Burlington Northern Railroad, who relocated the town on the opposite bank of the Platte and called it Kearney. Misinformed that I was following the family trail, he was angling for me to send him a photocopy of my argonaut ancestor's diary. The request was symptomatic of the desperate retrieval process caretakers of America's abused heritage are compelled to undertake.

Despite Fort Kearny's leading role in the epic narrative of westward expansion, the outpost was torn down after it had fulfilled its military purpose and, in 1871, the land was opened up for homesteading. Fifty years later, Nebraska decided that hadn't been such a great idea, and bought the land back. Had somebody paused long enough to think further than making a buck, the original buildings might still be in place. As at so many historical sites, Americans were left with reproduction buildings, static displays and a turgid audio-visual show to bring the conquest of the West to life. This possibly explained why those who devised the displays were obsessed with statistics. Every wayside historical marker and exhibit in a Visitors Center groaned under the weight of how much, how many and how often.

In fact, most diarists wrote very little about their time at Fort Kearny. Some noted that travellers outnumbered residents by as many as ten to one, and that their camp was surrounded by thousands of grazing cattle, also on the road west. While some in the companies pestered the army for intelligence about the way ahead, others dived into the sutler's store to buy provisions, or called in at the mail room to deposit letters for dispatch to the States. By June 23rd, 1849, the last of the wagons had moved on and it was estimated some 23,000 people had passed through Fort Kearny that summer, driving about 6,200 wagons. The year before, the Oregon-California Trail had attracted just 100 wagons.

In many respects, the month it took the overlanders to reach Fort Kearny had been a shakedown experience. By no means arduous, those 320 miles were sufficient to convince waverers to turn back before things became really sticky. For those more determined, it was a period when men learned driving and animal handling skills, became proficient at setting and striking camp, and decided they were grossly over-burdened. Between Fort Kearny and the river, the land was trashed with piles of discarded goods. With no idea of what they were getting into beyond the Missouri, Easterners had loaded their wagons with all manner of featherbeds, rocking chairs, chests of drawers and other luxuries which had no place on an expedition. It reminded me of journeys I had undertaken with cyclists who produced dressing gowns and fluffy slippers from their panniers. For some, it takes many miles before they feel sufficiently comfortable with the wild to discard home comforts.

It was an unprecedented third fine day. Stratocumulus clouds sauntered east across a graded cyan sky like scrubbed Charolais grazing their way towards the water trough of the Missouri. My road beside the Platte River was pancake flat but, a mile to the north, gentle curves marked the southern edge of the Dissected Plains — ancient flatlands eroded by wind and water into smooth ridges and steep slopes. In the broad valley basin, plumes of dust indicated where farmers had finally managed to get into the fields to start ploughing. Mighty mammoths with double rear bogies and multiple plough shares scraped back and forth across huge acreages separated by the flimsiest of barbed wire fences. In some fields, irrigation systems were sprinkling land which four days ago had been soused by storms.

I was now hugging the line taken by the exodus of Mormons as they fled Nauvoo, Illinois, and tramped towards their New Zion on the 'Trail of Hope'. In a land settled by Europeans fleeing religious persecution in the Old World, New World settlers had successfully harassed the church clear across country. From its inception in Fayette, New York, the Church of Jesus Christ of Latter-day Saints moved to Ohio, then Missouri and on to Illinois in search of somewhere to settle. In Nauvoo, they helped build one of the largest cities in the State of Illinois, with a population in the early 1840s of over 11,000 people, but strength of numbers and solidity of brickwork only increased the suspicions and resentments of the non-believers in town. In 1844 their founding father, Joseph

Smith, was murdered by an angry mob, and a year and a half later the great Mormon migration began.

Between me and the screen of cottonwoods hiding the swirling river, Interstate 80 and the railroad made a bee line for Wyoming. Ankling down Route 30, I cycled beside the ghosts of Latter Day Saints trudging along the Mormon Trail. On the opposite bank of the river, going our way, were the ghosts of gold seekers and pioneers following the Oregon-California Trail. In the eighteenth century, this was the Great Platte River Road used by St. Louis fur traders hauling out beaver pelts, and for thousands of years before that, Native Americans exploited the same natural corridor into the mountains. In a landscape as unyielding as the prairies were before the Industrial Revolution, lines of communication didn't stray far from the topographical freeways.

The road to Lexington was unwaveringly straight, flat and boring. I leant on the handlebars and surfed through the wavebands. Though I was over a thousand miles from the Tex-Mex border and California, a Mexican station blasted through the speaker loud and clear. I cranked into town humming to a *mariachi* and turned right onto a deserted main street unusually well endowed with Mexican restaurants and Latino craft shops. I asked a guy in a new Explorer 4x4 if he could direct me to the police station.

"Sorry, man, but I don't speak American."

I asked another who was white and mowing his lawn. He pointed the way, recommended I watch my "ass" and told me the town used to be a nice place, before the Californians moved in. "These days, you gotta be some kinda dumb fuck not to lock your dog in if you don't want it ending up in a damn *tortilla*, y'know?"

Through an intercom secured behind steel bars, a cop told me I could camp at Plum Creek Park. He then laughed. As I neared the park, the sound of people at play swelled to fill the empty approach road. The park was buzzing with families playing volley ball, picnicking, playing soccer, courting, and fooling with kids. It was the first town park I had visited which was packed, and it made me nervous. Everybody was Mexican. Since St. Louis I had heard nothing but bad things about Mexican-Americans, no doubt prejudiced things. When a football ran loose, I dropped my rig and dribbled the ball back to the game, impressed that I managed to beat two tackles before a third youth whipped the ball from under me.

"Not bad," the youth said, surprised a *gringo* could play.

"Yeh, well, it's our national sport," I replied, "second only to losing."

The lads formed a semi-circle round me and began firing off the names of English teams and players. I was in the presence of Lexington's youth soccer squad and struggling to hide the fact I knew sod all about football.

"I'm confused," I said, changing the subject. "I've travelled hundreds of miles across white America and suddenly I find myself in a Mexican town?"

It was explained that their parents had moved here from Mexico and California to work at the IBP meat packing plant. "Fuckin' stink hole, man." Now they mentioned it, there was a whiff of minced beef about Lexington. "Shit work for shit wages, and there's nothing else round here 'cept farming." In the middle of expressing horror at the prospect of following their parents into IBP, the team fell into whispers. Pointing out three youths walking across a bridge over the lake behind me, they warned that the gangsters were out. "They're killers, man." "Y'don't fuck with them." "You gonna camp in the park? Tonight? Man, you gotta be crazy. Those dudes will have you."

At their meanest, the three gangsters looked capable of pilfering candy from an unattended store but, when they left, they drove away in a customised Cadillac which would have ploughed a furrow had it's suspension been a centimetre lower. As it prowled round the perimeter of Plum Creek Park, it issued a menacing growl specifically aimed at me. Maybe Lexington wasn't such a great place to put up for the night?

Possibly because the trails stretch further across the Cornhusker State than any other, most towns allow travellers to camp overnight in the local park free of charge. On the edge of Plum Creek Park, I came upon a large hard standing where two enormous trailer homes and an Excalibur coach were plugged into a line of hook-ups. They were owned by three people who had spent the last eight months on the road showing and training dogs. On the grass before the car park, a row of temporary cages confined five huge Bouvies and a coondog which went ballistic when I approached. That night I pitched as close as I dared and came to appreciate the acrid reassurance of dog breath.

Chapter 17

The Mormon and Oregon Trails were family affairs. Men, women and children were travelling towards the land of their dreams, expecting to start new lives free from the poverty, persecution or plain boredom of their old lives. In the course of their epic journey, new friendships were made which blossomed into love and marriage. Children were born on the trail. People became orphans on the trail and died on the trail, and parents buried their parents. At day's beginning, middle and end, there were domestic routines and mundane tasks apportioned no differently to families living at home. People observed the sabbath and the Mormon's religious practices never faltered. Undoubtedly they journeyed under extraordinary circumstances, but an entire community was on the move, with all the complex social relationships and banal interactions found in any village. Not so with the Forty-Niners on the California Trail.

Crucially different, the Gold Rush was a male phenomenon. Hardly any women and children were among the army bound for El Dorado in 1849, and by 1852 they still constituted less than 15% of the traffic. Essentially the trail was a crocodile of blokes ambling west. They were not migrants or pilgrims on the road to the promised land, but opportunists. Their promised land was what they would buy when they returned stinking rich. For most of the men, there was family tying them to home, eager to reel them in as soon as they struck gold, if not before. The hundreds of diaries were written as much to combat homesickness as for the later edification of those left behind. Considerably fewer were kept on the pilgrim trails.

Most of the diaries barely qualified for the title, but some were well written, well observed and informative. Many authors recorded how rash and combative the men rapidly became without women around, and how mean spirited they were without children amongst them. Despite Articles of Agreement or constitutions, hardly a company escaped without something triggering a dispute which escalated into a brawl, knifing or shoot out. The outcome of card games and whether or not to observe the sabbath were the most common flash points, and company constitutions rapidly became meaningless as large companies fractured into smaller units. But the guys were having a big adventure — at this stage, the time of their lives. The folks who were really going through the mill were those back home left to handle the business, bring up children, bury relatives, and struggle on without husbands, brothers, lovers and fathers around. Those left behind clutched at every straw of information, every whisper of gossip, and every letter received by themselves or others in an effort to get an idea of where their men were and what they were going through.

It was my idea to send friends and family in England densely written postcards detailing different incidents from my unfolding adventure. Knowing each person would contact Sandy with news from the cards, I thought this would alleviate her loneliness and paint a broader picture than anything I could contain in a single missive to her. There was precious little time to write communiqués as it was. As the Forty-Niners discovered, between covering the miles and feeding yourself, there isn't a lot of down time on the trail. Those that kept detailed diaries wrote brief letters. Those that sent home long epistles wrote brief diaries or none at all. Nobody had the convenience of being able to talk on the phone or the problem of important faxes which don't arrive. At Gothenburg, outside the cattle market, I placed my weekly call. My wife was in tears.

Contrary to what I thought when I flew back to Dayton, Sandy was not close to finding her way out from under the avalanche that buried her when her mother died. She was still upset about my premature return to the trail, but her voice betrayed a deeper depression. Abandoned by Pauline and now by me, she sounded close to despair. She was managing to hold together the household and business, but while she was doing everything to support me, I was doing nothing to support her. Each minute of our conversation made me feel increasingly guilty, increasingly the selfish bastard. I was covered in road grime and surrounded by cowboys herding beef into auction. Men in chaps were doing manly things and I was on a mission. I didn't know how to deal with the waves of distress coming at me from down the phone.

By the time I hung up, I felt like liquid shit. I rode the thirty or so miles to North Platte wallowing in self recrimination, oblivious to what was happening around me. What the hell did I think I was doing deserting my wife and partner like that? And what was I supposed to do now? Somewhere beside the road there had to be a squalid little hole I could crawl into and die.

There wasn't, largely because I was now in a busy town riding down multiple lanes of traffic, struggling to concentrate on agitated drivers who shot out of nowhere. I was being bombarded by flashing neon signs which should have excited me. If I didn't already know it, Cody Liquors, Buffalo Bill Avenue, Scout's Bar and numerous other titles incorporating 'Scout', 'Cody' or 'Buffalo Bill' drove home that North Platte was a bit proud of its most famous star, William F. Cody, aka Buffalo Bill.

Of all the heroes featured in the comics I read as a kid, Buffalo Bill was my favourite. To grow up and discover he was a real person who spent much his working life with one foot in showbiz was something of a let down, but if anybody from the Wild West lived a life scripted for Hollywood, it was Buffalo Bill. He was an army scout, Pony Express rider, stagecoach driver and buffalo hunter. He was also a ruthless killer of men and buffalo, credited with bagging over 4,000 bison in just eighteen months. Between rip-roaring escapades in the West, he was the star of stage melodramas in the East and books further sensationalising his already sensational life. Thanks to a profitable and furtive relationship with dime novelist Ned Buntline, Buffalo Bill transformed the historic West into the mythical Wild West of the Western.

Because it was there, I rode round to Scout's Rest Ranch, Cody's retirement home, a beautifully ornate but quite modest eighteen room mansion. Trimmed with French Second Empire features and topped with a low turret, it was set beside a creek in the pristine grounds of a State Historical Park dominated by the scout's original barn. But the ranch was built in 1878 under the supervision of his wife. Cody was in New York during the ranch's construction, absorbed in the production of a new play mythologising some outrageous event in his life. According to his dreadful autobiography, he was married to 'Miss Frederici' in 1865, after which, but for a single line mentioning her and their daughter, Louisa disappears from his story until the final chapter, by when there are two daughters. While Louisa and the kids stayed home, Bill went out to play with the boys — for 365 action packed pages. Cody arrived at his new ranch in North Platte just in time to disappear again for six weeks, rounding up cattle with the guys. Thirteen years after getting married he decides, 'This work being over, I proposed to spend a few weeks with my family at North Platte, for the purpose of making their better acquaintance, for my long and continued absence from home made me a comparative stranger under my own rooftree.'

Compared with Buffalo Bill, I was a clinging husband, but I was in no frame of mind to appreciate the domicile of a man who was America's quintessential frontiersman, mythomaniac and absentee father. I still needed that squalid little hole.

That night I didn't erect the tent or bother to wash and feed myself. Feeling wretched, I laid my sleeping bag on the bare earth of a stubbled field and stared up at the emerging stars. My watch showed quarter to seven. In Nottingham, Sandy was sitting down to lunch on her own.

Neither of us had ever felt more in need of the other and less able to comfort one another. Whatever Sandy was going through had to be horrendous for her to break the first rule of a support unit. As an experienced traveller, she knew the last thing somebody out on a limb needs to be worrying about is anything other than being out on a limb. I knew she would now be feeling guilty for having burdened me, and that to beetle back home would only laden her with more guilt — my own. The situation was impossible. I convinced myself that I owed it to her mum to stay focused on the task at hand so at least one of us came out of this dreadful mess in one piece. From Hershey westwards, I was as driven by the thought of scooping Sandy into my arms as the Forty-Niners were of scooping up gold.

North Platte lay at the junction of the two rivers which flowed from the west to form the Platte River. 'The Forks' was where the Mormon Trail left the Oregon-California Trail and travelled north-west along the banks of the North Platte River. I rode south-west along the north bank of the South Platte River, following no particular historic line. The Oregon-California Trail still clung to the south bank but was obliterated by I-80, which had switched riversides soon after Gothenburg. Those rolling south-west crossed from one river to the other at one of two points. I chose to ride north at the earliest opportunity, from Ogallala, to join the North Platte at Ash Hollow. The second line across the wedge of land between the two tributaries began twenty-five miles west of Ogallala, arching north via the modern city of Sidney. By a quirk of mixed fortune, in a couple of days I was to find myself beside the western link nursing a buggered knee and separated from my bike by seventy miles.

A little over a hundred years ago, Ogallala was a trail head for cattle drives tramping north from Texas to meet the Burlington Railroad. It was Nebraska's Dodge City — a hell-raising town where cowpokes let off steam after months of herding their Longhorns and Herefords across the prairies. When I rode into Ogallala, the only hell being raised was by the Highways Department resurfacing Route 30 through the centre of town. Beyond the printed word, the exploitation of Ogallala's colourful past amounted to a block of stores on Front Street which could have been the left-over set from *High Plains Drifter*. The boardwalk was concrete but the street was covered in sand to appeal to tourists who strolled between the Cowboy Saloon, the Cowboy Café, the Cowboy Museum and, *de rigeur* in any cowboy town, the Cowboy Gift Shop. At seven that night, the tourist authority was staging a 'western shootout' on Front Street. I couldn't wait, and didn't.

I struggled up the climb out of Ogallala and the river valley, amazed that anybody could believe Nebraska was flat. Half way up the steep introduction to Route 26, a curious signpost prompted me to disappear into a grid of suburban bungalows in search of Boot Hill. Every cowboy town had its Boot Hill. The most famous was Dodge City's, largely because marshal Wyatt Earp and sheriff Batt Masterson ensured it was also the most populated and mythologised graveyard in the Wild West. Boot Hill, Ogallala, had only survived because it was a mound which developers of the surrounding subdivision had problems building on. For nearly seventy years it served as a dog walk and a great toboggan run in winter. In the 1950s, the authorities suddenly woke up to the possibility that the graves children dodged as they pelted downhill might have some historic value.

The knoll was a scrubby lump with a flight of concrete steps leading up to a couple of dozen wooden 'headstones' and a clumsy statue of a lonesome cowboy. An information board told me that this Boot Hill was the last resting place of only forty-five souls, though more undoubtedly died in the town before the graveyard was abandoned in 1885. The first to be buried were three hapless tracklayers for the Union Pacific Railroad. Among the round, pointed or flat-topped markers, a centenary capsule had been buried due to be opened in 2088, if the town council doesn't forget it's there.

While contemplating the grave of one J.C. Hill, I was collared by a couple of crinklies who looked like the sitters for Grant Wood's *American Gothic*. They were on their way home to Illinois after visiting the Montana battlegrounds of the Indian Wars, particularly the Little Bighorn.

"I couldn't believe the conditions in which the Indians live," Willis McCracken said, talking about the Crow Indian Reservation. "I've never seen poverty like it, not even on the television. It was appalling."

"They weren't very friendly," his wife muttered. "The Indian guides were really quite hostile."

"I'm not surprised," Willis turned on her. "I just can't believe we allow our own people to live like that."

"Maybe the folks on Capitol Hill don't see Native Americans as their own people," Mrs. McCracken sheepishly suggested.

Noticing the flag on my hat, Willis mentioned that they had visited Scotland a few years ago to trace his ancestors. His family tree had two trunks, Scottish and Polish, and he had charted both sets of roots back to the sixteenth century. I told him that if I had a dollar for every American who told me their genealogy..., and asked why he thought his countrymen were so keen to unravel their European roots yet so noticeably disinterested in their American ones.

"Yeh, I guess you're right. We've only recently gotten interested in American history ourselves, kinda as we got older." He thought for a moment. "You know, I just don't know about that one. Maybe we're like adopted kids — kinda curious about our real parents."

"What about your American history?" I pressed him. "A lot of people seem to know a bit about the Civil War, but I've met an awful lot more who haven't the foggiest who the Forty-Niners were."

Willis McCracken looked baffled. "I dunno. All I can tell

you is, after our trip up to Montana, I am ashamed of our history. All this stuff in the news about Kosovo and ethnic cleansing. Hell, Milosovic is a spit in the bucket compared to what we did to the Indians."

"It's hard to be proud of your country when it's has done such terrible things," his wife said. "I guess it's just easier to forget our past."

"Well, there isn't a nation on the planet that hasn't done something to be thoroughly ashamed of," I reassured her.

"Yeh, but this was supposed to be the New World!" the old boy said with a twang of bitterness.

Although the pioneer trails carved through a vast wilderness of grassland, those heading west crept forwards in a gentle stream of traffic which negated any possibility of feeling lost and alone in the landscape. As more folks gave up and turned for home, the flow of wagons and walkers began running both ways. Those who were returning provided those going forwards with intelligence of what lay ahead and a means of sending letters back east. Many returned by night, purely to avoid being continually pestered. In the middle of the Great American Desert, it was difficult to get away from people. Once the company had set up camp, argonauts frequently took themselves off for long walks and climbed high bluffs to gain a sense of the 'wild and undiscovered country' they were transnavigating.

It wasn't until I crested the northern escarpment and pedalled away from the South Platte valley that the true quality of the wide open prairie impressed itself upon me. The link over the high wedge between the two rivers was barely twenty-five miles across, but I had never felt so isolated and exposed on this journey. Farmsteads were as rare as trees, and I only noticed one tree. Unmarred miles of wheat and corn fields stretched to infinity — a great swathe of green brushed velvet folded over high benches and into deep rounded valleys. But for the Panther stroking a paw over the cloth, nothing moved — no birds,

212

no vehicles, no cattle.

The drop off the far side into the valley of the North Platte was prickly with flowering cacti and pine clumps and bedevilled with sharp outcrops of magnesium. This was the first really challenging descent the overlanders faced. It required locked wheels and winches to inch their wagons down the water scarred steps of Windlass Hill, an operation which ripped skin and muscle and crushed bones. At the foot of the bluff they followed the sandy bottom of Ash Creek on a smooth road down to the spring at Ash Hollow. What took them a full day, I plunged down in a matter of minutes, steaming past two miles of fence posts sporting hundreds of upturned cowboy boots.

The mouth of Ash Hollow opened wide to reveal a large graveyard of white headstones embedded up one side of the slope. In the glare of the evening sun, they looked like teeth. Whatever semblance of a community once stood here had long disappeared, but the size of the cemetery suggested Ash Hollow had been more than a camp site for passing wagon trains. Among the headstones was a roughly hewn stone preserved in a perspex box and engraved '1849' (the '4' cut back to front)

RACHEL E. PATTISON.
AGED 18
JUNE 19th. 49.

Since leaving Illinois, I had come across several pioneer graves at the roadside, but none from the year of the Forty-Niners and none quite so poignant.

I had been riding for seven days straight and needed rest. Tomorrow was the start of the Memorial Day Weekend, America's three day holiday paying homage to their war dead. I didn't know what to expect, but was certain it made sense to be around people rather than stuck out in the backwoods. While eager to spend a night at the spring where the Forty-Niners took time out to wash, hunt and mend their wagons, Ash Hollow was some distance from the sort of facilities I needed. Since Lincoln, my dicky knee had been giving me constant gyp and the lightning bolts of pain had become alarmingly frequent. At night it throbbed and flexed like crushed concrete. Each morning it started out as a pumpkin and had to be coaxed into bending. Ideally I needed a week out of the saddle but figured three days of good eating and tender loving care would set me on the road to rights. Across the river, the village of Lewellen was cute in a dilapidated sort of way, but the gas station was not going to provide a healing diet.

None of the villages over the following fifty-seven miles were any more appealing than cute in a dilapidated sort of way. There were only three, of which the first and largest, Oshkosh, had a world reputation for its goose hunts but didn't have a grocery store. In the second, Lisco, there was an adequate mini-mart but the population would have struggled to find a fourth hand for bridge. At Broadwater, I crumpled into a heap outside the scabby gas station and nursed my banging knee. The ride between villages had been tedious, gruelling and into a Force 8 gusting at 46 mph, if the radio was to be believed. There had been no shelter, no relief, and a stream of juggernauts charging down Route 26 had enveloped me in a continuous blizzard of grit. I felt as burnt out and blackened as Broadwater's charred bungalows. Overhead, a string of lighting for the forecourt batted around, clanking in the gale. Black polythene covering gaps in the ruin of a motel flicked and thwacked. The Panther howled through the broken panes of buildings crumbling into the earth, scraping up a dust storm with its paws. Considering the place was a gasp away from a ghost town, Broadwater was noisy as a head-banger's rave.

Beside the road out of town, a huge billboard informed me I was fifty miles from Alliance and something called Carhenge. I desperately wanted to visit this zany sculpture which reproduces Stonehenge in car bodies but, there and back, it was sixty miles out of my way, north of Bridgeport. I could count my blessings if I managed to make the fourteen miles to Bridgeport.

Two and a half hours later, my spirits were lifted by the sight of Jail and Courthouse Rocks. To the south of the river, the edge of the high prairies had whittled down to a gentle escarpment, leaving the two buttes sticking 120 metres out of the plains like stacs in an open sea. As with several isolated promontories I would pass between here and the mountains, the rocks were signposts and mile markers for the overlanders. Each had its own significance. At Courthouse Rock, the different overland routes taken by Mormons, pioneers and gold seekers came together again for the final push across the prairies. The Forty-Niners were 560 miles and a little over six weeks from the trail head at Independence. If it had only taken me two weeks, it felt like two years the way my body was giving out.

Chapter 18

Bridgeport's State Recreation Area comprised a sprinkling of chemical toilets, stand pipes and picnic tables set round a cluster of artificial lakes in a bulge of the flood plain just north of Jail and Courthouse Rocks. In a state which is the length of Britain away from anything approaching a sea, it attracts Cornhuskers like wildebeest to a savannah watering hole. I bathed my swollen knee in the soothing waters, shaded beneath Russian olives, and watched Nebraska dig in for the Memorial Day Weekend. Campers and caravanners staked their claim to the lakeside with barbies, sun shades and boat trailers ready for a lazy three days of honing the melanoma. It was Friday, May 28th, and one of America's rare bank holidays had begun.

On her way back from fetching water, a vivacious young lass with blond bouncy hair and a spring in her step called out, "Yow! How y'doin'? Whatcha doin'? Why don'tcha come over and have a drink with us?"

By their ruby faces, Lori Borchert, husband Mike and their two daughters had been at the lakes for several days entertaining boyfriends and family friend Rob. Parked beside their small and noticeably down-market encampment, a 1976 Ford Bronco caught my attention. Whoever owned it was either broke, retro or knew style when they saw it. I hoped for the latter. Mum and dad didn't look old enough to be parents of teenagers, though both were on their second marriage. Stephanie was Lori's by her first marriage and Lindsay was Mike's from his false start. Fortunately, when the parents came together, the girls gelled. There were step and illegitimate daughters in Mike's past, but the relationships were already complicated enough.

During Memorial Day Saturday, I dipped in and out of their company and the lake. They drove me into town to do a spot of shopping at a supermarket which actually sold fresh vegetables, and introduced me to the taste bud tremor of Terrioki beef jerky. Sympathetic to the severity of my limp, they encouraged me to spend a couple of days recuperating at their pad outside Sidney, forty miles to the south. I assembled my gear and joined them as they were being booked by a Ranger packing a side arm.

Rob and Lori had been drinking beer indiscreetly from cans, a finable offence in a State Park. Had the cans been in brown paper bags, there would have been no problem. The Ranger was lenient, issuing only one ticket to cover the two misdemeanours. The on-the-spot fine was $123, but the problem was the publicity. In Nebraska they operate a name-and-shame system, publishing a list of offenders in the local rag. Rob was a village school teacher and Lori worked for the City of Sidney. The impending smear was bad news, though likely to lead to little more than malicious tittle-tattle. But Lori was annoyed. The Borcherts were a powerful dynasty in Cheyenne County, though Mike and Lori had disassociated themselves from the family and tried their best to maintain a low profile. They even pronounced their last name differently.

Mike Borchert looked like a young Martin Sheen, except he walked with a gamy leg and had a limp right arm. One of six brothers, he was the black sheep of the family, whose empire encompassed oil, real estate, construction and golf courses. The pressure to tow the line and join the corporate clan was intense. Mike believed it caused one of his brothers to commit suicide, though father and despot R.V. Borchert refused to accept the inquiry's verdict. Mike left home early to work in a lumber yard, desperate to gain his independence and retain his sanity, but he married a woman who received R.V.'s seal of approval. Eventually coaxed into the family oil business by his wife, he earned big bucks that went straight up his nose or into the till of a liquor store. Mike drank himself into a seizure whilst still in his twenties. Returning from the dead a cripple, he blamed no one but himself.

217

"I was young, dumb and full of come, man. I gotta take a whole heap of pills now and there's days I feel like the fuckin' livin' dead, but I'm real glad to be alive. Hell, I'm a walking time bomb. Bang my head and I'm one dead dude."

After his divorce from the "wicked witch," Mike entered Alcoholics Anonymous's twelve step programme. Lori was somebody he vaguely knew from his youth who, as far as the dynasty were concerned, came from the wrong side of the tracks. She was detoxing from a drinking habit picked up from a barn-storming youth and hardened during a bitter marriage. They were made for each other. Two years later, they were dried out and married. Lori was now head of accounts for city utilities, and Mike worked as little as possible, keeping his hand in with a few of his own oil wells. "Nothing big," he said, "About thirty barrels a day on reserves of three million." He employed one hand, Rob's father.

I stashed my gear at Starvation Acres, a ramshackle joint at the entrance to the State Park, offering showers, bait, tackle and anything else the owner could make a buck or two out of campers from, and jumped into Lori's Cherokee Jeep. Mike and the others brought up the rear in the cute little Bronco. Twenty-eight miles due south of Bridgeport, as we entered the village of Gurley, Lori asked if I would mind our calling in at the graveyard. Paul Ernest, the young son of a friend of hers, had recently been interred and she wanted to see the headstone.

"It was a real tragedy," Lori told me. "He was sat on the back of his grandpa's ATV when it hit a dip and turned over, killing little Paul. Riding on the back of the four-wheeler was one of his favourite things. His death has destroyed the family. You can't imagine how his grandpa feels. My friend is now separated from her husband and doesn't look like getting over Paul's death."

We hung a left at the cross roads and drove past the school where their friend Rob taught. Two blocks later we were back in the countryside bouncing up a dirt road to a quiet resting place surrounded by corn fields. Paul's gravestone was the only one decorated with flowers. He was five years old when he died. On the plinth stood a toy tractor. Set in the stone was an oval photograph of the youngster wearing a cowboy outfit and a proud smile. It was genuinely moving and I could see the tears welling up in Lori. I gave her space, and thought about the cruelty of one so loved and loving being taken before his life had really begun. Beyond the headstone, the sea of corn stretched to the horizon and rippled in the breeze. It could have been a graveyard in the Lincolnshire Wolds, where we buried my mother-in-law. At sixty-nine and with still much to give, Pauline had likewise been taken before her life had justly run its course. A day early, Lori and I commemorated our own Memorial Day.

The ugly ducklings of the Borchert dynasty lived six miles east of Sidney and a couple less from where the western leg of the Oregon-California Trail turned north to cross the benches to Jail and Courthouse Rocks. Mike and Lori had bought the town of Colton, much to the chagrin of R.V. Borchert. The town was a dead end and no bigger than a farmstead, but it used to be a throbbing little place with a store, garages, a couple of houses and a grain elevator beside the main line to Ogallala. Mike's father owned land on three sides of it originally belonging to grandpa Kruger, R.V.'s father-in-law. The Kruger farm house was a hundred yards back down the track from Mike and Lori's place and was now a home for children at risk.

"In a rash moment, R.V. donated the building to the City of Sidney," Lori told us as Rob and myself were shown round the grounds. "But for his uncharacteristic generosity, these kids would've been shipped out to Gering, over seventy miles from home."

Despite cars in the driveway, the house looked empty. Whatever activities staff engaged the youngsters in during the national holiday were silent and didn't extend beyond the front porch. The grounds had fallen into terrible disrepair and felt damp and creepy. Weeds and rotting branches suffocated what was once a smart lawn, and round the back of the house, Kruger's Lake was now a muddy pond choked with algae and fallen trees.

"In the old days the waters were deep and used to freeze solid in winter," Lori expounded from her perch on a three-bar fence. "Grandpa K. would chop the ice into blocks, haul 'em out using horses, and slide 'em down these channels to the ice house over there near the tracks. The railroad was his biggest customer."

The channels and remains of the underground limestone cooler were still in place. It was an impressive production line which guaranteed the rail company supplies of straw wrapped ice from late winter right through to September. To one side of the lake there were further indications of the sort of imaginative enterprises prairie farmers dreamed up to survive the Depression. A long low barn sagging under the weight of damp timber looked like it had grown out of mangrove swamps. During the prohibition era it was a speakeasy, catering for customers who drove out from Sidney to take refuge from a crazy law. The Kruger family served home brewed rotgut and bootleg whiskey, and laid on slot machines, gaming tables and touring dance bands. Mike and Lori had a soft spot for the maverick from Mike's mother's side of the family, and had named their Labrador after him.

My knee had frozen solid. When Mike and I hobbled around the spread together, we were mirror images. While he wheeled out the tractor-mower and set to work on a lawn the size of a paddock, Lori drove me up to visit Cabela's, a retail legend in its own profit margin. Perched on a hill between Sidney and Interstate 80, the store claims to be the 'World's Foremost Outdoor Outfitters' and is Nebraska's most popular destination. No bigger than an average Ikea, the car parking occupied a plot equivalent to a small industrial estate. There were separate bays for truckers travelling I-80 with orders to pick up gear for folks from all over the States. The goods were no different from any other well stocked outdoors store but, where tents would occupy a large proportion of a European shop floor, it was the means to kill which dominated one full side of Cabela's. I had never seen so many guns, rifles, shotguns, flintlocks, duelling pistols, sabres, knives, cross-bows and bows — none of them reproductions simply for show. Watching a boy of fifteen getting the feel for a rifle (and I don't mean an air rifle), it was freaky to realise the kid was a mind warp and bullet away from his fifteen minutes of fame.

The ease with which the American male destroys life was emphasised by the other aspect of the store — the 'Free Wildlife Display' or, more accurately, the 'Bagged Wildlife Display'. The moment I entered I was confronted by the stuffed carcasses of majestically poised wapiti. Every pillar was adorned with the head of a dead stag. Running the full length of both sides of the store were hundreds of trophies of beheaded quadrupeds, in some places two rows deep. Flocks of stuffed geese were strung from the ceiling. Amongst the clothing and camping equipment, separate displays featured elephants, tigers, wildebeests and polar bears. I was in taxidermy heaven and the worst was yet to come.

Dominating the store was a mountain setting which reached to the roof and stretched forwards from a skyscape for maybe twenty yards. Among the species featured were moufflons, wolves, moose, pronghorns, grizzlies, big horns and on and on. But it had to be said, it was a magnificent display. These weren't rigid corpses. There was animation in every creature. The pronghorns galloped, the mountain goats jumped and the kid licked the mule deer mother. Some bastard had killed Bambi!

According to Lori, every animal was a trophy of hunting expeditions undertaken by Dick and Jim Cabela, owners and founders of the firm. Weeks later, mouths were to drop when I told people I had shopped at Cabela's, but I had seen enough.

Against the run of predictions, the weather was miserable on Memorial Day Monday, the day I was supposed to set off again. A buddy of Mike's dropped by, and the three of us disappeared into his den to play. A sailfish Mike had caught off the coast of Mexico graced one wall, though apparently only the sword was real. It was his one and only trip outside of the country, and he hated it. He didn't know the language and thought the locals were talking about him behind his back. While the friends smacked pool balls around, I practised on a shuttle board and lapped up the loud driving Texas blues. Through the shop windows, rain dribbling down the grain elevator sparkled in a thin shaft of sunlight which projected reflections across dark puddles in the yard. The rail lines were fluorescent lighting tubes, stretching away to someplace where they fused with the glistening spider's trail of telegraph lines. I watched the Panther race across the corn, delighted I couldn't feel or hear it. Over the sound system, Stevie Ray Vaughan ripped through *The House is Rockin'* and a Union Pacific freighter rumbled by with a blast of the horn. The moment I first clocked the Bronco back at Bridgeport, I knew Mike had class. I was in a goddamn Wim Wenders movie!

With the weather showing no signs of improving, Mike decided to run Lori and myself up to see Carhenge, a round trip of nearly 150 miles. He was amazed anybody from Europe had heard of the sculpture, let alone could hobble for joy at the prospect of visiting it. He ignored my polite protestations that it was surely too far. By their standards it was just down the road. They had difficulty getting their heads round the idea that, from my doorstep in England, they would pass a handful of cities, a basket full of towns and maybe thirty villages in the equivalent distance to Alliance. We passed through two small towns and four hamlets.

Locked on cruise control, the black SUV purred over the empty prairie like a yacht riding a swell. From Sidney up to Bridgeport we followed the western link of the Oregon-

California Trail, across draws and benches which had barely altered since. On the skyline, artificial humps similar to one I had seen on my way into Hastings located bunkers for nuclear weapons. A couple of pump jacks nodded like restless mules in the distance and a herd of buffalo were laying down. Another band of rain was moving in.

As we turned into the car park at Carhenge, the shadow from a mat of clouds slid across the prairie and the sun broke through, spotlighting a grey pile of scrap Chevys, Caddys and Plymouths. Close enough for pop art to the size of the real sarsen blocks, the 'carstones' were impressive. Unlike the English original, we could wander around the pillars and beneath the lintels. In the stark environment of the windswept sand hills, Carhenge was imbued with a serenity Stonehenge hasn't possessed since it was pinned between two main roads and fenced off from the public. Here the steel carcasses of the modern conveyances which zip either side of the sacred site had become the henge itself. It was a wonderful homage to motormania but it's appearance had offended the Nebraska Department of Roads and a number of Christian fundamentalist groups, who sincerely believed it was a pagan temple. Fortunately the Friends of Carhenge successfully combated calls for it to be torn down and the installation is now almost as big a tourist attraction as Cabela's.

Built by geologist Jim Reinders and family in 1982 as a memorial to his father, Carhenge was another example of the unexpected streak of artiness I discovered running through Nebraska. In no other state had I seen such an abundance of murals, sculptures and screwball folk art like the garden in Lisco packed with mobiles made from horseshoes, cartwheels and cowboy boots. The first paper I picked up in Nebraska was a free sheet stuffed with arts listings. Then there were the lavishly decorated towns like Friend and the hundreds of boots on the Ash Hollow fence posts. Maybe it was the boundless horizons and limitless skies which inspired creativity. Rodin's these works might not have been, but J.M.W. Turner would have had a field day with Nebraska's skyscapes and subtleties of light.

On our way back from the steel henge, Mike pulled over on the edge of the high benches for me to survey the western aspect of the North Platte Valley. The pink and orange wash of the evening sky was swilling into a bowl with a ragged lip. It was the first angular profile I had seen on an horizon since entering America. Like the Forty-Niners before me, I was convinced the Rockies were barely a day away, and for a change looked forward to returning to the road. Mountains meant shelter from Ga-oh the Panther.

The Wildcat Hills emerged with a stern face from the high prairies south of the river and veered west to run parallel with Route 26. The most striking of buttes stood bolt upright in the valley floor. Originally called Elk Penis by the natives, the stack stood 110 metres above the plain during the Gold Rush years. Erosion has since whittled it down but the tip still reaches over 1,200 metres above sea level. Looking like a Victorian smoke stack thrusting out of an enormous mound of ash, Chimney Rock was another milestone for the migratory trails, and probably the most misleading. Sighting the Brule clay steeple, the argonauts became excited. They believed it marked the end of their haul across the Great American Desert. Whips cracked and wagons accelerated as the teams playfully raced each other to the landmark. Considering the top speed of a team of oxen is a brisk walk, they didn't reach the foot of the rock until three days after clapping eyes on it. Once camp was established, many climbed the chimney and carved their monickers in the top rim. In no fit state to follow their example, I defaulted to the Visitor Center.

After three days of molly-coddling by the Bercherts, my body felt much improved. Riding west into another infernal headwind, the knee flexed without pain or the sound of crunching but was still stiff, hopefully more from lack of use than continuing complications. Taking every opportunity not to use it, I sat through the AV show at the

Chimney Rock Visitor Center twice. The packaging of America's heritage was taking on a familiar format — first the light entertainment then the hard work of the exhibition. If there was ever a question about low levels of literacy in this country, park authorities were in no doubt Americans would happily read galleys of text amounting to the word count of *Moby Dick*. To their credit, all the historical sites I had visited to date were remarkably free from crass commercialisation. I expected at least a Fort Kearny McDonalds or a Pizza Pony Express Hut. You couldn't get a cup of coffee at any of them for love or money.

And now historical sites were appearing more frequently than pit stops. Twenty-four miles further on, beyond the town of Gering, a finger of the Wildcats sidled up to meet me at Me-a-pa-te — Sioux for 'hill that is hard to get around'. Now called Scotts Bluff, road and trail climbed through a broad cleft between Sentinel and Cap Rocks. The sun was low in the west, playing hide and seek behind curtains of clouds. Leaping out to animate the dazzling yellows and greens of the sandstone rock face, it threw shock waves of amber across the tops of the corn. To the north, Cap Rock was a 240 metre slice through prehistoric highlands and a godsend to geologists. Its sedimentary layers were a unique chest of fossil trays chronicling the last fourteen million years. For the overlanders, it was simply another promontory they could climb, peer into the future and carve their initials in. For the modern day pilgrim, Scotts Bluff National Monument was another tramp through a Visitor Center I could do without.

I climbed the pass in the company of a middle-aged woman riding a pinto, pausing on the grade to check out the wheel ruts of the estimated 350,000 migrants who eventually trudged this way. To Americans, the wheel ruts of the pioneers are what the ridgeways of the Neolithics are to the British — the first marks in the landscape left by the first civilisation. They have survived the ages better than almost everything which might remind Americans of earlier indigenous civilisations, and are now treated with great respect. Horses and vehicles are not allowed on what remains of the Oregon-California Trail, but the ruts looked very rounded, as if smoothed by tyres.

"I used to ride along that track all the time," the woman on horseback told me. "The farmers really carved it up. It ain't what its made out to be, y'know."

I had already ascended several thousand metres since leaving the Missouri and the incline up to the pass was nothing exceptional, except that I could only see blue beyond it. As we approached the brow, the overlanders and I expected the Rockies to rear up before us. Reaching it, I paused. To the south, the edge of the Wildcat Hills continued westwards, now a striking Black Forest gateau of volcanic ash layered with seams of rich yellow sandstone. Crumbs of ponderosa pines were piled at its base and sprinkled across the flood plain, a cake board spread in an arc round to the north. The road bounded down to the floor and kinked right across a flat checker board of little farmsteads and tight fields. I could feel the disappointment welling up from my toes. In the distance were more hills and more plains, but the Rockies were nowhere to be seen. The thought of spending more days grinding through the Great American Desert did not fill me with joy.

I crossed the state line. A sign assured me Wyoming was 'Like Nowhere on Earth'. Wyoming looked exactly like Nebraska except for the herd of ostriches, llamas and camels which raced me down a field, . The bike still went Ba-Dum Ba-Dum and the landscape kept its quiet roll, but there were subtle differences. Stetsons replaced baseball caps and guys walked with a John Wayne lope, a condition brought on by the satellite dish buckling their belt.

Another day, another town, another grain elevator later, the low grey mass obliterating the horizon shed its load, lifted and revealed a mountain beneath the cloud base. It was an archetypal pyramid peak dominating a long sawtooth range. My heart leapt, but they were the Laramies not the Rockies. After twenty days and twenty nights in the prairies, I was grateful for anything which got in the way of the wind, but it took me two full days to reach their foothills. I was moving into a part of America where the discrepancy between perceived and actual distances played evil tricks on tired travellers.

Aside from tracking the Great Platte River Road, I was also linking the line of forts established to protect migrants. Conjuring CinemaScope images of Jimmy Stewart out to catch gun-runners, none was better known than Fort Laramie, though the town I rode into was a thousand miles from where the movie was set. In the log cabin which served as the tourist information centre, I tried squeezing sense out of a biddy who reminded me of Old Mother Reilly. Twenty or so miles ahead, Route 26 stopped dead at the toes of the Laramies and a T-junction with Interstate 25. There I would turn north and head for Casper, paralleling the course of the North Platte River. According to my map, the only artery between the junction and Casper was I-25 and off-limits to cyclists. I was trying to ascertain if there was a county road which the interstate had replaced but not smothered.

"Have you a map?" Old Mother Reilly asked. "This is a good map."

She handed me the same one I was holding.

"Casper, you're going to Casper, right? How about this leaflet? Oh, and here's one on the Medicine Bow National Forest. That'll be useful. Douglas," she pulled out another leaflet, "You'll be going through Douglas. Ah, yes, there's a really good map in the Cheyenne leaflet and what about a 'Highway Guide to the Mormon Pioneer Trail'?"

Cheyenne was in exactly the opposite direction to Casper and the map of the Mormon Trail was 152 years out of date, but I could have walked into a recycling plant and made a tidy profit from the leaflets she gave me.

Down the main road came a police car. "Ooh, ooh, he'll know!" The old dear was stood on tip toe at the entrance to the log cabin, pointing at the cop car and flicking her hand up and down. "Ask the nice policeman."

The officer got out, listened attentively and rubbed the side of his face.

"I think you gotta ride up the interstate," he said. "Y'asked James?"

"Ooh, James'll know for sure," Mother Reilly gushed. "He's English, you know."

James ran the Fort Laramie Trading Post, a log cabin full of souvenirs and trinkets and walls decked in 'ethnic' posters, paintings and blankets. James Stewart didn't get a look in, but James the Englishman was dressed for the role of fort sutler and was about as English as Dick van Dyke. He hadn't a clue what happened to the old two-lane blacktop running north. I left him arguing with the cop over a recent bet. As I made to ride away, Old Mother Reilly came trotting up and breathlessly said, "Here's a couple of leaflets for Fort Laramie. You'll be going there, of course."

I thought I was there, but this was the village of Fort Laramie, consisting of '250 good people and 6 sore heads' according to the town sign. As with Fort Kearny, the original settlement was relocated to the north bank of the river when the railroad came through. The Fort Laramie Mother Reilly meant was the heritage site on the other side of the tracks and a couple of miles down Jim Bridger Avenue. In 1849 the fort was an American Fur Company trading post. The military garrison was several years off, by when its role had become more about 'dealing' with the Plains Indians than supporting the wagon trains.

Two years after the Gold Rush started, around 10,000 natives from eleven different tribes assembled in all their finery near Horse Creek, a few miles back down the North Platte. It was the largest gathering of aborigines in the history of the West, organised by the Department of Indian Affairs to settle their growing hostility to white immigration. The Horse Creek Treaty mapped out 'colonies' where the Plains Indians would be safe from encroachment and might be coaxed into becoming good Christian farmers. Jim Bridger was the key negotiator for the government. Jim, a famous trapper, guide and scout, probably knew more about the geography and peoples of the Wild West than any whiteman alive. He was as close as the frontier got to somebody who had 'gone native' and knew efforts to pen in nomadic tribes were doomed before the ink had dried. But the United States had a different agenda.

The treaty lasted two years before a calf from a Mormon wagon train strayed into a Brulé Lacota encampment and was shot. Chief Conquering Bear apologised and offered to pay for the animal. Brushing him aside, a platoon of twenty-five U.S. soldiers marched into the camp to arrest the culprit. After a forty-five minute stand-off, the troops cracked and opened fire. Only one survived long enough to crawl back to Fort Laramie and raise the alarm. The revenge exacted was devastating and marked the beginning of the Indian Wars, the 'final solution' the army had been itching to get stuck into for years. Of over 200 treaties federal representatives made with the Native Americans, not one was honoured.

I crossed the old army bridge over the North Platte, crested the hill before Fort Laramie and was immediately drenched by a wet wind. In the heavens, a black bubbling cauldron was suspended over a firey dance of yellows and oranges. Thunder rumbled like it was ready to belch. Beyond the entrance kiosk, the famous fort looked more Legoland than Western frontier. Weighed against what was coming at me from the south-west, I took a rain check on military history, turned and pedalled like a man on a mission. Whether I could cover the thirteen miles to the next large town before the heavens rent asunder was debatable but I needed a bar. The Forty-Niners broke out the rum to celebrate completing the prairie crossing. With the Laramies in sight, I was prepared to put a lot of effort into maintaining that fine tradition.

A couple of miles before Guernsey, I noticed aircraft circling over the town practising 'circuits and bumps'. They were military aircraft — C-130 Hercules troop carriers. Beyond the tanks, trucks, half-tracks and helicopters lined up in the National Guard compound on the edge of town, Crazy Tony's looked like a bar the military would frequent. Decorated with a montage of cattle brands, the decor inside turned out to be strictly cowboy and the two dudes holding up the bar aimed their sights squarely at game rather than enemies of the state. I gulped down a couple of swift Buds, the second complementary of Crazy Tony with the comment, "Anybody insane enough to do what you're doing deserves to find gold in California." He pushed a tray of breaded elk in front of me, killed on Memorial Sunday.

On my fourth can, one of the bar-flies thought it wise to clue me in on the local police situation. "We got more cop cars in this town than road space," the one with the bushy white sideburns and frayed Stetson told me. "They sit outside, waiting for the bar to empty at night, and reel in anybody who happens to trip over the doorstep. They catch you drunk on a bicycle, you'll be parting with 700 bucks before you leave this fucking town."

A couple of hours later, I slew out of Crazy Tony's, crashed into the door frame, and tripped over the doorstep. Low and behold, there was a cop car in the car park. Wheeling my bike in a broad arc up to the driver's side, I again inquired about the logistics and legality of riding up I-25 to Casper.

"You're not going to cycle it tonight? Not in your condition?" I wasn't sure if he was asking or telling.

"Nope!" I blurted out, "I'm gonna walk it, like a good boy."

Singing *Home on the Range* to an empty main street, I pushed as far as the bridge at the western edge of Guernsey. There I mounted, pressed down on the left pedal, slipped and found myself slumped at an angle against the handrail staring down at the dark waters of the North Platte. I reminded myself of Lee Marvin and his cross-legged horse leaning against the wall in *Cat Ballou*. I chuckled and promptly threw up.

Chapter 19

"If you think Nebraska's bad," Mike Borchert had warned me, "wait until the winds in Wyoming hit you."

My first morning in the Cowboy State I was awakened by the downwind flap of the tent whipping and cracking like a demented spinnaker. In the process of crawling out, a sudden gust hurled me to the ground. From my snake's eye view, the best course of action was to slither back into my sleeping bag and try vacating again in half an hour when the gale had blown over. It was too early for the wind to be this strong. Generally the Panther didn't peak until around mid-day. It had to be an aberration.

Inevitably the animal grew stronger and, to my utter dismay, came billowing straight in from the west. That morning my route lay due west, then north for a hundred miles up to Casper, a town reputed to have the highest suicide rate per capita in the country. Nobody knew exactly why so many residents topped themselves, but psychiatrists suspected amenomania — literally, wind madness. It was small consolation that I only had eight miles to ride before veering right, out of the full frontal and into the shelter of the Laramies.

A voice drowned the drum beat of flapping canvas. "How about breakfast?"

Warily I peered out to find John Turk stood tall, hands on hips, braced against the gale. From high-heeled boots through stay-press jeans, a huge belt buckle, check shirt with buttoned down collar, and a broad rimmed Stetson, he was every inch the Marlborough man without the cancer stick.

"How do you guys keep your hats on in this wind?" I asked, staggering to my feet.

"What wind? This is a breeze." His shirt was stretched over his chest like cling film over a dead chicken. At the back it ballooned full of air. For an American in his sixties he was in good shape.

I had insinuated myself on John and Susie Turk the previous evening because theirs was the only ranch of the three I passed beyond Guernsey which was less than a mile from the road. A painfully slow climb winding through a shallow limestone gorge had sobered me up sufficiently to fend off their Australian sheepdog and string together my patter. The Rafter-T3 Ranch amounted to a large galvanised barn, a small brick house in the process of renovation, and acres of open range without another building in view. While building their dream home, John and Susie lived in a small caravan parked in the barn.

John was born and raised on a dairy farm in New York State, but always fantasised about becoming a cowboy. He had been through at least one previous marriage he was prepared to tell me about, and a succession of jobs in construction and long-distance trucking. His last job was more localised deliveries for a haulage company which went bankrupt while still in profit. Without any notice, the owner simply shut up shop and walked away, screwing workers out of two weeks wages and their redundancy package. Meanwhile, John and Susie hadn't a cent coming in. Until a week before I arrived, it hadn't entered John's head to apply for welfare. He was of that generation, but desperation finally overcame pride.

Susie was a "mighty handsome woman," as they say in the Westerns, and the picture of a cowgirl. She had curly blonde locks, an attractively lined face and a figure made for blue jeans. Previously married to the Kodak genius who developed the short-lived circular film, she had spent much of her life as a company appendage, biting her tongue and wearing frocks, which she hated. Courtesy of Mr. Kodak, she had seen some of the world, but her heart's desire was to rear ponies in the West. Both divorcees with adult families, she had bumped into John, fallen in love and was married by the words of an Apache ceremony. They had only been wed a year, and recited the blessing for me with a sparkle in their eyes.

Now you will feel no rain,
for each of you will be shelter to the other
Now you will feel no cold,
for each of you will be warmth for the other
Now there is no more loneliness,
now you are two persons, but there is only one life
before you
Go now to your dwelling place to enter into the days
of your life together
And may your days be good and long upon the earth.

What they were doing together was raising horses, particularly pintos or 'paints' and American Quarters, named after their domination of quarter mile races through frontier towns. Their ranch was 160 acres of beautiful rolling Wyoming and they leased twice that much off neighbouring ranchers, the Frederick brothers. What would eventually become their home was the brick house erected by the first homesteaders, George and Rebecca Ethridge, back in the early 1900s. "Our first plan was to tear it down and build anew," John explained, but he had since become a local history buff. He was chuffed that the Oregon Trail ran through their property and was modelling their house on the Lieutenant Colonel's Quarters at Fort Laramie, with a porch for rocking chairs where they could while away an evening gazing at their open range. Every morning they woke up and walked out of the barn, John and Susie probably had to pinch themselves.

At the Trails Inn, Guernsey, the "liars' club" took up two tables. At one, a couple of civilians sat chatting with the Chief of Police, whom I dimly recognised from the previous drunken evening. He winked when we were introduced. At the other, John Turk and I joined the Frederick brothers, Doug and Charles — a couple of weather-beaten fortysomethings who chewed tooth picks and slouched in their seats as if they owned the place. They might well have. As Mike Borchert would have put it, their family tree grew straight up.

In 1879, great grandpa Fredereck took early retirement from the U.S. Army at Fort Laramie, rode west, forded the North Platte and staked a claim to a whole lot of prime pasture around Warm Springs, across the river from Guernsey. He built a ranch house in the lee of the limestone gorge running up to the Rafter T-3, raised a family and entertained local Indians at his table to keep the peace. Since then, five generations of Frederecks had worked pretty much the same acreage, raising ever decreasing herds of cattle and horses. They were the second most powerful family in the valley. The most powerful were the Guernseys, who still farmed east of the town they built. Historically they had strong mining and railroad interests which somewhere down the line involved them in shotgun politics and the abduction of a group of U.S. senators. But it was the Fredereck family the incomer John Turk had most to fear from.

The previous tenant of the land John and Susie leased had lasted but a short time before the brothers cold shouldered him out. The newcomer had made efforts to prevent his herd straying onto the Frederecks ranch by stringing electric fencing round the entire perimeter, but a few loose steers blew his chances of currying favour with the brothers. Of course, in a town of battered pick-ups and sweat stained Stetsons, it didn't help that the tenant was into motor bikes and tasselled leathers. Worse still, he showed no interest whatsoever in joining the liars' club. Living out his childhood dream of becoming a rancher, John Turk was eager to fit into Guernsey like a Colt .45 in a hand tooled holster, and I think my presence at the breakfast table was a feather in his Stetson.

The conversation turned to hard times down on the ranch, and both tables expressed bitter frustration with "damn tree-huggers." In Wyoming, tree-huggers meant liberal, city based conservationists like the Sierra Club, rather than radical eco-warriors. A popular car sticker summed up local feelings — 'Hungry and Out of Work? Eat an Environmentalist'.

"If they had their way, we'd be baby-sitting open range and it'd be empty as a new spittoon," Doug said.

"And they're getting their way," the woman on the other table waded in. "Buying up small ranches and merging them…"

"Ain't that the truth," Charles said. "Ted Turner…"

As if the Devil himself had been invoked, mention of the media mogul's name solicited a Mexican wave of nodding heads and gnashing teeth around the two tables. Apparently Ted had been buying up ranches in Montana, tearing down fences and introducing large herds of buffalo. His sudden interest in conservation was laid firmly at the feet of his then wife, Jane Fonda, and his motive was encapsulated by Charles as, "Well, it's somewhere to invite your rich buddies to go a-hunting." What any of this had to do with struggling Wyoming ranchers went over my head, unless there was a tie-in with the conversation I had the evening before at Crazy Tony's bar.

According to Al, the bloke who warned me about the Guernsey cops, property prices in Wyoming were going through the roof. From as far away as San Diego, city types were buying up ranches for weekend retreats and allowing the land to go wild. "They know zip about ranching. And if'n they ain't second homes, we got speculators buying cheap and sitting on what they figure's gonna be a golden egg," Al said.

Caucasian Californians were relocating eastwards in droves, apparently fleeing the intractable tensions and gang violence of mixed-race suburbs such as in Orange County. They brought with them their urban ways, including an incurable romance for the Wild West. They wanted it wild, and as rapidly as they unpacked the U-Haul trailer, undesirable critters were moving in on their empty pastures. Both migrations were proving a major headache for natives of Wyoming, particular for youngsters like Al's son trying to afford a first-time home, and for ranchers like the Frederick brothers trying to keep out predators.

Back at the Rafter-T3, Susie greeted us and asked if I'd had any trouble during the night with the mountain lion she saw prowling round the barn. I wasn't sure if she was being funny. One particular big cat was certainly proving to be a scourge. For a little under a month, I had been locking horns with the west wind. From bitter experience, I had come to recognise three forces — windy, 'owlie' (what Lincolnshire folk call a howling gale), and winded. Winded was when I stopped and got off my bike before the Panther started pushing us backwards. Light, moderate or fresh breezes did not feature. Winds west of the Mississippi were either half on, full on or knock out. Battling to pull away from the Rafter-T3, I was one blow away from being down for the count.

Anywhere else, I would have taken refuge and waited for the Panther to back off, but the terrain had changed again. While I continued west towards the Laramies, the North Platte had curved north at Guernsey, taking with it the deep valley which provided a degree of shelter. Beyond the barbed wire, Wyoming was now wide open and empty, without a shrub taller than a foot above bluegrass height. I crouched behind some kind of utility box and watched the meadows being whipped to a frenzy. In the vain hope it would provide protection, a herd of Angus clustered in the lee of a thin concrete pylon and looked to me for sympathy. In an hour I had covered less than five miles, my knee was registering complaints, and I was straining to turn a cog geared for riding up the north face of Big Ben. I was knocking myself out to measure progress across America in rotations not miles. Plan A was to drag my sorry butt into Dwyer, the next town on the map, hole up in a gas station, store or café, and work out Plan B.

The Stars and Stripes flying over Dwyer Cemetery strained manically at the pole. Between the cemetery and a sign which said 'Dwyer — El: 4835' coffin bearers have walked faster than I pedalled. After the sign, on the left of the rise into town, there was a shabby bungalow, a rambling barn, a derelict pig sty and two horses, one a pinto. There was nothing on the right bar infinity. Over the hill, I expected the town to be no bigger than twenty or so buildings, but I had come across smaller places with fabulous ice cream parlours. I heaved past the barn, bracing myself for the back-draft from a juggernaut which overtook and kicked grit into my eyes. Turning to shield them, I noticed a small sign on the opposite side of the road between myself and the barn. It said, 'Dwyer — El:4835'. Between the two signs, the town of Dwyer consisted of a shabby bungalow, a rambling barn, a derelict pig sty and two horses, one a pinto. There was no ice cream parlour and no Plan B.

I dropped my head, half-heartedly sobbed, and ground forward. There was nothing else to do and nowhere to hide. It took me another hour to cover the three miles to the interstate. Turning north out of the headwind, I felt my pace quicken. For a short stretch of I-25, the Laramie Mountains protected me and I dared to hope. But the Panther was still out there, changing tactics, mustering its strength to hit me with a volley of broadsides. When they landed, I was flicked off the road like a tiddlywink and came to rest in a heap at the bottom of the highway embankment.

Until you have spent all day, every day, in varying degrees of gale force, it is difficult to appreciate the frustrations it brings to the simplest tasks. As with the overlanders, lunch was my big meal of the day and the only time I cooked, but feeding myself had become a struggle requiring hands, elbows, knees, feet and teeth to trap everything the Panther tried to whip away. At a Rest Area outside Lingle, I watched full cans of chilli slide across the table top and land in a heap with my cooker, pans and the heavy pannier bags cunningly erected as a windbreak. West of the Kansas River it was only feasible to cook in the evening, after the wind died down, by when I was too knackered to bother.

And it is impossible to appreciate how damaging this dry version of Chinese water torture can be to your mental health. As much as the noise of it boxing my ears, tugging at the hood I invariably had to wear, it was the continual flaying of exposed flesh which drove me crazy. From left cheek bone round to right, for twenty-four hours a day, the frontal arc of my face smarted as if a sparring partner had been jabbing punches at the speed of a cartoon pugilist. Now I was on the ropes, buckling under the pounding. There was no getting away from the Panther. In Wyoming the evil bastard charged straight through granite.

But a new mental torture lay before me. With cruise control set at seventy, good sounds emanating from the stereo and a flask of freshly squeezed orange juice in the cup holder, I-25 would have been a pleasure to drive. Traffic was light and the interminable grey ribbon swept through a soft-fingered landscape of juniper ridges and lush draws. At the top of long smooth gradients you could see into the next state, and the road itself was a python to the grass snake of an English motorway. Developers could have built a subdivision on the reservation separating the two carriageways. The interstate was a big highway carving through a big country with big vistas. In other words, for a little cyclist busting a gut to hit five miles an hour, I-25 was a bastard. I had to get off it and find a cosy country road.

A trickle of tarmac emerged from beneath the interstate and tracked it. Nothing travelled on the road and there were no indications where it led but, if I could get down to it, I figured I could always climb back onto the expressway should the ribbon wander off in the wrong direction. Unfortunately I was penned in by barbed wire which would have impressed a concentration camp commandant. Fencing gangs had managed to run the wire into places only a desperate cyclist would attempt squeezing through.

They ran it across bogs, up rock cliffs, tucked it into cattle tunnels and wrapped it in bundles between river banks. All of it was perfectly tensioned without a sag or loose strand. I was stitched in and up, with nowhere to go but the full ninety along Hell's own highway.

Things might have been bearable had there been a few wayside distractions but, between where I entered the interstate and the suicide capital of America a hundred miles north, the highway brushed only two villages and one town. I felt despair tangible as a toothache. Six soul destroying hours later, I limped into the Orin Rest Area. I had hit the wall beyond the wall and was blundering around in a daze. I craved caffeine but there were no drink machines. I staggered into the men's room and threw water on my face. In the mirror dripped a picture of abject misery. I paced back and forth, holding my head in my hands, cursing and ranting that I'd been sentenced to life on the long grey line. People threw me worried glances. I flopped to the sidewalk and quivered like I was still being pummelled. I had seen the elephant and it had stamped all over me.

In the nineteenth century, there was a story about a farmer in the East who heard the circus was coming to town. Having never seen a circus parade, he loaded up his wagon and set off to watch it. The extraordinary sight of jugglers, clowns and caravans being led into town by an elephant caused the farmer's horse to suddenly take fright. It spewed its load and bolted. "I don't give a hang," the farmer reportedly said, "for I have seen the elephant."

'Seeing the elephant' was a popular expression during America's antebellum years, but it had a special resonance for the Forty-Niners and pioneers. It is one of those sayings which defies precise definition. For Malcolm J. Rohrbough, author of *Days of Gold*, 'it is supposed to mean adventure. Seeing the elephant is meant to characterise something that happens to people which is so remarkably different from anything they have previously experienced.' John P. Reid, the professor of law who wrote

Law for the Elephant, understood it meant 'to face a particularly severe ordeal, to gain experience by undergoing hardship, to learn the reality of the situation first hand, or to encounter the unbelievable.' And a contemporary commentator took it that 'when a man is disappointed in anything he undertakes, when he has seen enough, when he gets sick or tired of the job he may have set himself about, he has seen the elephant.'

I had caught glimpses of the heffalump all the way across the United States, but on the road to Casper the whole scary monster filled my vision. For those on the migratory trails, the sight frequently broke their spirit and dashed their hopes. They turned for home despite having more miles behind them than ahead. On some parts of the trail there were more wagons returning east than travelling west, a demoralising sight for those going forwards.

Exhausted to the point that my legs wouldn't stop shaking, I lay on the sidewalk sobbing. I couldn't begin to consider what I would do next. What small roads there were led to Douglas then on to Casper and involved a three day detour in the best of circumstances. There was a railroad meandering along the banks of the North Platte which I could have tracked for sixty odd miles, but I didn't have the strength to undertake off-road work. Whatever else, I definitely wasn't going back onto the interstate. Short of the hand of God scooping me up and depositing me on the slip road to Casper, I-25 was my only way out of Orin.

"Tough ride?" a silhouette standing over me asked.

The question came from a dumpy character wearing a grey gilet, grey shorts and rubber sandals. He had a shaved head and looked like Buddha might after a month at a health farm. He approached me with caution.

"The worst," I croaked, wiping away tears. "I've had it."

"Yeh. Passed you coming up the interstate couple of miles back and thought you looked kinda done in."

I took a swing of tepid milk, tossed the container in the general direction of a bin, flopped back on the sidewalk and prayed for Scotty to beam me up.

"I'm driving that white shuttle over there, heading up to Thermopolis," the little Buddha said. "You're welcome to sling your bike in the back."

At the far end of the car park stood a brand new transit bus. As I eased myself onto one elbow, the sun bounced off it like the flash from a magician's wand. Above it circled cute Walt Disney doves with olive leaves in their beaks, and a rainbow formed an arch. The Hallelujah Chorus welled up from behind its iridescent form.

"'You sure?" I almost managed a smile.

"Sure. Got mine in there."

More than Buddha's bicycle was wedged inside the Magic Bus. By the back door, between bike and Bob trailer, his Thermarest and sleeping gear were strategically arranged next to his kitchen. Scattered across the seats, were panniers and holdalls, his wardrobe and an Amtrak bicycle box. Fanned around the driver's seat, were supplies of munchies, a cooler and numerous polythene bags containing rubbish. Despite the chaos, the interior was immaculate and smelt of virgin plastic.

"Careful of the upholstery," he said as we loaded on my gear. "It ain't mine. Root beer?"

Larry Donovan Smith delivered shuttle buses, RVs, school buses and anything else large enough to carry his cycling clobber. He had a house in Phoenix, Arizona, but spent spring through to autumn on the road. After each leisurely delivery, Larry loaded up the bike and pedalled off to explore some new part of America. When the money ran out, he turned to what he called "hitch-biking," thumbing a ride in pick-ups which transported him and his gear back to the nearest distributor to collect another delivery.

"This here shuttle's destined for Seattle, Washington. It's already three days late but, hey, provided it arrives... Thought I'd take in Yellowstone on the way, maybe ride

242

down the coast after delivery. Supposed to be real pretty up there. Where you headed?"

Beyond the windshield, I-25 was a smear on the foothills of the Laramie Mountains like the high water mark of an oil spill on a rocky beach. Ahead I could see clear into next week. I turned to stare out of the side windows, sick to my stomach. Bent by the wind, the pines of Medicine Bow National Forest were like lines of drawn longbows. I wasn't headed anywhere which involved stepping outside the Magic Bus.

"You want to get off in Casper? Okey-dokey. Let's see. Somewhere here I've got a map of Casper's hot-spots."

Larry passed me the fistful of leaflets he must have been handed by Old Mother Reilly. Sensing I wasn't feeling communicative, he eased his way into a monologue.

Marrying young and begetting a daughter, Larry Smith managed to avoid the clutches of the Vietnam draft. The relationship ping-ponged along for a handful of years before becoming destructive. They divorced and the draft board pounced. Entering the war late, he opted for the U.S. Marines and was posted to Danang, to a watch tower where he spent most of the worst phase of the war either soaked to the skin or coughing up dust whipped up by Chinook helicopters. Through the radio waves of the 'Wolfman of Nam', each morning broke to strains of George Harrison singing *Here Comes the Sun*, a track he had recently revisited and now "makes me puke."

By the time Larry took up his position in the tower, what once was a peaceful coastal strip of Vietnamese farms and villages had been transformed into the largest single military base anywhere in the world. Aside from the usual concessions to war like military hospitals and quatermaster's stores, Danang had cinemas, ball parks, bowling alleys, supermarkets, restaurants, tennis courts, bars and a drug dealer on every corner. Called the 'Dog Patch', it predictably became a special target for enemy fire, which Larry took very personally.

"After a year of dodging hot lead and whacking every hallucinogen going into my body, I kinda lost touch with reality and was shipped back to the States a basket case. I spent five years on a funny farm recovering from one year in Nam. When I was diagnosed sane, they released me into an America that cared shit about the psychological impact of war on its vets. I then spent five years in therapy getting over the five years on the funny farm."

One more failed marriage followed before Larry gave up on permanent relationships and settled life style.

"I've come to the conclusion it's easier to get a woman into your bed than out of it," he said. "When I get the urge, I just cut me one out of the herd."

The bright lights of Casper hove into view around seven. Flying over the interstate, we scanned the neon blaze beneath us for some place, any place, serving something other than tacoed travesty and Kentucky fried garbage.

"I normally hit the local deli and raid their salad counter," Larry said, slipping off I-25 and easing the Magic Bus along Center Street. A dull glow from uninviting bars was the only sign that life still breathed in downtown, but if it took until morning to find a 24-hour deli it was alright by me. Anything to delay climbing back on the saddle.

That night I slept in the aisle of the Magic Bus in a line with Larry. On the outskirts of town, in a bend of the North Platte, we found Riverside Park had a turnout where a zinc white bus wouldn't appear out of place or be vandalised. Sleeping between seats piled with bags, bikes and boxes, it was unlikely the beam of a patrolman's torch would pick us out. I had never been more grateful to see a day come to an end, nor convinced that a steel floor was a feather mattress.

Chapter 20

What a difference a day makes. On the haul out of Casper, I had to stop and check I wasn't imagining things. The absence was disarming. I licked my finger, thrust it above my head and didn't know what to make of it. The air was still. This *was* 'Suicide City', the town where the Panther takes no prisoners? Bizarrely, it was the first morning since crossing the Mississippi when there wasn't a wind in my face, but initially I failed to notice.

Larry had insisted on joining me for the leg to Independence Rock, the next natural waymarker on the Oregon-California-Mormon Trail and a ride of over fifty miles. Despite reminding him that I had seen the elephant and knew he would never complete the round trip in a day, Larry pulled on lycra and unloaded his bike. I think more to try out his new cycle helmet than give me moral support, he led the way to a leisure trail along the north bank of the river. The mock-metal skid lid made him look like General 'Blood and Guts' Patton, a hero of his.

Twisting through scrubby park land, we wove between joggers and power walkers, mostly women. With each set of bouncing bosoms Larry's eyes extended further. When we came to a section washed out by flooding, they shrivelled. I suggested we wade through, but a better way to road test his shiny new helmet had presented itself. Half an hour after setting out, Larry turned back to "cut one out of the herd." I continued alone, and pushed on through white water at the river's edge. The ferocious undercurrents nearly swept my feet away.

Two years before the argonauts reached this section of the North Platte, Mormons had established a ferry crossing at what was then called Upper Ferry. Never ones to miss an opportunity to turn a buck, their steady trade would have boomed had they been able to cope with 1849's unexpected surge in demand. By the time the main body of the wagon train joined the queue, the impatient had already hacked down cottonwoods and built their own rafts. For thirty miles downstream from the established ferry, the swirling waters of the North Platte were frantic with teamsters cajoling herds and hauling make-shift ferries precariously laden with heavy wagons. Having passed through several hands, some rafts were the worse for wear, and the crossing was the most taxing and dangerous operation the overlanders had yet undertaken. Every day men, mules, oxen and horses drowned in the process of trying to gain the north bank.

Following a line along the south bank, the map indicated I would ride through three communities in the next 150 miles, none with populations large enough to merit a store. Heavy with supplies, I was cycling into the really Wild West, into mountains which still weren't the Rockies. At the northern limit of the Laramies, the ridge overhanging Casper ended with a sharp edge like bad teeth in blackened gums. Squeezing between the sentinel peaks of Bessemer and Coal Mountains, the North Platte turned south and sucked in. Where the overlanders took the high road over a ridge on the north bank and left the river behind, I happily took the low on the south, more recently hacked through the gorge. There was no knowing what mood the Panther would be in when it woke up, and I wasn't about to tempt fate.

Beyond the natural gateway, the landscape dramatically and suddenly became desert. A few cedars survived, but the grass of the ranges east of Casper gave way to sagebrush and sand with a vengeance. As if entering a store selling pot pourri, the smell hit me with an intensity which turned my stomach. I was surrounded by high blue-grey hills and, behind them, low layered mountains, but the road I travelled was a line drawn from Nebraska — gently undulating across a broad plain. The distant ridges were blue, the river was blue and the sky graded up to an azure blue. It was a blue blue day but I felt in the pink. The wind that rushed through my hair came from speeds I thought would never again be achieved in America.

Climbing through the limestone hills penning in Alcova Reservoir, it started to spit. Large thunderheads slipped across the sky and became gridlocked. Within ten minutes, the mantle above me was solid and threatening. The temperature plummeted but the rain let up. I honked up a long steady incline, disturbed that the Panther still hadn't begun its daily prowl. It was mid-afternoon. At the brow, an enormous basin walled by mountains opened before me. From base to tip, the peaks were probably no higher than a thousand metres, but the road was close to 2,000 metres above sea level. Every quadrant of the firmament displayed a different temper. To the south, it was black and angry, hurling down sheets of rain. To the north, it was clear and inviting. Nothing moved on the desert floor except a few cattle searching through the sagebrush for isolated shoots of buffalo grass.

I paused to pull on another layer of clothing and discovered the wind *was* out and about but blowing from behind. The Moose had been nudging me along and I hadn't appreciated it. Too good to be believe and too advantageous to ignore, I leapt back on the saddle and sped across the basin. On the far side, an arm of the Rattlesnake Mountains forced a bend in the dead straight, bringing into view the distinctive bulge of Independence Rock. After all I had read about the 'Register of the Desert', the landmark was a sight less impressive than its significance.

Supposedly named by a group of fur trappers who camped here on July 4th, 1829, Independence Rock marked the midway point of the westward trail from Independence. It was another milestone adorned with graffiti, this time mostly inscribed by Mormons who charged for carving your initials on the high granite dome. Relieved to have reached the rock, many travellers were inspired to celebrate Independence Day once again, regardless of what day it was. The belief that they were writing a formative page of American history remained as strong as when they left home, but the trail from Upper Ferry had proved an eye-opener. The hills and desert I pounded through in a day took them nearly a week to cross — a week in which forage for the animals was scarce and drinkable water almost nonexistent. It was what they called a 'jornadas' or 'dry drive'. The dwindling course of the North Platte was a day's walk south of the trail, and surface water tended to be pools of liquid alkali. By mid-July, the trail was lined with the bloated carcasses of poisoned oxen. The stench of putrefied flesh and the sight of hundreds of swollen or exploded cadavers was something they would become familiar with but, at Independence Rock, the real cause for jubilation was the aptly named Sweetwater River emerging from behind it. Mormons, gold seekers and those bound for the promised land would stick rigidly to its course for the next hundred miles, all the way to the continental divide and South Pass.

I clambered over Independence Rock looking for evidence of the Mormons' enterprise. To the south-west the Sweetwater carved a deep slit known as Devil's Gate in a spur of the Rattlesnake Mountains. Snaking up to the gorge, the river turned to crystal in a beam of evening sunlight, its mercurial trace winding through lush meadows which provided ravenous oxen with their first juicy meal since Upper Ferry. Beyond Devil's Gate lay another enormous sagebrush plain.

The county road hiccuped over a col and brought me down to a freshly painted ranch whose orderly yard was solid with SUVs. The Sun Ranch was originally home-steaded by Tom Soliel in 1872, but it was now called the Hub and Spoke Ranch. Bought by the Mormon church in 1996, it had been converted into an interpretive centre commemorating the travails of the Willie and Martin Handcart Companies on the 'Trail of Hope'. There was a cottage museum which would reveal all about Willie and Martin but it was late and I wasn't in the mood. On the doorstep stood Elder Raab, a charming gentleman in his late sixties, smartly dressed in a black suit, white shirt and cowboy bow tie. I asked him why the car park was full but the ranch was deserted.

"They're down at Cherry Tree Creek campsite, 'bout three miles away. See those handcarts?" He pointed to four rows of maybe ten wooden carts per row pushed into one other like shopping trolleys in the corner of the compound. "They've unloaded their vehicles onto a handcart then pulled it down the side of the road to the campsite. When their visit's over, they load up again and pull it back. During their stay, they can explore the area and get an insight into what it was like for the handcart companies."

I had arrived at a Mormon theme park and presumed the camp site was exclusively for the brethren but worth a try. I told Elder Raab my story and his eyes lit up.

"Oh, I'm sure it'd be okay. If you hurry, you'll be able to join in the barn dance."

At Cherry Tree Creek, some folks had cheated. A handful of Chevys and Fords lined the entrance, one of them providing power for the knees-up. While a circle of dancers in nineteenth century costumes threw their hands in the air and jigged forwards shouting "Yee-ow!" I pegged out my tent. Aside from a couple of stand pipes and five chemical toilets there were no facilities, and the square of desert was divided into four encampments, each clutch of tents apparently from a different town. The brethren threw curious glances in my direction while I pitched. Nobody was rude, but nobody talked to me. I must have had 'Non-Believer' stencilled on my fly sheet. Finally I was approached and invited to join the folks from Logan, Utah, for dinner.

I entered a circle of twenty people, teenagers through to grandparents, huddled round a camp fire. On a handcart chocked level, a large pot of beef stew was simmering over a gas burner. On another ring, dumplings were being fried in a vat of bubbling oil. A corn-fed earth-mother handed me a bowl and invited me to get stuck in. The evening had quickly become night under a thick blanket of cloud and the wind had swung round to the south-west. As the Panther picked up speed, the temperature dropped below freezing and frost started to form. Between telling my story and answering their enquiries about sections of the Mormon Trail I had followed, I devoured three helpings of stew.

Dinner over, the Logan Saints came together around the pathetic fire. After a prayer and one verse of a hymn, they went round the group, each person relating the story of an individual member of the Martin Handcart Company. Some read from a script, others told their allotted tale in their own words. Despite the biting cold, the first half dozen histories were compelling, particularly those told by descendants of survivors from the original company.

The great Mormon migration to Zion lasted for twenty years. Most of those who travelled west in the years after the pathfinders were new converts from Europe, and several sat round the fire were of English ancestry. While wagons were still used, two-wheeled handcarts modelled on those supplied to street sweepers were the most common method of transporting essentials. They were faster, easier and cheaper than an ox team and wagon. Capable of carrying 500 pounds of gear, street carts might have been fine on brick roads and gentle tracks but they were totally inadequate for the desert, particularly when the pressure of demand meant knocking them together from unseasoned wood.

Late in the trail season of 1856 and despite severe warnings, Edward Martin's Handcart Company left Winter Quarters (Omaha) on the Missouri. Many of their handcarts rapidly fell apart, and those which remained were grossly overburdened with redistributed loads. Food, clothing and blankets had to be discarded. By the time Martin's pilgrims reached Devil's Gate it was October. Winter had set in, the snow lay deep, and blizzards engulfed the totally ill-equipped party. The harrowing tale of the company grinding to a halt, taking shelter beneath a granite overhang not a mile from where we sat, and watching friends and family die from exposure and hunger was the substance of the camp fire recital. By the time the twentieth variation on a theme of dire straights was read out, I had lost the sensation in my feet and my legs were shivering uncontrollably. 150 Mormons died in the temporary refuge of Martin's Cove before they were rescued. If the meeting went on much longer, I feared I would be joining them.

Just when I thought we could all hit the sack, earthmother rose and invited the congregation to bear witness. Up jumped a spotty youth in his early twenties, pouring out ecstatic affirmations that Joseph Smith was his main man, the Book of Mormon was his Way, his Truth and Light, and so on. A young lassie took to the desert floor. More self-righteous affirmations were followed by, "And if I was in a handcart company caught in a blizzard, I could hope for no better company than the brethren gathered about me."

"Can I say a few words?"

Before anybody else could take to their feet, I heard myself interrupting. I might have stood up, had I not been frozen solid, but I doubt it. For a couple of minutes I dribbled on about my horrible experiences in the face of the elements, and how proud they should feel about their ancestors' titanic achievements. I explained why some of us still choose to travel vast distances under our own steam, how it brought us closer to Mother Nature and thus to ourselves and our gods, and how I could see myself getting a little too close to my god if I didn't go to bed immediately.

It was a load of drivel, but the brethren seemed appreciative. Two hours after my head hit the ground sheet, however, I was convinced of three things — that the Saints were reeking their revenge, that somebody up there was livid with me, and that this desert plateau was no place to be when a storm blows up.

Montezuma's Revenge isn't a patch on what Joseph Smith can inflict. When it struck, it struck fast and furious. I awoke with a start, already tugging at the zipper to my sleeping bag. Barely was my bum out of the inner tent than my innards shot out. Huddled in the bay, half asleep and searching for Baby Wipes, it slowly dawned that I was being attacked by something vicious the other side of the fly sheet. While further disgusting deposits splattered south, the tent twisted and buckled like somebody was trying to drive the pair of us into the ground. I removed my ear plugs and was instantly deafened by the roar of a ferocious storm. Outside, the desert was airborne, filling my ears with sand and grit the moment I crawled out. Somebody's jumper wrapped itself round my leg. Before I could make a grab, it flew off towards the Granite Mountains. Leaning into a near hurricane, I staggered across to where my bike had been hurled to the ground and fished out guy ropes. Spitting sand and trying to protect my face behind the collar of my jacket, I grabbed the ridge of the tent, attempting to restrain it. It snapped free, writhing and jerking like a psycho in a straightjacket.

Two involuntary cow pats and a lot of aggro later, I had the tent secured. Through the grey of the dust storm, I could just make out loose canvas whipping above tent frames and people jumping about trying to make a grab. Some tents had totally blown away. Torches and people were running around catching items born on the wind. Chaos ruled over believers in strict order. Finally convinced my bowels were settled enough to slide back in the sack, I lay suffocating under a tent buckled down to ground level.

The wind was steady but light the following morning. Around the tattered remains of their encampments, the post-disaster *bonhomie* was tinged with relief that the brothers and sisters were all leaving today. A weary elder from Logan approached and squatted on his haunches. "How d'you get on? Godforsaken place this, yeh?" I turned down his invitation of a fried breakfast, claiming I wanted to be first in line when the Hub and Spoke museum opened.

Back down the road, Elder Raab introduced me to Sister Ose, who would be my guide around the exhibition. Housed in the original ranch house, the cottage museum was a continuous walk round four corners which brought you back to the front to the building. As one might expect of the Latter-day Saints, the exhibition was impressive, if a little creepy, and the first I had visited which took children into consideration. The story of Mormon persecution and the 'Trail of Hope' was entertainingly told using quotes from diaries, authentic relics and epic oil paintings specially commissioned for the exhibition. The word count was still mega, but this was cancelled out by Sister Ose's running commentary. Every visitor or group who followed behind me were accompanied by a spouting sister.

The *pièce de résistance* was the film show at the end of the tour. The screen flared into life and a roar reminiscent of last night's storm rattled the speakers. With production standards eclipsing BBC costume dramas, director Heber McBride had stuck scantily clothed extras in a raging blizzard and ordered them to look like they were freezing their nuts off. Hauling handcarts through icy creeks and impenetrable snow drifts, no acting was needed. It was a awesome piece of propaganda. There were tracking shots and dolly shots, expensive lap dissolves and an original soundscore. All this for a one-off AV installation at a little interpretive centre in the wilds of Wyoming?

The road to Muddy Gap was another long straight steaming across an undulating desert, except today heading straight into a bitterly cold wind. The plateau was a triangle shaped by low mountains and delineated by two roads and the Sweetwater River. The river departed from the road at the apex of Devil's Gate, flowed along the foot of the Granite Mountains and joined the base of the triangle at Split Rock, once the site of a Pony Express station. The line to Muddy Gap was flanked by Sentinel Rocks, which were a range more than an outcrop, and the bottom road from the gap to Split Rock bounded over the foothills of the Green Mountains, which were actually slate-grey. Within the vast triangle, there wasn't a lot going on except, beside the road, three cow punchers were branding heifers in a small corral.

I warmed myself at the propane burner heating up the irons. A mounted cowboy in chaps and straw Stetson cut one out of the herd, roped its rear legs and dragged the animal across to the wranglers. While one held its fore legs, the other burnt the brand and castrated the calf with a pen knife. They were Mormons from the handcart ranch, but the brand wasn't the circle and three rays of the original Sun Ranch. That had stayed with the Soliel family whose descendants now farmed the Diamond Hook Ranch beside the road to Split Rock. Offered up a bloody knife, I gracefully declined the opportunity to try my hand at castrating. "Not before breakfast, thanks."

Grinding into Muddy Gap a couple of hours later, my stomach had finally settled, hunger gnawed and plates piled with hash browns floated across my imagination like a screen saver. The hamlet comprised a handful of houses spaced quarter of a mile apart and, at the junction, the Three Fork Services — a large galvanised shed serving nothing that needed a fork. Between bites of something cook-chilled and disgusting, I chatted with Teresa, the owner of the gas station.

In her early thirties, perky and no doubt a tease for the local honchos, Teresa originally bought the business with her husband. They settled into the flat upstairs, but hubby didn't take to living in the outback. She loved the isolation of Muddy Gap and couldn't imagine living someplace where you couldn't keep tabs on your neighbours without the use of binoculars. (Hers were beside the till and well worn.) Now divorced, she had custody of their son and daughter, who went to different schools, one involving a bus journey of 120 miles a day.

I asked if she knew a short cut to South Pass. Having begun the day cycling into a south-westerly, I would now take Route 287 north-west along the base of the triangle to Jeffrey City. Beyond the town and a bridge over the Sweetwater, the road continued up to Lander, where I would have to hang a left to come back down to Atlantic and South Pass Cities. It was a day's detour my spirits didn't need. Teresa was confident there was a dirt road paralleling the Sweetwater to Atlantic City, but didn't know details.

Three very hairy and gnarled young men came in cussing and cursing their way through a blow-by-blow account of a punch up at some bar the previous Friday night. Teresa waded in with a raft of her own expletives. A tall, muscular and strikingly handsome Amerindian truck driver joined us, looking for directions to the Diamond Hook Ranch. As if Mother Teresa had entered the store, the swearing immediately stopped. He laid a state road atlas on the table. The county road I needed was BLM 2302 lurching across the Antelope Hills. The turn off was over a hundred miles away.

"After the storm last night, it'll be real shitty," one of the hairies told me, "And it's a fuck of a long way on a bicycle, dude. Hey!" He turned to the trucker. "Sorry, man."

Was there something about Native American sensitivity to swear words I wasn't party to?

It was twenty-one miles along the base of the triangle to the next town on the map, Jeffrey City. Thanks to the Panther, it was twenty-one miles ridden at the blistering pace of a mile an hour slower than walking. In that distance I passed a couple of pronghorn antelope, a dozen cattle grazing in a field the size of Dulles Airport and a mess of empty mobile homes half buried under sand and secured with steel hawsers. The only person I saw was a young lad on horseback rounding up mustangs. Within seconds of appearing from a dry gulch he was enveloped in dust and gone.

Chapter 21

Some towns I had been through might have felt like ghost towns, but Jeffrey City was the real thing. Most of it was boarded up or bulldozed down. A dirt service road running beside the highway provided access to a row of commercial outlets, mostly still standing and a couple still trading, though barely. Behind the front line, rows of abandoned apartment blocks awaited the ball and chain. A tarmac grid flocked with weeds and lined with unstrung telegraph poles extended a quarter of a mile into the desert. Beside it, only foundations and sagebrush remained. Tumbleweed rolled past residual occupancies and, behind the saloon, one man was doggedly mowing the desert. I wondered how many lost souls inhabited this sorry excuse for a town.

"I'd say about 200," the redhead behind the bar estimated, "if you include all the dogs and cats, and there are a lot of dogs and cats. It used to be a rip-roaring place. About 2,000 folks lived here when it was a mining town, before the tree-huggers stepped in. East of the Green Mountains there are big uranium deposits and humungus quarries. The apartments were for the miners. There are a few of them left doing restoration work but since the big downer on nuclear energy, nobody mines any more. All we've got out here is a little ranching."

Red was born and raised in Jeffrey City. She wished she was still living in what remained, but there was no work. She had moved to Lander, sixty miles away, and now was employed on the Wind River Indian Reservation as a social worker.

"Every weekend I come home to play," she said "Help my boyfriend run the bar." (He was the one on the mower.)

If I had to do the detour through Lander, I planned to pedal up to the reservation and poke around.

"Don't go there, man." She was emphatic. "You'll hate Americans."

"Actually, I rather like Americans."

"Not after visiting Wind River. Sure, I see the worst side in my job, but all this garbage about the Indian's cultural revival — man, those people are well and truly broken. There's drug abuse, alcoholism, abuse in the families — hell, you ain't seen low self-esteem until you've been to the Wind River. Y'know, the Shoshoni reservation used to be the size of Wyoming before it got took away. There's ranches round here bigger'n it now, and they've gotta share it with the Arapaho, f'Christ's sakes. Hell, they're traditional enemies. They ain't exactly killing each other, but one lot are Jesuits and the others are Episcopalians. They sure don't mix too good."

Red explained how reservation Indians had been snared by the myth of the noble native living in harmony with nature. While convenient for white liberals and their right-on ideas about conservation and the environment, "it's a tragic distortion of tribal history and sets the bar too fucking high for the average Joe." The so-called 'cultural revival' was something those with craft skills could earn a dime from, but when an American invests in a blanket or pot, he's "buying into all that 'Ecological Indian' crap," perpetuating a myth which keeps those without craft skills knocking back the booze. "What they really want is to be ordinary Americans," Red said. "They want RVs and hi-fis and microwaves and power boats, just like every white American."

The overlanders called the Shoshoni 'Digger Indians', a disparaging term applied to any Amerindian who didn't fit their stereotype of a near naked savage galloping through a dust storm of stampeding bison. Two hundred years earlier, the Shonshoni were Plains Indians and buffalo hunters, before they were driven into the mountains by their enemies. Forced to roam the Great Basin's harsh monotony of sagebrush and sand, they became superb 'resource generalists', scavenging plants and hunting small game to fill larders, medicine chests, tool kits and wardrobes. Annual gatherings of the tribe were an occasion for communal drives to catch antelope and jack rabbit, but their methods and superstitions were anything but benign. In the belief that an antelope stalked with respect would return to be killed several times over before finally giving up its soul, they set brush fires to corner herds and slaughtered well beyond their needs. Death and regeneration were a common theme in Shoshoni rights, and each hunting binge was preceded by a religious homage to the animal spirits. They appeased plant spirits before anything was uprooted, and a stone was sometimes left in the hole to re-seed. Heavily into immortality, they also practiced suttee, frequently demanding the wife commit suicide on the death of her husband. As Red observed, it wasn't the soundest footing on which to build the myth of the noble native.

The mass migration which began in 1849 quickly threatened the very survival of the desert tribes. More than the killing of antelopes or rabbits, it was the huge numbers of hungry oxen, cattle and mules which had the most startling impact. To survive the vicious winters, the Shonshoni relied on seeds laboriously collected during the summer months by the women and children. Not only did the overlanders' harvest or their livestock consume the vegetation before it went to seed, but the continuous stream of wagons shadowing the banks of the Sweetwater made the most fruitful margins of the desert a no-go area for the natives. If they occassionally stole a steer for dinner, it was to be expected, but they were stolen by stealth not by ambush. That was to come later, beside what was then called 'Mary's River'.

Somewhere between Jeffrey City and the hamlet of Sweetwater I twiddled through the radio dial and picked up a hurricane warning. Central Wyoming was in for a pasting. There had to be something more substantial than a tent at Sweetwater, if only a sand drowned trailer. I pulled out the stops to reach the hamlet before the hurricane struck, and hit a top speed of a brisk walk. Ice began forming on my beard and my extremities numbed up in the freezing wind.

I crossed Ice Slough, a desolate depression which emphasised the severity of the environment. Half a mile wide by maybe two long, the hollow looked similar to a peat bog except, beneath the surface, Ice Slough was permafrost. In their efforts to find water, the overlanders drove their spades in and hit solid matter beneath the surface. Out of curiosity, I took a chrome vanadium spanner to the slough and managed a seven centimetre dent. In the midst of this desert landscape, it was a remarkable natural feature and the only feature of any interest in over four hours of cycling.

Predictably, the Panther was adamant I wasn't going to make it to Sweetwater. Equally certain I wasn't going to suffer another night with the bastard sitting on my face, I gave up at a storm drain under the road. Slinging my sleeping gear into the corrugated tunnel, I prepared for a maelstrom which never came. Instead, sleep was interrupted by the patter of rodents scurrying either side of me through the night.

The severity of the Wild West had taken me by surprise. From the matinee stalls of my youth, I watched the butte and desert backdrops of cowboy films in awe. They were majestic, exciting, warm and spacious, but they never struck me as wild. Wild was jungle and ocean. Wild was what people got up to in the Wild West. Only two days into the sagebrush desert, I now understood how the unrelenting barrage of nature's forces drove the whiteman to do crazy things. The wind, the heat, the sand, the intimidating space — maddening sensations I never considered in a cinema in drizzly England. Europeans simply weren't built to withstand the maliciousness of this wicked environment day in day out. It undermined sanity and brought out the savage. I certainly was going bonkers and had psychotic fantasies of ramming my whole kit and caboodle down the black cat's throat.

I needed extra provisions if I was about to disappear into the desert up a dubious track. A packet of pretzels could prove a life saver, but Sweetwater turned out to be a bridge, a bungalow, a house within an empty RV park and a ramshackle gas station, which was closed. I dozed an hour away against a pump waiting for somebody to appear. At half eight, a ranger pulled up in a pick-up with the crest of the Bureau of Land Management on its door and black smoke billowing from of its tailpipe. "If'n he ain't here b'now, guess it'll be t'morrow," he said, crashing into gear.

Through binoculars, I surveyed the featureless desert for my dirt line. A jeep towing an Airstream caravan bobbed along the western horizon, apparently crossing open range. It turned onto the tarmac dripping great gloops of mud. I flagged it down. Yes, they'd just turned off BLM 2302 and the conditions were "muddy but passable, if'n y'got four-wheel drive." I had one-wheel drive but two feet I could take to if things got sticky. Atlantic City was about forty-five miles away, the fat vested driver said. By tarmac road, I estimated it to be half as far again. For better or worse, I turned onto the track. The old adage about a short-cut being the longest way round was about to come true.

Wilderness areas of America which aren't sites of special scientific interest or extraordinary beauty come under the control of the Bureau of Land Management (BLM). Those which are special tend to be State or National Parks, like Ohiopyle or Yosemite. The BLM manage bog standard wilderness, and millions of square miles of the stuff. The Antelope Hills were nothing exceptional to look at, unless you were trying to cross them with only muscle and sinew. Then they became daunting.

Initially the track was fine, its surface gritted. Most of the width was impossibly washboarded, but the margins were eminently ridable. I wound my way up to Beaver Rim and perused a bleak and barren cyclorama. Up the side of the slope, linear indentations marked the line taken by the wagons and handcarts, feet and hooves of the overlanders. They were the most unadulterated evidence of the passage of the Forty-Niners I would see, and they revealed that in high land like this there were many routes through.

At the very top of Beaver Rim, the Rockies finally revealed themselves on the north-western sky line. They were snow-capped and glowing but a hell of a long way off. I couldn't believe the sight of them was any more heartening for the wagon trains than it was for me. Before either of us would get an idea of their true proportions, there was mile upon mile of buckled desolation to negotiate. The prospect was depressing and I knew worse was to come. Weariness like I had never experienced before was beginning to blunt my brain and body. I could only believe blood continued to pump because my legs continued to pump, but I hadn't a clue what kept them going. I wasn't simply tired of the day. I was tired to the core of my being. No different from the overlanders at this point, every inch of my fibre was wrecked with fatigue. We all plodded wearily forwards on automatic pilot, and I knew what kept them going had nothing to do with promised lands or the lure of gold. Such dreams had fallen to the bottom of a wish list dominated by cravings for warmth, rest and silence, not for a day or a night, but for ever more. We blundered forwards because there was nothing else to do in this merciless place.

A day and a half after leaving Sweetwater I somehow hauled myself into Beer Garden Gulch. I could think of better names for this cleavage of barren sandstone at the tail end of the Wind River Mountains. The hills around the gulch were stripped naked and artificially shaped like coconut pyramids. Up the sunny side from Rock Creek, a small grid of dirt roads strung together a couple of dozen wooden shacks thrusting out of the steep slope. A few were modern A-frames, but most were as old as the hills, which were barely a hundred years old, having been sanded, scoured, blasted and generally hacked about by gold diggers from the 1860s onwards. The village was called Atlantic City, an even more unlikely name.

The population of Atlantic City had fluctuated between several hundreds and a grand total of three during its boom and bust lifetime. The first gold strike was made by panhandlers returning broke after a decade in the Sierra Nevadas. The thriving community which grew up around the mines included an opera house, brewery and a dance hall with a saloon and gambling tables. There was a school, church and fire station, but the tenor of the place is best illustrated by the local legend that Calamity Jane was employed as an escort at the dance hall. Until the cavalry chased them back to the shrinking reservation, the town was also subjected to periodic raids from the aggrieved Shoshoni. Since those rough and tough days, commercial and individual efforts to extract gold from the area had gone in fits and starts, all of it impacting badly on the landscape. At the peak of extraction, Atlantic City must have been a desperately ugly place to live in, except in winter under metres of snow, when it was just desperately cut off.

Gold mining was still carried out by individual die-hards and a recent find of a nugget worth $4,500 had raised hopes once again. The assured wealth was now in tourism, particularly fly fishing, hunting and cross-country skiing. Strolling around the hillside, it was interesting to see how the old stores, blacksmiths' shops and miner's homes had barely been modernised. Outside of one, a notice read, 'Welcome to Atlantic City. We really don't give a rotund rectum how you did it back home'. Whether this was a warning to incomers to curb their city ways or to tourists wasn't clear, but the residents were definitely a tight knit. At the Sagebrush Saloon, I picked up a copy of *The Mountain News*, 'Published by Women of Wyoming (Atlantic City and South Pass)'. The upcoming birthdays and anniversaries of local residents received prominent display, and Chris-Contracting offered to do maintenance on your log cabin 'at Christian prices'. Answering the question, "What do you do in winter?" the editor had written, 'Required reading — *The Shining*'.

The ascent out of Atlantic City was the steepest I had encountered in America. Slipping and sliding on the grit, I had to heave the bike forwards then jam on the brakes while my feet and breathing caught up. Either side of its high convex back, deep snowdrifts were grey and mucky with the splatterings from car tyres. The village had been hit by a blizzard on the night of the storm at Cherry Tree Creek. Protruding from a coconut pyramid topped in icing sugar, the shaky corrugated structure of a small working mine shuddered with something dangerous going on inside. A buckled shack propped on stilts was imperceptibly sliding down the hillside under the vibrations.

Less than a mile from Atlantic City, South Pass City was a fraction the size of its sister. I dropped down to the cross tracks in Hermit Gulch. Up the valley was a short cul-de-sac of cottages and the South Pass Trading Company, purveyors of period clothing. Down the valley was a small heritage park. I paid a dollar and went for a walk along historic South Pass Avenue, wandering in and out of the twenty-seven renovated log cabins, clapboard houses and stone buildings which made up a large percentage of the original gold town. It was a cold, comfortless place. In the two storey hotel, only one of the rooms had a stove. When all that separated you from sub-zero temperatures was a blanket and a plank of timber, sharing a bed with a total stranger was undoubtedly a plus. In the Sweetwater County Jail, you just froze to death standing up, in one of three dark cells akin to upright coffins. Here Polly Bartlett, the 'Murderess of Slaughterhouse Gulch', was shot dead by the vengeful relations of one of her victims. Polly was one of the West's earliest serial killers, thought to have robbed and poisoned over twenty miners who stopped by her family's way station south of town.

The most unexpected discovery I found at the far end of the row, in a cabin where Esther Morris and family once lived and produced a newspaper. Esther was America's first female Justice of the Peace. During the Wyoming Territorial Legislature of 1869, saloon keeper, miner and local representative William Bright steered through a groundbreaking women's suffrage bill which opened the way for Esther's appointment. Twenty years later, when Wyoming was negotiating entry into the union, the federal government had severe reservations based on the fear that Esther's position would set a precedent. Bright's reply was forthright. "We will remain out of the union a hundred years rather than come in without the women." This rough and ready frontier town in the back end of nowhere was the last place I expected to be at the forefront of women's rights.

In the Smith Sherlock Company Store, a modern frontier woman dressed in period clothing sat behind a counter displaying marbles, jaws' harps and liquorice sticks. Barbara Palmer sold toys and candy on behalf of the Friends of South Pass, but mostly she spent her time shooting the breeze with visitors. She was a powerful woman, self-assured and good at extracting information. I told her my tale, recounting my night with the Mormons at Martin's Cove.

"I bet they didn't tell you about the cannibalism?" I raised my eye-brows. "I thought not. They keep that under wraps. When they exhumed the bodies, they found saw marks on the bones. The Mormons were no better than the Donner party."

The story of the Donner party is the single most horrific episode in the history of the California Trail. Chancing their luck on a new route through the Sierras, George and Jacob Donner's wagon train became stranded in snow at Truckee Lake. With provisions for six days, a group of fifteen were sent forwards to fetch help. The journey took a month, during which time those left behind resorted to cannibalism when their food ran out. On the trail out of the mountains, the forward party likewise began consuming their colleagues as they dropped dead. Two Indian guides who refused to eat human flesh were shot and themselves eaten. The Saints hadn't gone that far but, if Barbara was right, they had gone a lot further than Sister Osage and the Hub and Spoke museum were prepared to reveal.

Peter Sherlock, the original storekeeper at the Smith Sherlock Company, was blind, but he could recognise his customers by their footsteps and knew where to lay his hands on any item in the shop. Barbara Palmer also had insight. In the middle of our conversation, she stopped, eyed me up and down, and declared, "You're a Libran, aren't you?"

"I am actually. October 3rd."

"Oh, my. Three is my number." Her car registration was 3.33, she lived at Three Forks Road and her phone number was all threes. Yep, Barbara had a thing about threes, but she also had the insight to realise I couldn't give a damn.

"You're exhausted, aren't you? And I bet you could do with a bath? Why don't you leave your bicycle here and come and spend the night at our place? We're not very together at present, but we've got a spare bed."

I didn't need convincing, nor did I appreciate quite what I was getting into. It's not every day one gets to wallow in a jaccuzzi in the middle of a desert watching elk watching you through the bathroom window.

I didn't see Barbara Palmer's house until her SUV was almost in the lounge. At the end of a rough track appearing to lead nowhere, the flat-roofed bungalow was dug into an isolated hillside and invisible on three sides. Made from Styrofoam blocks held rigid by concrete ribs, the house had been designed and built over six months by Dan, Barbara's husband, while they lived on site in a trailer. The outer surface was brushed with asphalt sealant, and the front clad in Moss Rock. About as attractive as a Normandy bunker, the Palmer home was equally efficient.

Wind power provided their electricity, supported by an 18 HP propane generator which echoed through the house when running. Eight heavy duty batteries stored the excess and kicked in to keep the rear of the place lit. Only the kitchen, chapel and bathroom received natural light. The enormous garage where the power was controlled also stored truck loads of caterers' tins and commercial freezers stuffed with packet food. Though last winter was mild, they expected to be cut-off for months at a time in a normal season. The skidoo and half-tracks for Dan's 4x4 pick-up had been called into action only last week, after the unseasonal blizzard.

Dan's confidence in the technology was based on his expertise as a military aviation engineer, but I was curious why an elderly couple would want to retire to such a remote and vulnerable location. This was not somewhere anybody would want to be in the depths of winter when the lights conked out.

"You've seen the chapel?" Dan asked, by way of a clue.

Barbara and Dan had fostered twenty-five children in their time. When the last child left home in 1995, Barbara got the calling and trained to become a minister for the Universal Brotherhood of God. Armed with a licence to go forth and proselytise, she had a vision of herself preaching in the wilderness.

"The following day, we received a phone call from a realty agent with an investment he thought would suit our purposes. We hadn't actually briefed any realty agents but there he was on the phone. The property was a forty acre lot overlooking Oregon Buttes. We came to look at the site and I instantly knew it was the right place. I walked around a bit and kinda tuned in. I just knew it was the right place."

Barbara located water, later confirmed by a professional dowser. They sank a well and raised a block house which included a simple chapel capable of holding a congregation of a dozen. She had conducted weddings there but mostly counselled disturbed souls who either sought her out or, like me, she picked up in the course of her day at the state park. I got the impression Dan was weary of sharing his home with Barbara's waifs and strays. A short, wily, affable sort of bloke, he seemed resigned to her over-bearing manner. While Barbara's head was firmly in the clouds, Dan's was full of nuts and bolts, volts and volumes, and a certain frisson underlined their relationship. They continually bickered and talked about each other as if they were the thankfully departed, but Barbara made no effort to beat me over the head with a Bible. She showed me the chapel and said it was there if I needed it. Over the altar were the words, 'Serenity Within'. Over the kitchen windows and closer to my needs were the words, 'Give us this day our daily bread'.

We dined on microwaved packets while relaxing in the windowless sitting room with Dan's slightly senile mother-in-law. Filling one wall was a modest library which was huge by comparison to anything I had seen in any other American home. Barbara showed me the work of William Henry Jackson, Dan's great uncle and a photographer whose early images are credited with enabling President Roosevelt to convince Congress to make Yellowstone the first National Park in the world. Jackson had taken pictures of Atlantic and South Pass Cities at the turn of the twentieth century. Then on a boom, the hills were either obliterated by the outfill from gantry mines or raw from the impact of hydraulic mining, a high pressure water process which ravages the landscape. The old towns were as grim and unromantic as I imagined.

Dan laid out the BLM map of the area to show me our location, a chart as detailed as anything the Ordnance Survey produces of our wilderness regions. Regardless of the lie of the land and the invisible lines of longitude and latitude, the whole of the Wyoming map was overlaid with a grid of perfect squares, each delineating 160 acres of BLM land. Every four miles there was a blue square representing land set aside for the state to locate a school house, administration buildings or whatever might be needed for future generations of desert settlers. Every other white square was up for grabs, and the Palmers were the first settlers of the rectangle abutting Spring Gulch. It was an astonishing testimony to the efficiency and invasiveness of the way the West was and continues to be won.

"A large percentage of the current population of the Sweetwater Mining District are artists, writers and musicians," Dan explained as he drove me back to South Pass City the following morning.

This threw new light on my reading of the sister villages, and probably explained how they had managed to fend off developers. I could see the isolated setting conspired with a romance for the Wild West, a fascination for industrial heritage and cheap property prices to lure Bohemians into the area. Gold has always held a strong fascination for creative people, particularly in the visual arts. It is an elusive colour, difficult to mix and challenging to use. It can be totally tacky or stunningly regal, and the myth that it was the matter of the bough which opened the Underworld to Aeneas only adds to its appeal. Less appealing is the harsh reality that wealth is as elusive for the majority of artists, including me, as it is for the majority of gold-diggers.

Wondering why I didn't stick to just trying to make it as a cartoonist, I hauled my weary bones out of the relative serenity of Hermit Gulch and back into the desolation of the Great Basin. The track curled out of the rocks and plonked me in the front stalls of the Saturday matinee. On screen, a sumptuous Technicolor desertscape of towering buttes lapped by soft swells just needed Ward Bond moseying over a sand hill to remind me why I was flogging my guts out on the trail to gold and not chained to a drawing board. My romance for the Wild West was flickering back to life, having been thoroughly beaten out of me over the past week. I had weathered the deep doldrums which every adventure suffers from somewhere down the line, and struck out for the Continental Divide with a discernible spring in my crank.

It wasn't to last.

Chapter 22

My plans for the new day were to ride through South Pass, the topographical feature beyond the village of South Pass, and take another BLM dirt road north-west approximating the line of Sublette's Cut-off, a diversion from the main course of the Oregon-California Trail. Since there was no easy route through the Wyoming and Wasatch Ranges of the Rocky Mountains, a number of alternative trails had been blazed by the few hundred migrants who traipsed to California between 1841 and the start of the Gold Rush. None were available to me as they crossed private land, but my proposed detour via the town of Big Sandy was a good approximation. Enquiries at South Pass City, however, revealed the track was impassable. It was the first week of June, summer was here, but Big Sandy was sealed in. In the previous three days it had received two metres of snow.

At 2,301 metres high, South Pass is not exactly a mountain pass, unless you can envisage a pass twenty to thirty miles wide, but it is still probably the most famous landmark on the westward trail. The grade up was gentle and across an exposed plateau. I was now in the Rocky Mountains but, except for deep gulches in the Sweetwater Mining District, I had yet to ride through mountains. I hadn't climbed a switchback or crawled along the edge of ravines. The pattern for crossing the Great Basin was shaped by the isolated ribs of unimpressive ranges protruding above a vast expanse of corrugated sagebrush. In prehistoric times, the cathedral spires of saw-toothed mountains might have dominated the area. Now the basin looked as if the hand of God had dribbled a stream of sand over the landscape, filling ravines to the midriff of mountains, wearing down sandstone peaks.

I crossed the Sweetwater River for the last time and cranked up the two-lane blacktop to the pass that wasn't.

Variously known by the overlanders as 'Uncle Sam's backbone' or 'the summit of the continent', the significance of South Pass lay in its position on the Continental Divide. To the east, all rivers flowed into the Atlantic or the Gulf of Mexico. To the west, they flowed into the Pacific or Gulf of California. It marked the furthest limit of the buffalo ranges and, although the watershed was topographically unremarkable, it was the point at which travellers symbolically severed contact with the East. The 'crossing over' invariably called for a party, much like crossing the Equator. People left Star Spangled Banners thrust in the sand in celebration of their achievement. Where I crossed over, a simple road sign bolted to a rough wooden post marked the divide.

The long deserted road forged across an empty wasteland paralleling Pacific Creek, the line the Mormons and remaining pioneers picked up. By now, the wagon trains were strung out across a thousand miles. It was early August for those on schedule and early June for me, possibly behind schedule to meet up with my wife in California. Sandy and I had begun discussing the details of a reunion planned while I was back in the UK. Since she was unable to accompany me on the first leg of my journey, we had agreed she would join me in Sacramento for the last. By August, some Forty-Niners had already arrived in the self-proclaimed capital of the gold country. For those still out on the trail, alternative routes and the thinning traffic reduced pressure on the land to provide unpolluted water and fuel for animals and fires, but the intimidating landscape now induced deep loneliness, particularly in those travelling with only a backpack or mule for company. As I was to discover, it was a loneliness born out of heartache, vulnerability and fear.

Overhead, the firmament had been acting out a drama as compelling as any Shakespearean tragedy and was now poised for the battle scene. To the north were ranged the forces of good — a deep blue sky lined with battalions of white clouds galloping north-east to gain an advantageous position. To the south, beneath the mass of dark forces, the horizon blazed as one fusillade after another were fired from Heaven's cannons. The front line of conflict was drawn up immediately above the line of the road, but it was moving quickly along the same angle the good guys were flanking round at. The rumble of hooves was the rumble of thunder sweeping across the plateau with increasing volume and speed. I bust a gut to pedal away from the battlefield, aiming for a thin wedge of blue which opened in the ranks of the enemy. For a moment, I thought I had ridden clear. An almighty explosion banged into my ear drums, deafening me. A second later, a jagged shaft of megavolts thumped into the ground maybe a mile away. Lightning zipped across the sky. More forks grounded, landing closer. I was the tallest element in the landscape and a sitting target.

The first wave of battle passed with only a splattering of rain, but the second attack charged in accompanied by a ferocious wind which stopped me dead. I edged forwards again, leaning into the gale. Without the warning of thunder, a blinding flash of lightning shot out of the clouds and thudded into the desert across the road from me. The earth shook, my ears popped, the wind was whacked out of my lungs and my brain fried as if a hot wire had been banged through my left temple and yanked out the right. I swerved uncontrollably across the road and came to a clumsy halt. Where the lightning had struck, a cloud of steam lingered.

Opening a sluice gate, the heavens rained down hail stones the size of gob stoppers. I dumped my bike, stumbled through the bouncing hail and assumed a crouching position beside the road, holding my hands over my head. There was nothing to shelter beneath, not even a bush. The best I could do was tuck myself into a ball and let my hands and back take the full force of the grapeshot. Close behind me, I heard another squib plunge to earth. The impact lifted me off my feet and threw me forwards. With bum higher than head, I knelt in a field of white gob stoppers, my brain reeling from another hot wire lobotomy. It started to bucket down with rain.

A shout came from the wound down window of a car which had pulled up on the opposite side of the road.

"Yo! Get in!"

A woman was beckoning me but I obviously wasn't thinking straight.

"I'm going the other way," I screamed. "Thanks."

Still dazed but aware I was saturated, I leapt on the saddle and pedalled away as fast as zapped muscles could cut the wind. My body temperature had plummeted and I desperately needed to build up a sweat. I carved through a freezing monsoon, flood waters streaming down my body. After half an hour trying to outrun hypothermia, the rain fizzled out, the dark forces parted, and the sun shone through. I started to steam, and shake uncontrollably with delayed terror.

The overlanders' diaries graphically describe being caught in storms which scattered their cattle and caused oxen to bolt and spill wagons. Backpackers were as alarmed and vulnerable as I was, holding their packs overhead for protection. Those who rode horseback shielded themselves from the fury of 'descending ice' by removing their saddles, hanging onto their mount and sheltering under the leather. Others 'clung to the reaches of the wagons and allowed themselves to be drawn along under them'. When 'the wrath of God passed over', wagon covers were shredded and cattle were found bleeding, 'cut through on the hips and back by the hail'. Thankfully I had been spared that much.

Ten miles further on, I climbed a low col. In the distance, a village was bathed in a warm glow which transformed the grey desert into a little Eden. It was a crossroads community of trashy trailer homes, junk strangled bungalows and ugly geodesic mishaps which stopped this side of the bisecting road. Down the other side flowed Sandy Creek, then more of the same grey desolation. The town sign said, 'Farson, El. 6580, Pop. 325'. Cats and dogs must have featured prominently again, but hopefully there was enough human traffic to merit somewhere I could get something hot.

In the Oregon Café, I fought the shakes while the waitress stood over me administering black coffee like it was unpalatable medicine. Through the window the washed out car park steamed and the bridge across Sandy Creek glistened like fool's gold. I apologised for spilling my drink.

"No problem," the waitress said, pouring a fourth cup while her colleague set down hot soup and cut my bread for me. "You just ridden through that god awful storm? Man, you gotta be brave or plum horse crazy."

"Er... Scottish," I grunted, wringing out my baseball cap.

A handful of miles beyond the river crossing, I crossed a cattle grid and entered open range, which is to say the road wasn't fenced in by barbed wire. A rush of wind and fanfare of thunder heralded a repeat of the empyrean drama. I thought to turn back but, in quick succession, rain storm followed hailstorm followed fork lightning. I tried curling my body into a drainage ditch less than a metre deep, hoping the levee might provide some protection from the driving monsoon. It did, until a trickle of run-off grew into a tidal wave. I remounted and rode into the maelstrom. The road had disappeared, its course marked by hovering snow poles whose bottom metre was invisible under spray and water.

Ten minutes which felt like an hour later, the rain stopped and a shaft of sunlight struggled through. Behind the crack in the grey ceiling, another front was moving in, and another behind that. The landscape was flat with nothing remotely approaching a building or shelter. I was in for a cold, wet, miserable night under canvas, and turned off at a shallow draw to find a modicum of protection at the foot of its mean edge. The wind gradually dropped, the grey sky thinned, and a double rainbow appeared as if by way of an apology. Undressing to dry myself down and rub warmth into a numbed body, I discovered my shoulders and hands were a mass of blotches.

It had been a bruising day, but the air was crisp and spicy when I emerged early the next morning. The sun was a bent thumb from the horizon set in a clear blue sky, and the landscape sparkled under a heavy frost. Having been destroyed in the storms, millions of spider's webs were being restrung between bushes thick with rime. I pissed on my bike to defrost the brakes and I struck out across the moribund plateau of the Green River Basin. Swelled by the conjunction of several streams near Farson, Sandy Creek had become Big Sandy River and etched a shallow valley to the south barely visible beneath the plateau. Beyond it, close to the horizon, the unexceptional contours of the Bad Lands Hills faded in and out through lingering mist. Peeking above the monotony, Pilot Rock was a pimple ten miles away which served as another waymark for the overlanders.

Along the highway, the only traffic was four-legged. Humorous billboards beside the blacktop featured an enormous elk ('Caution: Heavy Traffic Conditions'), a charging antelope ('Caution: Traffic Crossing at 55 mph'), and wild things zipping every which way ('Caution: Traffic Entering from all Sides'). Every year in America, the human death toll from drivers colliding with beasts on the hoof (or visa versa) runs into several hundreds. Just one state (Michigan) chalks up over 65,000 deer-vehicle collisions per annum. I soon found out why.

The road kinked and dipped into the Big Sandy Valley. A line of bluffs layered in orange, yellow and white defended my right flank from the north-westerly gathering pace across the range. On my left, a bounding pronghorn stopped and watched me cycle by. She bounded some more, overtook me, then stopped to check me out again. Four times she repeated this performance, gradually angling closer to the road. A stone's throw away and without warning, she made a dash for the tarmac, bisecting less than eight metres ahead of me before bouncing across the valley and up the steep sides of the bluff. Had I been in a car, one or both of us would now be pushing up sagebrush.

Highway 28 climbed back onto the plateau then swept off a ragged escarpment into the Green River Valley, site of many a fur trappers' rendezvous which so excited me back in St. Louis. The banks of the torrid river were thick with reeds and cottonwoods, and hundreds of martins darted beneath the bridge in a dizzying display of aerobatics. On the far bank, three white pelicans preened themselves, basking in the sun. The ultra violets were full on and the frost had melted, but the wind chill could have frozen the nuts off a penguin.

Fifty metres down-stream from the modern bridge, the Lombard Ferry was another Mormon enterprise invariably boycotted by the westward bound refusing to fork out $8 a wagon to cross. Such was the bottleneck in 1849, it took several days to get across. Meanwhile the encampments either side of the river vociferously debated the best route forwards. From the Green River, most pilgrims and gold seekers would cut south-east aiming for Fort Bridger, named after that trapper turned government peace broker Jim Bridger. There was nothing but an interstate for me to link with in the south, followed by several hundred miles of mind-numbing cycling to Salt Lake City. I bade farewell to the Mormon Trail for good and set off on a less popular line through the Rockies tracking the western leg of Sublette's Cut-off.

I turned north-west into a full frontal. An hour earlier the ground had been frozen solid but now dust was everywhere — on the ground, in the air, gumming up my gears. Behind my bandana, I could taste it and feel it running down my face in streams of cold sweat. My panniers and clothing were impregnated with it, and my glasses had to be regularly wiped clean. I could sympathise with the Forty-Niner who wrote, 'You may think that dust is a small matter... but it is one of the most serious difficulties on the route. I have eaten many a meal without daring to bring my teeth together on account of the sand. Sand wears away teeth and teeth are precious.' For a month now, everything I ate had crunched.

For the remainder of the day I sparred with the predator and didn't land a single blow, but then I couldn't see much through the dust storm. I turned onto a ridge route running along the exposed southern edge of the Slate Creek Valley and the onslaught subsided to occasional flurries. Beyond the valley and angled due north, the snow capped peaks of Commissary Ridge bore out a curious snippet I had gleaned off the radio. The Rocky Mountains were cloaked in 138% more snow than was typical for this time of year. Should a heat wave hit the Great Basin, as was usual at the beginning of summer, the authorities were concerned about the sudden surge of meltwater and the danger of flash floods which could charge down a gulch, overwhelm the road, and wash away the traffic. The frame of mind I was in, it would have been a blessing.

For no apparent reason, barbed wire reappeared between the road and the lip of the escarpment on my right. Out of the haze, a couple of blokes emerged walking the wire, checking its tension. They leaned into the wind, staring and pointing at me like I shouldn't have been there. Beyond a low rise, a team of labourers and a handful of plant were closing off the range on the opposite side of the road. Considering it is such a vast empty landscape, I had seen precious little open space in the Cowboy State. For hundreds of miles, barbed wire had hemmed me in as surely as brick walls, regardless that thousands of square miles of near empty desert lay the other side. It separated the public highway from public land in the shape of BLM land, and was erected by protectionist ranchers who had bought the grazing rights for herds I had yet to see.

Barbed wire similar to today's was patented by Joseph Glidden of Illinois in 1874, after experiments using a converted coffee mill, but there were 101 different designs of spiked wire in the nineteenth century. On the walls of cafés, I had seen boards displaying Brigg's Obvious,

Brinkerhoff's Riveted Splicer, Scutt's Arrow Plate and god-knows-who else's vicious contrivance. Historically a line of conflict between the romantic footloose cowboy and the prosaic grounded farmer, the desert was now penned in by the 'Devil's hatband' while the fields of Illinois lay unfenced. The freedom to roam which cattlemen fought to preserve by tearing down fences was a thing of the past, thanks to cattlemen erecting fences.

The Panther hammered me from the side with 50 mph incursions as I crossed a spur of Commissary Ridge. Time and again I had to thrust out a foot to prevent being toppled. I considered giving up and trying Larry Donovan Smith's trick of hitch-biking, but there was no traffic. I contemplated taking shelter and waiting for the evening lull, but there was nowhere to stick a tent this side of the shiny new wire. I was sick of cycling, sick of life, but my brain fixed on something my mother-in-law once said. Staggering into her kitchen after a particularly awful ride through a Lincolnshire snow storm, I commented that I was getting too old for this cycling malarkey. "You'll never give up riding your bicycle," Pauline observed. She hadn't meant it the way I now mentally chanted it, but the mantra kept me pushing onwards.

Pauline's words carried me out of the high desert, down through rounded hills chaperoning the furious floods of Fontenelle Creek and the Hams Fork River. In and out of the coal mining town of Kemmerer, the mantra prodded me to struggle up the side of the small mountain beyond, past open cast wounds. Finally, at day's end, I found respite several thousand feet below the high desert in a dramatic slash through the tail end of the Wyoming Range. At last I was in the midst of real mountains, crossing the Rockies the way ranges should be. High rock buttes and steep alluvial fans penned in the thorough-fares, forcing road, rail and river to compete for space. Tomorrow I would enter Utah, a state where the wind didn't blow, according to the Mormons from Logan I had shared a camp fire with. On the radio, the heat wave feared by those who measured the unseasonal snow cap was the late night headline. It had engulfed the east coast. Washington was wilting under 43°C and electricity companies were worried the rush to turn on air conditioning units would overload the system. A quarter of an hour later, in the wilds of the Cowboy State, hail scythed down and the temperature dropped below freezing.

Chapter 23
The California Trail

The state line was a rule on the map bisecting the eastern edge of the Bear River Valley. 'Utah — Still the Right Place', the sign assured me. It was indeed still, though I wasn't convinced the lack of wind had anything to do with the Joseph Smith's position at the right hand of God. I swept off Eli Hill, crossed the Bear River and carved through floods swamping a broad expanse of lush green water meadows, now following my own bearings. Though a few of the California bound did continue due west from the river, the overwhelming majority exploited the Bear River Valley to push into present day Idaho, arching north round the formidable barrier of the Wasatch Mountains. My objective was the Great Salt Lake Desert beyond and a heritage site which remembered a moment in American history that brought down the curtain on the wagon trains rolling west.

On a snaking line, I climbed through the bulbous sand hills of the Lake Ridge Mountains which were the forward defence line of the Wasatch. Rock-chucks (chipmunks) stood on hind legs to study my approach and lizards scurried away so fast their feet didn't touch the ground. Now and again, the warning castanets of rattle snakes basking by the road encouraged me to swing wide. On the far side of the hills, pelicans paddled contentedly in the washed out glazes of another emerald green tureen, and long-legged ibis gracefully swept the margins for snacks. To the north, the vivid blue waters of Bear Lake extended twenty miles into Idaho. The shoreline was edged with saplings and a froth which deposited something like salt on the narrow sandy beaches. I quizzed an angler and learned it was scum from limestone, apparently suspended in the water and responsible for the lake's extraordinary colour.

I had entered a little tourist area. On a hill behind the village of Pickleville, a colony of American *dachas* reminded me of the A-frame enclaves clustered beside lakes in landlocked Central Europe. Between the road and the shoreline a holiday village of small apartments stood stern as a communist housing project. The local store was newly stocked with beach balls, flippers and kid's fishing rods. The owner was building an extension to provide fast food for the expected surge of summer visitors, but he wasn't a happy man.

"Worst darn spring I can remember," he told me. "I spent all winter building that rear extension. Got a whole lot of wood and kitchen equipment I gotta pay off. I don't need this weather. Today's the first fine day. I sure darn hope it ain't fixing to change."

A jacked up pick-up with Big Foot tyres and mean looking bull-bars growled to a halt in front of the store. Two cool dudes in shades and designer long-hair climbed out. They might have been members of The Eagles.

"What *are* you doing?" the older of the two inquired, eying up my rig.

I told him.

"Shit, man, you've gotta stay with us tonight, or at least call in for a meal. Julie's gotta meet you."

The two were brothers and both lived in Logan, on the other side of the Wasatch Range. It was a town I was going through but not planning to stay at. Gary drew me a map to their place. It was at the corner of the crossroads where

I would leave town, right next door to where his parents lived.

"You can't miss it," Richard said. "There's a heap of pick-ups, cars and bikes out front."

The boys were a couple of fast talkers, self-employed and currently building a *dacha* on the hill for some fat cat from Logan. I said I might see them later, though it was unlikely I would get that far in an afternoon.

The climb over the Wasatch Range was a series of steep switchbacks which Gary thought would take me all day and him several weeks. It ascended 550 metres up the side of Beaver Mountain, zig-zagging past new cabins and condos. Two thirds of the way up, the road became shaded by the mature pines and silver birch saplings of the Cache National Forest. Over the summit of the pass, it dropped into a long treeless corrie called Swan Flats where large pockets of snow remained frozen to the grass slopes and skeletal broadleafs up the mountain sides had yet to discover it was well past spring. Hanging valleys were heavily shrouded in white and still providing good ski runs. On through a narrow granite incision and the highway took an earnest dive down to Beaver Creek. If this was the start of the descent into Logan, I would certainly be taking advantage of Gary's offer. The lads overtook me, passing a soda across as we plunged.

Where Beaver Creek tumbled into the Logan River, the bubbling waters swelled, the valley narrowed and the road began switching round smooth corners. Tall pines clung to steep convex slopes and mountain grasses held fast where trees couldn't. I swept into a narrow canyon of quartzite — sheer, naked and fractured at crazy angles. High above me, teetering towers of rock were poorly stacked like a child had been playing with building blocks. Then the parapets peeled away and the road plunged back into dark forest.

Spat out at the town golf course, I emerged on an edge overlooking Logan's 'Nob Hill'. In the background, across Cache Valley, the next snow-capped ridge of the Rockies was racked up. In the subdued light of evening it looked like sponge pudding with cream. I turned onto the grid extending down into town and freewheeled past the Mormon Temple, an austere Victorian brick edifice, three stories high and topped with battlements. Somebody flicked a switch and the upper quarter of the east and west towers were suddenly illuminated, dominating the townscape like the eyes of the Devil waiting at Hell's Gate.

Richard was right about Gary's place. On the corner before the railroad track out of town, the yard clogged with motors and trail bikes was difficult to miss but in keeping with the neighbourhood. Gary was on the lawn playing with his young step daughters, Taha and Lexi, and Richard was visiting, looking snappy astride a low-rider Harley. I turned onto the grass and was welcomed with a beer by Julie. Gary's partner was a trim thirtysomething with a homely face and mousy hair hanging in rat tails. From her embarrassment, I got the feeling she had never met a foreigner before.

The Fackrells were from Orange County, California, though they were not a good example of the white flight Al told me about at the bar in Guernsey. The family had moved east in 1980 to escape escalating racial tensions, but Richard and Gary had returned as soon as their independence allowed. They missed the pace of the Golden State.

"Man, for all the shit, there's a real buzz about L.A. you sure don't get stuck in this hole," Richard groaned. "Logan is like morguesville, man."

At forty-three, Gary was five years older than Richard and had clear, exciting memories of the Watts riots back in August 1965 when thirty-five people died and innumerable buildings were burnt to the ground. He wouldn't forget the flames lighting up the city and the soot falling out of an ashen sky. When the troubles began, his dad and himself joined a group of residents who commandeered dump trucks, disabling them to seal off either ends of their street. Equipped with guns, rifles and baseball bats, they patrolled the barricades in shifts throughout the riot, holding everybody at bay, including the police.

I stayed with the family for two nights. During that time, Gary recounted one story after another from his ghetto days, each more alarming than the last and always involving guns. There was a disconcerting matter-of-factness, but the respect he had for the twisted ethics of Mexican-American gangs shone through.

"When you can look into somebody's eyes and just see black — nothing — you know you're dealing with one mean motherfucker, probably a gang banger who'd waste you soon as spit."

When he walked the Orange County streets to go shopping, he packed an M-11 he called a "home protection device" and a pistol, in case the machine gun jammed. "But the best method of self-protection," Gary said, "was to show no fear." The slightest twinge of self doubt spelt trouble in an area patrolled by young bloods looking to earn their colours by picking off a white boy in a drive-by shooting. At school, he was the only Caucasian in his class. He knew and had the respect of a lot of gang members, which made him an even more tempting target for rival punks. At night, he slept with a shotgun and a pistol within reach, and still did. Richard told the story of his brother purchasing a water bed and lining the gap between mattress and bedboard with fire arms. "Damn thing burst first time he climbed in!" Richard said, howling with laughter.

For different reasons, both brothers moved out of Orange County five years ago. Richard missed it and would move back like a shot, except his partner was a bank manager and didn't ever want to go near the place again. Though still hyper, Gary was learning to slow down, but he found it difficult to sleep without the television blaring. Logan was simply too quiet at night. He was really getting into his "three ladies" and felt the kids were a calming influence. The way he was with them, it was difficult to believe Taha and Lexi weren't his own. As for

Julie, you couldn't hope to meet somebody from a more diametrically opposed background.

Julie was a farmer's daughter, born and raised in the neighbouring village of Newton. She had never been outside of Utah. Married at fifteen (as is not uncommon among Mormons), she left the relationship when her youngest, Lexi, was six months old (which is a lot less common). She met Gary while waitressing at a café down the road, and moved in with him four years ago. They weren't married and the closest she'd been to real fear was when a social worker from the Saints dropped in unannounced to see how the family were doing and why they no longer attended church. Fortunately, Julie's ex was also called Gary and Gary II wasn't stood around with a coffee in one hand and a ciggy in the other when the woman called. Although no longer practising, Julie's biggest fear was being excommunicated from the Mormon Church. Until I visited the Tabernacle in downtown Logan, I hadn't appreciated how deep their tentacles reached.

According to the Doctrines and Covenants of the Church of Jesus Christ of Latter-Day Saints (LDS), 'All who have died without a knowledge of (the) gospel, who would have received it if they had been permitted to tarry, shall be heirs to the celestial Kingdom of God.' In other words, if you drop dead before getting the chance to become a Mormon, don't despair. You can be baptised in your absence and thus be assured entry into the Kingdom of Heaven, a place rapidly filling up with more Mormons than were baptised in the flesh. It is a basic tenet of the Church that members should search out their ancestors through its world wide Family History database and pass on their names for baptism. That the religion didn't exist when they died or was rejected by them when alive was a mere technicality.

In less cynical tones, all this was explained to me by Brother Ephraim, stood beside the baptism pool in the cellar of the Tabernacle, next door to the Family History computer room. The chrome and perspex encased tub was where living beings were immersed and welcomed into the Church. The dead joined the immortal congregation at baptism ceremonies held in the Temple on the hill. Despite playing up my night with members of the Logan LDS at Martin's Cove, I hadn't managed to blag my way into the bastion with the scary eyes. I settled for a guided tour of the Byzantine meeting house where Church business and conferences were conducted.

Brother Ephraim was a conscientious guide, but his wife viewed me with suspicion.

"You seem very interested in the LDS," she said with raised eyebrow.

"I used to be a chorister at Rochester Cathedral," I explained truthfully but obliquely, adding nothing more than, "Sorry, Ephraim, you were saying?"

His wife politely but firmly hurried Ephraim through the remainder of my tour, reminding him of a prior engagement he seemed to know nothing about. "Maybe you would like one of our congregation to call on you?" she asked when we returned to the foyer and I made to leave. Brother Ephraim gave me a leaflet entitled 'The Family: A Proclamation to the World' and I gave his wife a false address.

Logan was a quiet, painfully respectable community — the sort of place where fashion stores had finally made it into the 1990s and the video shop eschewed racy movie posters in favour of historic photos of the town. While I queued in the Bank of Zion to cash traveller's cheques, I read the Proclamation. It was tough on families, tough on the causes of broken families, and I could understand why Julie was fearful of the Church finding out she was living in sin. 'Further, we warn that the disintegration of the family will bring upon individuals, communities and nations the calamities foretold by ancient and modern prophets.' It was a heavy responsibility for a loving mother and simple farm girl brought up in the strict ways of the Saints. It was unforgiving, coming from a faith which originally encouraged the taking of multiple wives.

When news of the Californian gold strike reached the LDS in Salt Lake City, President Brigham Young sternly directed his flock to stick to their tasks and ignore the temptation to desert Deseret (Utah) in search of greater riches. One of his trump cards was to order all waverers to take another wife. Readily available and officially sanctified sex with multiple teenage wives was a strong incentive to keep the male brethren in the fold. Why head for the flesh pots of California when you had concubines lined up at home? In his own household, the 'Lion of the Lord' had twenty-seven wives, the last of whom, Ann Eliza, became so outraged by her husband's meanness she mounted a nation-wide lecture tour entitled 'My Life in Mormon Bondage'. Ann Eliza blew the gaff on Mormon harems and helped precipitate the introduction of federal anti-bigamy legislation, though thousands of Mormons still practice polygamy.

On the other hand, strict rules governing the immediate and greater family made for successful, comfortable lives if you were a practising LDS living in Logan. The Mormons looked after their own, and Julie was concerned to keep the Church in ignorance for the sake of her daughters. Her own beliefs and practices might have slipped, but she was not going to let that hinder her girls enjoying the appreciable benefits of being an active member of the Logan Saints, should they so decide in later life. Somewhere in the distant past the Fackrells had flirted with the LDS, but nothing stuck and Gary was discovering the hard way what it was like to be a non-believer in a Mormon town. He found it difficult to get the contracts and the pay cheque he enjoyed back in California, where he worked for a company fitting out franchises like the Warner and Disney stores. He earned and spent big money then, but in Logan, seven dollars an hour was a good hourly rate for a skilled joiner.

"I've worked for a lot of local companies, but you soon find out this town's divided between peons and owners, and their ain't nothing in between. I mean, what fucking Mormon's going to invest in someone like me?"

'Peon' was a favourite word of Ma Fackrell's, used liberally when she held court in Gary and Julie's kitchen. Separated from next door by only a scrawny hedge, Gary's mum popped in about fifteen times a day — fourteen times more than Julie felt necessary, though she was quick to assure me she got on well with Ma. Thin, scraggy and dressed like a refugee from Haight Ashbury, Ma Fackrell was an intelligent, strongly opinionated republican, but she shrank into the shadows in the presence of Pa. Jim's big-boned brawn and abrasive machismo left nobody in any doubt whose genes Richard and Gary had. An ex-Naval fire-fighter who had seen forty years of action in and out of wars, Lee chain-smoked his way through everything including eating.

In a house where they had never thrown anything away, Lee's personal mess was his gun room. We entered through a locked door, though the window onto the street had no more security than a drawn curtain. The walls were wood panelled and covered with guns, pistols, rifles, shotguns, machine guns, muskets and bayonets. Gun cabinets and shelves heaved with more firearms. Under a pile of papers and tools, the table was covered with boxes of bullets and bits of dismantled side arms. Though he had taken pot-shots to test his weapons, Lee was more of an amateur gunsmith than a hunter, carving new stocks, renovating historic pieces and trying his hand at engraving barrels. His collection amounted to over 100 weapons.

All but four of them meant nothing to me. While father and son swapped anecdotes about M-11s and Saturday Night Specials, I picked up an original double-action Colt .45, famously known as the 'Peacemaker'. Unexpectedly heavy and uncomfortable in the hand, I couldn't imagine anybody drawing it at speed or hitting anything they intended. In the dying years of the Gold Rush, the Colt was a popular weapon but, in 1849, long muzzle-loading rifles similar to the Kentucky .45 on Lee's wall were the firearm of choice. Accurate up to a couple of hundred yards, they were good for hunting but inadequate if an enemy attacked in force. It sapped my strength just holding the flintlock level to my eye, so I exchanged it for a Winchester '73 repeating rifle, mythologised in the eponymous Anthony Mann movie. A sleek piece of engineering with simple lines and a snug grip, I felt confident I could hit the side of a barn with it. Lastly I tried a long six gun, shorter but similar to the 'Buntline special' supposedly presented to Wyatt Earp by Ned Buntline and reported to have a foot long barrel for whacking trouble-makers over the head. The imbalance of the one I held made it the perfect weapon for shooting myself in the foot.

I tried raising the issues of Columbine and gun control but Lee was more interested in my proposed route across the Salt Lake Desert.

"You do know there ain't nothing out there?" he said, unfolding a map on the gun table. "If y'turn off Route 30, there's a kinda store at Grouse Creek run by a Mormon woman, but you say you ain't going that a-ways?"

My route lay across large patches of tightly-packed blue dots signifying an 'Evaporation Basin'. I hadn't the slightest idea what to expect of the landscape, but knew towns marked on the map no longer existed. Gary had explored peripheries of the desert on his trail bike and spent much of our last drunken evening trying to dissuade me from signing my own death warrant.

"Man, the heat out there is ferocious. There been times I thought I was going to lose it, you know, like fading in and out, hallucinating. And the sweat! You gotta take a water tanker along to survive in that oven. It's bad on a motorcycle, but on a bicycle... man!"

He gave me their phone number, insisting he'd drive out and pick me up, even from Nevada, should I run into problems. Where he thought I would find a payphone in the middle of the desert I wasn't sure, but it was a generous offer.

Chapter 24

Tremonton was a morning's ride from Logan and the last supply depot on my route for going on 300 miles. It looked uncannily like the Mexican border town in *Touch of Evil*. Muddy pick-ups clogged the main street and blew dust-laden exhaust through the open doors of bars and stores whose names ended in 'o's'. But for a few adobe farms widely dispersed in the flatlands before the Blue Spring Hills, civilisation effectively ended at the town's western perimeter marked by I-84. The earth became progressively more parched and cracked as the road dog-legged towards the salt desert. Fields of wild grasses were speckled with white, like the fine dusting from an autumn snowfall. The tarmac took another ninety degree turn and a turquoise hat band appeared, wobbling beneath a heavy crown of blue-grey haze. I had reached the north shore of the Great Salt Lake and could feel the heat cranking up. The mucky white beach was animated by small whirlwinds of salt rising between three and fifteen metres into the air. I was entering a landscape where the extremities of nature were not to be trifled with, particularly not on this day. According to the radio, June 11th was going to be the hottest day of the year.

At Lampo Junction, where my road turned off into the salt desert, a curious noise like the toot of a steam engine emanated from the west. It seemed to come from behind a ridge where there was nothing but a vast expanse of wilderness and the Golden Spike National Historical Park, the objective of my long detour from the Bear River Valley trail. The spike was the last track pin driven into the most famous railroad in the country, and the heritage centre celebrated the route's important contribution to the story of westward expansion. According to my map, however, the lines had been ripped up decades ago, and the toot was too cute to belong to a ghost train.

During the period of great migrations, the call to link the eastern and western seaboards of America with a railroad grew ever louder. Aside from the internal benefits for a country the width of a continent, there was money to be made out of the Far East if the U.S. could drive a wedge between Europe and the Orient. As John Frémont observed, 'America will be between Asia and Europe, the golden vein which runs through the history of the world will follow the track to San Francisco, and the Asiatic trade will finally fall into its last and permanent road.'

In 1862, President Lincoln signed the act which provided for a continuous rail and telegraph line from the railhead at the Missouri through to the Pacific. It was to be built by two competing companies meeting somewhere in the middle. From Sacramento, the Central Pacific Railroad had the herculean tasks of crossing the Sierra Nevadas and part of the Rockies. From Omaha, the Union Pacific Railroad would forge west across the prairies and into the mountains. Construction was subsidised by Washington proportionate to whether they were laying on level ground, high plateaus or through the mountains, and from the start the project was riddled with corruption and sleaze. The two companies went head to head in a race which guaranteed the quality of the track fell hostage to the urgency for quantity. Covering distance brought in the bucks, and bold-faced lies about the nature of the terrain were told to federal funders 2,000 miles from gentle inclines paid for as mountains.

From Lampo Junction, my road wound steeply up to a saddle back. On the left, a knuckle of Promontory Ridge rose over 2,100 metres before plummeting down to the lake at a little over 1,200. On my right, deep scars in the backbone of the Promontory Mountains were evidence of the complicity of the two railroad companies. Parallel railbeds had been cut into the ridge where the lines overlapped. Where a col dipped below the grade, the Central Pacific had infilled and built an embankment while the Union Pacific constructed a trestle bridge, no longer standing. Before the location of the historic meeting was decided, the two companies had passed each other, continuing to earn dodgy money. Often grading crews of the two railroads were working so close to each other, nitro explosions by one gang would rain down rocks on the other.

Beyond the ridge, Promontory Hollow opened out and I found myself back in sagebrush country with a grit railbed running beside me. Another, louder, toot echoed around the hollow, though there was nothing man-made in the landscape save barbed wire and tarmac. The road took a left, flowed over gentle undulations, then crossed a couple of rail lines. A magnificent steam locomotive emerged from a shunting shed hidden in the foothills and moved towards the Golden Spike Visitor Center, where a second immaculate engine waited.

Twenty years after the Forty-Niners set out from Independence, the two railroads officially joined up at Promontory Hollow. Where the visitor's centre now stands, the last spike was driven home at a ceremony captured in the classic wet plate by A.J. Russell and relayed down telegraph lines to Washington (where they cheered) and San Francisco (where a banner proclaimed, 'California Annexes the United States'). The one item missing from the small exhibition was the eponymous golden spike, but the real stars of the show were the steam engines. Faithful in every detail, these gleaming reproductions of the two locos in the black and white picture were a sight to behold. The Central Pacific's *Jupiter* was a polished blue with shiny brass fittings and a large black stack shaped like a funnel. For the Union Pacific, *No. 119* was a stylish matt black and red, heavy on the brass and gold trim, with a pipe stack and white-walled wheels. They were lined up, cow-catcher to cow-catcher, as for the original photo shoot.

Finding them stuck in the middle of nowhere on an isolated couple of miles of track emphasised the extraordinary nature of America's great endeavour. Never mind that the Central Union had to scale higher peaks and blast through more miles of granite than any previous railroad builder in the world. In the rolling prairies, the task was difficult enough. Neither the wood for ties or sleepers, iron for rails and spikes, nor food and drink for the thousands of labourers were readily available in the Great American Desert. Everything had to be shipped up the Mississippi and Missouri Rivers, then carted or railed overland. As historical markers on my ride up the Platte River Valley indicated, crews and tracks were sitting targets for aborigines who rightly believed the 'Ironhorse' spelled an end to their way of life. Then there were the formidable social and policing problems presented by the 'Hell on Wheels' — the rolling city bringing up the rear, peopled by gamblers, prostitutes, saloon keepers and pimps who leeched off the rail crews.

I planned to follow the old railbed across the desert. Producing a BLM map, the ranger at the visitor centre said, "You can ride the grade all on through to Lucin and the steepest it gets is two per cent. The route's fairly obvious. You should find water at Locomotive Springs."

In a wasteland with no obvious landmarks a stranger might identify from a quick glance at his map, I wasn't sure "fairly obvious'" and the word "should'" were particularly reassuring.

"Have you cycled it?" I asked him.

"You kiddin'?"

I sped off down the gravel track beside the railbed, excited at the prospect of entering the salt desert. A liquid sun sat on top of the North Promontories to my right, and the blue hills of Dolphin Island rose like Dracula's castle from the lake ahead. Round the headland, the stone track swung off left to Promontory Ranch. Except for forty head of cattle and low hills furry with wild spring rye, there was nothing else out here. It seemed America's craving for beef encouraged people to farm in the most inhospitable of places. Throughout my crossing of the wasteland, I was to come across indications that optimists had tried and failed in their efforts to make the desert pay.

Where the grit track turned off I carried straight on and joined the dirt railbed to curve north round Spring Bay. The lake was a fantasy painting framed in white depicting a milky doppelgänger of the eerie landscape above it. Silhouetted citadels of rock kept a look out for enemy movement over the dark blue hills, but the stillness of the evening was unnerving. A soft humming noise like somebody had left a computer on suggested something invisible was about. The railbed cut across the tip of the lake and disappeared under water. When it was laid, the lake wasn't there. After a hundred of years of shrinkage, it was mysteriously filling up again. Keeping to the bank, I cut along a faint trace and punctured. Within seconds of stopping I was enveloped by as many mosquitoes as there are people in China. I had discovered the source of the humming and the nature of the enemy.

At sun-up the next morning I struck out across the white flats of the bay, throwing up a cloud of salt as I wove carelessly towards Monument Point. Pulling out a historic picture postcard bought at the visitor centre, I compared views. In the background were the distinctive stacks at the tip of the spit of land I was crossing. Where I stopped on the railbed, a man in the photo stood in front of *Jupiter* and a row of coaches. Behind us, a line of covered wagons were making their way west — the last of the ox powered migrants. Between the steam and the wagon trains, there was a second track in the picture whose railbed had since disappeared. The line from east to west was a single track but, at regular intervals, sidings had been laid so engines could cross. Travelling as an 'amateur emigrant' in 1879, Robert Louis Stevenson spent many an uncomfortable hour in these sidings waiting for the eastern bound locomotive to pass. He noted that those carriages leaving El Dorado were 'as crowded as our own'.

Beyond the rock outcrop, railbed and dirt track ran ruler-straight to a dust patch where the town of Kelton once stood twenty miles away. Under an unfiltered sun, the heat was beginning to give me cause for concern. Salt dust carried on a gentle south-westerly accelerated dehydration and every five minutes I had to sip water. By mid-morning it was evident I had sorely underestimated my liquid requirements, and the four mile diversion to Locomotive Springs proved fruitless. The spring was brackish and ringed with salt like a Margarita. When the argonauts drank from alkali springs, they invariably suffered a bad stomach for which their antidote was to eat spinach. I was right out of spinach and over a hundred miles from the next watering hole. With just three litres left to take me through a scorching hot day, a night, and the morning it would take me to reach Montello, Nevada, I was pushing it.

In the distance, unnatural white rectangles glowed above the scrub. As I crept closer, a cluster of caravan roofs revealed themselves and a woman on a trail bike screamed past me, showering me with sand. In a ragged circle of tents, caravans and 4x4s, hairy men bent over hairy machines, tinkering and tuning. Their molls lay about in shorts and bikini bras, reading bikers' mags and gently roasting. They were a trail bike club from Logan, out to rip up the desert. One of their number had ridden all over the salt wasteland and knew something about the way to Lucin the BLM didn't.

"It ain't obvious at all," he said, contradicting the ranger. "Stick to the railbed until it gives out, then switch to the track. At the first junction take a right. It don't look like y'ought, but if'n y'don't..." He drew his finger across his neck. "That right's, like, crucial. The track's shit but it'll take you back to the railbed in the Baker Hills, then you're clear."

With my water bottles brimming and better directions from somebody who knew the terrain, I rode away confident I would complete the crossing without a hitch. The surface of the railbed changed to crushed coke and crossed depressions over short trestles built by the original grading crews. A dirt road diverted around each rickety bridge, off onto the playa, then back up to the embankment. One diversion ran through a large puddle the width of the track. Not thinking, I rode into it. My bike stopped dead and threw me into the milky mud. We emerged covered in white slip — the sort of liquid clay potters pour into moulds. By the time we reached the crucial turn-off, we were fired and ready for glazing.

I was burning up and had to find shelter, but the sun was giving a good impression of being immediately over-head and the only shade was under me and the bike. The landscape was smooth and rolling, totally bereft of the sheer wall of rock needed to cast any depth of shadow. The rail embankment cast the slimmest of shadows. I scram-bled down, dug my heels in the base and flopped against its side with my toes sticking out in the sun. Immediately sweat gushed from every pore. I allowed myself ten minutes to cool down and rehydrate. With about eighty miles to go before hitting tarmac, I had to make the best of the lethal conditions. It was the fourth day of the weather cycle and another thunder storm was on the cards. Unless the heatwave was more than a blip, tomorrow it might pour down. I could find myself spending up to three days pushing through glutinous mud to escape the desert — three days I hadn't the supplies for.

The railbed curved wide and gently climbed into the Matlin Mountains. In a cutting, old sleepers had been dumped at the side of the track, and tin cans, rusty spikes and bent spoons lay on the jigger. Hovering in thin air above a distant ruled line, the flat bottom of Dolphin Island provided the clue that the Great Salt Lake was somewhere up ahead, indecipherable from the sky. In the scorched pan before it, the plumes of dust devils looked like the beams from disco lights mounted in the desert floor. If the weatherman reckoned Utah was bubbling at 45°C, I reckoned it had to be a degree or two higher where I was.

Twenty miles on, having wound through the Terrace Mountains, a graveyard appeared on my left. Covered in spring rye and impounded by a modern fence, the cemetery contained a small white headstone and a contorted wire cross. I could think of worse places to leave my mortal remains, but it was a hard road to travel for families to pay their respects. Despite a dramatic cross at the entrance made from old sleepers, I suspected the dearly departed were forgotten by everybody but their maker.

A little further on, a single plank of weathered timber stood erect above the sagebrush. It was all that remained of the largest rail town in Utah, born 1869, died 1910. A BLM sign explained that, at its largest, Terrace had between 200 and 2,000 residents, depending on whether you counted the Chinese population. I walked around finding broken crockery and shattered bricks, battered tin plates and rusting mugs. It took a major stretch of the imagination to picture an eight track marshalling yard and a town with a bustling main street, piped water from god knows where and people promenading through a civic park lined with trees. The only indication that anybody had ever settled here were large hollows in the ground, possibly the remains of where the Chinese lived, sensibly troglodyte like the Shoshoni.

Finding fewer than 600 of his white work force could be relied on to clock in each morning, Charles Crocker of the Central Pacific turned to the Chinese at home and abroad. They were an unknown quantity at this sort of labour, but Charles figured any nation capable of building the Great Wall had hidden strengths. Some came from the gold fields, where many of his white workers deserted to, but he 'imported' over 10,000 of them to work on the line and they proved to be a remarkable work force. They arrived already organised into gangs, usually from the same part of China and speaking the same tongue. Unlike the American and Irish navvies who worked for the Union Pacific, they were not prone to sickness. After a day's work, they bathed. They only drank boiled water in the form of tea, and their diet was a sight more varied than the beef and potato staple of the white workers, who drank from streams. Inevitably the Chinese were paid less and allocated the most dangerous jobs. Around 1,200 died during the building of the railroad, but it was unlikely any lay beneath the shadow of the Christian crucifix made of rail ties. Aside from the racism which denied them access to town cemeteries, the Chinese community was well organised. A kind of insurance policy came with the loan to buy their passage across the Pacific. In the event of death, it provided for their body to be returned home.

Though it allowed me to admire their carpentry skills, flicking on and off the embankment to by-pass the bridges made for hard riding. After clambering over a particularly well preserved trestle near Watercress sidings, I noticed strands of something like rye trapped between my rear rim and the tyre. On closer inspection, the outer casing of the tyre had frayed in two places, shredding the wall into strands which revealed the kevlar mesh.

I paced back and forwards, cursing myself for not giving my bike a thorough overhaul back in Logan. Where was my head? With over 2,000 miles of wear in them, what was I doing in the middle of a desert without a spare tyre? Had the Panther whittled away more of my brain cells than I cared to admit?

As far as I could remember, Tremonton didn't have a bicycle store, and it was over a hundred miles back to Logan, which did. Ahead of me, the nearest town that might supply a tyre was Wells, Nevada, the same sort of distance away. If not, Elko was fifty miles further on. I could repair the tyre but a bandage was not going to get me far across this sort of terrain. I was in trouble.

At the end of the ripped up railroad, Lucin was another company town which had disappeared off the face of the earth. Beyond the X that marked the spot, a short-cut was laid in 1904 which forged straight across the Great Salt Lake, sealing the fate of the desert loop. West of the X, the modern railroad stuck to the original course of the Central Pacific through to Montello, then Wells, Elko, Winnemucca and points west to Sacramento. Once again, a railroad was going my way, at least as far as

Winnemucca, where I would pull away from the main thrust of the California Trail to cross another forbidding cauldron.

Having spent the evening and morning repairing my tyre with an attention to detail worthy of a neurosurgeon, I followed the Southern Pacific railroad out of the salt pan. I could have drunk a swimming pool but had downed my last drop the night before. If the repair gave out, I had a full day's walk to the nearest tap. The sooner I reached smooth tarmac the better. The railway line converged on Route 233 at Montello, Nevada, about twenty miles away, but after four, a sign saying, 'Private: Trespassers Will Be Shot... DEAD' spurred me to cut across to the road early, free ranging through sand dunes on a strength sapping trudge.

I had switched the frayed tyre to the front wheel and the patch appeared to be holding up. Riding the newly-laid pavement, two little bumps rebounded through my palms each time the wheel rolled over the dressings. Into a dry gulch and out again, I crossed the state line and the road became a horizontal plumline across a glaring expanse of nothing. Through binoculars I could make out a small copse of trees, but no Montello. A pick-up zoomed past. Fifteen minutes later I could still see it dead ahead. I was back in the land of distorted distances, where the foot of mountains forty miles away appeared no further off than half an hour's ride.

The huddle of trees finally stepped back to reveal the village of Montello, 'Pop: 193. El: 4880'. The highway clipped the village and was the only tarmac road in a cross-hatch of rusty trailers and weathered bungalows. On one side was the railroad and some sheds. On the other, front street was a run-down motel, a gas station-cum-store, The Cowboy Bar, and a hundred yards of boarded up businesses. While I knocked back a couple of litres of water, the woman at the gas station told me the mishmash of residences were mostly retirement homes. Those who commuted worked in the slot joints, casinos and brothels of West Wendover, adjacent to the Utah border and handy for deviant Mormons. Aside from a little ranching and the surviving front street businesses, Montello's only other gainful employment was to be found at the "cat house" or brothel. I was more taken aback to learn that the woman I was talking to was married to a rancher who came from Chelmsford, England.

In The Cowboy Bar and Café, two old boys were yanking the hell out of a couple of slot machines and knocking back Buds. Good rockin' country music boomed from a live concert on the TV featuring a couple of artistes world famous in Nevada. A couple of hussies shoe-horned into Levis and Wonderbras jostled in behind me, taking time out from working on their back. While I waited for ham and eggs to appear, I studied the BLM map pinned to the wall next to a lurid portrait of Red Cloud, Chief of the Lacotas. The Forty-Niner's route had taken them on a broad arc through present day Idaho, forty miles north of my line, then back south along Goose Creek to Thousand Springs Valley. I planned to rejoin the trail at Thousand Springs, over fifty miles across the other side of the Toano Range, the western backdrop to Montello. Checking the contours and track, I decided it was pure madness to attempt the crossing. My injured tyre might survive the sands of the desert, but the rocks of the mountain pass would surely rip it to shreds.

My alternative was to stick to smooth tarmac. Ultimately all tracks and roads led to the Humboldt River, where the different branches of the California Trail merged to cross the final wildernesses. I ran my finger along the river valley, my spirits sinking lower with every mile. From where I picked up the line at Oasis to where I left it, 200 miles west at Winnemucca, there was just one road — I-80, another flaming interstate. There were short sections of country roads but, as with the interstate to Casper, I had no way of knowing if they linked up. The only other possibility was to take the rail company's service track along the valley line, but my morning's trudge didn't auger well for that idea.

I set off down Route 233 to join the dreaded interstate. Beyond the rail crossing the road deteriorated. Sprayed with tar and sprinkled with grit, loose pebbles had been swept into annoying little levees snaking across my path. Within a couple of miles, the last vestiges of the dressings were flayed from the bottom of my tyre. The walls remained fine, but I had other problems. For some reason, I couldn't get my legs working properly. They flopped beneath me like a string puppet's, bereft of all strength. My tongue kept sticking to the roof of my mouth and a peculiar crust sealed my lips. Despite downing a full breakfast and several litres of water, I was still severely dehydrated. At the top of a col, ten miles from Montello, I took a quick break in the shade of a juniper tree. The moment my head hit the sand, I fell into a deep sleep.

All things considered, my body had remained remarkably healthy throughout the second stage of my American odyssey. I hadn't experienced sickness or sunburn, been stung or badly bitten, and my left knee had settled down to being weak but usable. I rode in fear of catching encephalitis or some stomach bug from the ghastly tap water but so far, so good. If any organ was experiencing terminal breakdown, it was my brain. Perpetually locking horns with the Panther, I was suffering from repetitive head-butting injury.

Three hours, a good siesta and ten miles further on, I was standing at the junction with the interstate feeling physically improved but mentally ill-prepared for the 200 mile grind ahead of me. I honked up the slip road, entered the flow of traffic and was immediately faced with a 600 metre climb up through Pequop Pass. At the summit, I looked back and for the first time had a clear view of the Great Basin's metre. Bleak, empty deserts were followed by high broken backbones, followed by more bleak desert and another unimpressive range aligned north to south. So it went on through Nevada, Utah and Wyoming. The panorama was made the more disheartening by the two thick black lines of the interstate ruled straight to the horizon like twentieth century Nazca Lines. Purgatory was a better name for this blind corner of God's Own Country.

I charged down the mountain, my front wheel shimmying wildly under the distorting influence of the repairs. Reverting to the unenthusiastic plod which now typified my pedal across Nevada, I crept across the desert floor of Independence Valley. In the middle of the wasteland was a small compound of white dormitory blocks. Within a heavily fenced compound, a group of men in white fatigues stood smoking outside a white blockhouse. A couple noticed me and pointed, but nobody waved. A large sign said, 'Prison Area: Nevada Dept. of Prisons'. I fancied the sight of me inching across the desolation momentarily made their incarceration a lot more bearable.

Chapter 25

The moment I clapped eyes on Wells, Nevada, I knew it wouldn't have a bicycle shop. A soulless dive of a town, it's *raison d'etre* was encapsulated by a huge mock Mexican service station called the 4-Way Casino which dominated the intersection in the valley. The four ways appeared to be gas, gambling, booze and sex. On the counter, the *Best Cat Houses in Nevada*, a book which had nothing to do with felines, was displayed in a titillating dispenser. In the restroom, the first condom machines I had seen in an American toilet offered French Ticklers, Passion Plus and Hot Fudge — nothing standard. You couldn't move for people pumping money into slot machines, and that was in the convenience store. The gaming room was thick with sweaty truckers and overweight tourists clutching fistfuls of E numbers in one hand and cups of cash in the other. Round the back, a trade show of forty big rigs were lined up in the truck park.

After weeks on the road, hauliers could usually get a bath and a haircut at the barbers down the road, except he was away 'On an ambulance call out', the note in the window said. Clean and smelling sweet, they were ready to play with the cats at Donna's Ranch and ride one of her fillies. On the way back, if they had money and energy to spare, they could try their luck at the Ranch House Casino Café or the Chinatown Casino Motel. Finally cleaned out and feeling guilty as sin about the wife back home, they might wish to beg forgiveness at the St. Thomas Aquinas Church, strategically located in the middle of Main Street. St. Thomas' was one priest who was never short of work. I couldn't get out of Sin City fast enough, but looked forward to the morrow like one looks forward to curing a toothache by extraction.

It was fifty miles to Elko — fifty of 175 miles before I could quit the interstate. The trip would be boring in a

Formula One Maclaren, but on a bicycle... Elko was also fifty miles further than I could reasonably expect my front tyre to survive. With no option but to proceed, I made a point of not inspecting how the patches were holding up. To know they weren't wouldn't have helped. If they were, there was still every chance the tyre would explode, either from the heat or the unavoidable rumble strips which ribbed the hard shoulder.

Most gold seekers wrote unusually little about their days trudging down the Humboldt Valley. Between the state of the diarist's mind and the sorry condition of the company, there wasn't anything new to say about the scorching sun, tiresome terrain, lousy food and mind warping wind. "'My God, McKinstry,'" one noted of a colleague's reaction to his scribbling, "'why do you write about this trip so you can remember it? All I hope is to get home alive as soon as possible so I can forget it!'" Until I cycled across Nevada, I didn't know what sensory deprivation meant.

For most companies, 'each day's events were substantially a repetition of those of the day before', but a few had the misfortune to be preyed on by the local Paiute Indians, who had a taste for beef and mule-meat and, in 1849, found it a lot easier to raid the wagon trains than track fresh meat in the desert. The natives did not, however, attack the whites in the way depicted by Hollywood, galloping round wagons drawn up in a circle, offering themselves as easy targets. The Paiutes weren't stupid, nor were they sufficiently cohesive as a tribe for any one family to mount much more than a small, covert raid on the overlanders. Most stories concern the loss of no more than a handful of animals driven off under cover of night and maybe a shoot out in the hills where the Indians had settled down to cook up their booty. While incredibly frustrating for the wagon trains, particular for those who lost a full team of oxen in a single raid, the confrontation with the Indians of the middle Humboldt was a lot less dramatic than the myth would have us believe.

303

Eighteen miles from Wells, I crossed the web of sluggish rivulets lacing through swamp land which comprised the famous Humboldt River, originally called Mary's River. Somewhat appropriately, the 'Humbug', as some diarists called it, starts nowhere in particular near Wells and, 290 miles later, ends nowhere in particular at the aptly named Humboldt Sink. Described by different overlanders as 'nothing but horse broth seasoned with alkali and salt' and 'the meanest and muddiest, filthiest stream', little had changed about Nevada's longest river except its colour and clarity. If there was no shortage of running water along this indescribably turgid valley, there was also no shortage of piss bottles. This late in the great trek, Forty-Niners were still dumping non-consumables overboard. In modern day America, it was soda bottles full of frothing urine which long distance drivers jettisoned. Spotted beside every length of tarmac since leaving Lincoln, Nebraska, their frequency shot up crossing the deserts. Thanks to motorists too lazy to stop for a slash, an entire medical history of America lies bottled beside its interstates waiting to be analysed.

The sprawl of Elko started fifteen miles before the town limits in the dirt diggings of Ryndon. It defied understanding why anybody would want to live in this ugly blotch of trailers, part built bungalows and piles of scrap vehicles. A handful of miles further on, another hard desert hollow contained a second ghastly sleeper community. Osino was that much closer to Elko and that much older. Between the mounds of twisted metal and bleak trailer homes, some bungalows actually had roofs instead of polythene.

As the pulsating neon of the big city (population: 14,800) hove into view, an enormous billboard welcomed me to the 'Home of the Annual Cowboy Poetry Gathering'. Elko is one of the last remaining kosher cowboy towns in the Wild West, and their annual jamboree of campfires, country music and rhyming couplets was an attempt to preserve the traditions of a way of life which was riding into the sunset. Angled up the talus slope footing the southern range, the trace of a checkerboard had been platted and clouds of dust issuing from the wasteland indicated bulldozers were digging foundations. The town was evidently expanding and mining was now the core industry, along with get-rich-quick tourism. The Silver Dollar Casino was up for sale, but at the Stockmen's, Commercial and Red Lion Casinos the car parks were full.

With a massive sigh of relief, I slipped off the interstate late in the afternoon and collapsed outside the first gas station I came to. I felt filthy and looked like I had been rounding up steers for a month. In a town which wore its wealth on its sleeve, I had a feeling my saddle-tramp appearance wasn't going to earn me cowboy credibility, even if I could recite a witty limerick. I asked a child on a BMX where the nearest bike shop was. He told me the one and only closed down last Christmas.

Undeterred, I set off along the main drag, Idaho Street, to find the tourist information office. After a lengthy discussion cross referenced with a woman in another office, the two young women behind the counter confirmed there was no longer a bicycle store in Elko. "If'n it's just a tyre you'll be wanting, try K-Mart or Western Auto."

I pedalled back down Idaho Street to rifle through the rack of bicycle tyres stocked by Western Auto, opposite the gas station where I started out. They had nothing to fit. Following a lead from an assistant who seemed unusually curious about when I last slept in a bed, I cycled back up Idaho Street, beyond the tourist information office, calling in on various stores at the Plaza Forty Shopping Center and the Rancho Plaza Shopping Mall. Nobody had anything remotely suitable for the wheel of an average mountain bike but, at K-Mart, the assistant had a buddy who was "massively into bicycling." He made a phone call.

"He says there are two bicycle stores in the vicinity." The assistant imparted the information with a broad grin which said my problems were over. "If it's still trading, there's one in Winnemucca, 140 miles that a-way." He jerked the thumb of his left hand. "But there's several in Salt Lake City, 250 miles that a-way." His right thumb jerked.

On the way back down Idaho Street, I called in at a garage cunningly called Auto-Truck Repair. They were closing up, but one of the fitters inspected Kenobi's front tyre and gave me his assessment. The inner tube bulged through tears in the kevlar in a way that reminded me of my hernia of the previous year. How far did he think I would get?

"If'n y'got the Lord on y'side, end of the next block. You sure ain't gonna make it to Winnemucca."

So it was back down Idaho Street and back into the tourist information office to enquire about public transport out of Elko. The girls gave me a town map and pointed out the Amtrak station. The whereabouts of the Greyhound terminus was more of a challenge involving several phone calls.

It was hard to miss the Amtrak station, but not because it was a grand edifice. Elko's railroad station consisted of two bus shelters, one beside the westbound track and one beside the east. No train timetable was displayed, and there was no ticket office or information booth. Their whereabouts was a question nobody on the street could answer. Round the corner, along from the Stockman's Casino, I went in search of the Greyhound terminus. Directed down a urine stained alleyway, I entered an airless office where a queue of bored customers drummed their fingers while a gargantuan woman in a ripped quilted jacket argued vociferously with the desk clerk. A large sign made it clear I would only be allowed four items of hand luggage on the coach — two inside and two underneath — not exceeding fixed dimensions. It would require powers of compression I didn't have.

That left me just one possibility for getting out of town — Larry Donovan Smith's patent hitch-biking. Different states have different laws covering hitch-hiking and it is wise to be informed, so I pedalled back up Idaho Street to find the police station. It was locked and in darkness. Through a squawk box, I was invited into the reception area to wait for the ring of a red telephone which would connect me to Traveller's Aid. Half an hour later, a charming female voice informed me that hitch-hiking was allowed everywhere in Nevada, except on the interstates and slip roads. If I had a couple of hundred dollars going spare, she recommended taking a taxi to Winnemucca but, to the best of her knowledge, the nearest bicycle store was in Reno, just this side of California. She didn't recommend setting out tonight. "There are some wild people in Nevada."

Unlike Wells, Elko is a family town. On the city park opposite the police station, folk took advantage of the cool evening to picnic while their kids played on the swings and slides. In the Ball Park, Elko Junior High were training, watched by the critical eyes of mums and dads on the look out for the next Mark McGuire. I made to ask a middle-aged man sat reading at a table what the situation was regarding camping in the park.

"Excuse me, sir..."

"No!" He turned his back and buried himself further into his book.

"I was just wondering if..."

"No! I ain't got no money." He arched deeper over the page.

"I'm sorry. You misunderstand. I'm from England..."

"I don't care if you've come from God. No!"

In a town where a man can go from riches to rags at the roll of a dice, I guess it was fair to assume I was begging. Either that or I was one of the notorious "wild people." As I pushed my way towards an expensive night in a motel, a gravel voice called from inside a Chevy van whose dented bodywork had been attacked by chisels.

"Looks like you've been travellin' some."

Ray Mabella was a poker-faced man in his fifties, with a pot belly visible between the buttons of his shirt and hair swept over a shining crown. He was sat at the wheel of his

Chevy behind a mess of litter spilling from the dash board. I leant in on the passenger's side and told him woes. The van was piled to the roof with boxes, papers, files, clothing, a mattress, two sleeping bags, diver's weights, fishing rods, golf clubs and a bicycle.

"Don't recommend sleepin' in the park," Ray hissed. "It ain't the cops y'gotta worry 'bout. It's the young Mexican element. If they choose to fuck with you, y'on your own far as the cops' concerned. Y'could try the river bank, south of the city. That's where all the transients sleep, but they's mostly drunks, smackheads and tweekers (speed addicts). Don't fuckin' trust drunks myself, and the smackheads and tweekers'll strip y'bare."

It was fairly obvious Ray was a '76 Chevy away from being a transient himself. Transients without wheels were called 'footies'.

"Fuckin' footies lower the tone of the place and make it tough for the rest of us. Me? I got me a little patch of ground down off Errecart Boulevard where I pull off for the night. Private property next to the river, but y'couldn't put a tent there. An' y'ain't gonna getta ride out of Elko. No fucker goes to Winnemucca, 'cept to get laid. Got the biggest red light district on I-80, Winnemucca."

Mulling over the possibilities, Ray finally agreed I was up Shit Creek.

"Tell you what. You pay for the juice, I'll run you over." He made it sound like we were nipping across town. "Give me a chance to ask you lots of questions about Britain. Kinda curious about Britain."

Ray had nothing better to do with his time. He was an unemployed miner, laid off a couple of years ago when the price of gold suddenly dived. His helmet and overalls hung in the van. Before that, he was a painter-decorator and before that, a golf caddy for former Governor Ronald Reagan of California, whom he detested. It was difficult to believe, but he said he survived on a weekly food coupon of $10. Before he pulled up at the city park, he had begged five bucks off a Presbyterian priest. Three had gone on gas

308

and the remainder on a bottle of milk and couple of hard boiled eggs. He said he was just waiting for a call before starting back down the mines, though exactly where the call would be directed puzzled me. Ray had a hi-fi, TV and a computer on board, but no mobile phone.

Having rearranged his chaos and made space in the van for my clobber, we drove back down Idaho Street to the garage where my search for a bicycle tyre began. Like a fool, I didn't think to ask how big the Chevy's tank was. While I went into the store to get grub for the trip, Ray filled up round the blind side of the van. Having read every label and map in the kiosk waiting for him to finish, I leant over the cash desk to read the digital display. It registered fifty-eight flippin' bucks! And 36¢...and 37¢... The numbers took forever to change.

Paid up, I walked round the van to find Ray with cupped hands scooping dribbles of petrol back in the tank. Filled right to the brim, petrol squirted everywhere when he tried to replace the cap. More dripped from rust holes in the filler pipe. The forecourt was awash with gasoline.

"Better get out fast. He's a nice guy," Ray said, referring to the Latino sales clerk. "He knows me. Lets me buy little squirts of gas. Don't wanna push it."

The sales clerk did know Ray. I had checked with him that the old gold miner was sound, if a little loopy.

I would like to say we roared away from Elko, wheels spinning, but Ray Mabella didn't roar anywhere.

"Don't like to take it above forty-five," he said, spluttering up the slip road onto I-80. "That's fast enough. Get the best fuel economy at forty-five, y'know. It'll make it to Winnemucca okay. Went there once before in the ol' Chevy. Forty-five gets you the most for your dollar. Gonna enjoy this. I love the Nevada sunset. Look at those blues and greys and French blues."

Ray's passion for the Nevada landscape was contagious. The glow of warm sand lit by a becalmed sun and the chartreuse mounds of smooth mountains set before an orange and grey cloudscape did look spectacular, this side of a windscreen.

"Look at that sunset. Isn't it awesome? And look behind, in the mirror. I sure hope those Republican fuck-wits behind are appreciatin' this beauty rather than gettin' steamed up 'cos I ain't goin' a dot over forty-five."

The interstate was being repaired at that point and we were backing up vehicles for a mile, an achievement on a motorway where traffic volume could best be describes as slight.

Ray could talk the hind legs off a mule. He had four monologues which he repeated and embellished throughout the night, though not always recounted in the same order. Firstly, he repeated everything he had said before about the benefits of driving at forty-five, mostly when he had "Republican fuck-wits" on his tail. Secondly, he was in training for the triathlon.

"That bike of mine — it's a tri-bike. I'm trainin' with a guy from Austria. My running's not goin' too well. Got me a femur problem, but reckon we'll be competin' up in Canada this Fall."

His tri-bike was an ancient tourer and his femur problem probably had more to do with his weight problem.

The third monologue followed his flashing every truck which overtook us.

"They appreciate the courtesy of flashin' lights, y'know. I wanna work for them — Swift — the blue rigs. Gonna get my CVL (commercial vehicle licence). Get it in Winnemucca. It's a little easier there. Then get me some experience drivin' dumpsters."

His last monologue was about the love of his life, Kimberly, who was "from good British stock. Gonna marry her some day, have kids, build a home. I've already designed it. Got the plans in the back. Gonna be at Paradise Valley. Gonna get married as soon as I find my mother's weddin' ring. Kimberly lives in Orange County. Works at the sports store where I get my triathlon kit."

Fifty-eight bucks was cheap to bring a little happiness into Ray Mabella's life. The man hadn't driven further than between the town park and his night stand off Errecart Boulevard in two years, and it would have been good to hear his life story. With 140 miles to go at a break-neck forty-five, we had no shortage of time, but I was exhausted. Grateful he wasn't asking any questions about the UK, I faded in and out of his monologues until the lights of Battle Mountain flickered in the distance and I died.

We pulled into Winnemucca around one in the morning. The town was uncommonly dark for a hotbed of vice. Store security lights projected pale yellow rectangles onto deserted sidewalks, augmented by the diluted beams from weak standard lamps. The pixilated neon of Winners Casino beat out a hypnotic rhythm, but there was nobody on the strip to be compelled towards it. A coyote crossed our path, stopped, stared into the headlights, squatted for a pee, then trotted off towards the rail sidings.

It took me two hours to get rid of dear old Ray. I bought him a McDonalds in the only place still open, and had to drag him away from a courting couple who didn't know where Harry Jay's Fishing Store was, had never heard of the man and had no interest in listening to a nutter banging on about fly fishing in Paradise Valley. Having levered him back in the van, Ray insisted on trying to find the cycle store for me.

"Cheers, Ray, but I'm not going to get a lot of shopping done at this hour. I'd just as soon get my head down and worry about it tomorrow."

He wasn't listening. For an hour we drove around gloomy streets before stumbling on Bikes & More three blocks from the town park. Winnemucca wasn't that big, but Ray was a creature of habit. He took his bearings from the town park. After every sortie, he homed back on the green before setting out for a different side of town. Wearily, I thanked Ray for the lift and we parted, or almost. Leaning out of the window, he asked, "Is it true

311

what they say? The English eat roast beef and somethin' called Yorkshire pudding?"

Finally, he had asked me a question about Britain.

"Is it good? That's what I want to do. Go to England and eat roast beef and Yorkshire pudding."

After three attempts at different hotels to raise a night porter, I gave up on dreams of a bed for the night, cycled back to the park and slung up the canvas wherever. Awoken ten minutes later by a loud clatter, I struggled out of my sleeping bag to discover morning had broken. It was barely 6.00am, but golfers and grass cutters were doing the rounds. Three insufferably jolly men striding to the next green waved their clubs in the air and shouted, "Great morning." I had pitched on the edge of the eighth freeway and the club's lawn dog had trimmed a neat oval round my tent.

Chapter 26

By the time the Forty-Niners reached the ford which became Winnemucca, they were in a dreadful state. They were approximately four months out from Independence and, if their timing was right, it was now mid to late September. More than their outward appearances had taken a battering. Men who spent most of their lives in books and in pushing pens had now crossed three deserts and several mountain ranges, and battled through tempests and insufferable heat. Men who were never starved of a good meal now knew deep pangs of hunger and raging thirst. Men who espoused moral indignation had now scrapped with comrades over card games, food and the allotment of tasks — petty disagreements which flared into matters of life and death. The Forty-Niners were shadows of the honourable men who set out with pride, purpose and a great fanfare from their home towns. I understood their bitter transformation and thought a clean shave might make me feel a little closer to my old self. With an hour to kill before Bikes & More opened and I found out whether I could expect to be cycling that day, I strolled into Club Barber on Fourth Street, climbed into a seat and ordered a shave. I was their first customer of the day.

"Where'y headed?" asked the dapper little barber groomed to perfection and swathed in cologne.

"Gerlach, across the desert."

"Whoa!" He put down the electric shaver and thwacked his hand against his forehead. "You're not cycling to Gerlach? Hey, Sandy...!"

He made rapid strides to the back of the shop and parted a curtain. I heard mumbling, then a different voice said, "You serious?" He returned with a thin man twice his age but equally well groomed. They wore matching tops and hair gel, and could have been a comedy double act called Julian and Sandy.

"You really don't want to do that, y'know." Julian began stripping off two months of bleached growth. Sandy hovered close by and added, "People die out there. Gotta gun?"

"Why would I need a gun?"

"There's some real crazy people out there, man. Like, the whole place is just empty desert. Nothing but sand and sagebrush, and not a lot of sagebrush. I drove through there once, y'know, when I was going through a bad patch and needed to take off. I was on my own alright. Just driving it nearly killed me. Took me a week to recover."

I couldn't work out if Sandy was laying it on thick or the route was lethal and he was genuinely concerned I didn't know what I was getting into.

A sheriff's deputy walked past on patrol and waved through the window. Julian frantically beckoned him in and related my proposed insanity as if I was already dead. Sandy asked if the sheriff's department patrolled out in the Black Rock Desert. The deputy shook his head. "Most definitely not! And, I ain't never heard of anybody cycling further than the gold mine at Sulphur and back."

Neither had the ranger from the Bureau of Land Management, the next person Sandy solicited to try and discourage me. I took the phone off him at the far end of the shop, pleased the guy on the other end couldn't see me hovering uncomfortably in my pastel cape and half shaven face.

"It's a tough one, but you should be okay. You'll need plenty of water. There are hot springs along the way, but I don't know if they're drinkable."

Hot springs in an area where there is a mine called Sulphur? If they were the same springs the gold seekers wrote about, they were poisonous and twenty miles out of my way. This was beginning to sound like the kind of wasteland I really should avoid. But it was the route the

Forty-Niners took, or some at least — the ones who arrived here later than August.

The established trail to the gold fields followed the Humboldt into the great quagmire of the Sink, then across the 'Forty Mile Desert' sandwiched between the Trinity and Stillwater Mountains. Having crossed the open oven, the argonauts picked up either the Truckee or Carson Rivers and followed their whisking tails to the backbone of the Sierra Nevadas. By the time the middle of the Forty-Niners' crocodile reached the ford in the Humboldt bend, intelligence about the horrendous difficulties which lay ahead had filtered back down the line. Stories of hundreds of ox carcasses putrefying in the heat and men emerging from the wasteland like the living dead were frighteningly graphic. But a new trail had been blazed arching north, said to reduce the final leg to California to just ten days. Off it, there was thought to be a 'middle route', more difficult but even quicker. Although nobody had yet returned with a verdict on either of the short cuts, it was assumed what became known as Lassen's Cut-off couldn't be any worse than the California Trail.

Bikes & More was now open and they had a tyre to fit my front wheel. The owner, Chuck Austin, was a relation of Julian the barber but didn't bat an eyelid as I outlined my plan to follow the trail across the Black Rock Desert. He walked me across to the back wall of the store where large plan, shadow and topographical maps were pinned. He had done the journey to Sulphur and back, and warned me about mining trucks which batted down the dirt road spitting pebbles.

"Just get out of their way, but the road's good. What it's like after Sulphur, I have no idea. Don't think anybody's ever ridden that far."

Chuck's ambition was to cycle the length of Lassen's Cut-off, which started further round the Humboldt bend at Lassen's Meadows, bisected the Black Rock Desert, then crept north through High Rock Canyon. Today, there are few recognisable tracks along its length and certainly nothing mapped. My proposed route joined the original trail near Sulphur, then turned west to cross the desert length-ways along the 'middle route' later known as Nobles's Road, before realigning north to parallel Lassen's line through the mountains. I could have stuck closer to the historic thread but Chuck confirmed it was unlikely I would live to tell the tale. Equipped for riding where trails were no more, he and a colleague had managed to get no further than Sulphur before reaching for their mobile phone. He was currently trying to work out the logistics of completing the remaining two thirds.

"The problem's water. Over that sort of terrain, that sort of distance, you just can't carry enough for the sweating you do. In this sort of heat, I strongly recommend you don't set out until late afternoon."

With such conflicting reports of the journey ahead, I felt as confused as the gold seekers must have been when their companies reached the fork in the California Trail and had to make a decision. At the junction, they found a crude notice board and a large barrel labelled 'Post Office' where previous pioneers had left scrawled notes directing delayed companies and backpackers. Most strongly recommended taking the Lassen trail, but it was the first and only year of the Gold Rush when anybody did recommend it. Some companies camped at Lassen's Meadows and sent an outrider north to check the lie of the land. Having seen the Black Rock Desert, they returned with a firm thumbs down.

Outside it was nudging 46°C. I changed the tyre in the shade of a willow tree while chatting to Wilfred, a Paiute Indian who was tipsy and taking a siesta in the park. When he worked, Wilfred punched cattle for a local rancher, but the season was over and he was currently trying to stay out of the way of his wife. Since I was Scottish, he said, I probably wouldn't have heard that the white man stole his lands. In fact, it was an insult that the town was named after a Paiute chief. There was a photo of Chief Winnemucca on the front of the town's 'Walk

316

Through History' guide. Dressed in a mock military uniform several sizes too big, 'The Captain' cut a pathetic figure set up to be ridiculed.

It was only a few degrees cooler when I finally took off south-west along the Jungo road. As it kinked west round the base of a mountain sheltering the town, the tarmac crumbled into a dirt road the width of a dual-carriageway and climbed over a smooth ridge beside the rusting super-structure of a deserted mine. A couple of trucks and pups (trailers) rattled past and engulfed me in a sand storm. At the brow, the wind hit me with the force of an Amtrak and threw me to the ground.

"Give us a goddamn break!" I screamed, punching the air in the vain hope of clipping the Panther's jaw. "What in Hell's name have I done to deserve this?"

Beyond the ridge, the road curved down to a flat-bottomed expanse and trundled past sand blasted steel structures which once upon a time had something to do with ranching. A line of dust clouds swirled towards me at a rate of knots. The mines were turning out and mouths gawped and eyes tracked me as the lads rumbled past on their way back to town. From Winnemucca, it was thirty-five miles to Jungo. For six painful hours I juddered across the washboard spitting sand, the hood of my windtop smacking my ears like a sadistic school master. I willed the sun to hang fire in the sky but it was in league with the beast. An eerie afterglow settled as it sank behind the Jackson Mountains, transforming mile upon mile of deadpan desert into a snowfield.

If only to reduce the distance I would have to undertake the following day, I was determined to reach Jungo. There was nothing there but, where the old mining town once stood, the track swung left to cross the railroad. In this miserable vacuum, it was something to aim for. Up ahead, the headlights of a truck and pup crossed the line and turned towards me. They appeared no further than a few hundred metres away. After what seemed like a week, the driver dipped his lights and showered me with dust.

317

Resigned to falling short of my goal, I turned off the track and crunched across cracked alkali to spend the night in the shelter of a scrubby iodine bush beside the railroad.

I fell asleep to the painful whine of the storm racing through the growth, and woke the next morning to the same nerve-racking shriek. I couldn't have felt more distraught if I had come to in a dentist's chair with the drill stuck in an old filling. Without stirring a loin, I unzipped the tent. The wind ripped open the curtains on a raven trying to fly west above the course of the railroad. It was tumbling backwards chased by billowing clouds of sand. In my soul, I surrendered and was resigned to spending the day cowering under canvas. In my mind I knew that, if I did, I hadn't the water to survive an extra twenty-four hours crossing the desert.

Daylight revealed I was three-quarters the way across the width of a playa which stretched south to a finity sliced dead by the blade of an azure guillotine. Flanked by the grey backbones of barren mountains, only the nipple of a lone stack rose above the ocean of alkali. Behind this landmark ran the Lassen trail, heading for the Antelope Hills and Rabbit Hole Wells, the last watering hole before the Black Rock Desert. With great reluctance, I squared up to the Panther and cranked into the Antelopes. Sagebrush and wild rye returned, along with human settlement. Huddled in an amphitheatre of granite, a sagging bungalow, a trailer home and a handful of beaten up vehicles were dwarfed by some kind of crushing machine. Five miles further on, a couple of stranded trucks stood hub deep in sand beside four wooden shacks haphazardly located on land staked with marker posts. Were these the Shangri-Las of the crazies Sandy the barber warned me about? A fingerpost pointing to the Rosebud Mine confirmed there was only one reason anybody would want to live out here, and the continuing traffic of trucks and pups confirmed you needed to shift an awful lot of dirt to extract precious little gold.

My first sight of the starched white sheet of the Black Rock Desert reminded me of those Westerns where the villains are stood at the edge of the playa, weighing their chances of surviving the crossing against the slim chance that the posse would follow them into the furnace. The distance to the Black Rock Mountains on the opposite side didn't appear far, but the heat haze wobbling at their base indicated I was looking at another demoralising foreshortening.

Traversing the desert was the most desolate and demanding section of the argonaut's epic journey. There were no precipitous bluffs to negotiate or flooded torrents to ford, but there were mud flats and sand dunes to delay them, an incinerator's heat to drain them, at least twenty miles between brackish water, and no grazing for the animals. Where they trusted in God, I relied on covering at least twice the distance the Forty-Niners achieved in a day to get me safely to the other side. Unfortunately the wind had slashed my speed to their walking pace. Unless I could find fresh water or put in a mean turn of speed, I was buggered.

The trail followed the dramatic cliffs edging the Antelope Hills round to the zeugen of Pulpit Rock. Beyond the outcrop, the sharp butte on my left became a smooth escarpment of mining debris. Tucked between mountainous dumps was the Crowfoot and Lewis Mine, from where the trucks and pups emanated. Unlike the renegade operations I had passed in the Antelopes, this was a commercial gold mine, with brick offices, a cavernous hanger housing the winding gear, and tight CCT security hanging off every high fence post. I pressed the intercom. Somebody pushed a button and the electric gate rolled back.

"Gee, we don't get a lot of cyclists passing this way," the receptionist said, filling my *bidons* with spring water from a cooler.

"When was the last time?" I asked.

319

"Actually, we never get cyclists passing this way. Help yourself to coffee."

The track beyond the goldmine which Chuck Austin couldn't give a verdict on was terrible. Heavily wash-boarded and narrow, it was edged with grit levees which skewed the front wheel and dumped me in a heap. By the time I reached the remains of the historic mining town of Sulphur (a grounded shingle roof and one shack the size of a 'thunder box'), I had decided to ignore the track and make a bee-line for the playa. I struck out across the margin, dragging my rig through the dunes, wondering if I wasn't making a big mistake by leaving the BLM trail.

The sun was at its peak and sweat flooded out of me. Beside the railroad line, telegraph poles provided a sliver of shade and a track-light control box projected a little more, but neither shadow was sufficient to shelter a body. Quarter of a mile down the line stood a shiny oblong the size of a small garden shed. Stretched along the foot of it, I ate and rehydrated myself ready for the dash along the desert. A freight train rattled past. As the last flatbed rolled down the track, a voice piped up behind my head. My teeth locked on a tuna sandwich. Somebody in the box was informing somebody else that the train had passed checkpoint 456 doing fifty-six miles an hour. I walked round the box to find the entrance and discovered the unit was totally sealed. A second train passed and the comput-erised voice announced it was travelling at sixty-four.

Lassen's Cut-off was originally forged five years before the start of the Gold Rush in order to spirit migrants from the east to Peter Lassen's ranch, a hundred miles north of what became Sacramento. Later renamed 'Greenhorn Cut-off' or 'Lassen's Horn' (implying a harrowing route on a par with sailing round Cape Horn), the detour was not what the argonauts hoped it would be. From the start, it steered them away from the gold fields on a slow collision course with the most northerly tip of the sierras. While many companies sensibly travelled at night, the crossing of the Black Rock Desert was still a journey through Hell.

Like an incubus guard of honour, the route was lined with hundreds of festering cadavers, piles of discarded goods, burnt out and abandoned rigs, and human graves. They passed desperate people pleading for water and a ride out of the inferno, but nobody could help them. It really was every man, woman and child for themselves, but some who found themselves in difficulties still had the perverted presence of mind to think ahead. Firmly believing that, having reached the gold fields, they would return to collect whatever they had been forced to eject, they buried superfluous gear in false graves and marked them with a fictitious name. As if one crossing of 'Lucifer's Anvil' wasn't enough in the lifetime of people who entered it thin and weak, and emerged emaciated, sick and swollen tongued.

Except for the wind, I was having a great time riding across the hard baked pan of the playa. There were no corpses littering my way, the sky was clear and I had plenty of water. Since the oasis of Gerlach lay at the southern tip of the Granite Mountains tapering down before me, I could even see my goal. For a bit of fun, I closed my eyes and rode blind, curious to see if the right foot rule of wandering held true for cycling. This is the principle that, given a featureless desert to walk in, right footed people will naturally veer gently in the opposite direction to their strongest leg, ultimately prescribe an anti-clockwise circle. I'm left footed but the bike still swung anti-clockwise. I blamed my weak knee.

Other people also have fun in this terrible but stunningly beautiful desolation. There is an annual diary of desert attractions which include a golf tournament, hot-rod racing, dirt yacht regattas, and the Burning Man Festival, a sub pagan rave which annually attracts over twenty thousand cyber-heads and hippies. Without lashings of technology trundling in to provide life support, none of these events would be possible of course, and there was currently great concern from conservationists that the playa was being spoilt by trash which becomes permanently embedded in the surface.

I saw no scars in the playa except a few tyre tracks, but the fun was rapidly ebbing. After an hour the windswept pan became samey, after two it got boring, and after three it was driving me round the twist. A combination of wind resistance and my distorted perception of distance meant I was monitoring progress purely by watching the wheels go round. The landscape either side barely changed. If I forced myself not to look to the right for half an hour, it was just possible to detected a slight shift in the aspect of the distant mountains when I turned back. Looking ahead, my eyes were like a camera moving forwards while the zoom lens opened out. The depth of field was tearing open, but the subject wasn't getting any closer. I tried the radio for something to occupy my mind and picked up only one station. I opted to let the desert drive me crazy, rather than the Christian fundamentalists.

I was slow to realise it, but the heat and dust were taking a toll on my body as much as my mind. My tongue began sticking to the roof of my mouth again and stuff like dried snot sealed my lips. My skin turned soapy where I sweated and itchy where I didn't. Initially I was taking a sip of water every fifteen minutes. By the time what I believed to be Gerlach shimmied to the horizon, I was sipping every twenty turns of the pedal and running dangerously low on liquid. What appeared to be a lake lapped at the foot of the Granite Mountains, possibly the same lake which drove cattle ape when the wagon trains crossed. The animals sensed water and stampeded away from the trail towards a trick of the heat which augured their death.

My water dried up as I crept past the mirage of Gerlach. The town turned out to be a line of low hummocks like the backbone of a buried dinosaur, topped with shrivelled sagebrush. On one mound, a desert vixen watched her cubs rough and tumble around the lair. Ahead, white rectangles in a green blur suggested this time I really was approaching Gerlach, but very slowly — so slowly I had to discipline myself not to look to the front. On my left, the railroad was closing in on the town. I fixed on the telegraph poles to monitor my progress, counting them off for something to do. An hour and a half later I was close enough to confirm the blur was the oasis. Between me and the gallon of root beer I had fantasised about for most of the day lay a moat of porridge. Whichever tack I took, I ran into gloop. Finally I gave up trying to pick my way through and slopped straight across three miles of alkali mud dragging the bike, never thinking I was wallowing in something vicious. It was another hour and a quarter before I crawled up the beach to the isthmus of sand on which Gerlach rested. From knees down, my skin was on fire.

I staggered into the Texaco station like Swamp Thing emerging from the quagmire. It was more a workshop with a broken drinks machine than a service station with a mini mart. The mechanic pointed me in the direction of Bruno's Restaurant and Bar. I tried to saunter in nonchalantly, but blew it when I fell against the bar and whispered, "Beer."

"Wassat? Where you ridden from?" Bruno asked.

I muttered.

"Ha!"

Bruno was a man of few words and those he shared were short. The woman sat next to me at the bar explained his attitude problem was probably a product of Italian-Basque parentage. She cleaned the motel for him, "The blockhouse you passed after the gas station."

"I did?"

"You're in a kinda state, huh?" she observed.

The cleaning lady took charge of me. She ordered another round of drinks, handed over the key to a room in Bruno's Motel and sent me away to sort myself out. Leaning on my bike, I teetered back down the road to the blockhouse and flopped onto the bed. I could have drifted into oblivion but badly needed to attend to my burning flesh. Stripped and aiming for the shower, I stumbling into the bathroom and immediately jumped back in surprise. There was a skeleton in the cupboard.

I hadn't seen myself naked in a full length mirror since Paul and Arlene's place back in Nebraska. My collar bones protruded like granite mountains from a playa of stretched skin the colour of terracotta. When I moved an arm you could see every sinew operating. My face, arms and legs were dusted in white compact and streaked with rivers of sweat. My eyes were blood red and, around my mouth, it looked like I'd eaten a meringue off a plate without using hands. Except for stinging skin, a ringing in my ears, a mouth washed out with kitchen cleaner and utter exhaustion, I felt better than I looked. In ten days time I was due to meet my wife at Sacramento. I imagined Sandy taking one look at my emaciated body and calling Oxfam.

Chapter 27

Gerlach was uncommonly pro British. In 1997, Richard Noble used the village as a base for his bid to reclaim the world land speed record on the Black Rock Desert. According to an autographed poster hanging in Bruno's Bar, his vehicle had the combined pulling power of 141 Formula One cars and clocked 850 mph — 100 mph faster than the speed of sound and 846 mph faster than my crossing of the playa. Next door, in the restaurant, I was invited to breakfast with Beth Osborne, who ran the Miners Club two buildings down the road from Bruno's. Two years earlier, Beth had been the Mrs. Fix-It for the speed team, scouring the village to accommodate them. Her club had become the social and merchandising centre for the bid and she had albums of photographs chronicling every detail of the event, from the British landing with all their gear in Reno, through to her stay in England with members of the victorious team — a token of thanks. Concurrent to Noble's successful attempt, an American team was in the desert threatening to outrun the British, but they were a self-contained unit, had nothing to do with the town, and their star driver was a "know-all," Beth maintained. Not surprisingly, Gerlach was the only place in America at that time rooting for the Brits.

We were sat at the table with a retired couple — two of Beth's friends. They had heard the stories and seen the pictures a million times before, but Jack and his Canadian wife also had a soft spot for the British. Jack had always wanted to take "a horse drawn sleigh ride through Nottingham Forest," properly known as Sherwood Forest, and "plant a big wet kiss on the Queen's cheek." He was well impressed that I lived at the southern tip of what used to be the royal forest, but disappointed I hadn't met Her Maj.

"But I've pressed the flesh with Princess Anne and Princess Margaret," I told him.

Jack waved his arm in the air and called to the waitress.

"Another coffee for my friend. He's slept with royalty."

Jack was born in Gerlach eighty plus years ago, when the town's population was closer to 3,000 than its current 300. He remembered it as an important maintenance depot for the railroad, with extensive sidings, a turntable and locomotive sheds. Directly opposite Bruno's, where an unobstructed vista now opened onto the desert, there used to be a large dormitory block for the workers, but all that remained of the glory days of steam was a wooden water tower. Beef and sheep farming in outlying hill spreads was also more productive back in the Twenties and Thirties, and long before it became reliant on desert fiestas to bring in extra cash, the town was a popular stop-over for motor tourists en route to Reno. Though I couldn't think of anything about the place which might be beneficial to longevity, Gerlach was now a retirement community.

Where Jack and his wife had chosen to end their days was originally called Boiling Springs by 'Pathfinder' Frémont. Along with road names like Diablo Street, Boiling Springs about summed up an oasis clinging to a spit of bondu trapped between the two raging white cauldrons of the Black Rock and Smoke Creek Deserts. To be fair, there were trees all over the shop and the community boasted four bars, the Miners Club, and Bruno's empire — the restaurant, bar, motel and Texaco station. I wasn't convinced these amenities were sufficient to persuade any sane person to spend their twilight years in Nevada's equivalent of Death Valley. Jack said it had been blowing a gale since his childhood, but he thought the last couple of years had seen a marked increase in persistency and velocity. He could remember his mother cursing the wind when she hung out the washing, but their whites were always whiter than white.

I was wasted and badly needed rest, but I couldn't face another day in the desert. I desperately wanted to be in

California relaxing by a sparkling stream, rolling like a puppy in lush green grass, relieved to see the back of the Panther. For no reason, I thought everything would magically change the instant I crossed into the Golden State. I made a bid for the relative protection of the mountains to the north and began the long arduous slog up through Jones Canyon. Gradually the mountains wrapped round me, urging me deeper into a fissure carved by a hibernating creek. Coarse grass appeared on the mesa's slopes and black granite outcrops projected ugly faces. It was a relief just to have horizons limited but, from the top of the pass, I surveyed another irksome Nevada basin, hopefully my last. The road hit the bottom and charged unflinching across the scrub until it reached halfway, where it took a 45° lurch to the right and disappeared behind more blue ridge mountains. Knowing this was my last day in the Silver State, I put every effort into observing the scene without the prejudice of having experienced its hardships. Many desert lubbers subscribed to the belief that the wilderness simply reflects whatever is in the soul of the viewer. I'm not convinced. The landscape before my eyes was bitter and had the power to make that of the staunchest of souls.

Floored again by the Panther, I settled for a final night in Nevada on the cracked canvas of Duck Flat. I would have given anything to be in California but, as the evening drew in, Nevada turned on the charm. The blue mountains which had been the skirting boards of every desert floor I had crossed quietly turned a deep crimson. High in the sky, the alto stratus lid became blue-black as polished rust. Between its base and the tip of the western range, a narrow gap glowed like Darth Vador's sword, lighting a solitary wisp of fluorescence sneaking away from the cap. On one side, the cloud was fiery orange turning to green. On the other, white as heat. A coyote howled somewhere to the north and was answered by several from the west. A couple of startling booms announced that prairie chickens were out courting, and

the spluttering hum of what I took to be a zillion mosquitoes hovered around two on the volume control. When I
stopped however, nothing pounced. Maybe the buzzing
was the sound of silence? They say we hear our bodies
ticking over when the world about us provides nothing to
listen to. Even in a vacuum, there is no such thing as
silence, only quiet. If this was the sound of my engine, it
was in urgent need of a mechanic.

Rather disturbingly, everything did change when I
crossed into California a couple of hours after sun-up.
Emerging from a tight pass through the southern tip of
the Hays Canyon Range, the floor of Surprise Valley was
suddenly, eponymously ripe with fields of alfalfa. A
combine harvester was already hard at work. and ponies
padded around the corral of a ranch stacked with giant
toilet rolls of hay. Peering down from the roadside, I unin-
tentionally interrupted a couple skinny-dipping in a large
wooden barrel fed by a mountain stream. She clasped her
breasts, he emerged from beneath her and I knew I was in
California.

But Surprise Valley wasn't truly Californian. It was a
nowhere land between two radically different landscapes, mostly filled by three large areas of salt water —
the Upper, Middle and Lower Alkali Lakes. California
proper lay the other side of the impressive Warner
Mountains to the west. The line I rode squeezed between
foothills and lakes, mirroring the argonauts' route into
what they thought were the Sierra Nevadas but was
actually an off-shoot of the Cascades. What had taken
me four days to cycle took the companies twenty days to
walk, and the better part of a month lay ahead of the
Forty-Niners before they would reach the Mother Lode.
In front of them, 20,000 gold diggers had already staked
a claim.

I slipped into Eagleville before anybody was up and
about. It was the sort of sleepy hamlet where, if folk were
up, they would probably not be about, but rather in the
village store, sipping coffee and shooting the breeze. I

walked in past a tray of freshly baked cinnamon slices and a note saying, 'Just Help Yourself'. At a table in the middle sat three men and the proprietress. They were as welcoming and friendly as I had experienced everywhere else in the States, west of the Ohio River, but Eagleville was the last place for several hundred miles where casual contact with the locals felt comfortable. At Cedarville, further up the valley, I received a surprisingly frosty reception in both the restaurant and store, and where I turned west for the 600 metre hike up into the Warners, a fat slob leaning against a sign made a stinging remark about my chances of riding up the pass.

The climb was tough on the knees but a stimulating change from slogging across the Great Basin. I entered a deep gorge chiselled out by Cedar Creek, my shoulder brushing the footings of gaunt crags which blocked out the sun. A handful of miles on and so much higher, the cut opened out on snow-dusted peaks and dark troughs thick with pines. After the sour stench of sage, the air smelt sweet and I stopped to dabble my feet in the swift bubbling waters of a crystal stream. Another 600 metres above me, Cedar Mountain looked like a little Matterhorn. The Warners reminded me a lot of the European Alps, a familiarity which lifted my spirits by a smidgen. But if the landscape changed the moment I entered California, the wiles of the wind were unaltered west of the watershed. With scant protection from the Modoc National Forest, I forced the pedals downhill, crest-fallen that the Panther had yet to be caged.

I plopped off the edge of a rift into the North Fork valley of the Pit River. At the lip I could see a hundred miles ahead, across broad green flatlands threaded with blue creeks and irrigation channels. At the bottom, a battered GMC was parked on the roadside with a mongrel bouncing and barking while fetching sticks thrown from inside the van. It was one of the blokes from Eagleville. His engine had overheated going up the Warners and hadn't cooled down sufficiently coming down.

"Beer?" The man flicked open a cooler and tossed me a six-pack. "Sure I can't give you a lift anywhere? I'm going south."

Patrick Hammond was a gardener, currently landscaping the weekend retreat of a Superior Court Judge who had bought Patrick's mobile home for $38,000, shifted it 200 miles over the mountains, and now wanted something to look out on. Patrick spent three days a week up in Eagleville, kipping in his van overnight, and two working back home in Blairsden, in the northern sierras. In a little under a week, I was scheduled to ride through Blairsden and was tempted by the offer. A couple of cans later, Dutch Courage got the better of horse sense. I accepted his card, promised to call in for dinner, and wiggled off towards the 'bug station'. I was entering the final, most disheartening section of the argonaut's odyssey.

Since crossing the Mississippi, I had met a remarkable number of people who were hard pressed to say anything good about California, many of them Californians. Time and again I was warned that the state was like no other; that the people were self absorbed, the cops were bigger bastards, prices were astronomical, and any hospitality was given grudgingly. I was expecting it. Long before the lands between the Golden State and the big river joined the Union, California had a PR problem.

Writing in the 1860s to encourage Americans to visit the Far West, journalist Charles Nordhoff observed that, 'Probably twenty Americans go to Europe for one who goes to California'. It was not somewhere Americans knew a great deal about, even during the Gold Rush years. As far from Washington as Israel is from London, it was *terra incognita* until the transcontinental railroad was built. Hearsay, half-truths and lurid tales were fuelled by a discrepancy between the glowing reports sent east by journalists like Nordhoff and the downbeat letters sent home by miners struggling to find their pot of gold. In papers like *The Washington Intelligencer*, the conflicting stories often appeared on the same page.

Easterners held Westerners in contempt, particularly since so many white immigrants married into Mexican families. According to Nordhoff, Americans thought *californios* were 'vulgar and commonplace at best, shiftless, malcontent and positively dangerous at worst'. When American-Californians became overwhelmed by a united nations of gold seekers, character references didn't improve. Influential commentators like Henry David Thoreau thought the Gold Rush was 'a touchstone which has betrayed the rottenness, the baseness (of men for whom) the hog that roots his own living, and so makes manure, would be ashamed of such company.' Others like Nordhoff believed the incomers were made of nobler stuff. Man, woman and child had to be resourceful, determined, confident and blessed with vision to survive the crossing of land or sea and then build a new life out of a carpet bag. 'You ought not to wonder that they are above your Eastern average in intelligence, energy, and thrift,' he observed.

Gold or no gold, California was always going to be viewed through mud-splattered glasses by those in the East. It was, after all, a spoil of war and a captured enemy territory with its own history, an established culture and an entrenched population of Mexicans and Indians. By contrast, the rest of America was a thoroughfare for migrants from all kinds of different backgrounds seeking to put down roots. Unless to Asia, you couldn't 'Go West' from the Golden State, and once in 'this fine country of fertile soil, abundant water, dramatic landscapes and beautiful weather', many had no reason to return east. During the early years of the Gold Rush, this further tarnished California's reputation because the incomers weren't supposed to be here to settle down. They had come to rape and pillage the mountains then bugger off home laden with booty. That hundreds of thousands stayed only increased the resentment felt by those left behind. For as long as there has been a United States of America, California has been a different country, but I didn't expect to enter it through a border post.

The official at the Agricultural Inspection Station leaned out of his kiosk window, frowned and said, "Are you pissing me or what?"

Every vehicle on my side of the road drove through the bug station and paused for inspection. Why should a cyclist be any different? Then I noticed the list of proscribed items and realised my panniers weren't cut out for smuggling cattle.

Route 299 tracked the Pit River on a course through sumptuous green meadows where the gaps between ranches and towns were measured in minutes rather than days. Back in a land of the living, I was eager to blag a night in a bed and put Californian hospitality to the test. Beyond Alturas I knocked at four doors with no response and was intercepted halfway down the track to a fifth by a farmer driving an ATB who had no space for me on his thousand acre spread but still wanted to hear my tale. When I finished and tried him again he said, "Uh huh. Don't want nothing to do with that. Usually I lock the gate across this time of night."

Dusk descended and I reverted to looking for somewhere flat to camp. Since I was now riding across the depression of Warm Springs, everywhere was flat but also saturated. A cloud of mosquitoes swarmed across the wetlands, directing my attention to a bank where I could spend the night and they could suck me dry. Seeing the squadron coming, a muskrat burrowing in a levee took cover, back-flipping into the creek. A row of shacks displaced from Soweto ran at right angles a short distance from the road. Turned away from each of them, it was finally suggested I try the farm across the fields, "'cos they's new round here."

Steve, Donna and their teenage son were caught on the hop but welcoming. They insisted I kip in their spare room rather than sleep out and get bitten to death. Inside or out, we were all camping. They obviously hadn't been resident for long. The clinker-built house was damp and topsy-turvy, but in a lot better condition than when they bought it.

"There were sheep grazing in the lounge," Donna said, "And we're still trying to get on top of the damn vermin."

Though barely in their forties, the couple had bought the spread with the intention of taking early retirement from a lifestyle which had become too fast for their liking. Steve was some kind of engineer and Donna some kind of teacher, but they had no intention of breathing new life into anything other than the buildings.

"We got 400 acres we rent out to a local farmer," Donna explained. "There's no money in farming these days, unless you got thousands of acres and the machinery to make it pay. All round here we got folks moving up from the cities to take over farms, but they either commute or compute and go into the office once a month. They sure don't become farmers."

Sat on the decking outside the back door waiting for dinner, Steve stared across at the lava outcrop of Rattlesnake Butte, stroked his beard and offered nobody in particular his comments on the evening news filtering through from the kitchen radio. American peace-keepers in Kosovo had opened fire after being stoned by youths.

"Hey, if there's killing to be done, we're the guys to call in," Steve said, rolling another Bugler cigarette. "Dunno what the hell we're playing at. Ain't nothing there but a pile of rock. Ain't got no oil or nothing. Guess it's just time we flexed our muscles again."

Aside from smoking roll-ups, listening to national broadcasting and wearing a beard, Steve was unusual for an American in having travelled extensively outside the country, including spending time in the Balkans. Though he didn't approve of it, he could understand why the U.S. steamed into the Gulf. Kosovo bewildered him. It was the first time America had become entangled in Europe since World War II.

"Maybe Washington sees Yugoslavia as some sorta front line between Christians and Muslims?" he wondered.

Steve was highly critical of his country's foreign policies but saw America's meddling as a symptom of the state of its civilisation.

"America's kinda withering on the vine. Shame really 'cos it seems to me it's only just got going. Problem is, we're running out of things to have. We can't invent or reinvent things fast enough for Americans. We're digging ourselves into a hole — or kinda piling stuff up around us. We keep piling on the goodies and the damn hole just gets fuckin' deeper. American's got no idea what the hell they're doing in there, 'cept chasin' their butts. So much for the American fuckin' Dream."

For Steve, the American Dream was "no different to a Kosovan, Iraqi or Vietnamese Dream. Every fucker wants the same — family, home, security and fun. 'Cos it's the American Dream, sounds like we got that and better. What we got's a big damn hole."

The sun had yet to rise above the horizon, but a pale blue glow behind the Warner Mountains and a weak layer of condensation hovering above them suggested the new day was going to be another scorcher. In the wetlands surrounding the spread, farmers had turned on their sprinklers bright and early. The country was definitely locked in a heatwave. Since leaving Logan, every new day had been the hottest of the year.

I pulled back onto Route 299 following the dream that long ago had turned to a never ending nightmare for the Forty-Niners. In the flatlands of Big Valley, alfalfa, barley and beans grew in huge open fields occasionally interspersed with rectangles wired for cattle. The youngest, most successful hybrids pushing up in the landscape, however, were the 'For Sale' signs. It seemed United Country Realty and Knight Realty had almost every farm in every valley on their books. Fields were still worked but many farm buildings were simply abandoned, as Steve and

Donna's had been, and most of these farms were less than a hundred years old.

Villages mirrored the demise of the countryside. Visibly poor and run down, they were typified by Fifties gas guzzlers with flapping fenders and smoky pick-ups riding low on shot suspension. Shiny SUVs were notable for their absence. Only Bieber had anything about it to suggest the village was more than another reluctant sleeper community in waiting. At the Big Valley Lumber Company, circular saws screeched like worn brakes as they pushed through the units. Neubieber, the next community along and the 'New Bieber', was Big Valley's railroad depot, once a noisy goods yard handling timber and farm produce. From the top of the railroad bridge, I looked down on an ambitious village platte of mostly empty rectangles. Neubieber wasn't so much dying as stillborn.

Outside a craft shop in the village, I sipped coffee while the mother of the owner told me about her Scottish-German roots. She explained how, in the 1850s, her father's side of the family were on the trail of gold when they staggered into Big Valley and gave up, reverting to the farming life great grandpa left behind in Germany. The conversation wasn't so interesting for its content as the fact it took place at all. I wasn't sure if the stonewalling I received in the communities along R-299 was the infamous Californian cold shoulder or just the locals' reluctance to engage with a vagabond in the terminal stages of anorexia nervosa.

From the top of Big Valley Mountain I could see clear across sixty miles to Mount Shasta in the north-west. At over 4,200 metres, it's classic volcanic cone and glacial cap belittled the mountainous skyline, but today it was feeling jocular. Pulled down over its eyes, a cluster of clouds formed a high crowned Stetson reminiscent of the ludicrous hat Bob Hope wore in *Son of Paleface*. To the south, smaller volcanic peaks dripping with ice poked above forested highlands. The tallest was Lassen Peak, whose contours I would be scaling in a couple of days. I was entering the Ring of Fire, one valley away from climbing onto the rim of a Pacific wide pressure cooker. The mountains before me were so many valves and beneath them the earth bubbled.

The floor of the Pacific Ocean is forever growing and expanding outwards until it hits the continents containing it. Unable to make further headway, the oceanic crust slips beneath the margins of the continental plates, grinding back down towards the Earth's core. Deep beneath the land mass, the crust remelts, forming pockets of magma which become the feeding chambers for the hundreds of volcanoes ringing the Pacific. The Cascades and Sierra Nevadas were small links in this 24 carat chain. The origin of gold isn't fully understood, but low concentrations of the ore are widespread in all igneous rock. Carried to the surface in a fountain of magma, it precipitates and sets into the yellow veins which drive men crazy. I was looking at the roof of El Dorado and it glowed.

Mind and body were now several pegs beyond weary. Like the embers of a dying fire which glows brighter when poked, each morning I prodded myself into life and glowed a little weaker for a little shorter. Every nerve and muscle was burnt out, reduced to ash. Any last chips of fat and twigs of imagination had been thrown on the fire weeks ago. I was cycling purely on willpower. Increasingly I cared less about maintaining body and soul, monitoring my fuel intake, checking the bike, and being vigilant on the road. Logging trucks, the bane of the Californian blacktop, had twice blasted me off the road. I desperately needed downtime and pulled off the road a couple of miles after Saddle Mountain to set up camp on the north bank of the Pit River. I planned to spend two days recuperating but discovered I was missing one essential ingredient.

There is an unwritten law of free range travel — if you need it and see it, get it. Do not presume the next place will have it or better it. At McArthur, the store boasted full shelves, locally baked bread and fresh fruit, but I couldn't face the bustle of the amateur rodeo stars stocking up on six-packs and charcoal for the evening celebration of their moment of parochial glory. I pedalled on without a meal in my larder, hoping the grocery store at Fall River Mills would be less popular. It was, largely because it stocked sod all.

Regardless of the food shortage, I wasn't moving the next morning and lay in bed watching a couple of turkey buzzards spiral over Sixmile Hill. On the radio, Anne Page's *Radio Daily* phone-in raised the ugly spectre of Columbine once again as a prelude to the day's Senate debate on gun control. On cue, rifle shots echoed round the wooded bowl of the river bend. They were sporadic but moving closer. When an automatic rattled off thirteen rounds in rapid succession, I began to worry. I hadn't noticed before, but there were shotgun cases and bullet shells on the ground. I knew nothing about hunting seasons or the status of the land where I lay, but I knew for sure that Americans have a long tradition of shooting each other accidentally. 30,000 die each year from gunshot wounds and as many as a quarter of them just happen to be in the wrong place at the wrong time.

Aside from sickness, drownings and wagon accidents taking life, those on the California Trail were equally prone to being shot to death or badly wounded. Precious few Indian ambushes or violent crimes occurred over the months, but an awful lot of firearms were carried by an awful lot of inexperienced gentlemen who thought the best way to protect themselves against the wilds was to arm themselves to the teeth. In one company of sixty men it was recorded that every member had at least a rifle and a revolver and started out with thirty pounds of lead and 5,000 percussion caps. Reading the diaries, I got the impression the retort of rifles and pistols accidentally discharging serenaded the wagon train like musak. There was no instruction in rules of safety and any proposals to regulate firearms were met with scorn in the companies. Now Americans have lashings of firearm regulations, continually scorn them, and thousands of by-standers still take an wayward bullet each year. I had no desire to swell the current statistics by one, and moved out.

Every atom of the bicycle and I rebelled against another damn day on the road. A handful of miles before Clint Eastwood's home town of Burney, we hung a left and aligned south for the final push into the sierras. On the gradual climb from the Shasta to the Lassen National Forest, signs began appearing to curious cross culture tourist facilities like the Celt-Mex 'Rancheras Angus RV Park' somewhere deep in the forest. At the desperately inadequate Maacooatche Store in the hamlet of Hat Creek, Sheila TenEyck elaborated on why grocery stores in a tourist area are the last place I should have expected to find groceries.

"When Americans go away for the weekend, they carry enough provisions to survive Armageddon. Then they can't face cooking, so only the restaurants do good business in this valley."

Sheila and her husband were more refugees from Orange County, moving up to Shasta County back in the 1970s. They had once undertaken their own, modest historic journey inspired by the book *Land of the Grasshopper Song*. It told of two women employed by the Bureau of Indian Affairs who, at the beginning of the twentieth century, were sent out West to help aborigines living on the Klamath River Basin reservation, west of the Cascades. Equipped with a couple of mules, these early social workers walked all the way from the Missouri. Towards the end of their journey, they came across a TenEyck Mine.

"I thought the book was fiction. It's not the most common of names — it's Dutch — but at the back there was a map. I was kinda curious so my husband and I drove over to the coast. We went along this terrible track. I was terrified. I didn't think the Cherokee would hold up. The weather didn't help none. It had been raining for a week and the track was a river, but we found the mine. It wasn't working anymore, but it was still owned by a TenEyck —

a sorta mountain man who lived in a shack out back. We had to spend the night in the car. Didn't dare move in the downpour. It was kinda exciting and frightening at the same time. Guess you've had a few of those moments?" She leaned back and squinted at me. "Sure. You've had 'em."

Chapter 28
Gold Country

I was on the countdown to Sandy arriving in Sacramento. It was June 20th and I was a week away from holding her in my arms. Leaving a day to make myself respectable and allowing time for weak limbs to struggle up severe inclines, I worked out a travel itinerary — my first since leaving Washington. Up to that point, I knew where I was going and was flexible about when I arrived. Knowing my gammy knee and the blasted wind had set me back, I panicked in Nebraska and plodded on blindly through Wyoming, Utah and Nevada hoping fewer rest days would make up for lost time. They had, but at what cost? There were no more stretches of off-road to spring surprises, and while the Panther still padded about, he would find it significantly more difficult to stalk me in the mountains. Logging trucks were now the principle threat to life and limb, though I was about to enjoy thirty or so miles without them. On the road into Lassen Volcanic National Park, a large sign prohibited commercial traffic.

Of the volcanoes on the North American length of the Ring of Fire, Lassen Peak is the one plate technologists believe is most likely to let rip in the not too distant future. Currently the world's largest plug volcano, it last blew in 1915, emitting a seven mile high plume of ash which rained down debris on Reno 120 miles away. Because of its significance as an active volcanic landscape, 79,000 acres surrounding the peak were made a national park the following year. For the scientific community, Lassen's importance lies not in what might happen in the future, but in monitoring what's happening today. As a case study of how devastated landscapes recover, the area is what the British would call a 'site of special scientific interest', but the park has limited appeal for the general public. Anybody other than a committed backpacker would find Lassen severely restricting by comparison to the access and facilities afforded at Yellowstone or Yosemite. Aside from anything else, the highway through Lassen offers less than an hour's drive. Knowing how reluctant Americans are to get out of their cars, I hoped this meant the hordes stayed away.

From the store near the entrance by Manzanita Lake, I called home. Sandy and I had been incommunicado for a couple of weeks. She had been on holiday with friends and I had been crossing deserts, but we needed to refine the details of our linking up.

"Are you excited about arriving?" I tentatively asked.

"Not really." There was still an edge to her voice. "I'm only flying in to be with you. I can think of a 101 places I'd rather be going this summer."

Twenty years ago, California had been the destination of Sandy's first foreign excursion. It hadn't been a good experience and I could understand her reluctance to return, but I was missing the point.

"It's alright for you. You've been swanning across America doing your own thing, having a high old time. I've been stuck here going through hell. You haven't a clue what's been going on, have you?"

"Hey, it was you're idea to join me on the final stages," I protested, now missing the point by a mile. "I was quite happy to complete on my own."

"Precisely! Self-Contained Man…"

It was some time before I got a handle on what Sandy meant by that comment, but everything else she said immediately rang true. I might have been driven mental, fried to a crisp and drained of all my strength, but there was no denying I had been through a remarkable adventure. By the same token, Sandy couldn't begin to imagine how desperately I wanted this godforsaken journey to end.

With serious doubts that my body was up to it, I began what would become a 1,200 metre continuous climb up the flank of Lassen Peak. Where terra firma was previously an occasional nut of white rock peeking above a springy forest floor, the earth was now smothered under a chaos of jagged boulders. Lodgepole and pine saplings forced a way through gaps between the gunmetal rocks. Lording over them was the gnarled black rim of a range of stunted volcanoes called Chaos Crags, their reaches drenched in iron grey scree. Facing them, debris was layered in waves up the foot of Table Mountain like levees on a shingle beach. Called the Chaos Jumble, the rocks were brought down some 300 years ago by an avalanche which slid off Chaos Crags. Riding on a cushion of air, it thundered across the valley I now cycled along and climbed 400 feet up the other side before losing its head of steam and slumping back into the valley. For any Yana Indians who witnessed the terrifying spectacle, the mountain was shedding its skin.

Reaching the edge of the devastation, a dark forest of damp conifers rapidly enveloped me. It was the stuff of creepy fairy tales. Occasionally the sun penetrated down the length of short stretches of tarmac, but mostly I rode in deep shadow and shivered. Looking up, a narrow trench of flame blue indicated America was experiencing its latest hottest day of the year. Where I pedalled, the temperatures were sub-zero.

As I plodded towards the fifth Emigrant Pass of my journey, the trees began to thin, revealing Lassen Peak. Dazzling white with shadowy darts of grey, the cracked volcano rose 3,187 metres above sea level to a thin and ragged line of black rock windswept clean of snow. The road crossed diamond-studded streams bringing down rich volcanic soil to gradually fill each valley. Soft green grasses and lanky reeds had taken root, and meadows were being formed. Higher up in Lassen's destruction zone, the earth remained grey and stony, but young latchpoles had somehow found a way to strike out. In the scabby landscape left by the molten inferno, nature was healing just fine.

Beyond Hot Lake (silting up and now more of a puddle), the ascent began in earnest. Large patches of melting snow started appearing beside the road. Amongst the trees, clearings were submerged under meltwater and the road was streaming. The snow patches joined up like white mercury and became levees. By Summit Lake (nowhere near the summit), they were two metre walls of compacted snow and the landscape had turned Alpine. Grinding up the side of Reading Peak, a vista opened out on my left. Already higher than I had ridden before in the States, I looked across to a layered horizon of cut-out mountain ranges, each theatre flat painted a percentage lighter than the royal blue of the first. In the foreground, now set in white cement, Corsican pines had slid south to clog the mouth of a corrie damming back the glacier. To my right, a wedge of trees had been smacked by an avalanche and grew at an angle. I slipped down another gear. A man standing on a snow wall shouted, "Keep it up! Not far to go!"

Knowing America's definition of "not far," I steeled myself for another hour of labour and left the tree line behind. The angle increased and the road doubled back on itself, crossing a saddle-back between peaks like ice cream sundaes. Finally I reached the top of the pass, sandwiched between concave ice walls four metres high. Still in the saddle, I flopped against the glacier and welded. Either side of the col, meltwater was turning to black ice as the afternoon temperature dropped. Another seven hundred metres above me, Lassen Peak stood quietly superior, waiting for me to come a cropper.

I freewheeled the first mile of the descent with feet extended like stabilisers. I gathered speed, clipped into cleats, and the world turned black and white. Bumpass Hell was surrounded by the slumped remains of the ancient caldera of Mount Tehama, a stratovolcano which imploded thousands of years ago. Like a monochrome photo of soap suds draining down a plug hole, compression marks belied the imperceptible slide of the névé. Somewhere below the ridge, Cold Boiling Lake described what really was going on beneath this geothermal cauldron. Whether pronounced 'Bump ass' or 'Bum pass', the Hell was appropriately named after a pilgrim who lost a leg trying to cross it.

The blacktop ripped down the western flank of the caldera, switching back on itself, jumping arètes and sweeping round scoured rills. I owned the road, but round the flutings of Diamond Peak the Panther sprang an attack. At a speed matching my descent, my heart thudded against the roof of my mouth. On the off-side was a sheer drop. I lost it for a second, swinging too wide on a bend. An on-coming car braked and honked. I zipped between it and the edge, somehow regained control, and was immediately assailed with the pungent smell of sulphur. The road bottomed out in a steaming dip reeking with rotting eggs. In an ochre stained hollow, a couple of fumaroles spat erratic fountains of boiling water. A short walk from the highway, the Sulphur Works, thought to be Mount Tehama's original vent, glooped and steamed, but I didn't hang about. Between the fright and the stench, my stomach needed sweet smells to settle it.

For over twenty miles, from the summit to Mill Creek, I barely touched the pedals. I swept out of the park and dived through thickening woods, bombing back into a landscape reminiscent of Germany's Black Forest. At the junction with Highway 36 I was welcomed back to the fray of traffic by a stream of logging trucks which appeared to have a wager on who could take my elbow clean off. Like stampeding dinosaurs, they were racing for the mill carrying their rear bogies piggy-back. Girders designed to hold in the timber projected from their cabs like the horns of a triceratop.

Long shadows slipped across a meadow, dipped into a stream and painted zebra markings across the road entering California's Black Forest. Every motel, restaurant and café in the holiday village was either up for sale or sold, yet to be renovated into something even more garishly Bavarian. Chalet rental homes lined one side of the road, accessed through bolted and barred covered bridges. On every conceivable upright the word 'PRIVATE' was hammered home, and electric or razor fencing was *de rigeur*. I ended the day by a sluggish brook feeding into Lake Almanour, at the back of a realty development which had progressed as far as ripping up trees and laying down kerb stones before losing its way and its backers.

Where the Pit River swept round the foot of Big Valley Mountain, the companies steered their drained bodies on a tighter curve south than the one I was forced to follow up Hat Creek into the Lassen Volcanic National Park. They trudged up a parallel depression to the east, then looped round the back of Lassen Peak to pick up a tributary of the Feather River at Big Meadows. Rejoining the trail, I found that where they were 'in camp all day cutting hay' was now several hundred metres under Lake Almanour. They scythed Big Meadows 'for the desert to come', apparently unaware the sands were behind them, but then none of us knew quite what lay ahead. It was inconceivable the terrain could be more exacting than the barren wastes of the Great Basin, but America had a way of dishing expectations.

At Big Meadows, exhaustion in the camps was tinged with relief. After early reports of the tortures endured on the Lassen Cut-off, a Californian supply convoy had struck out north to assist stragglers. As late as the beginning of

October there were still 10,000 people on the trails, and while relief trains had been dispatched along the Truckee and Carson routes, by far the worst deprivations were found on the Lassen trail. The incomers were destitute, discouraged and half starving, and many were suffering with scurvy and dysentery. Aid was distributed in the form of 'coffee, hard bread, rice, etc.', but just hearing about the relief party lifted the morale of men who, on learning how far they were from the gold fields, now added panic to their list of woes. But they had reached the mountains and were within striking distance. For the first time since leaving the prairies, conversations returned to the object of their epic voyage. Gold fever came back to galvanise drained bodies. They were strong but weak with exhaustion, determined but demoralised by the trail, aware they had achieved something great but unable to find anything to celebrate. Didn't I know it.

Beyond the reservoir I called in at Canyondam and blagged breakfast at the store. Symptomatic of the state I was in, I had run out of cash two days ago but the store keeper was sympathetic. He was a bit of a Gold Rush buff, he said, but then everybody I was to meet in the sierras was a bit of a Gold Rush buff. He endorsed my proposed route to Sacramento, "but watch out for them loggin' trucks. We gotta lotta them in Plumas County — northern tip of the old gold minin' area, y'know. You'll begin to recognise the names, if'n you've read the books. There are still die-hards in these hills diggin' for gold, but mostly recreational. In July, Greenville holds an annual Gold Digger Day — kinda fun, if you're gonna be around. You'll find a bank there."

It was high noon when I swept into Greenville. Main Street was a hotplate and empty. A photograph of the road circa 1878 hanging in the Chamber of Commerce window showed little had changed since the miners' camp matured into a town and became a fixture. The old stores, warehouses and artisans shops were archetypal Western and I half expected Gary Cooper to be loping down the middle of the street. Instead, I found a decrepit Mexican who insisted on chaperoning me to the bank. Half an hour later, emerging from a supermarket with supplies for a week, he was sat on his haunches, "Keepin' an eye on y'wheels, man. Can't trust no one in this goddamn town." I stood him a Coke.

"I come up here from Reno 'cos my brother, he said it was real good here," the old man said, his face as sad as a rotting sack. "It's real good, if'n you got work. Been here six months. Going crazy as a coyote under a full moon. Ain't nothin' happen 'cept trucks rollin' through." A couple crawling down Main Street still managed to raise a dust storm. "Could get some sorta work in Reno, anytime, but Mexicans in Greenville? Shit."

"Maybe things'll pick up when the season really gets going?" I suggested.

"This *is* it really going, *amigo*. Look at it. It's a fuckin' fly trap, man."

Beyond the Mexican's fly trap, the Alpine walls which funnelled Wolf Creek through Greenville snapped open to reveal the broad meadows of Cache Valley, renamed Indian Valley by pioneers who found an unexpected concentration of native farmers tilling the fertile basin. At its southern tip crouched the hamlet of Crescent Mills, referring to mills which crush rocks rather than crops. Beyond the old gold processing plant, converging streams from Indian Valley fed into the East Branch of the North Fork of the Feather River. I entered the gorge with an inane grin on my chops. Nearly a year after I set out from Washington, I had finally arrived at the first of the great rivers coursing through El Dorado.

If the name of the upper tributary was not very colourful, it provided the argonauts with a good mental picture of their position relative to the great scheme of the sierras. A cheroot shaped range of high mountains running two-thirds the length of California, the Sierra Nevada lies at the same angle to and 160 miles inland from the coastline. From the west, they climb gently out of the

Sacramento and San Joaquin Valleys for forty to sixty miles, before rising steeply for an equivalent distance up to the peaks. East of the backbone, they fall sharply and dramatically though not as deeply, down to the high deserts of Nevada. West of the backbone, they are lacerated by strong torrents such as the South Fork of the American River where the gold was first discovered. As far as the Forty-Niners were concerned, each of these flows was a vein carrying yellow corpuscles from the heart of the Mother Lode. In the rivers they dug for their dreams. Beside them, seedy camps became shabby towns knocked together in a week. Along their tight valleys, thorough-fares were carved and complementary enterprises set up shop. The rivers of the sierras quickly became Main Street, California.

Ten key rivers were exploited by the early gold diggers, most with a North, Middle or South Forks, some with East or West Branches feeding into the forks. All pour into the Sacramento or San Joaquin Rivers, which merge at Sherman Island before surging into San Pablo Bay and out through the Golden Gate to the Pacific. Reverse the flow and you have the route taken by more than 41,000 sea-faring argonauts who landed at San Francisco in 1849 having sailed round Cape Horn or taken the short cut across the Isthmus of Panama. From San Francisco they sailed upstream to Sacramento or Stockton, then travelled on foot or by donkey to the river beds laying the golden eggs. In the so-called 'gold fields', they joined the leaner, fitter overlanders who had not spent the last four months stewing in steerage. By the end of the year, mountains and valleys previously populated by a few 'Digger Indians' and a handful of *californios* were totally over-run by around 90,000 Americans, Europeans, Mexicans, Chinese, South Americans, Russians and Hawaiians. No other event in the history of the world had attracted so many from so far.

For me, the North Fork of the Feather River was especially significant. Many diarists from the overland trail put down their pens for the last time on reaching the river.

Five months of almost daily entries were not rounded off with a neat conclusion or a summary of all they had been through. The writing simply stopped, left hanging on some banality, but I had no trouble imagining what they saw which brought their entries to a sudden halt. Though arriving late in the season, they found miners still working the river bed, living in tents, cedar shacks and benders. The sides of the canyon were raw, stripped of timber for fuel and building, and sagging with mud flows. As they proceeded further down stream, the river-rat population increased and the course of the river became more distorted, channelled by man-made levees and edged by crude flumes and sluice boxes called 'long toms'. Like a mismanaged quarry, the floor of the valley was a pile of debris, shattered boulders and chaotic dams rimmed by a high water mark of faeces which seeped into the river, their source of drinking water. Trails blazed along the valley sides were more rocky, precipitous and strength sapping than anything the newcomers had previously encountered. If their groans of disappointment joined the ring of pick and shovel echoing round the chasm, the new arrivals were soon caught up in the frenzy to find an empty spot and stake a claim.

Beyond my imagining, I saw none of this and felt cheated, not to mention a total wally for thinking I might. For over a hundred days and nights, I had been on the trail of men who had something to look forward to at the end of their road — something they believed made the struggle worthwhile. As long as I was travelling, I could pretend I was one of the boys. Now I had arrived, the bubble burst. A surprising number of overlanders felt the same when they saw the squalor and competition in the gold fields. They made a beeline for Sacramento and civilisation, or at least a more refined squalor, and reverted to their original occupations.

Rather than face hauling wagons over the tortuous trail beside the North Fork, many overland companies disbanded here and went their separate ways. For my iron horse and myself, the line along the river bank was smooth, snaking and initially down hill, demanding little more than a wary eye for logging trucks. To my left, the force of the river was unbridled. White water rocketed through the canyon, shooting over rapids, spinning back in whirlpools, tumbling and hurling itself against the pre-stressed concrete supporting bends in the roadbed. Each spring it undoubtedly smashed through the dams and levees argonauts piled high to deflect its course, bouncing the boulders downstream like so many pebbles. Within a few years of the miners leaving the sierras, any evidence that there ever was a Gold Rush would have been washed away from the valley floor. Although they took longer to heal, the walls of the canyon had also repaired. As far as the eye could see, tall strong pines and wispy conifers covered every inch of the interlocking slopes from river bed to col and crest. The second growth in the Sierra Nevadas was a lot denser than the forests described by the Forty-Niners.

Just before Paxton, I hung a left at the river junction and began the steep ascent up the side of Spanish Creek. I was experiencing something of the pain the argonauts felt on those final miles, digging for reserves of stamina buried under the cellar of my being. I now pedalled on the outside of the road, with a ninety metre sheer drop an arm's length away. Between me and my Maker, fifteen centimetres of raised tarmac was the best protection California could offer me. Fighting back vertigo, a painfully long ascent dragged me through linking canyons before the road gently angled down to American Valley and slipped me into Quincy, the liveliest town in California thus far.

I cooled down under the umbrella of a picnic table opposite the Gold Pan Motel, hopeful I would find more authentic evidence of a time when the town was a string of wooden shacks and gambling marquees either side of a pig trough of a road. Beaming in on the Pumas County Museum, I smoothed back sweat soaked hair and entered.

"My, would you look at you!" an attendant exclaimed.

351

Two women sat behind the museum counter. When the rakish one balked, the tubby one looked up from her keyboard and audibly inhaled. An elderly gentleman flicking through periodicals looked me up and down, and said, "Come a-ways, huh?"

The skinny woman needed to verify my story. She lifted J.S. Holliday's *The World Rushed In* from the sales rack, flicked it open and presented a panorama sketched by an argonaut during his September crossing of the Black Rock Desert.

"What, you crossed that?" she said in an admonishing tone. "Well, you've read the diaries. You know what condition the pioneers were in when they arrived here. You're *supposed* to feel weak and exhausted, and if you aren't, you sure look it." She pointed out of the window to a lawn. "You go and lie down out there in the shade and get some rest. Take as long as you need, but go lie down. Please."

Chapter 29

One of the first opportunists to work the American River in 1848 was a man from Canton called Chung Ming. Like many of the earliest gold panners, he struck lucky and wrote home with the news. That year, around 300 Chinese shipped out to what they called 'Gold Mountain'. Four years later 20,000 crossed the Pacific, sometimes 2,000 landing at San Francisco in a day. Mostly farmers from Guangdong Province, they were contract labourers working for sponsors back home who paid their passage and took a cut. Because they had to be, the Chinese were more successful at mining than the whites, often striking pay-dirt in tailings abandoned by Americans. And if they didn't do well in the gold fields, they capitalised on business opportunities in the service sector, setting up hash houses, opium dens and clothing, hardware or food stores. The Chinese laundry might be a movie cliché, but it was good as a gold mine in 1850s California. Until the likes of Wah Lee went into business, San Franciscans sent their clothes to Hong Kong or Honolulu for laundering, but however quickly they became an integral part of the Californian business community, the Chinese just as quickly came to feel the rifle butt of American racism.

California entered the Union a slave free state in 1850, though this apparent liberalism had more to do with the argonauts' fear of competition than anything so noble as their subscription to the Rights of Man. Miners would rather be working shoulder to shoulder with ethnic minorities than be barged out of the river valleys by gangs of black slaves owned by businessmen with clout. In the remote canyons of the sierras, miners exacted their own law, which afforded minorities less protection than the laws governing slavery. Referring to anybody who wasn't Caucasian, the *Annals of California* declared, 'These people need not, and most probably cannot, be swept from the face of the earth; but undoubtedly their national characteristics and opposing qualities and customs must be materially modified, and closely assimilated to those of the civilising and dominant race.' Part of that civilising process was to intimidate the Chinese from their mining claims and burn their shacks. Under Californian law, they weren't allowed to own property or testify in miners' courts, and summary justice included beatings, floggings and cold-blooded murder.

But not in Quincy, the exhibition at the Pumas County Museum assured me. Arriving in 1850, the Chinese were apparently treated better in Quincy than anywhere else in the gold country. A display card proudly informed me they even had their own graveyard, tucked 'behind the large blue-gray building' on the road out of town. I walked the length of the road several times, but couldn't find the plot set aside by a community outraged that a Chinese girl was to be laid to rest in the town cemetery a little beyond the blue-grey building. Another card explained how inter-racial marriages were forbidden by local laws and how, since there were so few Chinese women in the vicinity, most of the men lying beneath the soil died lonely. 'Several of the dead who lie here were victims of murders,' the paragraph ended.

Outside of the fusty little museum, Quincy was a colourful town, gaily decorated with murals depicting its exotic history and ill deserving the muddy logging trucks coughing soot over Main Street and drowning sidewalk conversations. It had sprawled over a finger of Bachs Creek Ridge into East Quincy, and a few of America's favourite throw-ups had staked a claim on an excuse for a strip. Between the two, Highway 70 expanded to six lanes then shrivelled back to a thin grey ribbon which scurried away from the head waters of the North Fork of the Feather River to intercept the Middle Fork.

For twenty miles I clawed my way over mountainous razorbacks crossing the nerve ends of creeks pouring off Grizzly Ridge, the sierra watershed. Either side dense forests camouflaged wildcat prospecting, or so I imagined from a large graffiti splashed across a cliff face stating 'Mineing Prohibted' (*sic*). Occasionally I passed through a town, though without the road sign one would never have known. Since it only consisted of four houses, 'Spring Garden Pop: 80' was somewhat over-crowded, and the former mining camps of Sloat and Cromberg had developed into little more than holiday trailer parks. The road took a gruelling south-easterly line along a buckled depression which peaked at 1,352 metres and consumed me with loathing. Beyond the hurdles carved out by the Middle and South Forks of the Feather River lay Blairsden, the home of landscaper Patrick Hammond, who I had shared a beer with before foolishly checking myself through the Agricultural Inspection Station.

I came upon Patrick's Landscaping by accident, but he wasn't in. His yard was the sort of 'back knockings' littered with old railroad ties, rusting plant and piles of rubble you find kicking around the rough end of town. Blairsden itself began a hundred metres further on and ended five hundred beyond that. One side of the road was a run-down gas station, a broken tarmac strip and a long buckled shack containing a laundrette. On the other, a covered boardwalk fronted four smart pine buildings housing a restaurant, realty office, hairdressing salon and a bakery-cum-coffee shoppe, all pandering to a clientele more monied than those living in the surrounding shacks appeared to be. Even the Pizza Place take-away had pretensions.

A couple leaving the Grizzly Grill said they were local, "from Reno," but didn't know Patrick. In the restaurant, all the staff knew Patrick but not where he lived, and in the Pizza Place they said, "Oh, Patrick…" as if he was the flu. They confirmed he was hard to track down, but thought I might find him boarding with the "little old lady up on the hill." In the four houses up on the hill there was no little old lady. Back on the boardwalk I collared a woman closing up the estate agents who told me the best thing to do was wait in his yard. "He generally comes back about now and cracks open a beer."

As I rode back to Patrick's Landscaping, his old GMC coughed into town. Signalling to meet him at the yard, he turned the rig around, backed onto a garbage can, crushed it and drove forwards dragging it down the road until the two separated when he hit a bump.

Patrick Hammond was a gentle giant, facially similar to a haggard Kenny Rogers, and desperately in love with his constant companion, Pebbles the dog. He hadn't lived with the old lady on the hill in two years and was happy that the people of Blairsden saw him as elusive and cranky. It was a snotty little place, he said, and he had no wish to fraternise. He now resided a handful of miles away up at Sierra Springs, on a pine-sheltered trailer park which seemed to be populated by lonely middle-aged men from failed marriages. You couldn't swing a church mouse in his trailer and it looked like I would be sleeping in the wagon that night. His kitchen was a bachelor's mess containing everything unnecessary to make a meal, but on the decking outside stood a cool-shed stocked with beer. Patrick flicked on some blues. While I scrunched up in a shower the size of a budgie bath, he and Pebbles set off to buy us a take-away.

For the first time in twenty years, Patrick had a life. With clever footwork by lawyer and client, he had walked away from his divorce with a single alimony payment of only $8,000. Having just settled, he was now trying to rebuild a relationship with his two adult sons. Since his wife was a Seventh Day Adventist who "brainwashed my boys against me," it was going to be a long haul up a high mountain, but Patrick was determined. He had no illusions about the ground he needed to make up and readily admitted his culpability. He had been through a protracted rough patch which began when he returned from the Vietnam War, and was only now getting on top of his problems.

"Three types of guys come away from a war," he told me, "those who are okay, those who are physically fucked, and those who are mentally fucked. I was mentally fucked."

He took another wizened drumstick, dipped it in something yucky he'd whipped up from packets which had gone solid, took a bite and swilled it down with red wine.

"I was in 'Nam '66 through '71. I was an ordinary grunt — a common rifleman in the infantry. You listen to people talk and they're always something grand in 'Nam. Get's like nobody was ever an ordinary soldier doing the fucking fighting."

He was in D Company, 2nd of the 5th, Ist Cavalry, the outfit greatly misrepresented in *Apocalypse Now*. To my surprise, Patrick had seen every Vietnam movie going. Only *Platoon* came close to his experience of the war.

"On one day — one damn day — forty-two were killed in my company. These guys were my next door neighbours. We went to school together. We were called up together and trained together. I was walking next to my best friend when he took a bullet in the throat. What do you do? You stick them in a body bag, new guys come in, and you move out is what you fucking do. All in a day's work. It don't hit you 'til fifteen years later. I spent fifteen years without proper sleep — sort of cat-napping, ready to jerk into action. Two years ago the medics diagnosed me PTSD (with post traumatic stress disorder). They give me these tranquillisers to help me sleep — keep me mellow through the day. They help stop the spasms I get in my legs."

Patrick took fifteen pills of six different varieties a day, smoked a bong and drank wine and beer in the evening. The wine made him maudlin, he said. When he spent evenings on his own, he found it difficult not to think of Vietnam. The memories were too powerful.

"We did some terrible, terrible things. We shot women and children. They carried mortars on their backs. What do you do?"

Some nights he cried himself to sleep stroking Pebbles.

"I probably won't vote Democrat again but, say what you will about Clinton, for a couple of guys whose privileged families kept them out of the war, Gore and Clinton did a heap for vets. They were the first to recognise the mental impact of war on vets, and they speeded up the payments."

With the help of Vietnam Veterans of America, Patrick now received $600 a month from the federal government and was booked into regular review boards with a view to increasing the payments. Until two years ago, he hadn't bothered with the money or the medical treatment.

"I was too fucking angry with this country for the war," he said, whacking back the last drop of wine.

I left him listening to love-sick blues with his best friend curled up on his lap and crawled into the back of the work wagon. In the morning, Pebbles found me under a Pick-a-Stick pile of gardening tools and dug me out like I was a buried bone. His master looked like he'd spent another night in the foxhole coiled like a spring. He drove us back to the Blairsden Bakery for breakfast on automatic pilot. Inside, the coffee shoppe was busy with local people who didn't live locally but had second homes in the valley. On the wall was a world map with pins representing where visitors hailed from. While Patrick ordered breakfast and regaled the clientele with exaggerated tales of my adventures, I stuck a pin in Lincolnshire and whispered, "We did it, Pauline."

I was headed south-east to pick up the North Fork of the Yuba River and begin my descent down to the Sacramento Valley. Back at his yard to collect my bike, Patrick recommended a shortcut across the snow peaks looming over Blairsden. "It's a stiff climb up the side of Mount Etwell," he said, pointing to a pinnacle which looked more like K2, "but you won't have any problems with trucker fuckers."

Anything which nibbled away at the miles I was now happy to take, but 'Patrick's Cut-off' was an unexpected treat. It would steer me past Gold Lake, and I began the ascent with an inexplicable bounce in my legs. Within minutes a landscape of jewelled cathedrals embraced me. At every corner a different aspect of the ice crusted sierras revealed itself — sometimes volcanic and a chaos of rocks, sometimes a creek gushing from a clearing where deer grazed. The Panther was gusting at 40 mph but for once it didn't bug me. 1,830 metres up and surrounded by celestial spires, I stood on the stone shore of Gold Lake leaning into the beast, refreshed by the spray lifting off breakers.

According to the Chinese legend, trapped within the volcanic rim of 'Gold Mountain' (California) lay 'Gold Lake'; a crock of treasure dribbling nuggets and dust into the rivers of the sierras. 'Gold Lake' was the Chinese equivalent to the Mother Lode and the idea that there was an inexhaustible repository of the yellow stuff hidden somewhere in the mountains. But long before these myths were conjured up by nineteenth century argonauts, California was christened in the name of rumours of gold. Writing about a land north-west of Mexico, Conquistador Hernan Cortez appropriated the name from a popular sixteenth century Spanish novel set on 'an island called California very close to the Terrestrial Paradise'. Ruled by the Amazon Queen Calafia, the fanciful paradise abounded with 'gold and precious stones and upon it no other metal is found'.

That California's treasure only revealed itself nine days before the defeated Mexicans handed over Alta California to the United States has to be one of history's greatest ironies. The hand of God had to be at work, Americans reasoned, offering up the earth's bounty as a sign that the young nation was in His favour. As far as the Forty-Niners were concerned, it was God's will that they go forth and plunder the sierras. It was their Manifest Destiny, as articulated in a famous editorial in the *New York Morning News*. 'Our claim is our claim... by the right of manifest destiny to overspread and possess the whole continent which Providence has given for the development of the great experiment of liberty.' Manifest Destiny was the engine which powered American expansionism in the nineteenth century, and still does.

Myths, rumours and unsubstantiated reports of fortunes found were the life sustaining viruses which raised the temperature of gold fever. In the numbing waters of mountain runoffs, men who were poorly fed, inadequately housed, lonely, prone to violence, and vulnerable to disease, injury, depression and being ripped off had only gold fever to keep them going. Those same runoffs now provided a long list of life enhancing recreational activities for the leisured classes. For tourists camped beside Salmon Creek and the Yuba River, it seemed basking in the sun and poking the barbie was the limit of their Manifest Destiny.

The North Fork of the Yuba River was as powerful and destructive as the forks of the Indian River, and the line along its side no less pleasurable to fly down. Mile after mile of mighty canyon and secretive gorges rushed past my ears as I stormed into Sierra City. A linear hamlet of clapboard shacks pinned between valley wall and spuming river, it appeared the whole place was held upright by a cat's-cradle of telephone and power lines strung between buildings and anchored to the ground. There wasn't the space for roadside parking, and little reason for tourists to stop. Sierra City was possibly the most authentic old mining community I had ridden into, but a couple of cranks on the pedals and it was gone.

Thirteen miles on, Downieville was more the sort of place where the Timberland boot brigade spend time and money. Beautifully renovated, the historic gold town was still mutton dressed up as lamb. Miners' shacks had been transform from squalid hovels into bijou residences and riverfront restaurants. 'Authentic gold nugget jewelry' was displayed in windows which once hawked picks and shovels. Like Atlantic City, Wyoming, it had a touch of the Bohemian about it, except this was California and there was money. I had a poke round the museum, and saw the usual Gold Rush relics and mildew stained photos of crusty gold miners posing by their long toms. In Downieville it seemed everybody had a shave before being snapped. The elderly woman behind the desk told me a tale presumably designed to impress visitors with the town's colourful frontier history. I wasn't so sure the story of Juanita was something to be proud of.

In July 1851, after a particularly feisty evening of beer swilling, a bunch of the Downieville boys made a raucous tour of the poor end of town, kicking in doors and assaulting the occupants. They eventually got bored, broke up and went home, but one, a mountainous Scot named Jack Cannon, went back for a second helping. Some argued Jack returned to apologise, except a witness had heard him address Juanita as a *prostituta*. A married woman of twenty-three, Juanita flew into a rage and plunged a knife into Jack's breast, killing him instantly. At the kangaroo court which immediately convened in the town plaza, Juanita's young lawyer was kicked from the barrel he appealed to the crowd from and passed hand-to-hand overhead, away from the proceedings. A local doctor attempted to save her by endeavouring to prove she was pregnant, but three others said otherwise. Finally she was taken by the crowd to the Jersey Bridge I rode across on my way into town and hung. The American press roundly condemned the miners and the story received coverage in *The Times* of London, but mob justice in the gold fields was only to get rougher in years to come. As rapidly as the gold being extracted decreased, so racism in California increased.

On the climb out of Downieville I stopped to look back. The town clung to the banks of a fork in the Yuba River where the Downie flowed in. Old photos in the museum showed the junction at the foot of ravaged mountains, stripped of all cover and scarred with small landslides. I could see the original line of the barren slopes, but now thirty metres higher and green with the quiffs of conifers. According to the lady on the desk, the trees started growing back around 1903. Her mother was one of the

361

volunteers who planted saplings to protect the town from land slips which regularly choked the rivers and precipitated flooding. Now the Yuba just has a surge once in a blue moon. She showed me photographs of the valley in 1997, when forty-nine people were killed by a tidal wave which ripped up the concrete road bed and destroyed everything in its path.

I deserved at least one night camped in a river bed pretending to be a Forty-Niner. Where Fiddle Creek Ridge was summarily cropped by a cutting for Highway 49, I slipped across a walking bridge beyond a National Forest camp site and surreptitiously planted the tent on a sand bar of the Yuba. It was an idyllic spot on the inside of a bend which ricocheted off a fifteen metre granite wall before racing off downstream in a series of shallows. Upstream, evening sunbeams burnt through the fine mist shrouding a section of rapids, creating shimmering traces of the spectrum. Armed with my dinner plate, I strode into the icy waters. Had my nuts not instantly shrivelled to peas, I might have lasted long enough to make a stab at panning for gold.

The next morning, in the lee of Montezuma Hill, I watched a man wearing waders up to his knees in Shady Creek wielding something which looked like an overgrown car vacuum cleaner. When he took a break for a smoke, I clambered down the side of the gorge, introduced myself and cautiously asked him what he was doing.

"I's dredgin', but ain't legal. Didn't think y'could see me from the pavement."

I assured him you couldn't unless you were riding a bicycle, and since I hadn't seen a cyclist in 500 miles, he was pretty safe.

"This run's Class H, but I reckon I'm on some dude's claim. Gotta be careful hereabouts. Guy was found shot dead by a camp fire a week back. Reckon it was the guy owned the claim did it, but he got an alibi."

The old man looked like Fagin in denims. His hands were deformed with arthritis and he had the shakes. He explained he was using a suction dredge to filter the floor of the river for the yellow stuff. I had met my first prospector.

"Find me 'bout 500 ounces a year — 'bout enough to get by, but its more a hobby. Weather ain't conducive for an ol' river-rat like me. We gets five months rain or snow, four of high water and three when I can work, 'cept it's too damn hot by noon."

That much hadn't changed in 150 years. Yet again, the morning report had forecast the hottest day of the year, and the news warned of river flooding as the snow caps melted. From the mid-West, reports of a drought were coming in, with farmers baying for emergency hand-outs.

The prospector showed me a tatty handout produced by the California Department of Fish and Game. It ran to twenty sides of A4 and contained the rules and regulations for suction dredging. The hoops and hurdles to getting a licence were formidable, and the rules of deployment detailed where, how and with what any one river bed could be exploited. Every river in California was classified A through to H, giving dates when they were open for dredging and precise instructions regarding the condition each should be left in. The Gold Rush might have petered out a decade after the Forty-Niners arrived, but there were still many prospectors out here hoping to strike it rich. 4,000 suction dredgers were currently registered.

"Six years ago down Jamestown way, they's found a sixty pound nugget worth a million bucks," Fagin informed me with a glint of gold fever in his eyes. "A week later they's dug up another $2,000 worth."

Chapter 30

My goal for the day was Nevada City and a B & B called The Parsonage. With prices in excess of $100 a night, I couldn't afford to stay, but had heard it was run by the great grand-daughter of a Forty-Niner. When I dropped down the hill into town, it seemed I had gate-crashed the wrong party. For the first time I felt thoroughly embarrassed by my appearance and conscious I was being watched. As I wheeled my rig down Broad Street, waves of immaculately groomed visitors parted, bustling each other off the sidewalk to give the stinking hobo a wide berth.

Clasped within hills of pine and straddling Deer Creek, the town was a living museum of beautifully preserved architecture and an expensive tourist trap. Originally settled in 1849, little remained to suggest Nevada City was once a rip-roaring gold town which exploded from a handful of tents to 17,000 residents in a couple of months. Many of the buildings on Broad Street were original, though built later in the century. Now they were sugar coated and painted in pastels. Mock gas lamps lined smart streets thronged with promenaders who wove between twee coffee shops, fancy restaurants and designer boutiques. The ubiquitous strings of power lines had been tastefully buried and galleries exhibited pueblo pottery alongside romantic water-colours of the good ol' days. If you needed something useful for the home, Nevada City was not the place to find it, but there were three theatres playing *Rigaletto*, a farce called *Angry Housewives* and Bram Stoker's *Dracula*.

I sat beside a huge hydraulic mining nozzle displayed like a ship's cannon in the small park on Union Street and wondered what to do. The town was far too smug and memories of its gold days were too well packaged for anything useful to be gleaned without staying longer than my money allowed. A hundred bucks for bed and breakfast represented nearly ten days living on the road.

I strolled back up Broad Street and happened upon The Parsonage. It was pure Frank Capra and mom's apple pie, but I fell in love with the place. A round-faced woman with short hair answered the door wearing a Bermuda shirt and slacks. She confirmed she was the great grand-daughter of a Forty-Niner. Profusely apologising for my appearance, I asked if she could spare me five minutes to talk.

For several hours, I sat in Debbie Dane's exquisite sitting room — period decorated and furnished with family heirlooms — listening to her extraordinary tale.

"My great grandfather, Ezra Dane, wrote down his story when he was 91 years old. It could have been the story of any of a thousand Forty-Niners, except Ezra set out from the Missouri in 1852. What happened to him bore out the uncomfortable truth that a guaranteed fortune was not to be found in the gold diggings. If a man wanted to get rich in the California Gold Rush, he dealt in something the miners needed, like food.

"Ezra learned this almost immediately he left the Missouri. He had bought into a company led by a Mr. Barton. How Ezra put it, Barton was 'in for making money off us'. He saved the grub they had paid to eat, filled them with *penola* (roasted ground corn) and sold their food to others on the California Trail. The company carried large barrels of brandy on Barton's behalf. He also sold this along the trail, but the level in the barrels never went down.

"When he reached Hangtown (now Placerville), Ezra was hired to mine the American River. The claim was only a modest success before floods drove them out. With enough gold dust to see the year through, he set off for Tuolumne County to work in the Southern Gold Mines. Ten miles from Sonora, he was taken ill. For $16 a week, he spent the winter huddled behind the bar room stove of the Mountain Pass Ranch. During his convalescence, he worked in the hotel's vegetable garden and built it up into a thriving business. He cut wild hay and sold it in Sonora. He went into poultry, cattle and sheep, bought into the ten acre vegetable plot and began planting fruit orchards."

Debbie's great grandfather became an extremely successful market gardener, feeding the stores and hash houses which fed the miners. An etching on her wall of the orchard estate left for grandpa George Byant Dane to run depicted a country mansion surrounded by thousands of regimented acres of orange groves. After Byant's death, the estate became too much for grandma Beatrice. She sold up and moved to San Francisco, where she started the first garbage round in the city and became a multimillion-airess. On another wall was an excellent charcoal sketch of an old gold miner drawn by Debbie's father, George Ezra Dane, who committed suicide at the age of thirty-six. George's story was even more fascinating and possibly explained Debbie's warm disposition towards me.

"My father was very bright and highly talented. He was pushed towards becoming a lawyer by grandad, but was turned down by Harvard for being too young. So he set off to spend a couple of years in Europe. He studied languages at the University of Geneva and travelled around the continent, collecting folk tales and sketching local people. He was fascinated by customs and traditions. Linking up with trains, George used a bicycle to explore away from the beaten track. He wrote a book, *With Bike and Bag from Carassonne to Cadiz*, but it was never published."

Debbie's smiling eyes peered deep into mine and she tapped the couch with embarrassment. I was more than a nosy writer to her and she showed me a small wooden box, never revealed to her B & B guests. It contained neatly wrapped mementoes of the father she never knew except through his work. She unwrapped each item like a jeweller revealing priceless gems.

Finally graduating from Harvard Law School, George's interest in folklore and personal histories grew. He was a founding member of a fraternity called E Clampus Vitus, and began writing and illustrating oral history books

366

about the Gold Rush. He was collecting first-hand material for a definitive study of the notorious robber Black Bart when he killed himself. Ascribed to a nervous breakdown, Debbie thought her father's inability to square the boredom of his day job with frustration at not being able to travel, sketch and write probably lay at the root of his self destruction. She was barely five when he died and fourteen when her mother, Yvonne Harley, succumbed to cancer. Among the legacy of letters they left her was a five page, limited edition booklet entitled *Deborah Dane : A Biography — Containing a Full Account of Her Arrival in California and Early Experiences There*. Written by her mother with an introduction by her father, it was Debbie's birth announcement, presented as a humorous parody on the story of the Forty-Niners arriving in the Sierra Nevadas.

Debbie was intelligent, erudite, university educated as a nutritionist, and a fine example of the strong, resourceful women typically attracted to the Mother Lode. Contrary to popular myth, the overwhelming majority of women in the gold fields were not prostitutes. If not miners, they ran respectable businesses similar to Debbie's, capitalising on the numbers drawn to the mountains. They were seamstresses, cooks, store keepers, landladies and wives like Louisa Amelia Knapp Smith Clapp. Better known as 'Dame Shirley', Louisa was a teacher and the wife of Dr. Fayette Clapp, who set up a practice at Rich Bar on the Feather River in 1851. At that time, over ninety per cent of the non-native population of the mountains were male, but Louisa Clapp's articles in *The Pioneer* remain the most perceptive contemporary accounts of what it was really like living in the gold fields. In a world full of men, it was the words of a woman historians now relied on.

Deborah Dane was more than the perfect hostess. By the end of our conversation she was insisting I stay overnight in her house — not the Bed and Breakfast, but the small private residence newly erected at the back of

The Parsonage. I protested my poverty but Debbie wanted no money.

Bonnie, Brent and baby daughter Bethany welcomed me into the family home with open arms. Debbie's daughter and family were staying over on a flying visit from Indonesia, where they were missionaries. Bonnie was another formidable woman — an internationalist, at ease with and endlessly curious about travellers. It was too soon to tell if baby Bethany was blessed with the same forthright female genes, but she had mighty powerful lungs.

I showered, treated myself to clean clothes and came downstairs to find I was included in the family's preparations for dinner. This was going too far, I graciously protested. Bonnie was only home for a couple of nights before the family began a tour of the States to raise funds for their Ecumenical mission in the Far East. With the pressures of the B & B, they would see little of mum. The least I could do was allow them quality time together.

On the scrubbed streets of Nevada City the day-time clamour had been replaced by a sprinkling of overnight guests leisurely making their way between restaurants, bars and theatres. They were dressed casually but costly. I walked in the opposite direction, out of town, up to the Pioneer Cemetery on West Broad Street. On a grassy knoll overlooking a formal graveyard, a scattering of wooden crosses and small headboards poked out of the untended ground. A few headstones and slabs carried weathered inscriptions remembering people born in places an ocean away. Most died in the 1850s and all died young, the oldest making it to just thirty-two. It was a pitiful yet tranquil sight, possibly the only slice of history in Nevada City not smothered under treacle. Debbie told me the tour leaflet didn't explain that the cemetery at the foot of the knoll was Catholic. The Pioneer Cemetery was a bit of spare land where anybody who didn't bend a knee to Rome got dumped.

I grabbed a bite at Friar Tuck's on the corner of Commercial Street, at the edge of the original Chinese quarter. The waitress was most impressed I came from the land of Robin Hood. "Y'mean, there actually was a Friar Tuck?" She had seen me earlier in the day sketching the ornate frontage of the National Hotel (built in 1854), and was herself a Gold Rush buff with hands-on experience.

"Came out to the Yuba from Iowa in 1975. Bought me a suction dredge and started scouring the river, cleaning the hidden crevasses. Never found nothing but I stayed. It's a kinda neat town, y'think? Lotsa real neat people live here."

She explained the neatness was mostly due to a bunch of West Coast intellectuals in the Forties called E Clampus Vitus — George Ezra Dane's bunch. Reviving a fraternal order from the Gold Rush years, they managed to achieve serious things without taking themselves too seriously. Unfashionably into American heritage and preserving historic monuments, the fraternity discovered the ramshackle old town before the developers did, and fought to defend it from molestation. Around the late Sixties, West Coast hippies began moving up. A few opened 'head shops', but mostly the Flower Children just hung out and got stoned. At that time, the majority of residents worked in the timber industry and the two cultures clashed, sometimes violently.

"In the early Seventies, the loggers got so pissed with the dopers they got together and threw the hippies outa town — bodily. Course the freaks moved back in once the dust died down. This town is run by old hippies. They don't look like hippies no more, but underneath the Armanies..."

In 1985, having staved off developers for decades, Nevada City became unique in having the whole of the downtown area listed in the National Register of Historic Places. Debbie said the civic bylaws were strictly tailored to preserving the town in aspic. You couldn't paint your house a different colour without the town council meeting.

All around Nevada City there were historical parks, gold mining museums and sites of special interest. In a car, I might have been tempted, but there was little appeal in a fifty mile round ride to see where miners water-blasted a gorge 100 metres into a mountain side. I could imagine it and the historical parks where guides in authentic reproduction costumes toured visitors round authentic reproduction mine workings. I had been there before.

But my curiosity was aroused by a heavily burdened mountain bike propped outside a store selling mining equipment on the back road to La Barr Meadows. Peeking from the panniers was a tin plate and what looked like a bedroll lay across the rear rack, cowboy style. Amongst handbooks, sluices and racks of shovels, I found Justin Seals locked in an esoteric conversation about metal detectors with the proprietress. Justine was a gold panner on a bicycle, an opportunist and somebody the Forty-Niners would have called a 'pocket hunter'.

"I cycled up here from Texas," he told me, "Used to work as a window cleaner for my brother. Poor bastard's going through a messy divorce and closed up the business, temporary like, until he gets himself sorted. I thought I'd come up here and try my luck."

Justin was in his mid thirties, tubby but strong and healthy. He panned on private land, slept wild and had amassed eight ounces of gold dust in the last two weeks — a good day's haul in 1849. At current prices it could have bought him a soft bed at The Parsonage for a good few nights. Back then it was worth about $128, the cost of a boat trip back to New York.

"I carry the tools of my trade to fall back on," Justin said.

Along the length of his bicycle he strapped the poles to his window cleaning gear, but he hadn't had a great deal of success in that department either.

"What the hell! It's sunny, the water's good, I've lost buckets of fat and you never know — tomorrow I might strike it rich."

Justin was amazed I hadn't gone hunting for gold. He offered to take me to a spot said to be ripe for metal detecting.

"Come on, man! After your expedition, you gotta pan for gold."

Scanning river bars with a metal detector wasn't exactly my idea of gold panning, but I really couldn't get enthusiastic about looking for gold by any method. I started this journey eager to end it knee deep in the American River, but a lot of strong emotions had since flowed under the bridge. Truth be told, all I hoped to find at my journey's end was a whole lot of forgiveness and understanding from my wife.

Within a month of labouring in the squalor of the gold fields, a lot of Forty-Niners wished for nothing more than the same. California wasn't matching up to the dreams they had before setting out, and letters home began preparing families for the possibility of them returning empty handed. In an effort to counter the wild inaccuracies of glowing press reports in the eastern papers, they tried to dissuade people from crossing the continent. 'Say to all my friends stay at home. Tell my enemies to come,' one wrote, while another told his family, 'The more fools the better, the fewer to laugh when we get back home.' By 1850, the vast majority of prospectors were lucky to find slim pickings in the gold fields, if any.

Since Blairsden, I had dropped over a thousand metres and was now riding south towards the Sacramento Valley, descending down the foothills. I swung onto Highway 49, which rims the central section of the Sierra Nevadas like a tide mark. Immediately I was caught up in heavy traffic speeding towards the western section of I-80, the interstate I cursed all through Nevada. I had left the forests behind and was now bounding through swollen hills and ranching country where pastures had already turned the parched yellow which gives California the title of the Golden State. The blacktop was the filthiest road I had travelled in America — littered with ripped tyres, smashed wine bottles, strewn newspapers and the ubiquitous soda bottles of piss. Ten miles later it fed me into Auburn along a token cycle lane which doubled as a linear truck park.

At the bottom of a steep decline, the old town was dwarfed by a huge brutish sculpture of Kenneth H. Fox, the fruit farmer who hit paydirt and started the mining camp which matured into Auburn. Unusually, brick buildings dominated the crossroads and, as everywhere else, they were occupied by antique and collectables stores with titles like 'As Time Goes By'. Outside 'Gypsy Wind Beads', somebody handed me a leaflet outlining the mining ordinance of the town, maybe thinking I was a 'pocket hunter'. I made a note not to prospect after '7.00pm or dusk, whichever occurs earlier' and only to do it 'at least five feet from city improvements, including but not limited to bridges, culverts, pipelines and retaining walls'.

It was straight down the North Fork of the American River to Sacramento, but there was one last place I needed to visit on my tour of the gold fields. A dozen miles southeast of Auburn, Coloma was where the first gold washed up in the South Fork and where the clumsily titled Marshall Gold Discovery State Historical Park immortalised the event. I knew enough not to expect the original buildings would still be in place. Gold fever had men tearing down every standing structure so they could rifle through the earth beneath, but I was curious to see how the state remembered what many academics regard as the single most formative event in American history. It seemed several hundred motorists were equally curious. I rode into a stream of metal flooding towards the American River and descended steeply and, for me, perilously into the river valley. Pinned to the drop side by motorists who clearly felt tarmac was not a fit surface for cyclists, I crossed the bridge spanning the junction between the North and Middle Forks to begin the long taxing crank up the ten per cent to Cool. The small mountain pinched in the V of the tributaries was stripped of all cover and smooth as a mammary. It didn't seem possible but it looked as if it was still recovering from the ravages of hydraulic mining.

I had seen hose nozzles the size of Howitzers in Nevada City and the Quincy Museum, and studied photographs of their terrifying ability to remove and reshape the landscape. Spewing out a million gallons a day with a force which could cut a man in two, nothing illustrated the doctrine of Manifest Destiny more brutally than the hydraulic process deployed by mining companies in the latter years of the Gold Rush. Largely because of the devastation wrought on the sublime beauty of the sierras, the United States was to become the first country in the world to officially conserve parts of its landscape. It was a twist of irony symptomatic of the great contradictions in the American spirit.

In the same year aspiring Forty-Niners set sail from the British Isles, an eleven year old Scot crossed the big blue with his parents to settle in Wisconsin. Eighteen years later, his university education completed, John Muir set out on the first of many treks through the wildernesses of America and Alaska. His travels were to convince him that something had to be done to protect the majesty of God's Own Country before the hand of Man despoiled it for good. On seeing the legacy of hydraulic mining, he wrote, 'The hills have been cut and scalped, and every gorge and gulch and valley torn and disembodied, expressing a fierce and desperate energy hard to understand.'

Decades before the word 'ecology' entered the lexicon, Muir was writing and talking about how all of life was inter-connected. He was a founding member of the Sierra Club and a formidable influence on three presidents. By the time of his death at the start of World War One, he had been instrumental in the creation of fifty National Parks, 200 national natural monuments and over 140 million acres of National Forest in the United States. It was another thirty years before Britain established its first National Park in the Peak District, over the hills from where I live.

As I scaled what I hoped was my last loathsome climb, I took solace in the symmetry of knowing that the John Muir Trust in Scotland were the caretakers of Britain's highest peak. My ascent out of the American Valley would have taken me to the top of Ben Nevis and beyond.

Chapter 31

The South Fork of the American River swung up parallel to the winding highway and for five miles the banks of the river were monopolised by the camp sites of whitewater rafting companies. Before I realised it, I had ridden through what I presumed was Coloma. I doubled back to check this drab hamlet was indeed the place which had inspired the world to rush in. On one side of the road was the Coloma Club Café and Saloon. On the other, a small L-shaped plaza contained a sports store, deli and the local farm agent for Nutran Feeds. There was a gas station, camp site and a few holiday cabins further down the road, but if this was what had become of the gold town where it all began, it was criminal.

I ordered a couple of compensatory Sierra Nevadas at the Coloma Saloon and took them to a secluded spot round the side of the bar where I pitched on a bit of waste land used for target practice. Clearing the ground of shells, I settled down for a night under a full moon not a hundred metres from where I figured the gold was first discovered. Across the road, in the official camping ground, an amplified crooner howled through *American Pie*. I waited for the ghost of James Marshall to appear with hands clapped over his ears.

In August 1847, James Wilson Marshall was sent to a bend in the South Fork of the American River to build a saw mill. His employer, Johann August Sutter, ran a fortified trading post in the Sacramento Valley and needed planking for further expansion. In the course of deepening the mill race, Marshall's 'eye was caught by something shining in the bottom of the ditch... I reached my hand down and picked it up; it made my heart thump, for I was certain it was gold. The piece was about half the size of a pea. Then I saw another...'

Marshall rode down the mountain and showed the samples to his employer, who confirmed it was gold. Immediately Sutter swore Marshall to secrecy, at least until his mill was completed and the title to the land secured. Amongst Marshall's workforce were a Mormon family, the Wemmers, whose son let slip about the find. Initially the news didn't spread far. There had been previous discoveries in places like present day Colorado, but nothing came of them. Finally the news filtered through to another Mormon, Sam Brannan, an acquisitive entrepreneur who owned a flour mill and California's first newspaper. Brannan opened a store next door to Sutter's sawmill and stocked it with everything a budding prospector might need. He then caught a boat to San Francisco and walked through the streets waving a quinine bottle full of gold dust shouting, "Gold! Gold! Gold from the American River!" It was May 1848 and the secret was well and truly out.

I rode down the hill from Coloma looking for the State Historical Park and swept into, er... Coloma. It seemed I had spent the night in Lotus, on a bend of the American River but not *the* bend. My disappointment evaporated at the sight of Sutter's mill standing tall and solid a short distance from the river. The original structure was torn down in 1856 to make use of the wood, but its foundations were uncovered seventy years later and the replica I photographed from every angle was reconstructed from Marshall's original drawings, albeit in a different location. It was the most impressive exhibit in an otherwise unab-sorbing open-air collection of rock crushers and mining tackle. Considering I was visiting the heritage site in the sesquicentennial year of the big event, I expected more of a splash.

By comparison to the Mormon's block buster screened at the Hub and Spoke Ranch, the docudrama of life in the gold fields was a hammy, scratchy B-feature liberally sprinkled with inaccuracies and stereotypes. The only exhibit in the visitor's centre I learned anything from was a daguerreotype of Coloma before it was inundated. It appeared the barren rounded knaps I had seen at the junction of the North and Middle Forks were not much different from the barren rounded knaps of before the Gold Rush. The only other item I could get excited about was a plastic tub on the ticket counter containing 'prairie rings' — copies of the bent horseshoe nails used by the overlanders for wedding rings. I bought one to slip on Sandy's finger at our reunion.

Opposite the Visitor Center, a row of shacks pretended to be the Coloma of old. At the one selling drinks and home baked cakes, I slipped into conversation with a local chap who looked miserable and spoke American with a heavy accent. On Friday, Finn Schmidt's wife had passed away. He had just been to church, which only reminded him of the 101 things he needed to organise for his wife's funeral. She was a popular lady in the neighbourhood and Finn had received special dispensation for his wife to be buried in the Pioneer Cemetery. One of the last people to be buried in the historic graveyard was Matt Sugarman, the former superintendent of the State Historical Park. Finn told me about Matt and explained why the sesquicentennial celebrations failed to make a mark.

"Matt was passionate about the park. He believed it was the most important historical site in America. When Pete Wilson became State Governor, he set up a fund of $2.5 million for the special anniversary and for improvements to the museum, but Wilson froze Matt out. He set up a commission and blew the money on junkets to Europe and contracts for his buddies. They came out with lousy, half-baked ideas. In the end, all there was to show for the money was a load of glossy publicity."

Hoping they would dig into the scandal and lay it open for public scrutiny, Matt Sugarman called in the press. The commission proceeded to intimidate him, threatening to withdraw all state funding from the park.

"At the time, Matt was dying of cancer," Finn went on. "The commission were totally unaware of his illness. As

377

far as they were concerned, he was a meddling employee playing a game of political brinkmanship. Forcing him to attend the opening celebrations, Matt took the opportunity to publicly embarrass the governor. The opening went off like a jammed gun, but Matt cornered Wilson into announcing a further 300,000 bucks to go direct to the park. You want to go up and take a look at the graveyard. The epitaph on Matt's headstone just says 'Truth Speaker.'"

I didn't cycle up to check out the Pioneer Cemetery, principally because I wasn't cycling anywhere I didn't have to, least of all up hill. All I wanted to do was finalise details with Sandy and beat a hasty retreat down to Sacramento. Several times I tried phoning home but she was engaged.

If you are stood at around forty metres and your destination is roughly fifteen above sea level, you would imagine your road would be downhill all the way. Had it followed the American River valley and the route taken out of the mountains in the nineteenth century it might have been, but the tarmac road to Sacramento first had to haul itself through the Himalayan foothills of El Dorado County. For anybody who had a nano erg of energy in them, the ascents were less than grievous. I had been riding on empty longer than I thought humanly possible. At the foot of the first climb disappearing into the clouds, I burst into tears.

Ten agonising, detestable miles later, I was saved from myself by a friendly little store-cum-café in the tiny wooded hamlet of Rescue.

"It's named after a guy who struck gold," the woman behind the breakfast bar told me. "He was rescued from heavy debts of the life threatening kind. Hey, you're from Ingerland, right? D'yar know Def Leopard — the band? I'm a friend of the drummer's. D'yar know him — Rick Allen? Been to Sheffield, 'n all. *Full Monty*, wahey!" She lifted her apron and jigged to the till.

On a phone in the café which was a hand-me-down from Alexander Graham Bell, I finally got through to Nottingham. There was an unexpected bubble of excitement in Sandy's voice.

"I can't believe this is really happening. In twenty-four hours I'll be in San Francisco," she frothed.

"You're excited, yeh?"

"Too right. I'm out of here. I can't wait to see you." More cautiously she asked, "How do you look?"

I had spent a long time worrying about what Sandy and I would do when she arrived in California. She was bringing her bicycle and we vaguely planned to explore more of the gold towns together. I could think of nothing I would least like to do, but the next three weeks had to be Sandy's time. I owed her that much and probably a lot more, but how to make it a reunion to remember when all I wanted to do was sleep for a hundred years?

Hills of frizzled grass gradually gave way to subdivisions of skeletal timber. Both were yellowing. Detailed down to porticoes and cornices, near complete condominiums of plywood awaited plastic sheeting to transform them into homes less desirable. The population of the Sacramento Valley was spreading up over the toes of the sierras like athlete's foot. Dwarfed by the dirt dam of Folsom Lake, I rolled into Folsom town on a six lane blacktop looking for a sign post to Sacramento which didn't want to steer me onto I-50. At a gas station I asked directions. Nobody knew how to get to the big city without taking the freeway.

More by accident than directions, I crossed the American River again. On the far side, a buckled cycleway sign pointed down to a tarmac trail hugging the north bank. Disorientated as a tracker dog sniffing in a creek, I had nothing to lose but the traffic. I wove my way through the thickets of Negro Bar and out onto shingle banks bristling with wild rye. The trail took a dive down to river level and meandered beside Lake Natoma — a bulge in the river like dinner in a snake caused by a dam five miles downstream. Beneath bright orange cliffs supporting the

379

sprawls of Folson and Orangevale, I rode through evening shadows cast over a lazy current, impatiently scanning the skyline for signs of the high steel of Sacramento.

The riverside trail added eight miles to the straight into the city. For the pleasure of a traffic free route, the added distance usually wouldn't have bothered me, but I was petulant to finish and would have jumped onto the interstate had it presented itself. The cycleway wandered through parks and picnic areas where kids whacked baseballs and Muslims bowed towards Mecca. It picked its way through endless boulder bars and cottonwoods pungent with fennel. Except that the finishing line appeared to be receding, my odyssey was over. There were no more surprises, except the wrong turns I took in my haste. Frustrated and angry, I resigned myself to cycling into Sacramento in the dark.

Amongst commuters and evening exercisers pedalling the thin grey line, I came upon a family of eight hogging the strip. As I dallied behind, poised to overtake, it struck me this was a sight to behold, even in Europe. The oldest child was about fourteen and the youngest about four. There were three boys and three girls — a balanced family balanced on bicycles.

"Is there anybody left at home?" I quipped, pulling alongside mum.

"Nar. The whole family's here, present and correct, if Junior would just hold his line." The woman spoke perfect American with a guttural accent which sounded Central European. "We're on our way home. They're a little tired."

They had every right to be. According to Nelly, the children had cycled a round trip of over forty miles. The youngest solo rider pedalled a single speed, small wheeled machine never designed to go further than the end of the block. The baby of the bunch sat behind dad, trying to stay upright in a kiddie seat. Each time he slumped, Jim swung an arm round his back to shake the lad awake. He said the family took a ride most Sundays. They were six miles from home, straight down the bike trail.

Nelly was an English interpreter from Timisoara, Romania. She was there in December 1989 when the revolution kicked out Ceausescu's local lackeys. Jim was a relief worker trucking aid into Timisoara when they met seventeen years ago. Nelly was now an American citizen, but I didn't get their full story and couldn't work out if the children were all Jim's. He was softly spoken, polite and courteous, and the kids were certainly the same.

Number one daughter had been listening intently to my conversation with Nelly. "Excuse me, Mr. John. Nottingham? That's where the Sheriff lived, yes?" She too spoke with an accent.

Like a detective checking her facts, number one daughter told me that Robin Hood was probably a compilation of several real people, that the first story was written down a century or more after their death, and that Robin of Sherwood was a hero of the dispossessed. I was dumb-founded. "I've read a few books," she explained.

There was something odd about these children. Aside from anything else, they weren't whinging. Forty miles is a long way for the best behaved little legs, but what banter occurred between them revolved around identifying wayside plants. When Jim invited me to pitch in their garden for the night, curiosity got the better of my desire to have done with the argonaut's trail.

We were in the city, Jim said, but still I saw no skyscrapers looming over the cottonwoods. I followed them up a steep embankment onto an off-shoot of the American River Trail, and rode into a working class estate of scabby bungalows and dog-eared streets north of El Camino Avenue. Ours were the only white faces. In their driveway were a car and a pick-up which wasn't long for the wrecker's yard. "Going to have a problem transporting the wildlife," Jim said cryptically, tapping the pick-up as we squeezed past. "I'm extending the sides to take a higher load."

Jim, Nelly and the tribe were on the verge of moving to Michigan. They had sold their house and were boxing things up. "We need more space and more land, maybe a little farm," Nelly said. "We haven't bought anywhere yet. In fact, we've never visited the state. We plan to stay with Jim's cousin while we search for a house. There will be thirteen people living under one roof when we move in."

It was a recipe for tearing your hair out — or maybe not. I watched the children stash their bicycles, take a wash, change and settle down for the evening without any argibargy or instruction. Their behaviour was as exceptional as the family's back yard.

Where neighbouring gardens were grubby lawns blitzed with kid's toys, half of their's was cultivated and orderly. At the bottom stood a small orchard of apple trees and secret hiding places where the children played. Then came the chicken pen and bee hives, the province of number two son, who was an apiarist and expert on White Leghorns. The remaining area was a kitchen garden bordered with flowers and a little white picket fence. A path down the middle slipped under a Chinese pagola onto the lawn before the house. A miniature Dutch barn built by Jim and the kids out of scavenged wood housed the bikes and gardening tools, and a small pond allowed their free range ducks, geese and Newfy, the German-Newfound' cross, to take water. While explaining to Jim why it was a joy to see such a garden, I pitched next to the dovecote. "Of course, the fowl are illegal in the city, and we've had complaints," Jim said, nibbling one of their Granny Smiths. "Another good reason for moving."

In the kitchen, Nelly had been preparing dinner when she was struck down with a blinding migraine. All she could do was lie on the sofa in a darkened sitting room and grit it out. Jim lovingly caressed her brow and occasionally massage her neck. She was in tears of pain.

"I never ever suffered from migraines until I came to America," Nelly moaned. "I watch our diet like a hawk — everything we eat and drink. I have no idea what brings it on."

Without any prompting, number one daughter and son had taken over the cooking. I sat at the kitchen table drawing for number two daughter, and held a quiet conversation with the replacement chefs. They dismissed TV as boring but quite liked the Discovery Channel. They had both read the *Harry Potter* books and thought they were okay, for light entertainment. She was currently researching the State of Michigan and he was reading up on milk cows. What the hell was it with these kids?

It emerged they were 'home schoolers', taught principally by Nelly and supported by a movement which was gaining ground in America. Over a million kids were registered as being taught at home and fifty states had accepted the practice, albeit reluctantly. In 1997, home schooling received a major fillip when one of their number won the National Spelling Bee contest. Since then, home schoolers had consistently achieved significantly better results than private and public school kids, generally performing a grade higher than their contemporaries in the two systems.

Jim told me that school psychologists were talking up the fear that home schooling failed to develop the "socialisation skills" of pupils. They argued that children taught at home were introverted misfits who couldn't relate to other kids, "In the same way that Eric Harris and Dylan Klebold related to other kids, maybe?" The chefs told me they regularly joined other home schoolers from Sacramento for field trips, visits to museums and sporting activities, and they all had friends who went to mainstream schools. "Anyways," Jim said, "would you trust the opinion of a profession which prescribes Ritalin to children to keep them subdued in class?"

In the morning, breakfast was served by daughters one and two, and son number three. Nelly was sleeping in after a rotten night and Jim was off to earn a few bucks working for a pal. He made to leave, returned, dug in his pocket and thrust $20 in my hand. It was twenty bucks better spent on his family, but Jim was an irrepressible aid worker. I thanked him and handed back the money saying, "I'm only cycling a couple of miles down the road, Jim. I'm all done."

A shiver of relief rattled through me at hearing those three words. "Yes you are," Jim said, patting me on the shoulder.

When I left for the final ride, Nelly was still in bed and all six children were gainfully absorbed in reading, writing, drawing or building "Robin Hood's castle" out of Lego. The second stage of my journey had started with the slaughter of innocents at a high school. The massacre cast a shadow over the second year of the trip, particularly over those I stayed with who had teenagers. At trail's end, it was heartening to spend time with children who were bright, helpful, inquisitive, creative and genuine. Jim and Nelly's kids weren't going to need a machine pistol to get themselves noticed.

From Independence to Sacramento had taken the fastest wagon trains ninety-three days to complete what one diarist described as 'so tedious a journey'. It had taken me exactly eight weeks and a total of thirteen weeks from Washington. Hundreds of miles of my ride had been numbingly tedious, but their ordeals had given me a unique insight into what the overlanders put themselves through. The weather was mostly unforgiving, remarkably little of the landscape was seductive, and few built up areas were much more than bland. Where town or country was a bit special it was strikingly beautiful, sometimes sublime and generally surpassed my expectations, but it was the people who most astonished me. Travelling alone, I missed the comradeship of argonauts, pioneers and pilgrims following the same trail, but the readiness with which so many opened their door surpassed anything I had experienced elsewhere in the world. Of my ninety-one nights on the road, sixty-four were spent with families. Americans might not travel far beyond their shores, but their eagerness to learn about distant lands and how the world perceived them had resulted in many a morning suffering from late nights.

Of course the line I travelled was a single thread in a huge woven carpet, and as I rode towards my final destination, I mused on how frequently my attempts to generalise about America and Americans had been confounded. All I knew for sure was that the enterprise exhibited in crossing and colonising the continent in the second half of the nineteenth century made the United States what it is today, for good and bad. I now understood better than any history book could convey just how much the pioneer spirit of the nineteenth century forged the God given role the USA believes it has in the world today. Manifest Destiny is a mighty powerful driving force.

Where the American River flowed into the Sacramento, the curtains of greenery finally parted to reveal the skyline of Sacramento city, pleasantly under-endowed with steel and glass monoliths. What reached for the clouds were the turn-of-the-century towers, steeples and domes of a classically influenced architecture befitting a state capital looking to establish a sober identity after the raucous years of the Gold Rush. I crossed the American River and rode towards the shunting yard which once was the eastern terminus of the Central Pacific Railroad and now was the California State Railroad Museum. The cycleway across the tracks was closed for Railfair, a ten day beano for train spotters and one of the largest in the world. Following another cyclist, I dragged my rig through a tear in the chain link onto a fly-over into town. He cycled towards the traffic on the wrong side of the road, a malpractice I had witnessed in every major urban area since leaving the Appalachians. Now was as good a time as any to do as they do in Rome.

The second driver to approach hurled abuse at the guy in front and took aim at me. I squeezed into the high sidewalk, grazed my front pannier, corrected, was clipped by the car's front fender and fell against its side window.

Thrown back onto the sidewalk, I landed in an embarrassed heap with the bike sprawled across the on-coming lane. Smarting with grazes, I made a rapid escape along the footpath.

Sat outside the train station beyond the fly-over, I was consoled by an elderly business man who fished Kleenex from his briefcase to wipe away the blood. "Welcome to Sacramento," he said. "For what it's worth, in my experience, it's actually very safe cycling in this city... on the right side of the road."

Chapter 32

With a day to kill before Sandy arrived, there was one last heritage site I needed to visit to complete the Forty-Niners' story. It lay at the opposite end of town to Old Sacramento, the focus of the city's tourism, but was a blind spot in the eye of the tourist information officer. Considering Sutter's Fort was the original settlement, it appeared a serious omission. He had no literature and only the sketchiest idea of its whereabouts, but then the poor man was completely unaware this was the 150th anniversary of the Gold Rush from the East. Except for an autumn 'extravaganza' scheduled at the Memorial Auditorium entitled 'Gold Fever — The Lure and Legacy', I found nothing in Sacramento which celebrated the sesquicentennial year of its founding.

A German hailing from Switzerland, Johann Sutter arrived penniless on the West Coast of North America a decade before it became American. With Mexico's help, he established a trading post south of the American River and, over the years, staffed it with blacksmiths, carpenters, gunsmiths, coopers, bakers and candle makers. On the land around it, now the city, he grew everything the country's first industrial park needed to be self-sufficient. By 1848, when he sent James Marshall into the hills to build a new mill, Sutter had established a small fiefdom in the Sacramento Valley, but he was always hospitable and encouraged incomers to join his New Helvetia.

When I finally discovered it, Sutter's Fort was infinitely more arresting than the tacky theme park of Old Sacramento. Set in grounds the size of a block and cornered by stout bastions, the impressive rectangle of white adobe walls stood out against the greys of the surrounding metropolis like a polar bear against a herd of elephants. At the entrance the ticket seller said, "I'm sorry, but you can't bring your bicycle in here."

With palms still seeping blood, I was in no mood to be messed around.

"Let me get this right," I replied, before forcefully outlining the substance of my journey. "...and having arrived where the story begins, you're telling me you're not going to let me and my mule in?" I felt like squaring up to him, hands poised for a lightning draw.

The stand-off was resolved in my mule's favour by a member of staff who sported a thick white beard, rough cotton shirt, Bowie knife and calf-skin boots. Except that he was well nourished and not riddled with arthritis, Clancy epitomised the mountain man. One of a handful of workers in period costume who engaged visitors in educational demonstrations, he was fascinated by my trek and the details of how I survived. I was equally keen to learn the little tricks the role-players knew which made life more tolerable for nineteenth century travellers. Authenticity was the cornerstone of their demonstrations, and it was evident the public were often surprised to find Hollywood myths debunked.

"We had a wagon train come through here last Friday," Clancy told a small gathering sat on barrels in the East Yard of the fort, "one of those re-enactment groups. The men were dressed in tasselled buckskins and critter hats, like the coon-skin cap associated with Davy Crockett. 'Course he wore no such thing, at least not until the year he was killed. He saw one in a play in New York City and took to wearing it to impress Easterners. As for leather clothing, a trapper or pioneer wouldn't wear buckskins. Rasp the flesh right off a man, and what about when it got wet? Cotton was what they wore, like this." He peeled off his thong laced top to reveal cotton long johns, explaining why two layers were always worn, in winter for warmth and in summer for protection. "Not like our friend here, who cycled through the Black Rock Desert wearing just a T-shirt. Foolish, *hombre*."

That day, every visitor was made aware of the lanky Brit's endeavour and I found myself co-opted into the role of tour guide. "Dress him in rags and he'd be perfect for the part," the lass playing the pioneer woman quipped. "Them bones are real authentic, John."

The trading post was the best historic site I had visited. That it was the last and the most embracing of my experiences might have swayed my judgement, but visitors I questioned were similarly impressed and mystified why the city kept Sutter's Fort under a bushel.

When the world rushed in to rip gold from the hills, New Helvetia was trampled under foot. Only the central two storey block of Sutter's offices remained of the original fort, while the store rooms, workshops and quarters lining the inner walls were torn down to provide building materials for the new city. As his land was squatted and his work force deserted, Sutter's dream of seeing California become an agricultural and industrial centre of excellence turned bitter. 'I should have been the richest person on the Pacific shore; but it had to be different. Instead of being rich, I am ruined,' he wrote. Sutter died destitute and lonely in a Pennsylvania hotel room having spent his remaining years failing to convince Congress that the nation had an obligation to redress his losses.

In a lull between visitors, Clancy bent my ear. "You've gotta understand, John, the Gold Rush made America American." He rocked on his stool in the shade of an awning and sorted out fur samples ready for the next demonstration of trapping skills. "All those European ways of doing things brought in on the shirt tails of the immigrants — all that high an' mighty New England morality that came from the East — it all got dissed. Hang-ups 'bout class and privilege went out the wagon. All that mattered was gold. Y'either had it or y'didn't, and if y'didn't have it, maybe you'd have it tomorrow. Didn't matter who y'were, where y'come from or how y'tackled a knife an' fork. The gold diggers introduced a new approach to things — the democracy of the dollar. It became the business culture of our country, and American culture is business. We're incorporated — even the people. 'Course, now the whole world dances to the same tune — well, 'cept Cuba — but it was first played right here in California 150 years ago."

Clancy invited me to stay at his place for the night to continue swapping notes, but I had some serious laundry and troughing to do before Sandy stepped off the train. I made my way back down town to the International Hostel at the corner of Ninth and H Streets, and found myself stumbling open mouthed into the lobby of a mansion fit for *The Magnificent Ambersons*. If the Washington hostel was a seedy reminder of the over-crowded boarding houses the Forty-Niners set out from, this was the palatial residence they dreamed their gold would buy. A man couldn't wish for a more impressive setting for a reconciliation with his wife.

Many Forty-Niners had severely lowered their sights, within a year of labouring in the gold fields. Those who weren't greedy and had left family behind arrived with the aim of amassing something like $10,000 before pulling out and heading back East. After a season in the sierras, most would have been delighted to walk away with $400, but the more determined or bull-headed hung on in hope. Although the message was slowly getting through to the United States that El Dorado wasn't all it was cranked up to be, a lot of miners simply couldn't face the folks back home with the embarrassment of failure. As the months dragged on, an increasing number of wives, lovers, relatives and friends took the trail west to find their men. Some found graves. Some didn't like what they found and returned home unaccompanied. Others had joyous reunions and, under the steadying influence of their women, moved into different, more assured occupations. There were still plenty of fortunes to be made on the back of gullible gold miners. Three years after the rush started, over 50,000 immigrants arrived in California, mostly with no intention of getting their hands dirty in the riverbeds. It has been argued that the Dollar Rush following the Gold Rush didn't peter out until the turn of the twentieth century. Having visited Nevada City, I'd say it continues to this day, but with the arrival of the women, civilisation came to California.

Sandy's train had only travelled from San Francisco, but already Amtrak were running twenty minutes late. "Nothing unusual there," I was informed by a couple of train spotters bound for Chicago after the Railfair. Learning that I intended catching the train back to Washington to round off my journey, the woman warned me to "Prepare y'self for arriving in Chicago seven hours late an' y'll be real delighted when y'pull in four hours behind schedule. That's 'bout y'average."

At a pace slower than walking, the silver Zephyr finally appeared under the fly-over where I had my prang. Sandy stepped down onto the platform and I fell in love again. We embraced like ravenous leeches. We sat in the station foyer and stared longingly into each other's eyes, sharing a root beer. I slipped the 'prairie ring' onto her finger and we walked to the hostel hand-in-hand, skipping across junctions like young lovers. By tea time our euphoria had ebbed away, replaced by a cloud of discomfort. We had a lot of sorting out to do.

We spent three days in Sacramento, talking and walking and listening, trying to make sense of each other's stories. We hired a car and spent a week driving through Death Valley, the Mohave Desert and Yosemite. In the months apart, we had travelled difficult roads on different continents and battled through harrowing experiences alone. We were both damaged in a way each found almost impossible to convey to the other. Unless we could find a whole lot of understanding in our hearts, our situation was irreconcilable.

I was forty pounds lighter than when I set out from Dayton, Ohio, looked like a rake and suffering from acute amenomania. The mere sound of the wind made me agitated and the feel of it rasping against my skin triggered a sickness in the pit of my stomach I could only apportion to fear. Driving up a freeway on our return from

Death Valley, I was hit by a panic attack and had to swerve onto the hard shoulder before losing control. The interminable grey ribbon brought the horror of cycling across Nevada rushing back. I sat on my haunches hyperventilating by the roadside, shivering and gushing sweat over Sandy. She was beginning to get a measure of the toll of my journey, but my deep sense of failure — of failing her — only sank deeper. I didn't need to read their letters and diaries to know how wracked with guilt many an argonaut felt when their wives and lovers joined them in California. Their empty 'poke' wasn't the half of it.

It is impossible to be accurate about the total number of people who crossed the continent in pursuit of gold. In the decade historically recognised as the Gold Rush years, several hundred thousand set down in the Golden State. In any one year, however, as many as half the number disembarking in San Francisco climbed the gang plank to return home. Despite setting out with no intention of putting down roots, many did, mainly because they established successful businesses. For those less fortunate, there was something about California's remarkable landscape which inspired the belief that everything was possible. It was, after all, God's Own Country, possibly the most fertile of seedbeds for the American Dream. California remains spell-binding and is the one place where a nobody can become a somebody overnight, regardless of the weeks, months or years spent in the wilderness. Like the disappointed gold seekers before me, however, I couldn't get out of the place fast enough. Sandy and I beat a rapid retreat through San Francisco.

Writing about the argonauts' journey home, J.S. Holliday believes they 'had not faced the elephant until (they) had spent some time in San Francisco.' The quickest city to appear on the planet, it was also the biggest fire risk. Gutted and rebuilt four times in the course of 1850, the tinderbox town catered for a man's basic needs and preyed on his basest desires. With a ratio of one woman to thirty-five men, it rapidly degenerated into a den of iniquity. As one miner described it, 'Rows, fights and robberies are the order of the day, and the night too, and to see sin and depravity in its most glaring colors, the seeker after such pleasures has only to walk from one end of Long Wharf to the other.' With respectable businesses greatly outnumbered by gambling tents, drinking parlours and brothels, the morality of the place so offended the most hardened of prospectors, many who wrote their last letter from the port set down nothing but the itinerary for their journey home.

A lot had changed since 1850. I wasn't there long enough to do the modern metropolis justice, but it appeared to me a lot also hadn't changed in that time. Sandy and I spent most of our stay walking and talking and listening in the vicinity of Market Street, picking our way through streets littered with 'pan-handlers'. What the homeless and unemployed couldn't pack onto a liberated shopping trolley wasn't worth plucking from a trash can. Some had several — an articulated rig — and carried a mountain bike and midi system. Few begged, but those who did, did so aggressively. Each had a scam which made life a little more bearable. From a coffee shop, we watched a drugs damaged white woman carefully collect the dregs from styrofoam beakers left by staff rushing into an adjacent office block. With half a beaker of mixed slops, she shuffled up to the counter and said, "Can I have a refill, please? You can sling that. It's gone cold." In the evening, the dispossessed converged on the plaza of the Civic Center like the Children of the Dammed, but there was a festive feel to the cacophony of music, haggling and entwined bodies splayed across tatty sleeping bags. Thirty years ago it might have been a love-in.

I was in town to catch the Amtrak back across America and Sandy was there to fly home to the UK. I wanted to jet out with her. Our relationship had caught up to a point where we felt committed to taking it forwards again, but there was still much to sort out. After she left, I felt thoroughly dejected and impossibly alone.

Walking up Market Street to buy supplies for the three, possibly four day train ride, I became strangely aware of an austere state building over-looking Safeway's car park. We had passed it several times before without giving it a second glance. Double chain link fencing, portcullised gateways and a drab oblong elevation suggested a prison, but now I noticed that huge reproductions of American coins topped each of a dozen square columns. Above them, faintly reliefed stone lettering spelt out 'UNITED STATES MINT'. San Francisco was conspiring to rekindle my enthusiasm for seeing the trail of gold through to the bitter end.

The best estimates suggest around $6 billion worth of gold was extracted from the sierras in the ten years of the bonanza, but only a fraction reached the United States Treasury. Almost a year elapsed between James Marshall finding gold and the first shipment arriving at the U.S. Mint in Philadelphia. While California pleaded for a mint to be built in the Far West, Washington remained unconvinced news of the find was any more than a ruse to lure settlers. Meanwhile, the bounty was being sent to Mexico, Peru and Chile for minting, sold at a price barely a quarter of its true value. During the one year when gold was being scooped out of Californian river beds by the sack full and traded at a pittance, the United States Treasury didn't see a bean. While Washington was 'slumbering', gold to the value of as much as $15 million a day was being weighed in on the other side of the country.

For all the months spent in the saddle, I had seen neither hide nor hair of Californian gold. Of course I wasn't the only man who failed to catch a glimmer at the end of their 3,000 mile treasure hunt but, unlike my predecessors, I could cheat. On my first day back in the capital, I joined several thousand visitors pushing their way into the Smithsonian Natural History Museum. In the hope of finding a single lump of the sort of ore the Forty-Niners dug up, I jumped the orderly crocodile of families filing past the Hope Diamond, the Star of Bombay and numerous displays of colourful crystals. In a darkened corner, I discovered a row of yellow faces illuminated by the glow from a large cabinet containing twenty samples of sierra gold extracted between 1848 and 1852.

The largest and heaviest piece was the size of a man's shoe, weighing a staggering 101.76 ounces. Next to it, another was the size and approximate shape of a child's pelvic girdle. It weighed in at 64.48 ounces. More than size and weight, it was the sheer beauty of the mineral which beguiled me. It wasn't difficult to appreciate why a man would want to bellow "Eureka!" from the highest mountain after prizing one of these exotic specimens from the drab earth. Regardless of it's monetary value, the extraordinary appearance of raw gold was enough to trigger euphoria.

Fiery as molten larva, each lump in the cabinet fitted into one of four character types. Some were smooth, like nuggets of yellow barbecue charcoal. Others were pitted like pumice stone. One or two reminded me of folded pastry which had dried out, curled and cracked at the edges. The most spectacular were like congealed lumps of jumbo sized Corn Flakes which had been scraped up, leaving jagged holes where some of the flakes remained stuck to the bowl. They were all a brassy gold, with deep shadows of rose gold merging into hues of orange and daffodil yellow. They were exquisite and I drooled. Out of the corner of my eye, I noticed an attendant studying me, suspicious of the time I was spending leaning against the cabinet.

I pushed my way out of the building against the flow of tourists and plonked myself on the bench beside the steps of the museum. My cheeks felt flushed and my temples throbbed. Somewhat late, I had gone down with a touch of gold fever.

THE RIG

Bicycle Custom built Orbit Romany Expedition, 26" wheels, offset rear triangle.

Attachments 5 bottle/fuel cages, map holder, radio clamp, cable lock, tool kit, "bike god" (from Sandy).

Panniers Carradice Super Cs plus day sack bungie strapped to top rack with Camelback water carrier.

House (DAY SACK) Terra Nova Solar tent, Thermarest, 4-season sleeping bag, silk inner.

Kitchen (FRONT LEFT) MSR XKGII stove, 3 small pans, tin plate, Ka-bar kfs, Opinel knife.

Office (FRONT RIGHT) Notebook, sketchpad, drawing tools, maps, compass, whistle, radio, films, documents.

Wardrobe (REAR LEFT) 2 sets travel wear, 1 set respectable. Layers suitable for –20°C, Shimano SPD footwear, Gore Bike-Wear waterproofs.

Larder (REAR RIGHT) Whatever is edible locally from shop or field to top up emergency rations of jerky, dried vegetables, cous cous, oats, chocolate, stock cubes.

Pannier pockets Headtorch, cash, repair kits for panniers, tent, Thermarest, cooker, clothes, camera, shoes & body.

Hidden Passport, traveller's cheques, plane ticket.

Bumbag Credit card, press pass, camera, 3 lenses.

Attachments Dog Dazer, mini binoculars, dictaphone

Author's Website
www.brickbats.co.uk

Catalonia is a comprehensive review of Catalan history and culture from its classical and medieval origins to the Universal Forum of Cultures 2004. John Payne's personal tone brings alive highlights of Catalan history and leading personalities of its cultural life.

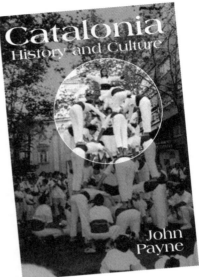

The book covers key periods in Catalan history from Greek and Roman times to the Spanish Civil War and modern times, including the mingling of Christian, Jewish and Muslim heritage and the popular street culture of processions, dancing and fireworks. Naturally, the author discusses Barcelona's extraordinary profusion of modern design and architecture, as well as aspects of Catalan life, language, environment and politics.

John Payne has lived and worked in Catalonia and visits regularly. He speaks Catalan and Spanish, and is the author of *Journey Up the Thames: William Morris and Modern England*, published by Five Leaves, and *Catalonia: portrait of a nation*. He lives near Bath, and is a freelance researcher.

328 pages, 0 907123 29 5, £9.99/$18.50
Five Leaves Publications
www.fiveleaves.co.uk, info@fiveleaves.co.uk